Methods, Moments, and Ethnographic Spaces in Asia

Methods, Moments, and Ethnographic Spaces in Asia

Edited by
Nayantara S. Appleton and Caroline Bennett

ROWMAN & LITTLEFIELD
Lanham • Boulder • New York • London

Published by Rowman & Littlefield
An imprint of The Rowman & Littlefield Publishing Group, Inc.
4501 Forbes Boulevard, Suite 200, Lanham, Maryland 20706
www.rowman.com

British Library Cataloguing in Publication Information Available

ISBN: HB 978-1-78661-248-9

Library of Congress Cataloging-in-Publication Data
Names: Appleton, Nayantara S., 1980- editor. | Bennett, Caroline, 1978- editor.
Title: Methods, moments, and ethnographic spaces in Asia / edited by Nayantara S.
   Appleton and Caroline Bennett.
Description: Lanham, Maryland : Rowman & Littlefield, 2021. | Includes bibliographical
   references. | Summary: "This book discusses the shifting landscape of field sites and
   the resultant emerging research methodologies and is aimed at both those who are
   already deeply immersed in fieldwork and those who are seeking ways to undertake
   it"—Provided by publisher.
Identifiers: LCCN 2020049676 (print) | LCCN 2020049677 (ebook) |
   ISBN 9781786612489 (cloth) | ISBN 9781538152652 (paperback) |
   ISBN 9781786612496 (epub)
Subjects: LCSH: Ethnology—Fieldwork—Asia. | Ethnology—Asia.
Classification: LCC GN625 .M47 2021 (print) | LCC GN625 (ebook) |
   DDC 305.80072/3—dc23
LC record available at https://lccn.loc.gov/2020049676
LC ebook record available at https://lccn.loc.gov/2020049677

To our families,
who help us make sense of this world and encourage us
to work towards a better future for all

COVID-19: (Re)Shaping the World and Research

Since early 2020, COVID-19 is reshaping the world we live in.

Not only is the loss of human life immeasurable, but the current way of life for migrants, jobless, vulnerable, and already marginalised people is deeply distressing. We hope our work, both in this book and beyond, helps contribute to a better world for all.

This new COVID-19 reality not only has implications for Asia, but also ethnographic research and methods in general. The bulk of the work on this book was done in 2018 and 2019. So while the chapters do not reflect this new reality, in re-reading these chapters in light of COVID-19 and the emerging socio-political landscapes, we see the conversations herein as vital stepping stones for ethnographic inquiry in and about post-2020 Asia.

Contents

Contributors

Nayantara Sheoran Appleton is a senior lecturer at the interdisciplinary Centre for Science in Society, Te Herenga Waka, Victoria University of Wellington, Aotearoa New Zealand. Trained as a feminist medical anthropologist and STS Scholar (with a PhD in cultural studies) her first project is a book manuscript titled *Demographic Desires: Emergency Contraception, Media, and the (re)Imagined Family Planning Project in Contemporary India* (under contract at Rutgers University Press). Her second project is on the ethics and regulations of stem cell research and therapies in India. She teaches, researches, and writes on ethnographic methods as a way to continually re-think disciplinary borders and boundaries. Having moved to Aotearoa New Zealand, she is now starting to conceptualise a project that explores relationship between immigrant and Indigenous communities – both within and beyond the medical space.

Caroline Bennett is an anthropologist specialising in the study of politics and violence, with specific research in the study of genocide, human rights abuses, mass death, and the politics of death and the dead. Her current research examines mass graves in Cambodia, exploring the use of political violence and mass death in projects of nation- and state-building. Caroline also researches the treatment of human remains following conflict, humanitarian crises, and disaster. With prior experience as a forensic anthropologist, her research intersects the practical and theoretical approaches to mass grave investigation and the recovery and identification of human remains.

Kathie Carpenter received her doctorate in Linguistics from Stanford University in 1987. Her doctoral research investigated children's first language acquisition of Thai numeral classifiers and was based on two years' fieldwork in Chiang Mai, Thailand. She joined the faculty of the Linguistics Department at the University of Oregon in 1989, and served as director of the Southeast Asian Language Programme there until 2000, when she joined Oregon's Department of International Studies, where she is now department head. Her current research is focused on children and social constructions of childhood in Southeast Asia, in particular, children in residential care in Cambodia.

Jia-shin Chen is associate professor and director at the Institute of Science, Technology, and Society, National Yang Ming Chiao Tung University, Taiwan. His research interests include contemporary addiction medicine and its policy manifestations, transformative impacts of neuroscience on society and culture, and the challenges of psychiatry in the modern world when dealing with human sufferings.

Lorena Gibson is a senior lecturer in Cultural Anthropology at Te Herenga Waka – Victoria University of Wellington. She specialises in the anthropology of hope and NGOs with an area focus on Melanesia, South Asia, and Oceania. Her comparative, ethnographic research focuses on the processes of development and social change, how social actors relate to the future, the politics of hope and agency, and creative practices. Her most recent work is concerned with the social impacts of community-based NGOs operating orchestral music education programmes in Porirua and Lower Hutt, Aotearoa New Zealand.

Paul Hansen is an anthropologist and Professor at Hokkaido University. His research focuses on social theory and non-human animal-human-technology relationships in Japan and Jamaica, exploring how forces of globalisation, such as the neoliberalisation of labour or trade, progressively alter both human and animal relationships, and how technologies of production impact human and non-human connections creating a hyphenated animal-human-technology, in essence a co-construction of being and becoming. He has published in many peer-reviewed journals, including *Critique of Anthropology* and *Asian Anthropology*. His latest book, looking at the Hokkaido dairy industry, is under review.

Graeme MacRae first discovered 'Asia' in the late 1970s and travelled there for a year. He returned in the 1990s for eighteen-month ethnographic research in Bali. Since then he has returned most years for a month or two and occasionally to India as well. His research focuses largely on the intersection of environment and development issues. He is currently working on a new project about food security in Indonesia, but he is also trying to develop ways of making sense of the extraordinary changes in Bali over this period. In between he teaches anthropology at Massey University.

Rimple Mehta is a lecturer in Social Work and Community Welfare, School of Social Sciences, Western Sydney University. She has previously worked at the Tata Institute for Social Sciences, Mumbai and Jadavpur University, Kolkata. She researches and writes on gender, criminalisation of mobility, trafficking, and incarceration. Her monograph titled *Women, Mobility and Incarceration: Love and Recasting of Self across the Bangladesh-India Border* was published in 2018. She has researched with women in prisons in Mumbai, Kolkata, and The Netherlands and also worked with organisations such as Swayam and networks such as Maitree against violence on women in West Bengal.

Till Mostowlansky is a research fellow at the Department of Anthropology and Sociology, The Graduate Institute Geneva, and an affiliated scholar in Anthropology at Monash University in Melbourne. His research interests include humanitarianism, development, Islam, infrastructure and mobility which he brings together in ethnographic and historical work on Central Asia, South Asia and associated diasporic settings. He is the author of *Azan on the Moon: Entangling Modernity along Tajikistan's Pamir Highway* (University of Pittsburgh Press, 2017) and has widely published in peer-reviewed journals and edited volumes, most recently in *History and Anthropology*, *Modern Asian Studies*, and *Political Geography*.

Sandali Thakur was research co-ordinator at the Resource Centre for Interventions on Violence Against Women, School of Social Work, Tata Institute of Social Sciences, Mumbai, until recently. She has taught Women's and Gender Studies, Social Work, and Sociology at various Universities in India, including Azim Premji University, Bengaluru; Rajiv Gandhi National Institute of Youth Development, Sriperumbudur; Savitribai Phule Pune University; Banyan Academy of Leadership in Mental Health – Tata Institute of Social Sciences, Chennai; and TISS, Mumbai. She has been part of anti-caste struggles and the Women's Studies movement for more than a decade. She co-founded an organisation to intervene in the area of social exclusion in higher education and helped set up the Women's Studies Department at Patna University.

Sarwat Viqar is an urban anthropologist and teaches in the Humanities, Philosophy and Religion Department of John Abbott College in Montreal, Canada. Her research focuses on the politics of urban space, gendered subjectivity, and informal urban governance in cities in the Global South with a special focus on Pakistan. She has published articles on Karachi's urban history, the dynamics of its low-income neighbourhoods, and fieldwork methodology. She has worked as a consultant and researcher on projects related to gender and violence, the politics of infrastructure, and access to affordable housing in various regions of Pakistan.

Lee Wilson is an adjunct senior research fellow at the Centre for Policy Futures at the University of Queensland. His BA is from the School of Oriental and African Studies, and his doctorate is from the University of Cambridge. His research interests include security and development, politics and power in Indonesia and Papua New Guinea. He is a staunch advocate of using anthropological approaches to help solve real world problems. He works with governments and organisations to reframe and overcome the challenges they face.

Yi Zhu specialises in business anthropology, organisational studies, and cross-cultural management. She published the book *Zhongguo de jingying fengtu yu jialefu de zhongguo bentuhua* (中国的经营风土与家乐福的中国本土化) *[China's Management Climate and Carrefour's Localization in China]* in 2013. Major journal articles include 'Reexamination of Japanese companies overseas: Anthropological critiques of ethnocentric management' (*Journal of Management Philosophy*, 2016, 14: 60–73) and 'Introducing Omotenashi to the World: Challenges of Japanese Customer Service in a Cross-cultural Setting' (*Transcultural Management Review*, 2016, 13: 47–63). She teaches management-related courses at Lancaster University.

Acknowledgements

Like academia, an edited volume is a collaborative process. We are thankful for the warmth and generosity of all who have been involved, and we would like to extend our thanks to all the people who have supported us and made this project possible. First and foremost, we thank the authors who contributed chapters – working with us, sometimes on short notice, and always with good humour. The other academics who have generously given time to this project through generous reviews, thank you. In particular, Anni Kajanus, Gordon Matthews, Atsuro Morita, Grant Otsuki, Thomas Reuter, Jonathan Silver, and Ayo Wahlberg. Thank you to our colleagues, friends, and students, in the School of Social and Cultural Studies, and Centre of Science in Society, at Te Herenga Waka – Victoria University of Wellington. We could not have done this without your care, support, and critical conversations. We would also like to thank Eli Elinoff and Philip Fountain in particular. Eli was instrumental in the early stages of the project, and Philip in the final days. Both are Asianists, and generous critics, who provided valuable advice for this project. Thank you also to colleagues at the Nordic Institute of Cultural Studies at the University of Copenhagen.

This book would not be possible without the warm and patient support of our editors and editorial support at Rowman and Littlefield, in particular Scarlett Furness and Gurdeep Mattu. We would also like to thank Suzie Tingley for her superb copyediting skills which helped bring our arguments in to focus.

Finally, to our families: thank you. Your constant love and support keeps us afloat. We give special appreciation to our parents – Lynda and Colin Bennett, and Raj and Neelum Shivrain, for always being there for us unconditionally. Thank you from Nayan to Samraj and Michael Appleton – you make so much of this possible.

For all its external credits, if the edited volume suffers from shortcomings, those, we assure you, are all our own doing.

Asia and Ethnographic Methods

An Introduction

Nayantara Sheoran Appleton and Caroline Bennett

This edited volume began as a series of conversations back in 2016, shortly after we both moved to the Anthropology Programme at Te Herenga Waka, Victoria University of Wellington (VUW) in Aotearoa New Zealand. As junior academics in a new programme, having lived, researched, and worked in Asia, we were glad to have each other to share observations on our fieldsites and former homes. As we discussed our time and research work in Asia, we started noticing similarities in the way our fieldsites in Cambodia (for Caroline) and India (for Nayantara) had changed over the course of our time there, along with shifts in the kinds of scholarship that was emerging from, and about, these spaces. Moving from some archaic anthropological renderings of Asian spaces, to the more contemporary, where 'natives' were returning from Euro-American spaces to participate in shaping the discourse about Asian countries, we saw interesting patterns that kept us up chatting over cups of tea, coffee, and glasses of wine.

After a few months of reflecting on and talking about Asia, we decided to embark on a collaborative project exploring these confluences and associations in greater depth. This volume is the result. Right from the start, the book has been underpinned by our desire to engage in a sustained and critical conversation about Asia between ourselves and with our colleagues. This book is an intellectual collaboration, and through it we have developed a friendship that enriches our lives and our scholarship. Working on this book has shaped the ways we think about our research, our relationships to and in our fieldsites, as well as the way we inhabit this world in and beyond Asia.

While working on this project allowed us to see Asia as a site from wherein we can imagine new paths for contemporary ethnographic practice (including our own), it was the pointed engagement with Kuan-Hsing Chen's *Asia as Method: Toward Deimperialization*[1] that honed our intellectual commitment to critical research methodology about Asia. We drew from this publication as an early inspiration for understanding how ethnography in Asia can reflect intellectual projects, but it also served as a political awakening for the kind of scholarship we wish to do – both as researchers and teachers. We both came to Asia as a geographical space by different paths (one was born there and the other is a committed researcher of Asia), and it was Chen's book that brought us to Asia together intellectually in Aotearoa New Zealand. This edited book is an articulation of what we have learned about how to enact Asia in our ethnographic praxis. The engagements rendered visible in each of the chapters have also been influenced by authors' own subjective experiences, both as Asianists and anthropologists.

Bringing our diverse backgrounds and research interests together, as well as a deep love and respect for each other (and each other's work), has made working on this volume a pleasure. We are lucky also to have been involved with our authors and other scholars across the globe on this intellectual project. These scholars pushed our own thinking, as well as each other's, and we imagine this edited volume a continuation, as opposed to an end, of a conversation on Asia and ethnographic moments and methods. We hope to contribute to this dialogue in textual form, so we can connect dots and build collaborations allowing us to think, work, and continue to talk via this critically important frame of Asia as method. This is a commitment to build alliances, as suggested by Chen at the start of his groundbreaking book.[2] For us, as for Chen in his work, this edited volume is more than an academic exercise; it is a wish to see conversations in and beyond anthropology that engage with an Asian experience – both as a physical location and intellectual conversation. While the conversations in *Asia as Method* began in cultural studies, these debates became a vital theoretical and political contribution to anthropological thought. For anthropologists in and from Asia, this analytical framework to recast our ethnographic practice and product through an Asian lens is important, particularly as the discipline continues to attempt coming to terms with its colonial legacies, and wrestles with the challenge of decolonisation in post colonial nations and settler states.

To that end, this book asks, and suggests answers for, a few key questions about ethnographic researchers and research in Asia. Some of these we address briefly in the introduction and include: Why Asia, and why now? What is gained by using 'Asia as a method' as a conceptual framework to think about ethnographic research in contemporary Asia? And what is gained (or lost) by studying Asia as a whole, and working towards a pan-Asian research ethic/frame?

WHY ASIA? WHY NOW?

In the first instance, the answer to this question is: because a decade ago, Kuan-Hsing Chen invited researchers and scholars to write about Asia as an intellectual project in and of itself (without necessarily always-already being relational to colonialism, neocolonialism, globalisation, and civilisationalism). Since Chen's book was published, we, and the other authors in this volume, have spent time across Asia, and have variously considered his invitation, or perhaps challenge – given the deeply complex ideas presented in the book – as a way to deepen our understanding not only about this space, but also our ethnographic practice.

The socio-political shifts in the world's economy, technological advances of monumental scales, and attempts at ongoing decolonisation projects across the region have created spaces in Asia that are confident and assertive of their place in the geopolitical sphere. Political and economic reassertion of Asian sovereignty in opposition to perceived Western dominance, and dramatic and rapid development in the region, destabilises relationships between the centre and the periphery, wherein new renderings and imaginations of hierarchies of identity and power come to the fore. This changing environment leads to emerging challenges for anthropologists working in the region – both those who have been working there for years, and new scholars starting fieldwork. An intellectual project that is *not* in opposition to the perceived 'West', but rather one grounded in multiple ways and from multiple locales within Asia, is a call put forth by Chen, to which this edited volume responds.

Some of the moves witnessed across Asia in the recent past have also given way to nationalism and nativism, as a way to assert a post-colonial identity. Our challenge as anthropologists and ethnographers of Asia is to account for, and engage with, this Asian ascent as a geopolitical and economic power, while also laying bare the machinations of a reductive nationalism. Chen writes:

> In the third world, nationalism has been a force forged in response to colonial conquest, and in order to eventually move beyond it, we must first dig into local histories and distinguish the different effects that nationalism has manifested in different locations.[3]

This call to 'dig into local histories' is what we, as ethnographers, do. This edited volume, launched in 2021, a decade after *Asia as Method*, aims to shed light on the histories of contemporary changing Asia, as a way to re-situate the region as a complex space that needs to be examined against and of itself. This book considers changes in the region, our accounting of it as an intellectual project, and the implications of this on our ethnographic practice.

By focusing on Asia as a site of enquiry, our contributors discuss tensions and opportunities arising in their ethnographic fieldwork.

The authors in this book provide deeply personal reflections on their fieldwork and power dynamics vis-à-vis Asia in the contemporary. They also consider how fieldwork is being negotiated within the changing dynamics of anthropology in the region, all the while trying to privilege a narrative that does not slip into a nativist or nationalist rendering. This book discusses the shifting landscape of fieldsites and the resultant emerging research methodologies. As such, it is aimed at those who are already deeply immersed in fieldwork, as well as those who are seeking ways to undertake it.

Asking researchers to think differently about the spaces that we learn from is a political project that requires continual engagement and effort. It requires a constant thinking through of our ethnography – not only at the stage when we write it up, but also when we are doing the very practice that makes anthropology possible. When Paul Rabinow wrote *Reflections of Fieldwork in Morocco*[4] it was simultaneously a celebrated and critiqued text. It raised the curtain on ethnographic practice and the nature of fieldwork, conversations that had thus far primarily been reserved for extra-textual consideration. Later *Writing Culture*[5] and then, in response to the exclusion of women in that text, *Women Writing Culture*,[6] further extended the desire to engage and unpack the complexities of anthropological research, and minutely examined the relationship between the researcher, the researched, and the fieldsite.

Clearly within anthropology there is a long tradition of edited volumes examining how the changing fieldsite and evolving relationships with interlocutors have an impact on the nature of anthropological inquiry and work.[7] Fortuitously for us, over time Asian ethnographers have trained the lens on themselves as scholars of/in/from Asia, albeit under different regional spaces including South Asia,[8] East Asia,[9] and Southeast Asia.[10] These recent publications across various disciplines are, like ours, attempting to think through the ethnographic research process. In explicitly engaging with 'Asia as a method,' our book engenders a revitalising conversation on methods and contemporary ethnography across and in Asia. In taking seriously Chen's call for an Asian studies from Asia, we have been careful not to do a subregional project, but rather, made available voices and narratives of ethnographers from across Asia. Here we bring together essays from senior scholars who have been conducting fieldwork in Asia since the 1970s, alongside those of junior scholars. These chapters trace changes in the region including, but not limited to, political change, economic liberalisation, and social migration. The diversity of our authors experience allows for a conversation to coalesce that while grounded in the contemporary, is cognisant of the histories of Asia and its disciplinary renderings.

By using Kuan-Hsing Chen's proposition of 'Asia as method' as a conceptual prompt, we aim to contribute to these conversations, while engaging with others within ethnography that aim to decentre Western hegemony of knowledge and practice. Thus, *Asia as Method* can be read alongside other texts, such as Linda Tuhiwai Smith's *Decolonizing Methodologies: Research and Indigenous People*,[11] Rita Astuti's lecture, 'Taking People Seriously',[12] and Nancy Chen and Aihwa Ong's *Asian Biotech: Ethics and Communities of Fate*,[13] that invite readers and researchers to reconsider how they approach their research, both theoretically and methodologically.

ASIA AS METHOD

Although it is couched modestly, Chen's *Asia as Method* is no timid intervention. Ultimately, *Asia as Method* seeks to move research beyond what Chen sees as the limits of post-colonial studies, globalisation studies, Asian studies, Area Studies, and their various offshoots in different fields. He encourages us to use multiple reference points for our intellectual projects, wherein the 'West' is not deemed 'best' or as the only referent. He challenges us to review our own post-colonial desires to always engage with our colonial ancestors, because for him even scholarship written in opposition to coloniality works to reinforce it. For Chen, the deimperialization project is a two-part commitment to first encourage inter-Asian referencing and create multiple reference points within Asia, thus breaking imperial ties; and second, to move the analysis back to the colonising spaces (some within Asia) where the project of deimperialization returns from Asian shores. On the second point, early in the book he writes:

> This must be performed by the colonizer first and then on the colonizers' relation with its former colonies. The task is for the colonizing or imperializing population to examine the conduct, motives, desires and consequences of imperialist history that has formed its own subjectivity.[14]

Beyond this global project, Chen focuses on Asia as a space from where to work, by critically drawing on Asia's own material histories as a way to explain its contemporary. It is a call beyond cultural studies to all Asianists to reposition Asia as the centre of analysis and decentre (or destabilise) canonical hierarchies.

Yet, as he asks for an Asian grounding, he also asks us to be wary of nativism and nationalism(s) in the face of reclaiming Asia in opposition to its colonial past. He is not the only one to see the resurgence in the 'us' versus 'them' rhetoric, mobilised across Asia by political powers to particular end goals (what he calls inter-colonialism in the service of capitalism). It is note-worthy that in the same year as *Asia as Method* was released, Nancy Chen and Aihwa Ong, anthropologists and STS scholars, released their book *Asian Biotech: Ethics and Communities of Fate*.[15] The book is a treatise on Asian biotech, and recognised the tensions that emerge when talking of a project that centres Asia as both a physical space and intellectual project through an anthropological lens. While writing about bio-tech, they were also engaging with the geopolitically volatile nature of contemporary Asia. They write:

> Asia is a region of political and ethical contradictions, of population surplus and bio insecurity, of economic backwardness and full-throttle capitalism, of memories of colonial humiliations and the cumulative force of resurgent nationalism.[16]

Thus for Asian scholars such as Ong and (Nancy) Chen, to understand and write Asia ethnographically is a tightrope walk. To see the space outside the confines of a colonial gaze, but not through the jingoistic nationalistic and/or nativist mobilisations, requires ethnographic attention to detail and complexity around regional patterns, alongside the theoretical nimbleness of a cultural studies project. This edited volume project, thus both requires and represents this tightrope walk.

It is this interdisciplinarity, when combined with attention to Asian interdependencies and independences, that makes it possible to account for a return to histories, Asian histories, and to recast the 'West' and its narratives about Asia through a measured lens. This also helps Chen develop his argument around the Cold War. For him, acknowledging both that the Cold War had very different spheres of influence in Asia than it did in the West, and that the consequences are ongoing, is vital in projects of deimperialisation that must accompany decolonisation. For many, the Cold War never ended, and to openly discuss and explore this allows for a chance to write Asia, through Asian narratives. Texts like Heonik Kwon's *The Other Cold War*, published in the same year as *Asia as Method*, make a similar claim about the Cold War being 'cold' only in the Western narrative, and only by seeing it as a bloody, and very hot war, can we (re)claim space for Asian narratives and experiences of/in the 'de-Cold War' project.

In one of his concluding chapters, Chen writes:

> The potential of 'Asia as method' is this: using the idea of Asia as an imaginary anchoring point, societies in Asia can become each other's points of reference, so that the understanding of the self may be transformed, and subjectivity rebuilt. On this basis, the diverse historical experiences and rich social practices of Asia may be mobilized to provide alternative horizons and perspectives. This

method of engagement, I believe, has the potential to advance a different understanding of world history. [. . .]

At the same time, the formulation of Asia as method is also an attempt to move forward on the tripartite problematic of decolonization, deimperialization, and de-cold war.[17]

This subtle move of taking a space, Asia in this instance, as a site for collective and critical theory-making is an intensely political and also deeply generous project. It does not deem other spaces as non-vital (say Africa, Aotearoa, or Latin America), but rather offers a guide map for collective, and progressive, research and engagement from and with/in Asia.

As is visible in the work of Beng-Lan Goh and Anna Tsing[18] 'Asia as method' is already being practiced.[19] However, this is an ongoing project of 'unsettling' and decentring, and ethnographic attention will only fine-tune this intellectual endeavour. There remains a sense among many scholars conducting research in Asia (be they scholars from Asia or Asian studies scholars from beyond Asia) that the time is ripe to further decentre 'Orientalising' narratives of Asian spaces. While the topical issues may differ, the logic underpinning the engagement with methodologies in this volume is a pushback to some methodological dictates handed down to us by the Global North. Here we bring together a wide range of scholars – some are researchers returning 'home' to do research, while others are researchers from the Global North doing research while staying cognisant of histories and this contemporary discourse. The cohesiveness of the intellectual project designed to push back against previous ethnographic engagements (be they post-colonial, feminist, or critical ethnography) is what brings these chapters together. This edited volume then becomes part of the 'Asia as method' intellectual move.

SPACES AND PAN-ASIAN RESEARCH

The question of how to define or consider Asia as a space of and for research has a long history. In the public sphere, media stories conjure images of 'Asia' as one of large spaces and economies such as China, Japan, or India; of contemporary political turmoil in places like the Philippines or Thailand; or spaces with complicated pasts implicated in their present, such as Cambodia, Indonesia, or Afghanistan. Until recently, scholarly endeavours have tended to bound Asia into subregions: South, Southeast, East, Northeast, and so on, with an idea that these regions held greater similarity within themselves – be it socio-culturally, linguistically, economically, or politically, than to other regions, and comparison, or even conversation, with other areas was incommensurable. More recently, the rise of India and China politically and economically has seen a shift in the focus of both scholarship and politics,[20] and Area Studies are changing from a subregional focus, to a wider focus on Asia as a whole, often centring on China and India as the points of strategic and scholarly interest. This is in line with the continued rise of Asia's economy (in 2019 it was 'the world's fastest growing major region, contributing more than two thirds to global growth'[21]), and as a major strategic area for political and military attention.

However, these regional divisions, often formed by political and economic interests,[22] cut across pre-existing relationships within and across Asia and other countries, and render invisible the ways Asia has been formed in the past as well as the present. As far back as the eight century CE (and across several centuries afterwards), Buddhism and its teachings reached across China, India, and parts of Central and Southeast Asia, creating cultural linkages across the region.[23] The Silk Road(s), and other trade routes, created networks of exchange of goods, religion, and knowledge, with and beyond the region, as far back as the second century BCE.[24] Even recent relationships are rendered invisible in these external renderings of Asia. For example, as International Relations scholar Manjeet Pardesi argues, the area now labelled as Indo-Pacific, and considered by many to be a 'new' area of geopolitical strategic focus, functioned as a single strategic area for most of the last two centuries, and during the first fifteen years of the Cold War, Asia was treated as 'a single strategic system'.[25] It was not until the 1960s that a combination of factors fragmented the region into smaller subregions. While Area Studies first emerged as a post-World War II American project responding to a perceived need for knowledge about the non-Western countries and people it was encountering,[26] the subregions of Asia that it focused on were largely a consequence of the Cold War, as Soviet and US alliances and conflicts created divisions and allegiances across the world,[27] and investments were made in Area Studies across the English-speaking world, including North America, the UK, Australia, and New Zealand. The persistence of some of these investments reflects contemporary political and economic forces, such as ASEAN, within the region as well as outside.

Chen insists that 'Asia as method' is not a project of nation-states. Nor is it a project of subregions. There have always been multiple Asias, and Asia has had linkages and divisions across itself for centuries. The ways of defining Asia are immense: a vast geographical region stretching across forty-eight nation-states; a geopolitical area of increasing strategic interest; an economic region constituted of networks of trade and exchange; a cultural space of socio-linguistic linkages. In their introduction to the recently published *Imagining Asia(s): Network, Actors, Sites*, Andrea Acri, Kashshaf Ghani, Murrari K. Jha, and Sraman Mukherjee visualize Asia as 'a discursive field of intensified interconnections intertwining almost every aspect of human society'.[28] This is more in line with how we, as editors, and the authors in this volume, approach Asia. Although this book encompasses the vast geographical area of Asia, we do not take Asia as a given, rather (drawing on Doreen Massey) as a space always in the making.[29] Thus, as Robin Bush, Philip Fountain, and R. Michael Feener comment, in their introduction to *Religion and the Politics of Development*:

> The value of "Asia" is not that it carves out a distinct, bounded unit of analysis, but rather that it calls for approaches that take account of this diversity on a scale somewhere between the national and the global. Further, "Asia" usefully broadens analytical frameworks beyond "The West," which all too often remains the implicit norm in scholarship on religion and politics.[30]

In this volume we approach Asia as an emergent, contested, multiple, and conceptual whole.

This is not to suggest that we consider Asia to be homogenous, or that we are reifying its difference to other parts of the world: to do so would be to continue the exoticisation that has underscored approaches to Asia as outlined in Edward Said's influential book, *Orientalism*, back in 1978.[31] Rather it is within the heterogeneity of the region that we see opportunities for productive discussion and new ways to think about our research. This is an opportunity to consider how the geographical space of Asia, which encompasses hugely disparate communities and socialities, has led the contributors to engage with moments and methods in the shifting fieldsite. Thus, we have chapters that consider mobility and altitude across Afghanistan and Tajikistan, feminist conversations in India, and comparison not only across Asia, but also between Asia and Melanesia. We see these collected perspectives as an opportunity to unbind the presumed bounded. Asia is vast, diverse, and changing in a multitude of ways, and this edited volume uses that multidirectional change itself as a point to continue a common, and sustained, conversation. The chapters in this volume furnish provocative and original contributions to the questions asked, though they also recognise the need for further research. Thus, all contributors have grappled with ongoing dilemmas and puzzles, and offer interpretations that may yet change.

Critics of Chen have argued that he reifies the distinction between Asia and the West (or Asia and the rest), or criticise him for focusing only on East Asia.[32] We do not read it this way. While Chen's case studies are East Asian, his challenges and propositions are towards a decentring and questioning of knowledge starting from Asia, but considering, and in relation to, other places in the world. In fact, Chen himself asserts that this is not just about Asia: while he urges academics within Asia to consider it as a referent instead of the West, he also proposes a multiplicity of connections outside the continent.

The inter-referencing he proposes is about considering places that share and address similar problems across the Global South, or from other positions marginalised by Western-centric academic and political discourse. Instead of approaching Asia through the frame of Euro-American theory as the main reference point, he argues we generate multiple reference points. This decentring and destabilising the 'one' absolute space from wherein theory can emerge opens opportunities for other engagements. This is a discussion that emerges from, and within, globalisation debates.

Using Asia as a frame allows us to consider a regional horizon beyond nationalist or localist projects, without relying on 'global' or Eurocentric classifications, while also enabling a consideration of inter-Asian connections and circulations. Thus, it provides a valuable corrective to some past framings, and an opportunity to think differently about how and where we do our research. The scholarship in our edited volume, deeply situated in anthropological debates, does not argue for the value or importance of fieldwork in Asia, but rather addresses the value of addressing the nature of shifts in fieldwork in a rapidly changing Asia, and the implications this has, not only methodologically, but also on the very way we conceive of the 'field' and of Asia as a place of enquiry and/or an imagined locality.

CHAPTER OUTLINES

When considering some of the complexities of fieldwork and the fieldsite itself, Akhil Gupta and James Ferguson in 1997 highlighted an anthropological complexity in defining the field at this contemporary moment:

> On the one hand, anthropology appears determined to give up its old ideas of territorially fixed communities and stable, localized cultures and to apprehend an interconnected world in which people, objects, and ideas are rapidly shifting and refuse to stay in place. At the same time, though, in a defensive response to challenges to its "turf" from other disciplines, anthropology has come to lean more heavily than ever on a methodological commitment to spend more time in one localized setting.[33]

This complexity is visible in each of the chapters presented in this edited volume. The authors understand that there is an inherent change to fieldwork[34] and take seriously the entanglements between their own positionality and the spaces where they work. Each chapter here is an invitation to our readers to see Asia as a methodological space rife with moments that shed light on ethnographic methods. The chapters are organised into three sections; however, with connections across these (imagined) boundaries imposed by us as editors. We thus encourage you, our readers, to read each section on its own, or across sections, to locate the rich ethnographic moments that inspire us all.

The first part of the book is titled 'Reflexively Re-reading the Field'. The four chapters in this section span from Afghanistan, Tajikistan, and Pakistan, in the West end of Asia, to India and Bangladesh in the Central parts, and Cambodia in the South East. These four chapters are a testament to not only examining Asia as a method for ethnographic practice, but also highlighting the value of a pan-Asian engagement. Each of these chapters takes as their object of analysis an already considered space, and re-illuminates it with a contemporary reflexive reading. The first chapter in this section, and of this book, is by Till Mostowlansky, drawing on his fieldwork in 'High Asia' (Afghanistan, Tajikistan, and Pakistan). Through an examination of fieldwork in the Pamirs, Till makes the case for studying verticality as a form of mobility and all this says about social life in the mountains. Playing with historical musings about mobility from his interlocutors, to the discourse around immobility effected by modern nation-state boundaries, Mostowlansky shows that despite limits, people meet familiar strangers and build new social relationships across boundaries in these locales. To then think of 'Asia as method' requires paying attention to the historicity of cross-border interconnectedness within Asia, particularly in the face of colonial and post-colonial nation-state borders that force a disconnect on mobile communities. While outlining the efforts to cross-borders, not only by his interlocutors, but also academics alongside non-governmental organisation (NGO) workers, travellers, and religious envoys, this rich ethnographic text shows the limits of this possibility within this high-altitude part of Asia.

Borders are a colonial legacy in parts of Asia and continue to shape contemporary lives, politics, and social relations. In chapter 2, Rimple Mehta and Sandali Thakur draw on their research on the borderlands on the Eastern part of India – shared with Bangladesh and Nepal. Rimple draws on her research with Bangladeshi women in Indian prisons caught on the Indian side of the border without proper documentation, but who had continued to cross into India, a space of their ancestors for work and/or making kin. Sandali draws on the borderland between India and Nepal, focusing on traditional Mithila artists working in both countries. Their interaction with their interlocutors allows both these scholars to also situate their own positionalities as regional border crossers. They offer a nuanced reading of contemporary borderlands, and their reflexivity about ethnographic identity, and generous ethnographic engagements, render visible colonial legacies that need to be examined for a decolonisation of Asia as a space.

The third chapter in this section, by Caroline Bennett (one of the editors), lays bare the legacies of the Cold War in Cambodia. Drawing on the prompt by Chen, in *Asia as Method*, to 'de-cold war', Bennett examines the ways global amnesia about the West's interventionist policies shape lives even in the contemporary. She considers the complex narratives among her participants, who see international intervention in Cambodia as an essential way forward for the country, while minimising the role of those same geopolitical forces in enabling the Khmer Rouge. By considering the way local and global forces continue to work to shape knowledge and praxis around, and about, violence in contemporary Cambodia, Bennett shows that the Cold War is not yet cold in Cambodia, and argues that the current regime could not be, and remain, in power, were it not for the legacy of the Khmer Rouge, which enacted a genocide as a direct result of the Cold War. Thus, contextualising the discourse and practices around the legacies of the Khmer Rouge, she outlines how this history continues to shape contemporary Cambodian lives and space.

This historicising approach to the contemporary is also undertaken by Sarwat Viqar in the last chapter of this section. Viqar lays bare the colonial violence that still shapes infrastructures in Karachi, Pakistan, through an examination of power relations around documentations and bureaucracies that have historically shaped and continue to shape post-colonial space. Like the other chapters in this section, Viqar offers a reflexive and historical lens, which she mobilises to illuminate three key factors that contribute to the way infrastructure projects come about in Karachi. She outlines privatisation, informality, and state fragmentations as the contemporary artefacts of colonial legacies, which have a direct (and troubling) impact on the way a 'modern' Karachi is being built. Connecting the dots between contemporary crony capitalism and historical colonialism, she considers how capitalism is re-shaped and translated into local contexts that produce distinct modernities. Her approach offers a consideration of the strength of a pan-Asian Asian studies that centres inter-Asian referencing. To understand the bureaucratic structures in Karachi, we are better placed to study post-colonial infrastructure projects in say Cambodia, than Brussels or Berlin.

The historicising, contextualising, and reclaiming from the colonial narrative a reflexive rendering of contemporary life, is an important ethnographic commitment, visible also in the next two sections of this edited volume. The second section of the book takes us 'across time and space', where comparison between an Asian past and present, alongside a comparison with Melanesia, grounds the intellectual project. In chapter 5, Kathie Carpenter outlines the changes over time in the way the discursive relationship between coloniser and colonised has shaped the way Childhood Studies articulate childhood in Asia. Revisiting her three decades of research with children in Thailand, Cambodia, and Indonesia, she argues that in the orientalist and Eurocentric rendering of Asia, as well as in other 'serious' scholarship, children have been missing. This lacuna can be addressed by examining the flow of ideas and knowledge in and about Asia. Carpenter suggests that a lot can be gained for Childhood Studies, both globally and in Asia, once the idea that is replicated between adult/child is unmoored from logics of the coloniser/colonised. Her comparative framework over the shifting fieldsites in Asia contributes to a complex and nuanced understanding of childhood, with responsibilities and obligations on the one hand from the children, and on the other hand, to the children. Carpenter candidly points out that the way she researched with children thirty years prior could not be repeated (for which she is grateful), but also goes to show the shifts in the field, and the conceptualisation of children, that allow her to ask, could we consider the child as method?

While Carpenter's chapter is a reflection on changing research within one area, in chapter 6, Lorena Gibson asks what can be offered by comparing understanding and action across Asia and beyond. While paying particular attention to 'Asia as method', Gibson also puts forward the idea of 'comparison as method', making the case for an intra-referencing, where to think about 'Asia as method' through a decolonial lens requires us to attend to the similarities and differences in Asian spaces against other former colonies – in this case, Papua New Guinea. While Chen, and those inspired by his work (like us), are looking at inter-referencing within Asia to create multiple reference points to learn from each other's histories, Gibson's chapter is a useful reminder to examine the value of referencing outside Asia, particularly when the referential point is another space with a similar history. She builds this comparison project by looking at NGOs in a slum in Kolkata, India, and in Lea, Papua New Guinea. In weaving this comparative narrative she takes us on a journey beyond Asia; however, never losing sight of 'Asia as method'.

In chapter 7, Graeme MacRae and Lee Wilson reflect on their fieldsite over three decades of ethnographic research. Deeply focused in the spirit of 'thick description', this chapter is part lyrical musing, part political economic analysis on Bali, but always extremely anthropological. By focusing on Bali as it changes over time, this reflection affords interesting ways for anthropologists to think about Asia in general. Working across scales of change, accounting for both the structural and institutional level, and also the local ethnographic everyday, MacRae and Wilson offer rich anthropological insights in what they call the 'new' Bali. As anthropologists of and in Asia, they make visible the value of comparison over time, as it situates the historicity of Asia as an important site of analysis.

The ability of ethnographers to take their readers on personal journeys is indeed the bread and butter of our trade. Sometimes the personal is about the people and places we research and at other times it is our own personal that bleeds into our ethnographies. In the final section, titled, 'Notes on Positionality', the four ethnographers situate themselves within their fieldsites and use their own sense of belonging - and/or not - as a method to think through and about Asia. In chapter 8, Paul Hansen plays with 'cosmopolitical conditions' as a way to highlight the fact that we, as humans (and ethnographers), are continually being and becoming with human and non-human actors. Thus, to be, become, and/or belong, requires a critical engagement that works against the simple logics of boundedness. Drawing on his own experiences of living, working, and making kin with/ in Japan, and focusing on his fieldwork on human–dog relationships in a demographically changing country, he asks us to look beyond the need to see difference as a classificatory tool. In this frame, to think of 'Asia as method' seems a reductive Area Studies experiment for ethnographers, which might strengthen, rather than weaken, boundaries that create 'us' and 'them'. For Hansen, the changing nature of ethnographic research in Asia needs to be situated in the embodiedness of the ethnographer (who often exists in boundary lands of belonging and not belonging) but not at the cost of artificially creating a bounded object of study.

Just as Hansen works against the boundedness of a field or area, in chapter 9 Nayantara S. Appleton (one of the editors) draws on her own experiences of being bound and unbound in various fieldsites. She uses moments from her research in India to think through some of the ethnographic methods and realities she came to expect based on reading classic ethnographies. In this chapter, she asks if Asia can serve as a feminist ethnographic method, in order to address some of the historically problematic representation of 'others' and disregard for power differentials even within 'women's spaces'. Drawing on two sites of fieldwork (contraception and stem cell research) she highlights the politics of decentring the narratives around 'studying up' and paying attention to women's mobilities in contemporary Asia. For her, viewing these ethnographic realities through the lens of her own insider/ outsider position enables a critical engagement – both on and from Asia - but also with feminist ethnography as a method.

The politics of belonging and/or not belonging, of being an insider and/ or outsider, and the shape shifting we sometimes do as ethnographers are examined further by Yi Zhu in chapter 10. Drawing on her personal journeys across China, Japan, and Hong Kong, alongside her fieldwork in a Japanese company in Hong Kong, Yi Zhu reflects not only on her own practice, but also on how she was perceived by the people she worked with – an important insight for ethnographers as they think through identities in the field. She shows that Asian identity (variously understood), like the ethnographer's, is co-constructed relationally between the researcher and the researched. The 'deep sharing' in this chapter serves as a generous example for scholars about to start fieldwork on how to respond to the expectations that are placed upon s a researcher. Yi Zhu outlines how the ethnographic everyday is underpinned by the theoretical and historical mappings in globalisation and Asian studies – with implications for anthropology and ethnographers in general. She offers an invitation to a very private space – both for the ethnographer, but also to her fieldsite: the often difficult-to-access space of a global corporation.

This critical engagement on positionality with a focus on the insider versus outsider dichotomy is taken up by Jia-shin Chen in the last chapter of this book. Titled, 'Comprador, Translator, or Cartographer? Thoughts on Methodological Positions', Chen's chapter is an examination of the researcher's position in the field, and in the writing of ethnography. In this chapter, Chen examines the discursive and practical engagements with the idea of insider versus outsider researcher, as well as how Taiwanese scholars draw from (and contribute to) scholarship both inside and outside the nation-state. Drawing on his own research on harm reduction policy in Taiwan, he shows the subtle ways he had to negotiate his position based on the demands of the ethnographic research process, and considers the dilemmas of being a writer of/from Taiwan trained in the West. He ascribes the role of a cartographer to an ethnographer: mapping or guiding understanding, while remaining cognisant of changing contexts, and with attention being paid to privilege the voice of the people with whom he worked. The spirit from which this chapter is written is one of honest reflection, and provides a nuanced (and poetic) glimpse into the dilemmas we often face as researchers of/in/from Asia.

CONCLUSION: ASIA AS METHOD IN ETHNOGRAPHY

As editors, we are grateful for the generous insights our authors have shared with us. We are also grateful for the response to the theoretical and methodological call of 'Asia as method' we put forth, alongside the request for ethnographic details from the changing spaces within Asia. The scholarship reflected in the following pages is a generous engagement with a multitude of ideas reflected in the various fields in Asian Studies, Area Studies of Asia, Anthropology, and Cultural Studies, all the while paying attention to ethnographic methods and moments. As we mention in the opening of this introduction, we see this edited volume not as an end, but rather as a hope for a continued conversation.

Our authors take 'Asia as method' as a prompt to reconsider their own research from another angle, be it a space as the ethnographic object (Viqar and MacRae and Wilson), the ethnographic analytical construct (Carpenter, Gibson, and Appleton), or the political invitation to re-centre marginalised realities and voices at the core of their work (Mostowlansky, Bennett, Metha, and Thakur). Further, thinking through the ethnographers positionally in Asia

(Hansen, Chen, and Zhu), the chapters offer insights into reflexive ethnography in and out of Asia. Chen's stance is political, and it sits alongside other texts encouraging researchers to reconsider their points of reference and the methods of research. As Gibson points out in this volume, this is not only an Asian endeavour but one scholars in other parts of the world have also been addressing. When Jean and John Comaroff wrote *Theory from the South*,[35] the anthropological 'establishment' took their call seriously. We hope, similarly, when we suggest that *Asia as a Method* is a challenge to ethnographers and anthropologists to reposition Asia as ground from where research and theories emerge about the continent, the resultant product is not just a better ethnographic text, but a more generous relationship between researchers and their communities of research.

NOTES

1. Kuan-Hsing Chen, *Asia as Method: Toward Deimperialization* (Durham: Duke University Press, 2010).

2. Ibid., 2.

3. Ibid., ix.

4. Paul Rabinow, *Reflections on Fieldwork in Morocco* (Berkeley: University of California Press, 2007).

5. James Clifford and George E. Marcus, *Writing Culture: The Poetics and Politics of Ethnography* (Berkeley: University of California Press, 1986).

6. Ruth Behar and Deborah A. Gordon, *Women Writing Culture* (Berkeley: University of California Press, 1995).

7. Nelson H. H. Graburn and Noel B. Salazar, *Tourism Imaginaries: Anthropological Approaches* (New York: Berghahn Books, 2014); Paul Dresch, David J. Parkin, and Wendy James, *Anthropologists in a Wider World: Essays on Field Research* (New York: Berghahn Books, 2000); James Davies and Dimitrina Spencer, *Emotions in the Field: The Psychology and Anthropology of Fieldwork Experience* (Stanford: Stanford University Press, 2010); Kathleen Musante DeWalt, *Participant Observation: A Guide for Fieldworkers*, 2nd Edition (Lanham: Rowman and Littlefield, 2011); Shalini Puri and Debra A. Castillo, ed., *Theorizing Fieldwork in the Humanities: Methods, Reflections, and Approaches to the Global South* (New York: Palgrave Macmillan US, 2016).

8. Sarit K. Chaudhuri and Sucheta Sen Chaudhuri, *Fieldwork in South Asia: Memories, Moments, and Experiences* (New Delhi, India: SAGE, 2014); Helen A. Kanitkar, *An Anthropological Bibliography of South Asia* (The Hague: Mouton, 1976); Saloni Mathur, "History and Anthropology in South Asia: Rethinking the Archive," *Annual Review of Anthropology* 29 (2000): 89; Sasanka Perera and Dev Nath Pathak, ed., *Intersections of Contemporary Art, Anthropology and Art History*

in South Asia: Decoding Visual Worlds (Cham: Springer International Publishing, 2019); Srila Roy, *New South Asian Feminisms Paradoxes and Possibilities* (London: Zed Books, 2012).

9. Shinji Yamashita, Joseph Bosco, and J. S. Eades, *The Making of Anthropology in East and Southeast Asia*, Asian Anthropologies (New York: Berghahn Books, 2004).

10. Victor T. King, *The Modern Anthropology of South-East Asia: An Introduction* (London: Routledge, 2003).

11. Linda Tuhiwai Smith, *Decolonizing Methodologies: Research and Indigenous Peoples*, 2nd Edition (London and New York: Zed Books: Distributed in the USA exclusively by Palgrave Macmillan, 2012).

12. Rita Astuti, "Taking People Seriously," *HAU: Journal of Ethnographic Theory* 7, no. 1 (2017): 105–122.

13. Aihwa Ong and Nancy N Chen, ed., *Asian Biotech: Ethics and Communities of Fate* (Durham: Duke University Press, 2010).

14. Chen, *Asia as Method*, 4.

15. Ong and Chen, *Asian Biotech*.

16. Ibid., 43.

17. Chen, *Asia as Method*, 112.

18. Anna Lowenhaupt Tsing, "Natural Resources and Capitalist Frontiers," *Economic and Political Weekly* 38, no. 48 (2003): 5100–5106; Anna Tsing, "What Is Emerging? Supply Chains and the Remaking of Asia," *The Professional Geographer* 68, no. 2 (April 2, 2016): 330–337.

19. Beng-Lan Goh, "The Question of Cultural Incommensurability: An Intercultural Interpretation Arising out of Southeast Asia," *American Anthropologist* 121, no. 2 (2019): 498–505.

20. Many scholars are considering the changing position of India and China globally, in the region, and to each other. For considering the strategic and political aspect, of note is Manjeet S. Pardesi: Manjeet S. Pardesi, "American Global Primacy and the Rise of India," *AsiaPacific Issues* 129 (March 2017): 1-8; Manjeet S. Pardesi, "Review Essay: Understanding the Rise of India," *India Review* 6, no. 3 (July–September 2007): 209–231; Sumit Ganguly and Manjeet S. Pardesi, "Can China and India Rise Peacefully?" *Orbis* 56, no. 3 (Summer 2012): 470–485; Manjeet S. Pardesi, "India in Asia: India's Relations with Southeast Asia and China, 1962–1991," in *India in the World: National and Transnational Perspectives, 1947–1991*, ed. Andreas Hilger and Corinna Unger (Frankfurt am Main: Peter Lang, 2012), 15–34. Peter van der Veer's recent work has begun to provide comparative sociological considerations of India and China, for example: Peter van der Veer, "Religion, Secularism and National Development in India and China," *Third World Quarterly* 33, no. 4 (2012): 719–732; Peter van der Veer, "Smash Temples, Burn Books: Comparing Secularist Projects in India and China," *The World Religious Cultures* 73 (Spring 2012): 17–26; Peter van der Veer, "The Comparative Sociology of India and China," *Social Anthropology* 17, no. 1 (2009): 90–108.

21. International Monetary Fund, "Regional Economic Outlook: Asia and Pacific. Caught in Prolongued Uncertainty: Challenges and Opportunities for Asia," *International Monetary Fund*, Washington DC [online] (Oct 2019), https://www.imf.org/en/Publications/REO/APAC/Issues/2019/10/03/areo1023

22. Manjeet Pardesi argues that 'regions are formed and transformed through politico-military processes, and "some of the most basic taken-for-granted 'regions' of the world were first framed by military thinkers" and other political actors (Lewis and Wigen 1997, xiii)', (Manjeet Pardesi, "The Indo-Pacific: A 'New' Region or the Return of History?" *Australian Journal of International Affairs* 2019: 8).

23. Iania Sinclair, "Sanskritic Buddhism as an Asian Universalism," in *Imagining Asia(s): Networks, Actors, Sites*, ed. Andrea Acri, Kashaf Ghani, Murari K. Jha, and Sraman Mukherjee (Singapore: ISEAS Publishing, 2019), 275–333.

24. Federica A. Brolio, "Interconnectedness and Mobility in the Middle Ages/ Nowadays: From Baghdad to Chang'an and from Istanbul to Tokyo," in *Imagining Asia(s): Networks, Actors, Sites*, 334–357.

25. Pardesi, "The Indo-Pacific," 8.

26. Jon Goss and Terence Wesley-Smith, "Introduction: Remaking Area Studies," in *Remaking Area Studies: Teaching and Learning across Asia and the Pacific*, ed. Jon Goss and Terence Wesley-Smith (Honolulu: University of Hawai'i Press, 2010), xi.

27. Pardesi does an excellent job of outlining these movements in his article 'Indo-China'.

28. Andrea Acri, Kashshaf Ghani, Murari K. Jha, and Sraman Mukherjee, "Introduction," in *Imagining Asia(s): Networks, Actors, Sites*, ed. Andrea Acri, Kashshaf Ghani, Murari K. Jha, and Sraman Mukherjee (Singapore: ISEAS Publishing, 2019), 3.

29. Doreen Massey, *For Space* (London: Sage Publishing, 2005).

30. Robin Bush, Philip Fountain, and R. Michael Feener, "Introduction," in *Religion and the Politics of Development*, ed. Philip Fountain, Robin Bush, and Michael Feener (London: Palgrave Macmillan, 2015), 3.

31. Edward W. Said, *Orientalism* (New York: Pantheon Books, 1978).

32. Goh, "The Question of Cultural Incommensurability".

33. Akhil Gupta and James Ferguson, *Anthropological Locations: Boundaries and Grounds of a Field Science* (Berkeley, CA: University of California Press, 1997), 4.

34. James D. Faubion, George E. Marcus, and Michael M. J. Fischer, *Fieldwork Is Not What It Used to Be: Learning Anthropology's Method in a Time of Transition*, Cornell Paperbacks (Ithaca, NY: Cornell University Press, 2009).

35. Jean Comaroff and John L Comaroff, *Theory from the South: Or, How Euro-America Is Evolving Toward Africa* (Boulder, CO: Paradigm Publishers, 2012); Jean Comaroff and John L. Comaroff, "Theory from the South: Or, How Euro-America Is Evolving Toward Africa," *Anthropological Forum: A Journal of Social Anthropology and Comparative Sociology* 22, no. 2 (2012): 113–131.

REFERENCES

Acri, Andrea, Ghani, Kashshaf, Jha, Murari K., and Mukherjee, Sraman. "Introduction." In *Imagining Asia(s): Networks, Actors, Sites*, edited by Andrea Acri, Kashshaf Ghani, Murari K. Jha, and Sraman Mukherjee, 1–16. Singapore: ISEAS Publishing, 2019.

Astuti, Rita. "Taking People Seriously." *HAU: Journal of Ethnographic Theory* 7, no. 1 (2017): 105–122.

Behar, Ruth, and Deborah A. Gordon. *Women Writing Culture*. Berkeley: University of California Press, 1995.

Bush, Robin, Philip Fountain, and R. Michael Feener. "Introduction." In *Religion and the Politics of Development*, edited by Philip Fountain, Robin Bush, and R. Michael Feener, 1–9. New York: Palgrave Macmillan, 2015.

Chaudhuri, Sarit. K., and Sucheta Sen Chaudhuri. *Fieldwork in South Asia: Memories, Moments, and Experiences*. New Delhi, India: SAGE, 2014.

Chen, Kuan-Hsing. *Asia as Method: Toward Deimperialization*. Durham: Duke University Press, 2010.

Clifford, James, and George E. Marcus. *Writing Culture: The Poetics and Politics of Ethnography*. Berkley: University of California Press, 1986.

Comaroff, Jean, and John L. Comaroff. *Theory from the South: Or, How Euro-America Is Evolving Toward Africa*. Boulder, CO: Paradigm Publishers, 2012.

———. "Theory from the South: Or, How Euro-America Is Evolving Toward Africa." *Anthropological Forum: A Journal of Social Anthropology and Comparative Sociology* 22, no. 2 (2012): 113–131.

Davies, James, and Dimitrina Spencer. *Emotions in the Field: The Psychology and Anthropology of Fieldwork Experience*. Stanford, CA: Stanford University Press, 2010.

DeWalt, Kathleen Musante. *Participant Observation: A Guide for Fieldworkers/ Kathleen M. DeWalt and Billie R. DeWalt*. 2nd Edition. Lanham: Rowman and Littlefield, 2011.

Dresch, Paul, David J. Parkin, and Wendy James. *Anthropologists in a Wider World: Essays on Field Research*. New York: Berghahn Books, 2000.

Faubion, James D., George E. Marcus, and Michael M. J. Fischer. *Fieldwork Is Not What It Used to Be: Learning Anthropology's Method in a Time of Transition*. Cornell Paperbacks. Ithaca, NY: Cornell University Press, 2009.

Ganguly, Sumit, and Manjeet S. Pardesi, "Can China and India Rise Peacefully?" *Orbis* 56, no. 3 (Summer 2012): 470–485.

Goh, Beng-Lan. "The Question of Cultural Incommensurability: An Intercultural Interpretation Arising out of Southeast Asia." *American Anthropologist* 121, no. 2 (2019): 498–505.

Goss, Jon, and Terence Wesley-Smith. "Introduction: Remaking Area Studies." In *Remaking Area Studies: Teaching and Learning across Asia and the Pacific*, edited by Jon Goss and Terence Wesley-Smith, ix–xxvii. Honolulu: University of Hawai'i Press, 2010.

Graburn, Nelson H. H., and Noel B. Salazar. *Tourism Imaginaries: Anthropological Approaches*. New York: Berghahn Books, 2014.

Gupta, Akhil, and James Ferguson. *Anthropological Locations: Boundaries and Grounds of a Field Science*. Berkeley, CA: University of California Press, 1997.

International Monetary Fund. "Regional Economic Outlook: Asia and Pacific. Caught in Prolongued Uncertainty: Challenges and Opportunities for Asia." *International Monetary Fund*, Washington DC [online] (Oct 2019) available at: https://www.imf.org/en/Publications/REO/APAC/Issues/2019/10/03/areo1023, last accessed 26 January 2020.

Kanitkar, Helen A. *An Anthropological Bibliography of South Asia*. The Hague: Mouton, 1976.

King, Victor T. *The Modern Anthropology of South-East Asia: An Introduction*. London: Routledge, 2003.

Kwon, Heonik. *The Other Cold War*. New York: Columbia University Press, 2010.

Massey, Doreen. *For Space*. London: Sage Publishing, 2005.

Mathur, Saloni. "History and Anthropology in South Asia: Rethinking the Archive." *Annual Review of Anthropology* 29 (2000): 89-106.

Ong, Aihwa, and Nancy N Chen, ed. *Asian Biotech: Ethics and Communities of Fate*. Durham, NC: Duke University Press, 2010.

Pardesi, Manjeet S. "The Indo-Pacific: A 'New' Region or the Return of History?" *Australian Journal of International Affairs* 74, no. 2 (2020): 124-146.

———. "American Global Primacy and the Rise of India." *AsiaPacific Issues* 129 (March 2017): 1-8.

———. "India in Asia: India's Relations with Southeast Asia and China, 1962–1991." In *India in the World: National and Transnational Perspectives, 1947–1991*, edited by Andreas Hilger and Corinna Unger, 15–34. Frankfurt am Main: Peter Lang, 2012.

———. "Review Essay: Understanding the Rise of India." *India Review* 6, no. 3 (July–September 2007): 209–231.

Perera, Sasanka, and Dev Nath Pathak, ed. *Intersections of Contemporary Art, Anthropology and Art History in South Asia Decoding Visual Worlds*. Cham: Springer International Publishing, 2019.

Puri, Shalini, and Debra A. Castillo, ed. *Theorizing Fieldwork in the Humanities: Methods, Reflections, and Approaches to the Global South*. New York: Palgrave Macmillan US, 2016.

Rabinow, Paul. *Reflections on Fieldwork in Morocco*. Berkeley: Univ of California Press, 2007.

Roy, Srila. *New South Asian Feminisms Paradoxes and Possibilities*. London: Zed Books, 2012.

Said, Edward W. *Orientalism*. New York: Pantheon Books, 1978.

Smith, Linda Tuhiwai. *Decolonizing Methodologies: Research and Indigenous Peoples*. 2nd Edition. London and New York: Zed Books: Distributed in the USA exclusively by Palgrave Macmillan, 2012.

Tsing, Anna. "What Is Emerging? Supply Chains and the Remaking of Asia." *The Professional Geographer* 68, no. 2 (April 2016): 330–337.

Tsing, Anna Lowenhaupt. "Natural Resources and Capitalist Frontiers." *Economic and Political Weekly* 38, no. 48 (2003): 5100–5106.

van der Veer, Peter. "Religion, Secularism and National Development in India and China." *Third World Quarterly* 33, no. 4 (2012): 719–732.

———. "Smash Temples, Burn Books: Comparing Secularist Projects in India and China." *The World Religious Cultures* 73 (Spring 2012): 17–26.

———. "The Comparative Sociology of India and China." *Social Anthropology* 17, no. 1 (2009): 90–108.

Yamashita, Shinji, J. S. Eades, and Joseph Bosco. *The Making of Anthropology in East and Southeast Asia.* Asian Anthropologies. New York: Berghahn Books, 2004.

Section I

REFLEXIVELY
RE-READING THE FIELD

Chapter 1

Astronauts of the Western Pamirs

Mobility, Power, and Disconnection in High Asia

Till Mostowlansky

ABSTRACT

How can we think about mobility between places in High Asia that are disconnected by complex national boundaries as well as by colonial and Cold War legacies? What does ethnographic fieldwork in these places reveal? And how can we connect this knowledge to other sites of anthropological investigation? This chapter approaches these questions, drawing on the author's own longitudinal fieldwork in and between multiple locations in Afghanistan, Pakistan, and Tajikistan. Looking back in the history of anthropology to Bronislaw Malinowski's *Argonauts of the Western Pacific*, it argues that – despite the many empirical differences between early twentieth-century Melanesia and twenty-first-century Central Asia – sea- and mountain-faring are not unrelated forms of mobility: navigating the verticality of the region, the stickiness of cultural stereotypes, new regimes of state power, transnational NGOs, and illicit forms of trade, the people of the Pamirs in the borderlands of Afghanistan, Pakistan, and Tajikistan meet familiar strangers and build new social relationships. Furthermore, this chapter argues that fieldwork on mobility in the mountainous margins of Central and South Asia offers alternate, yet complementary insights into contemporary anthropological research on an interconnected Asia. Stretching definitions of modernity, urbanity, and the centre, the 'astronauts' of the Western Pamirs make a case for their planetary perspective from the rarefied air of their high-altitude home.

* * *

In the region in High Asia in which I have conducted much of my ethno-graphic fieldwork – roughly covering the borderlands where Afghanistan, Pakistan, and Tajikistan meet – mobility across cultural, ethnic, linguistic, and political frontiers is of utmost importance to people. Thus, a focus on modes of connectivity (or the lack of it) in the region – which we can, broadly speaking, refer to as 'the Pamirs' – requires research in and between multiple locations. In the past two decades, this kind of anthropological research has usually been framed in terms of George E. Marcus's paradigmatic article on 'multi-sited ethnography', in which he argues for the 'translative mapping of brave new worlds'.[1] A decade later, in 'A Not So Multi-Sited Ethnography of a Not So Imagined Community' Ghassan Hage provided a rebuttal to the trend that Marcus's call set in motion.[2] Hage's article largely focuses on the difficulties of multi-sited ethnography in migration research, foregrounding the physical and psychological demands on the researcher that extensive air travel and overwhelming ruptures in social relations entail. Yet Hage also points to the fact that considerations of and reflections on multiple sites and circulations by no means simply belong to contemporary research in a global-ising world.[3] In fact, he argues, we could go back to Bronislaw Malinowski's *Argonauts of the Western Pacific* and the very foundations of anthropology to observe how mobility has informed research in a similar way in very dif-ferent times and places.[4]

In this chapter I take up this invitation to look at mobility and 'multi-sitedness' in a longer time frame, making an unlikely comparison between some of the world's highest places above sea level and Malinowski's field in maritime Melanesia. My reasons for reading mobility in High Asia in relation to Malinowski's work on the Trobriand Islands require some elaboration, both conceptually and in light of an increasing polarisation between the repudiators and defenders of anthropological classics.[5]

Malinowski's work on mobility and processes of exchange in the Western Pacific is structured around the depths of the seas – tiny, scattered islands and atolls and the great expanses of water between them – and examines technologies to overcome the disconnection deriving from these depths and distances. In this chapter, I take these themes – ever cautious of the political and epistemological context in which Malinowski's research was produced – to argue for their useful relocation to the high-altitude environment of the Pamirs. *Argonauts of the Western Pacific* tackles many issues that have remained salient themes in anthropology, but which are in need of extension and reformulation rather than mere repetition. In the following I would like to take up two points and build on them to make *three key arguments*.

The first point touches upon the questions of why, how, and where people travel, and how and to what ends we can follow them on the specific circuits and disconnections that arise along the way. The second point concerns processes of arrival, departure, disconnection, and (re)connection that are encapsulated in the opening sentence of Malinowski's ethnography, in which he calls the readers to imagine themselves 'suddenly set down surrounded by all your gear, alone on a tropical beach close to a native village, while the launch or dinghy which has brought you sails away out of sight'.[6] Modified versions of this image reflect widely recounted anthropological experiences of fieldwork as a rite of passage in which disconnection from old social relations and the establishment of new ones play a pivotal role.[7] Replace the 'tropical beach' with any other location of arrival, the 'native village' with a settlement with a name, and the 'launch or dinghy' with a different means of transport, and you might find yourself in any contemporary ethnography.

In the case of my own fieldwork, which I have been conducting in High Asia since 2008, my 'tropical beaches' were a road maintenance outpost and an orchard beneath a fort, the 'native villages' were the small towns of Murghab and Karimabad, and my 'boats' were a Russian car and an ageing Pakistani jeep. Yet what is more – and this is the *first key argument* that I would like to explore in this chapter – the experience of disconnection, arrival, and newly established social ties has never been unique to me as an anthropologist. My informants, too, whom I frequently accompanied on their journeys, underwent experiences of profound strangeness, exoticism, and disconnection in the process of crossing the multiple frontiers that mark their world.

People in the borderlands of Afghanistan, Pakistan, and Tajikistan are both separated and united by different languages, religious identities, ethnicities, temporalities, and the containers of the Afghan, Pakistani, and Tajik nation-states; by different colonial, post-colonial, and socialist histories; and by the verticality of high altitude.[8] While some of these factors have long been inscribed into the region – materially and socially – others are outcomes of Russian and British colonialism, Cold War interventions, and more recent violent political incursions. In everyday life, these factors are inextricably entangled, rendering mobility across difference a central part of a three-dimensional ontology in which the vertical is bound up with changing compositions of air, culture, and power.[9] Life and fieldwork in the Pamirs are subject to such changes, and the experience of the frontier is closely linked to elevation.

I would like to illustrate this chapter's *second key argument* with a brief vignette. When I met Mehmonsho in 2007 in Dushanbe, Tajikistan's capital, he was in his forties, worked as a driver for an international NGO, and had just sent his son off to work as a security guard in Moscow. Yet before all that Mehmonsho had lived 'many lives', as he told me, from a Soviet childhood in a serene village in the Pamirs to an opposition fighter in the Tajik civil war

(1992–1997) to a policeman to a driver for an NGO. During the war, he had ventured into the Afghan parts of the Pamirs, and after the war he sold cars in the less accessible, high-altitude parts of the region where, he told me, 'the air gets so thin that you can barely breathe, where you need the training of an astronaut [*kosmonavt*] to survive'. Later, in 2010, while conducting fieldwork in these parts of the Pamirs, I spotted Mehmonsho in the bazaar of Murghab, a small town at 3,650 metres above sea level, where he had brought tourists in his employer's car. 'Ah Tillo', he said, 'you got your training and made it to the moon [*luna*]'. When I asked him if such a trip with tourists was really worth risking his job, he laughed and said, 'This isn't just about the money. It's about going somewhere different. Look at all these Kyrgyz here, look at how close we are to the sun. We should get ourselves sombreros'.

Mehmonsho's experience is not at all an isolated one. In fact, many people I have met in the Pamirs – on all sides of the nation-state divides – have comparably complex biographies and spatial trajectories, albeit moulded into very different late twentieth-century histories. These diverging spatial and historical trajectories, as well as specific modes of mobility and immobility, inform the perceptions of people across political and geographical boundaries as either familiar or 'exotic others'. Very early on in my fieldwork in 2008, I noted that my preconceived idea of what constitutes an ethnographic site was challenged by my informants' rapid and continuous movements across difference and physical space, as well as by their insistence on *not going* to certain places. These movements (and the absence of them) were – not surprisingly – informed by economic opportunities and constraints, but also by kin networks, pilgrimage, political change, transhumance, education, health, and sometimes simply by curiosity, fear, or the desire for adventure.

In his book *Asia as Method*, Kuan-Hsing Chen argues that focusing on intra-Asian connections across cultural and political frontiers serves to decolonise, deimperialise, and 'de-Cold War'-ise the study of their people and places.[10] Following Chen, this chapter's *third key argument* is that studying mobility in the Pamirs across the frontier contributes to an understanding of its seemingly separate entities. However, looking at how modes of connection and disconnection work, at how people in the Pamirs manage to maintain relationships across vast geographical, temporal, and cultural distances, and at when they decide – or are forced – to abandon these relationships is not a mere academic exercise. At a point in time when the geopolitical legacies of nineteenth- and twentieth-century histories seem to fade, overshadowed by a future-oriented turn to an expanding China, such a focus does political work, too. In recent years, a great deal of literature has been written on the everyday implications of connectivity and (neo)liberalisation in Asia, often from the standpoint of urbanisation.[11] There is little doubt that this focus on the Asian metropolis, now often seen through the prism of Chinese investments connecting 'centres' across Asia, is likely to persist and grow.[12] In contrast, the Pamirs at large offer us insights into a very different story of contemporary Asia, a story that is marked by the spectre of remoteness, the weight of colonial and Cold War histories, the dynamics of contemporary geopolitics, and the ways people in the region organise their everyday lives amid these fragmentations.

MODERN ISLANDS IN A SEA OF TRADITION

In recent years few people have actually travelled overland between northern Pakistan and eastern Tajikistan, crossing Afghan Badakhshan. While there is published research on small-scale cross-border trade[13] and on Tajiks seeking refuge in Pakistan's Chitral District during the civil war,[14] physical journeys across nation-state boundaries are a relatively rare occurrence. Reasons for this include the complex border regimes enforced by all three countries, the continuing threat of war and violence on route in Afghanistan, and the lack of economic incentives to pursue such treks.

Nevertheless, during fieldwork in the area around Hunza and Gilgit in northern Pakistan in 2013, I heard intriguing accounts of such journeys from the few men who had travelled to Tajikistan since the disintegration of the Soviet Union. Their travels had been sponsored by NGOs that sought to revive regional connectivity. These organisations imagined that such connectivity had been in place before the closure of the Soviet border and Cold War competition had firmed up the frontier. Among them was the Aga Khan Development Network, whose presence in Pakistan, Tajikistan, and Afghanistan is rooted in the Ismaili Muslim communities of the region. There are also several smaller NGOs that have promoted the revival of cross-border connectivity, including an organisation that fosters such connections through the development of gem stone processing – a business very much linked to the region's mountainous geology.

Upon their return, the travellers had stories to tell about historical links between their homes and the places they had visited, but their observations were also focused on how differently places across the region had developed in the course of time. Niaz, a man in his fifties who had travelled to Khorog, eastern Tajikistan's largest city at the Afghan border with a population of around 30,000, put this perhaps most pointedly. He told me that his journey from Pakistan to Tajikistan had been one from his home to 'Europe'. Niaz based his argument on the fact that in Khorog one could see girls in miniskirts and 'European style' houses. Niaz's statement was both spatial and temporal. He did not mean to say that Europe actually began beyond the northern border of Afghanistan. He rather referred to Khorog as part of a different cultural space

– one that is more compatible with that of an imagined Europe than with that of an observed Afghanistan. While Niaz referred to Khorog as 'European', in the same sentence he pointed to the places in Afghanistan through which he had travelled as 'backward', using the English term. He based this observation on the fact that girls there did not wear miniskirts and that people still used donkeys as a means of transport. This view gave Niaz's account a temporal twist that largely resonates with the ways people in the Pamirs situate ideas of modernity and progress on a scale of time that allows for the perception of different places co-existing in the present, yet living in different times.

Like in many other settings of mobility around the globe,[15] even 'local' people crossing the Pamirs' manifold frontiers tend to encounter an abundance of 'exotic' places along the way. Malinowski's 'tropical beaches' are not limited to the figure of the 'foreigner' (*khoriji*) alone. Yet these encounters come with an important difference: what makes their setting distinct is that each of these 'other' places comes with a historical memory, a sense that underneath the sand of these 'beaches' is a fading connection that has been buried by the tides of the twentieth century. While the region's different nation-states have largely favoured and often actively accelerated this process of fading in an attempt to pull the borderlands more tightly into the state's orbit, some local and international NGOs have been engaged in cross-border revival activities. Meanwhile, scholarly research has been increasingly interested in how these different modes of connection and disconnection have come about in the first place.[16]

In parallel with other places throughout Asia, the Pamirs became infused with ideas of progress and modernity in the first half of the twentieth century. In this regard, the transformative, but slow, establishment of Soviet power in the region was certainly a driving force. At the same time, social activists embedded in Ismaili Muslim networks worked in a similar direction in the context of the late British Empire. While the ideological foundations of these projects were situated on opposite ends of the spectrum – Soviet socialism versus Islamicate (Cold War) liberalism – their engagement with people in the region was not entirely unrelated: both projects pursued the steady build-up of material and social infrastructures, of schools, pathways, roads, assembly halls, health facilities, and educational mobility on the territories of today's Tajikistan (Soviet) and Pakistan (Ismaili). This build-up accelerated in the second half of the twentieth century and took an unexpected turn when, after the disintegration of the Soviet Union, the Ismaili-run Aga Khan Development Network extended its influence into Tajikistan and Afghanistan.[17]

As mentioned earlier, in the account of his journey across the Pakistan–Afghanistan–Tajikistan borders and back, Niaz operated with the idea that not all places across the region had received their fair share of progress and modernity. As a result, one could observe material, temporal, and embodied differences between these places. My informants living along the border of Tajikistan and Afghanistan have expressed similar views over the years: this border meanders along the river Panj, which delineates the boundary between the two countries. For the most part, the other bank of the river is so close that, with good eyes, one can observe everyday life across the water. In the Soviet period, people on the Tajik side witnessed how, over the decades, towns, an airport, electrified villages, roads, and other signs of infrastructural development appeared on their bank of the river, while little change took place on the Afghan side. This image has persisted despite the fact that, in the wake of the international military intervention in 2001, donors made sure that Afghans received new roads and electricity generated by new micro-hydropower stations.

While Tajikistan's infrastructure has, in turn, crumbled such that the Afghan bank of the river sometimes shines brighter than its own, many of my informants in Tajikistan insist that Afghanistan is still 'old' (*qadim*) and enmeshed in tradition and religious fanaticism. It is important to note that such 'civilisational' differences are rarely mapped onto whole nation-states or the former Soviet Union per se. Instead, people identify very specific 'islands' of modernity, which are often surrounded by temporally and culturally different areas. In the case of the Soviet Union, such islands were created following the logic of enclosure, incorporation, and provisioning (*obespechenie*) of strategically selected places.[18] Considered a sensitive border area, the Pamirs were part of this scheme, colloquially known as 'Moscow provisioning' (*Moskovskoe obespechenie*), a term that refers to the direct cultural, aesthetic, and political connections to Moscow that this status implied.[19] To this day, many parts of the Pamirs are infused with a sense of urban lifestyle, and the residents cling to the notion that they are still somehow culturally and temporally different from people in other places in Tajikistan – even its capital Dushanbe.

In contrast, the inhabitants of Niaz's home town – Karimabad in northern Pakistan – draw on a very different sense of history. As mentioned earlier, ideas of progress and their material incarnation date back to the first half of the twentieth century, when social and religious activists fostered educational opportunities. In the second half of the twentieth century these efforts coincided with the construction of the Karakoram Highway. Previously, travel along the footpaths between Karimabad and down-country Pakistan was a harrowing and seemingly endless undertaking. With the completion of the highway, however, Karimabad, and the Hunza Valley in which the town is located, became a prime humanitarian laboratory for the Aga Khan Development Network. From the 1980s onward, multiple large-scale projects transformed the valley not only in terms of education and health, but also with respect to social organisation, agriculture, animal husbandry, and tourism.[20]

While Pakistani state and media discourse depict the country's north as overwhelmingly remote and exotic,[21] the people living in Karimabad see these transformations as the reason for high literacy rates in the area, for mobility, and for their worldly outlook beyond the borders of Pakistan. In contrast to places in Tajikistan that were hand-picked to be linked to the centre (Moscow), locales in Hunza have attained their status as islands of modernity through a complex interplay of NGO work, religious-humanitarian networks, and the expansion of Pakistani state power. Nevertheless, in both cases – socialist engineering on the one hand and humanitarian laboratory on the other – the basic idea has been that of distinction from the surrounding areas. This is what makes them islands in a vast sea of perceived temporal difference. A trip from one island to the other is therefore never simply a journey through space, but also one through time.

SHIPS OF THE DESERT AND OTHER LUNAR ANIMALS

The *Bar Varka* is located on Khorog's Ulitsa Gagarina, a street dedicated to Yuri Gagarin who – in his spacecraft *Vostok* ('East') – was the first human to venture into outer space. Dinners, and even lunches, at the *Varka* are usually intoxicating occasions, a feature that some of my friends in Khorog attribute to the outlet's heavy food, which, they say, can only be digested with plenty of booze. *Varka*'s seating sections are assembled along the windows and the inner wall, leaving sufficient space to dance between the two dining areas. Few guests resist the temptation to move their legs after a meal that has left them with heads and stomachs heavy from vodka and mayonnaise-laden dishes with alluring names such as 'Scent of Love' (*aromat liubvi*) and 'Parisian cutlets' (*kotleta po-parizhski*).

On an evening in mid-summer 2011, I sat with a group of Khorogi friends in the *Varka* and we talked about the higher parts of the Pamirs along the border with China, from where I had just arrived a day earlier. Manzura, an office clerk and, back then, about thirty years old, said, while trying to drown out a *Modern Talking* song, 'Tilljon, I think you're a bit crazy to keep going back there. What's there except for yaks and headaches?' While I was contemplating my response, Jamshed, a teacher in Khorog who frequently travels to his home village further up the Ghunt Valley, stepped in and replied for me. 'It makes sense to go to Murghab', he said. 'It's serene; it's peaceful there and you can eat meat every single day. You might have bad dreams from the lack of oxygen, but it's not like the city. I stayed there once in a yurt at a hunting camp for a few weeks, and I'd go back if I had the time'.

Manzura's and Jamshed's statements reflect common Khorogi viewpoints on the high-altitude parts of the Pamirs. To them, Khorog – located at the Tajikistan–Afghanistan border – is a city that, despite its small population of 30,000, has two universities, important administrative institutions, and the possibility of an urban lifestyle. To juxtapose the city with 'empty' high-altitude space is part of a common imaginary that resonates in both Manzura's undivided love for the urban and Jamshed's longing to escape it. Not surprisingly, people in Murghab – the district encompassing much of the area Manzura and Jamshed referred to – have a different take on this issue. Viewed from Murghab, the question of remoteness is no doubt an important one. It influences the way people experience the presence and absence of the state, for instance, through the lack of quality educational and healthcare facilities. Sometimes Murghabis also reflect the same dichotomy as Manzura and Jamshed by emphasising that their parts of the Pamirs are much 'purer' (*taza*) than those closer to the orbit of 'the city' (*shaar*), meaning Khorog. However, what marks Murghabi views on Murghab is that apparent contradictions can go hand in hand and allow for both the perception of an empty, lunar space and of that of an intensely connected region, populated by humans, animals, and spirits.

When I met him in July 2015, Sorbon, an engineer working for one of the major mobile network providers in Murghab, had just come back from his daily routine of refuelling the generator that keeps phone connections going in the small town. After rushing through the door of a friend's house, he sat down for a cup of tea and said, 'It takes so much fuel to keep mobile connections stable, to Dushanbe, to Moscow, and for you to Europe'. Sorbon had studied in Tajikistan's capital Dushanbe in the 1980s and ever since worked for different telecommunication companies. 'They've always listened in on what we say to each other here', Sorbon continued. 'Now they store our conversations and messages on servers in the capital. Back in the Soviet Union they installed big satellite dishes and antennas in Murghab with which they could listen to conversations from around the world. We don't call it "the roof of the world" [*kryshe mira*] for nothing. From here you can listen better'.

The act of listening is not only linked to surveillance and the presence of state power in this borderland. It is also a constitutive act in anthropology, and this intersection might be why anthropologists are frequently mistaken for spies in this and other parts of the world. Listening to others talking about listening and observing how others listen are activities that have long been part of ethnographic endeavours. Indeed, in *Argonauts of the Western Pacific*, Malinowski mentions the act of listening multiple times as an underlying theme that stands at the heart of his methodology. This methodology is not only centred around the ethnographer listening to people talking, but also around the observation of people listening. This observation, in turn, provides a window into social interactions that are linked to broader formations of historical memory, ritual, and hierarchy.

On the one hand, in Murghab, one can 'listen better', as Sorbon put it, because sounds overlap and interfere with one another less here than elsewhere. Once the Chinese trucks have passed through the settlement, the dogs take a break from their barking, and the children go to sleep, one can hear otherwise unheard voices: the 'fire talking' (*ot süloit*) in the stove, an ancestral spirit (*arbak*) rushing through the house, or – further away from the town – the sound of a lone Soviet car crossing the summer pasture (*jailoo*), yaks puffing in their sleep, and – if the wind blows in just the right direction – faint music from a far off, neighbouring yurt. On the other hand, listening to humans talk can sometimes be tricky in Murghab, not only because some mistake listening for spying, but also because people's lives in the high-altitude environment are extremely busy.

While Murghab lacks a proper entertainment industry, the often insufficient electricity supply, large families, the chores of cattle breeding, and the harsh climate make up for it by keeping people busy around the clock. Thus, catching Kamal, a government worker, was never an easy task, but when we managed to meet our conversations usually plumbed the depths of Murghabi history. During a meeting on a cold winter afternoon in 2010, I told Kamal about my research on the Pamir Highway connecting Murghab with Khorog and Osh in southern Kyrgyzstan. He listened carefully and then reminded me that Khorog and Osh had not always been the most obvious destinations for people in Murghab. He told me that prior to Soviet road construction, the path to Osh took almost twice as long as the route to Kashgar in what is today China's Xinjiang province. 'People from Murghab would take their cattle to the market in Kashgar and traders from there would come by camel to us to exchange cattle for goods'. He emphasised that camels could handle the high altitudes while horses – just as some people from the flatlands – were likely to suffer from ill health when ascending into thin air. 'Not everyone can stand the elevation of Murghab', Kamal stated. 'After the camel came the automobile on the road, and Soviet trucks, and then Chinese trucks and cars from all over the world'. When I asked him about other connections that the region's national boundaries had closed off from the 1940s onward, Kamal said, 'For our ancestors there was no Tajikistan, no Afghanistan, no China. They moved back and forth. Now there's very little movement in this area. Go to the hunting camps at the border with Afghanistan, lie still and don't look out for people. Then you can see Marco Polo sheep crossing without passports and visas. If you're lucky you'll spot a snow leopard, too, sneaking through, perhaps from as far away as Pakistan. They're the only travellers these days'.

POWER ACROSS THE WATER

Kamal's take on borders in the Pamirs largely corresponds to my own observations over the years: movement across international boundaries in the Pamirs is not primarily shaped by high altitude and other environmental conditions, but is channelled through shifting power relations between political actors and local populations. While humans are busy negotiating the conditions on which they build these relationships, wild animals indeed escape the picture and remain largely invisible. At the same time, these animals are closely involved in political processes through their inclusion in frameworks of species conservation, lucrative hunting camps whose owners profit from privileged ties to the government, and the consumption of locally popular game meat. Discourses on connection and disconnection are also linked to the mobile force of the elements, such as winds[22] that blow from Afghanistan into Tajikistan and which people in Murghab often attribute to 'black' (*kara*) religious rituals performed by mullahs on the Afghan side of the border, and water,[23] most materially and symbolically explicit in the form of the river Panj marking the border between Afghanistan and Tajikistan.

The river Panj splits the Wakhan Valley into a Tajik side to the north and an Afghan side to the south. Many people from across the Pamirs, as well as Tajik and international tourists, travel to the Tajik part of the Wakhan for its hot springs and pilgrimage sites. Some of my informants from Murghab travelled to the *mazar* ('pilgrimage site') of Bibi Fotima to perform fertility-enhancing rituals. I also met people from Khorog on holiday in small sanatoriums close to the valley's various hot springs. From all these places villages in Afghanistan are visible on the opposite bank of the river, whose water levels fluctuate throughout the year and are sometimes so low that people can walk across this still sensitive former Cold War boundary.

For people from other parts of the Pamirs the border river is still the final frontier, beyond which the land is considered wild and unknown. For those living in the Wakhan, however, the outlook onto the Afghan side is rather complex. While many see Afghanistan as eternally backward and dangerous, many family connections, spiritual lineages, and actual face-to-face encounters across the border have persisted to the present day.[24] During my 2016 fieldwork in a Tajik village whose fields are so close to the river that they are regularly flooded, I was told detailed stories of decades-long cross-border exchanges by foot or horse. These ranged from family visits to humanitarian aid during the Soviet war in Afghanistan to starving Tajik citizens looking for food in the villages of their distant Afghan relatives in the 1990s to more recent business deals in the trafficking of drugs and booze. At one point during my fieldwork, a long and expensive detour through the official border crossing at Ishkashim – the entry to the Wakhan – finally took me to the

Afghan counterpart of the Tajik village. I was tempted to simply walk across the river back into Tajikistan, but too much water and, more importantly, my fear of detention in this still uneasy borderland prevented me from doing so.

In the Afghan village, which grew substantially as a result of emigration across the river under early Soviet rule in the 1920s and 1930s, peoples' attitudes towards illicit border crossings were much more relaxed. To be sure, they depicted their walks through the river as adventurous and exciting, but this had less to do with the act of wading through the water than with the nature of the goods being transported. Prime objects of exchange, I was told by Rahim, a farmer in his mid-twenties, are opium and heroin leaving Afghanistan and booze entering from Tajikistan. Then, as he laid out the dinner he had invited me to, he stated apologetically, 'If there wasn't so much water in the river this summer we would be drinking *arak* [vodka] now'. As the evening progressed, Rahim explained how he visits Tajikistan under cover of darkness. 'I call one of the mobile numbers in Tajikistan', he said, 'and I make an appointment. Either somebody comes across from the Tajik side or I put on my chest waders and walk through the river. . . . Sometimes I buy some *arak* and a few cans of *Jack Power*. *Arak*, wine, and *Jack Power* are brought over here from Tajikistan. Opium and heroin are taken by the state [*davlat khati*] to Tajikistan further down the valley at Ishkashim'.

State institutions' close involvement in and exercise of control over opium and heroin trafficking is an open secret in both Afghanistan and Tajikistan. Goods are transported across bridges, inside tires, and by rubber dinghy. In the meantime, the regionally famous *Vodka Tojikiston* makes its opposite way through the river in plastic bottles, loaded onto male bodies. These male bodies are fuelled by what Rahim and his friends called *Jack Power* – a liquid substance believed to sharpen the senses, improve physical strength, and enhance virility. It took me a while to find out what *Jack Power* was and where it came from: when I eventually crossed back into Tajikistan and asked in one of the Wakhan's grocery stores for a can of *Jack Power*, the shop owner laughed and pointed to a large pile of black cans behind him. Red letters on the can said *Jaguar*, and a closer look revealed that *Jaguar* was a Russian-produced alcoholic energy drink. The shop owner asked where I had heard the name *Jack Power* and laughed again when I told him that this was the beverage's name on the other side of the river. Then he said, 'They're out of their minds over there. They drink this stuff like crazy [*divona*]! Hey! You've crossed the border. How do I know you're not a terrorist?'

Like many locales in the region, the two sides of the river Panj stand for the ambivalence of physical proximity, for the simultaneity of mobility and disconnection, and for the powerful legacy of historical identities. The transformation of a run-of-the-mill Russian energy drink into a mythical elixir is part of this complex: while the very opportunity to trade booze across the Panj is based on a deep sense of shared ethno-linguistic identities and kin networks, cans of *Jaguar* journey through the water only to reappear on the other bank as *Jack Power*. Almost a century of intermittent separation and othering have led to the establishment of binaries such as *Jack Power* versus *Jaguar*, tradition versus modernity, and terrorism versus security. These binaries are sticky labels and persist despite a multitude of circulations across the region. Thus, both the capacity to get rid of colonial, Cold War, and nationalist legacies and the impossibility of doing so sit at the intimate nexus of everyday life where the body, the matter inhabiting and surrounding it, and the categories used to describe their relations all come together.

CONCLUSION: 'ASTRONAUTS' OF THE WESTERN PAMIRS

Malinowski's *Argonauts of the Western Pacific* gives us a view from the boat that unfolds into cosmological verticality. Economy, social relations, and a taste for adventure emerge as inextricably linked across the relatively flat surface of the Pacific. In contrast, using cars and trucks instead of boats, the astronauts of the Pamirs ascend to physical heights from where the perspective is planetary. They navigate remoteness and attempt to overcome the obstacles of a dry and rocky land. Their pathways, however, do not simply lead them up and down. Pamirs also head east and west, north and south: large numbers of people from Pakistan's portion of the area work in the Gulf, Wakhis from Afghanistan make their way to Lahore and Karachi, Tajiks construct apartment buildings and stadiums in Moscow, and overall there is an increasing orientation towards China.

Yet, as I have argued, people from this borderland do not need to travel far to encounter the 'exotic'. In fact, the other is always close by in the Pamirs. It is in the neighbouring country, one valley beyond, across the river, one village further, next door, and sometimes even an experience within. Building on Viveiros de Castro's (1992) Amerindian perspectivism, Ghassan Hage notes the critical potential of the realisation that humans live 'continuously and concurrently in a multiplicity of realities' and that this offers an 'important meta-ethnographic consolidation of the critical anthropological ethos of "we can be other than what we are"'.[25] The Afghanistan–Pakistan–Tajikistan border region represents not only such radical difference enshrined in a history of colonial, Cold War, and nationalist separation, but also attempts to overcome this difference through various forms of mobility and references to history.

Against this backdrop, I have argued that some of the answers to the questions of why and by what means people depart, arrive, and establish new – or revive old – social relationships lie in both shared mobility and shared immobility. Much of Malinowski's work employs this methodology to capture a circuit – the *Kula* ring – which revolves around the exchange of bracelets and necklaces in the Western Pacific. So, is there a *Kula* of the Pamirs? The answer is yes and no. There are small, scattered, and interrupted circuits of exchange that are linked to shared belonging in this politically fragmented region. To grasp the meaning of this fragmentation and the lack of broader circuits, we might turn to Edward Evans-Pritchard's critique of *Argonauts*, in which he argues that 'Malinowski failed to see clearly what is perhaps the most significant feature of the *kula*, the bringing together, through the acceptance of common ritual values, of politically autonomous communities'.[26] Inverting this argument for the Pamirs, I suggest that precisely because the borderland populations of the region have been constantly pulled into settings of political dependency – colonial, socialist, nationalist – no overarching common ritual values are in place today. To be sure, local travellers, anthropologists, NGO workers, and religious envoys alike have continuously sought to traverse the many boundaries of this sea above the clouds. At the same time, however, this part of High Asia is still awaiting more profound attempts at decolonisation, deimperialisation, and 'de-Cold War'-isation, all of which would require conscious, and concerted, political and academic efforts.

* * *

ACKNOWLEDGEMENT

I would like to express my deepest gratitude to my interlocutors in Afghanistan, Pakistan, and Tajikistan, who have made possible my research over the past decade. To protect them I use pseudonyms throughout the chapter. For comments on earlier versions of this text I am also indebted to the editors as well as to Brook Bolander, Brian Donahoe, Philip Fountain, and Tobias Marschall.

NOTES

1. George E. Marcus, "Ethnography in/of the World System: The Emergence of Multi-Sited Ethnography," *Annual Review of Anthropology* 24 (1995): 114.
2. Ghassan Hage, "A Not So Multi-Sited Ethnography of a Not So Imagined Community," *Anthropological Theory* 5, no. 4 (December 2005): 463–475.
3. Hage, "A Not So Multi-Sited Ethnography," 467.

4. Bronislaw Malinowski, *Argonauts of the Western Pacific: An Account of Native Enterprise and Adventure into the Archipelagos of Melanesian New Guinea* (London and New York: Routledge, [1922] 2002).

5. For example, Anastasia Piliavsky, "Disciplinary Memory against Ambient Pietism," *HAU: Journal of Ethnographic Theory* 7, no. 3 (2017): 13–17; Paige West, "Introduction: From Reciprocity to Relationality," *Cultural Anthropology* (2018), online: https://culanth.org/fieldsights/introduction-from-reciprocity-to-relationality -west (last accessed 31 May 2019).

6. Malinowski, *Argonauts*, 3.

7. Janet Carsten, "Fieldwork since the 1980s: Total Immersion and Its Discontents," in *The SAGE Handbook of Social Anthropology*, ed. Richard Fardon et al. (London: SAGE, 2012), 7–20; Paul Rabinow, *Reflections on Fieldwork in Morocco* (Berkeley: University of California Press, 1977).

8. Hermann Kreutzmann, *Pamirian Crossroads: Kirghiz and Wakhi of High Asia* (Wiesbaden: Harrassowitz, 2015); Till Mostowlansky, "Faraway Siblings, So Close: Ephemeral Conviviality Across the Wakhan Divide," *Modern Asian Studies* 53, no. 3 (May 2019): 943–977.

9. Stuart Elden, "Secure the Volume: Vertical Geopolitics and the Depth of Power," *Political Geography* 34 (May 2013): 35–51.

10. Chen Kuan-Hsing, *Asia as Method: Toward Deimperialization* (Durham and London: Duke University Press, 2010).

11. For example, Erik Harms, *Luxury and Rubble: Civility and Dispossession in the New Saigon* (Oakland: University of California Press, 2016); Michael Herzfeld, *Siege of the Spirits: Community and Polity in Bangkok* (Chicago: University of Chicago Press, 2016); Pun Ngai, *Made in China: Women Factory Workers in a Global Workplace* (Durham: Duke University Press, 2005); Anne Rademacher, *Reigning the River: Urban Ecologies and Political Transformation in Kathmandu* (Durham: Duke University Press, 2011); Nathaniel Roberts, *To Be Cared For: The Power of Conversion and Foreignness of Belonging in an Indian Slum* (Berkeley: University of California Press, 2016); AbdouMaliq Simone, *Jakarta, Drawing the City Near* (Minneapolis: University of Minnesota Press, 2016); Li Zhang, *In Search of Paradise: Middle-Class Living in a Chinese Metropolis* (Ithaca: Cornell University Press, 2010).

12. See for example, Max Hirsh, *Airport Urbanism: Infrastructure and Mobility in Asia* (Minneapolis and London: University of Minnesota Press, 2016); Parag Khanna, *Connectography: Mapping the Future of Global Civilization* (New York: Random House, 2016).

13. Carolin Maertens, "'No Debt, No Business': The Personalisation of Market Exchange in Gorno-Badakhshan, Tajikistan," in *Approaching Ritual Economy: Socio-Cosmic Fields in Globalised Contexts*, ed. Roland Hardenberg (Tuebingen: University of Tuebingen, 2017), 159–192.

14. Magnus Marsden, "Muslim Cosmopolitans? Transnational Life in Northern Pakistan," *The Journal of Asian Studies* 67, no. 1 (February 2008): 213–247.

15. For example, Engseng Ho, "Inter-Asian Concepts for Mobile Societies," *The Journal of Asian Studies* 76, no. 4 (November 2017): 907–928; Magnus Marsden,

and Till Mostowlansky, "Whither West Asia? Exploring North-South Perspectives on Eurasia," *Journal of Eurasian Studies* 10, no. 1 (January 2019): 3–10; Alessandro Monsutti, "Mobility as a Political Act," *Ethnic and Racial Studies* 41, no. 3 (November 2018): 448–455.

16. For example, Kreutzmann, *Pamirian Crossroads*; Hermann Kreutzmann, *Wakhan Quadrangle: Exploration and Espionage During and After the Great Game* (Wiesbaden: Harrassowitz, 2017); Mostowlansky, "Faraway Siblings, So Close"; Martin Saxer, "A Spectacle of Maps: Cartographic Hopes and Anxieties in the Pamirs," *Cross-Currents: East Asian History and Culture Review* 21 (December 2016): 111–136; Nazif M. Shahrani, *The Kirghiz and Wakhi of Afghanistan: Adaptation to Closed Frontier and War* (Washington: University of Washington Press, [1979] 2002).

17. Till Mostowlansky, "Development Institutions and Religious Networks in the Pamirian Borderlands," in *Routledge Handbook of Asian Borderlands*, ed. Alexander Horstmann, Martin Saxer, and Alessandro Rippa (New York and London: Routledge, 2018), 385–395.

18. Madeleine Reeves, *Border Work: Spatial Lives of the State in Rural Central Asia* (Ithaca: Cornell University Press, 2014), 114.

19. Till Mostowlansky, *Azan on the Moon: Entangling Modernity along Tajikistan's Pamir Highway* (Pittsburgh: University of Pittsburgh Press, 2017).

20. Shafqat Hussain, *Remoteness and Modernity: Transformation and Continuity in Northern Pakistan* (New Haven: Yale University Press, 2015).

21. Hasan H. Karrar, and Till Mostowlansky, "Assembling Marginality in Northern Pakistan," *Political Geography* 63 (March 2018): 65–74.

22. Jerry Zee, "Downwind," *Cultural Anthropology* (2017), online: https://culanth .org/fieldsights/downwind (last accessed 31 May 2019).

23. Jason Cons, "Seepage," *Cultural Anthropology* (2017), online: https://culanth .org/fieldsights/seepage (last accessed 31 May 2019).

24. Abdulmamad Iloliev, "*Pirship* in Badakhshan: The Role and Significance of the Institute of the Religious Masters (*Pirs*) in Nineteenth and Twentieth Century Wakhan and Shughnan," *Journal of Shi'a Islamic Studies* 6, no. 2 (March 2013): 155–175; Suzanne Levi-Sanchez, *The Afghan-Central Asia Borderland: The State and Local Leaders* (London and New York: Routledge, 2017).

25. Ghassan Hage, "Critical Anthropological Thought and the Radical Political Imaginary Today," *Critique of Anthropology* 32, no. 3 (September 2012): 300.

26. Edward Evan Evans-Pritchard, *Social Anthropology* (London: Cohen & West, 1951), 95.

REFERENCES

Carsten, Janet. "Fieldwork Since the 1980s: Total Immersion and Its Discontents." In *The SAGE Handbook of Social Anthropology*, edited by Richard Fardon, Oliva

Harris, Trevor HJ Marchand, Cris Shore, Veronica Strang, Richard Wilson, and Mark Nuttall, 7–20. London: SAGE, 2012.

Chen, Kuan-Hsing. *Asia as Method: Toward Deimperialization*. Durham and London: Duke University Press, 2010.

Cons, Jason. "Seepage." *Cultural Anthropology* (2017), online: https://culanth.org/ fieldsights/seepage (last accessed 31 May 2019).

Elden, Stuart. "Secure the Volume: Vertical Geopolitics and the Depth of Power." *Political Geography* 34 (May 2013): 35–51.

Evans-Pritchard, Edward Evan. *Social Anthropology*. London: Cohen & West, 1951.

Hage, Ghassan. "A Not So Multi-Sited Ethnography of a Not So Imagined Community." *Anthropological Theory* 5, no. 4 (December 2005): 463–475.

———. "Critical Anthropological Thought and the Radical Political Imaginary Today." *Critique of Anthropology* 32, no. 3 (September 2012): 285–308.

Harms, Erik. *Luxury and Rubble: Civility and Dispossession in the New Saigon*. Oakland: University of California Press, 2016.

Herzfeld, Michael. *Siege of the Spirits: Community and Polity in Bangkok*. Chicago: University of Chicago Press, 2016.

Hirsh, Max. *Airport Urbanism: Infrastructure and Mobility in Asia*. Minneapolis and London: University of Minnesota Press, 2016.

Ho, Engseng. "Inter-Asian Concepts for Mobile Societies." *The Journal of Asian Studies* 76, no. 4 (November 2017): 907–928.

Hussain, Shafqat. *Remoteness and Modernity: Transformation and Continuity in Northern Pakistan*. New Haven: Yale University Press, 2015.

Iloliev, Abdulmamad. "*Pirship* in Badakhshan: The Role and Significance of the Institute of the Religious Masters (*Pirs*) in Nineteenth and Twentieth Century Wakhan and Shughnan." *Journal of Shi'a Islamic Studies* 6, no. 2 (March 2013): 155–175.

Karrar, Hasan H., and Till Mostowlansky. "Assembling Marginality in Northern Pakistan." *Political Geography* 63 (March 2018): 65–74.

Khanna, Parag. *Connectography: Mapping the Future of Global Civilization*. New York: Random House, 2016.

Kreutzmann, Hermann. *Pamirian Crossroads: Kirghiz and Wakhi of High Asia*. Wiesbaden: Harrassowitz, 2015.

———. *Wakhan Quadrangle: Exploration and Espionage During and After the Great Game*. Wiesbaden: Harrassowitz, 2017.

Levi-Sanchez, Suzanne. *The Afghan-Central Asia Borderland: The State and Local Leaders*. London and New York: Routledge, 2017.

Maertens, Carolin. "'No Debt, No Business': The Personalisation of Market Exchange in Gorno-Badakhshan, Tajikistan." In *Approaching Ritual Economy: Socio-Cosmic Fields in Globalised Contexts*, edited by Roland Hardenberg, 159–192. Tuebingen: University of Tuebingen, 2017.

Malinowski, Bronislaw. *Argonauts of the Western Pacific: An Account of Native Enterprise and Adventure into the Archipelagos of Melanesian New Guinea*. London and New York: Routledge, [1922] 2002.

Marcus, George E. "Ethnography in/of the World System: The Emergence of Multi-Sited Ethnography." *Annual Review of Anthropology* 24 (1995): 95–117.

Marsden, Magnus. "Muslim Cosmopolitans? Transnational Life in Northern Pakistan." *The Journal of Asian Studies* 67, no. 1 (February 2008): 213–247.

Marsden, Magnus, and Till Mostowlansky. "Whither West Asia? Exploring North-South Perspectives on Eurasia." *Journal of Eurasian Studies* 10, no. 1 (January 2019): 3–10.

Monsutti, Alessandro. "Mobility as a Political Act." *Ethnic and Racial Studies* 41, no. 3 (November 2018): 448–455.

Mostowlansky, Till. *Azan on the Moon: Entangling Modernity along Tajikistan's Pamir Highway*. Pittsburgh: University of Pittsburgh Press, 2017.

———. "Development Institutions and Religious Networks in the Pamirian Borderlands." In *Routledge Handbook of Asian Borderlands*, edited by Alexander Horstmann, Martin Saxer, and Alessandro Rippa, 385–395. New York and London: Routledge, 2018.

———. "Faraway Siblings, So Close: Ephemeral Conviviality across the Wakhan Divide." *Modern Asian Studies* 53, no. 3 (May 2019): 943–977.

Ngai, Pun. *Made in China: Women Factory Workers in a Global Workplace*. Durham: Duke University Press, 2005.

Piliavsky, Anastasia. "Disciplinary Memory against Ambient Pietism." *HAU: Journal of Ethnographic Theory* 7, no. 3 (2017): 13–17.

Rabinow, Paul. *Reflections on Fieldwork in Morocco*. Berkeley: University of California Press, 1977.

Rademacher, Anne. *Reigning the River: Urban Ecologies and Political Transformation in Kathmandu*. Durham: Duke University Press, 2011.

Reeves, Madeleine. *Border Work: Spatial Lives of the State in Rural Central Asia*. Ithaca: Cornell University Press, 2014.

Roberts, Nathaniel. *To Be Cared For: The Power of Conversion and Foreignness of Belonging in an Indian Slum*. Berkeley: University of California Press, 2016.

Saxer, Martin. "A Spectacle of Maps: Cartographic Hopes and Anxieties in the Pamirs." *Cross-Currents: East Asian History and Culture Review* 21 (December 2016): 111–136.

Shahrani, Nazif M. *The Kirghiz and Wakhi of Afghanistan: Adaptation to Closed Frontier and War*. Washington: University of Washington Press, [1979] 2002.

Simone, AbdouMaliq. *Jakarta, Drawing the City Near*. Minneapolis: University of Minnesota Press, 2016.

Viveiros de Castro, Eduardo. *From the Enemy's Point of View: Humanity and Divinity in an Amazonian Society*. Chicago: University of Chicago Press, 1992.

West, Paige. "Introduction: From Reciprocity to Relationality." *Cultural Anthropology* (2018), online: https://culanth.org/fieldsights/introduction-from-reciprocity-to-relationality-west (last accessed 31 May 2019)

Zee, Jerry. "Downwind." *Cultural Anthropology* (2017), online: https://culanth.org/fieldsights/downwind (last accessed 31 May 2019).

Zhang, Li. *In Search of Paradise: Middle-Class Living in a Chinese Metropolis*. Ithaca: Cornell University Press, 2010.

Chapter 2

Re-searching and Re-positioning the Self and the Field

Investigating the Nation-State Through Narratives from the Borders

Rimple Mehta and Sandali Thakur

ABSTRACT

This chapter draws on the work of two researchers, one with Bangladeshi women in prisons in India and another with traditional artists in Mithila in India. Though appearing diametrically opposite to one another, the research topics come together through the individual pedagogical and methodological journeys of the researchers and the presence of border narratives. The chapter seeks to use the context of these journeys and narratives to nuance the idea of 'Asia as a Method' through a feminist perspective that is not only cognisant but also constitutive of epistemological standpoints of multiple, intersectional marginalities. There is a need to pave the way for frameworks and perspectives that demolish hegemonic understandings of the nation-state and generate new insights for a transformative politics ahead.

* * *

The memories of partition and/or a shared past linger on in the everyday life of people who occupy the different South Asian countries,[1] especially those in the borderlands. Irrespective of the levels of security and control at the different borders India shares with its neighbouring countries, cultural and political connections continue to survive.[2] Therefore, in the post-colonial context, the question of identity continues to remain a complex one. This paper draws on the work of two researchers from India. Rimple did fieldwork in prisons in West Bengal – exploring the everyday lives of Bangladeshi women in prisons in India, and then went on to examine cross-border child marriages between men in India and women from Bangladesh in West Bengal villages, close to the India–Bangladesh border. Sandali's research, meanwhile, was in Mithila – a cultural region that cuts across the Indian state of Bihar, and parts of Nepal.[3] Sandali's fieldwork was an ethnography of social – gender, caste, class – relations among traditional artists of the Indian part of Mithila, after commoditisation of the art form by the Indian state. In the first case, the intersection of marriage, kinship, and gender formed the core of discussion around identity and in the latter religio-cultural myth and caste emerged as the cornerstones of the discussions around identity. Taking examples from these two researchers' work, this chapter argues that to understand the 'field' in the context of Asia, it is important to look at 'border' narratives. Further, it contends to nuance the understanding of 'Asia as a Method'[4] from a feminist standpoint,[5] which is not only cognisant but also constitutive of intersectional subjectivities and marginalities.[6]

Both of us began our research with different objectives, and borders did not occupy a central position in our early inquiries. For instance, the research on child marriages across the India–Bangladesh border emerged as a consequence of working with Bangladeshi women in prisons in Kolkata. The initial objective was to understand the experiences of Bangladeshi women in prisons in India through a feminist lens. Over the course of the research it was realised that to understand the experiences of Bangladeshi women in prisons in India it was imperative to understand their experiences of crossing the border. This led to further research on cross-border child marriages.[7]

In the case of research in the Mithila region of India, investigation into the evolution of an art style ingeniously 'invented' by *Dusadh*[8] artists led to the exploration of religious and cultural myths and legends which their art draws from. On further investigation, it was discovered that scores of people belonging to the *Dusadh* community from both sides of the Indo-Nepal border congregate annually at a pilgrimage site in the Nepal part of Mithila, to celebrate those myths and legends. In order to understand the connections between art and pilgrimage, the visit to the said site in Nepal presented a perspective of the border that was antithetical to its popular understanding as a line that divides. The Indo-Nepal border, from this perspective, presents an imagination of a seamless, borderless region of Mithila, across which social and cultural relations thrive as well as struggles around identity and representation prevail.

This chapter addresses the question of methodology in two ways: first, through locating the research question in one's own personal journeys; second, by locating the research question and process in the larger South Asian identity of the research participants and the researchers taking into consideration that the two are not mutually exclusive for the research participants or the researchers.

IDENTITY FORMATION IN MITHILA:

India and Nepal (Sandali Thakur)

My engagement with the Mithila canvas started during my master's degree in Social Work in 2004–2006 when I decided to write my dissertation on the social relations among traditional artists of the Mithila region. With its emphasis on how socio-economic locations and axes of identities, for example, gender, caste, class, structure 'self', the Social Work programme helped me and many others like me embark on the journey of exploring our own identities by attempting to dig out our roots, and ask the question: where have I come from? The context of multiple migrations – to different Indian cities for education – had already brought to surface the question of identity and belongingness for me. During years of interactions with people and theories, the self started getting defined more sharply in some senses. What I was, began to make more sense when I saw what I was not. At the same time, it also made me realise that the self is never fixed; it is essentially relational and ever-evolving. The journey towards the self is mediated, and any attempt to look for one's roots at any point in time only leads to multiple routes. Engagement with the field of Women's Studies eventually provided the tools to understand the process of identity construction.

The question of identity envelops within itself multiple layers, including language. I grew up in Patna – the capital city of Bihar state, where my parents moved for education and jobs from their respective native areas in Mithila, like several 'upper' caste people of the region at that time. Patna is located in Magadh – one of the three cultural-linguistic regions of Bihar, apart from Bhojpur and Mithila. Patna has largely been a Hindi-speaking region. As a consequence, even though my mother tongue is Maithili, I grew up speaking Hindi as my first language.

The trajectory of Maithili language during India's struggle for political independence from the British colonial regime[9] is fraught on multiple levels. On the one hand, Bihari elites fought for a separate province of Bihar to be carved out of the Bengal Presidency during the end of the nineteenth and early twentieth centuries, wherein various cultural regions within Bihar came together to articulate the said demand on the basis of a common language, Hindi. This obviously meant marginalisation of other languages spoken within Bihar, including Maithili. On the other hand, in order to prove allegiance to the nationalist movement for political independence from the British, attempts were made by the rulers of Mithila to actively discourage the use of Maithili (including Mithilakshar script) and promote Hindi as well as Nagari script. The slogans of 'Bihar for Biharis'[10] on the one hand, and 'Hindi-Hindu-Hindustan' on the other, thus put Hindi language on the forefront and obstructed the blossoming of Maithili and its embracement by several Maithils.[11] Thus, locating my individual life, in the context of larger historical forces in the search for my identity, enabled me to make sense of and come to terms with my identity of a Maithil, who spoke Hindi.

During fieldwork in Mithila, my identity of someone who 'belongs' to Mithila, yet who does not speak Maithili fluently, provided me with an important vantage point. Language in India is inextricably intertwined with caste. Vanguards of Maithil identity and language – some upper-caste men and women – reminded me of my lack of Maithili-speaking skills, yet opened up to me as I was the 'daughter' of Mithila, while for many others, my linguistic distance probably meant that I was less entrenched in caste hierarchies, and so felt comfortable sharing about their lives. In addition to region and language, I began to understand how other markers of my identity – caste, class, and gender in particular – have shaped my experience of the world beyond research, providing me with power and privilege on the one hand and restricting my choices on the other. My growing comprehension of the complex interplay of power, privilege, and disadvantage made me locate my research objectives within the framework of questions around equality and justice.

It became imperative for me, to then ask the questions: how an individual's socio-economic location creates, sustains, or delimits opportunities and life chances; and how the interplay of one's identities determines, to a huge extent, what one can do with those opportunities, how much one can achieve or even aspire for. For many, the promise of modernity – of equal opportunities – gets routinely undermined by traditional hierarchies, which are always already present within modernity. This understanding strengthened my praxis that had grown from my engagement with anti-caste struggles and those around questions of intersectional feminist knowledge production. During my doctoral and other research endeavours, I came face to face with the unequal and unjust social fabric of Mithila and decided to make sense of it all through the lives of the traditional artists of the region. I assumed that the lives of artists, who were navigating multiple worlds, would provide me the window to understanding social relations in a range of sites – religion, culture, art, labour, market, State – and see the shifts therein.

I had initially hoped that interrogation into 'my own culture' would provide answers to all the questions that I had about my identity. Instead, in the course of multiple visits to the region, notions regarding the existence of an 'authentic' culture as well as the belief that only a 'native' anthropologist can best capture and present the 'authentic' worldview of the 'natives' to the world outside got ruptured.[12] Neither I, nor the artists could neatly fit into the category of the native, not only because of the movements across boundaries of time, space, sensibilities, and worldviews that they[13] and I had been part of, but because *a* particular culture embodies endless permutations and combinations of multiple and shifting identities, relationships, and configurations, and that there is no single or singular 'essence' therein. The artists and I were at once insiders and outsiders in a culture we considered 'our own'.

Mithila is a cultural-linguistic region comprising the north of Bihar and the *Terai* region (foothills) of the Himalayas in south-eastern Nepal. Right from the Puranas[14] to modern histories, the boundaries of Mithila have been described in a similar way – that it is surrounded by the Himalayan range in the north, by the rivers Kosi in the east, Ganga in the south, and Gandaki in the west[15] – a tract of land locked by the topographical barriers of mountains and rivers. Mithila is one of the regions of the Indian subcontinent which has been considered to be an ancient civilisation. It has been labelled as the land of the most orthodox Brahmanical tradition. But this is also the same place where non-Aryan philosophies like Buddhism and Jainism flourished. Both Mahavira and Buddha have lived and discoursed in Mithila. But the non-Aryan/non-Brahmin streams always had strained relationships with the Brahmanical religion, prior to the almost complete takeover of the latter in the region. In the popular imagination, therefore, Mithila is known for being the birthplace of the mythical goddess Sita, who is believed to have been born in Punaura (Sitamarhi district), on the Indian side of Mithila, and grown up in the kingdom of her father Janak in Janakpur, on the Nepal side.[16] Sita is believed to have been wedded to Rama, the prince of Ayodhya – located in the Indian state of Uttar Pradesh.

The traditional art of the region is known as Mithila or Madhubani paint-ing,[17] and has been practiced by women of all communities on auspicious occasions and for the decoration of homes. In the 1970s, as a response to successive droughts that led to the downfall of the agriculture-based economy of the region, the Government of India introduced a livelihood programme that entailed encouraging women to paint on paper, which would then be sold by state agencies as a welfare measure. The programme was a huge suc-cess in providing immediate relief to people and catapulted Mithila art and the women artists onto the world map. Mithila painting is not a homogenous tradition and is practiced by women from several communities and various caste groups, who have developed their own distinct styles. Due to the domi-nance of upper-caste groups – particularly *Brahmins*[18] and *Kayasthas*[19] – in the region, the caste groups considered to be lower in the hierarchy were initially left out of the livelihood programme, as it was believed that the 'purest' form of art was practiced by women belonging to the said upper-caste groups. This belief had been discursively generated through scholarly and other writings on the subject,[20] some of which were written prior to the inauguration of the said governmental programme. Since the drought had hit the lower-caste communities the most, as is the case in most calamities, some *Dusadh* women attempted to paint figures of 'high' Hindu deities in order to join the livelihood programme of the state. However, they were not intimately familiar with upper-caste iconography and ended up depicting them erroneously, inviting affront from the upper castes. This made them turn to their own religio-cultural universe of myths and legends to draw inspiration for the depiction of themes and motifs. The experiment extended into inventing a unique *style* which was radically different from those practiced by the upper caste in the same region. What emerged in the process is a fascinating story of assertion of identity of a people and evolution of a unique aesthetic form and pictorial vocabulary.[21]

Of all the gods and goddesses that began to be painted profusely by *Dusadh* and eventually other Dalit artists, it was the legend of Raja (King) Salhesa that held the most prominence. Raja Salhesa is a mythical figure, a legendary god, loved dearly and revered primarily by the *Dusadhs* but also other communities in the Mithila region of India and Nepal. Engagement with the figure of Raja Salhesa, along with other gods such as Rahu, Ketu, of the 'little traditions', encouraged me to delve deeper into the pantheon of communities, who have historically been shunned from Brahmanical Hinduism through the ideology of purity and pollution.[22] I visited the villages of Jitwarpur, Ranti, and Harinagar around Madhubani town multiple times during my doctoral research. During one of my visits to Jitwarpur, I was informed about the annual pilgrimage fair of the *Dusadhs* that is organised in the Nepal part of Mithila on the first day of the Maithili New Year, which usually falls in mid-April. Significantly, the day is also celebrated as the birthday of Raja Salhesa.

I decided to make a visit to *Rajaji ki Phulwari* (Raja Salhesa's garden), an actual site located near Lahan district headquarters in Province 2 of Nepal, which inhabits the highest number of Maithili-speaking people in Nepal. The *Dusadh* leader of Jitwarpur Roudi Paswan, who with his wife Chano Devi, was instrumental in bringing in the *Dusadh* myths and legends in her artistic practice, accompanied me for a day-long trip to the Salhesa fair, having himself been to the site a few times. This trip to the Nepal side of Mithila was not part of my initial plan, but interactions with Paswan, Devi, and other artists in Jitwarpur compelled me to visit a place that held special meaning for them. The pilgrimage fair at *Rajaji ki Phulwari* turned out to be much bigger than what I had anticipated. I witnessed hundreds of people from the Indian part of Mithila seamlessly going past the Nepal border to be part of the annual event. The idols of Raja Salhesa, along with his brothers Motiram and Budhesar, as well as those of his consorts Reshma, Dauna, Kushuma *malins*[23] at the site were strikingly similar to the idols I had seen at several places in the Indian part of Mithila. In conversations with the pilgrims and local leaders, Raja Salhesa and his companions emerged as figures they took pride in and saw as a powerful and positive symbol of identity – in contrast to the humiliating and degrading reality placed on them by other caste communities.

The transformation of Raja Salhesa from a mythical god to a symbol of pride for the *Dusadhs* and other lower-caste groups has been happening simultaneous to the mobilisation of the said caste groups in the domain of electoral politics on both sides of the border. In response to the injunctions imposed on these communities by the Brahmanical social order with respect to temple entry, the lack of representation in political parties, high levels of poverty, discrimination in access to resources and opportunities, use of violence to perpetuate the status quo, and silence dissent, these communities are constructing an alternate narrative for themselves at the cultural as well as political levels.

If we turn our gaze to the more recent past, the Indian prime minister Narendra Modi has been visiting Nepal frequently since he was voted to power in 2014.[24] His third visit to Nepal was in Janakpur instead of the capital Kathmandu, where, in an impassioned speech, he emphatically reminded the citizens of Janakpur of their shared religious ties with India, besides congratulating them for their commitment to good governance and inclusive development.[25] He underlined the shared heritage of 'Hinduism' by invoking the mythical characters of Sita and her father – King Janak – said to have ruled the kingdom of Videha centuries ago.[26] Modi and his Nepalese counterpart KP Sharma Oli announced a direct bus route connection between Janakpur and Ayodhya. For the Indian government, Janakpur is part of the 'Ramayana circuit' – a set of fifteen sacred sites across India, chosen to be developed as sites for religious tourism. Within this context, the lack of attention to the Salhesa fair, organised only a few kilometres away from Janakpur, unmasks the exclusionary agenda of the Indian and Nepali government.

The question, therefore, that needs to be asked is about the exclusion of a people – *Dusadhs* and other Dalit communities – from the imagination of the Hindu nation. Communities that are most violated, whose people – men and women – have been most discriminated against, and continue to be exploited and oppressed,[27] but who are asserting their identity and staking their legitimate claim on the nation through means of art and political mobilisation, continue to be rendered invisible by the Brahmanical Hindu nation-states. Inflicting epistemic violence on discriminated communities by not giving their cultural expressions any recognition becomes a way for the nation-state to declare who is wanted and who is not. This story of exclusion of a people from the imagination of the Brahmanical Hindu nation should not be seen only as a reflection of the ascent of hardline Hindutva in recent times. Preceding governments have not been very different in their exclusionary impulses, primarily because most mainstream political parties have largely been peopled by Hindu upper-caste agendas. Despite this, the Salhesa fair continues to be organised every year and is growing in scale.

Apart from sharing my personal journey to show how I arrived at my research question, this narrative was also intended to bring to the fore the myriad complexities that are constitutive of the nation-making process. David Gellner[28] has implored researchers to look at multiple layers – issues of subnationalism, caste, ethnicity – while developing an understanding of the nation-making process, and to refrain from 'methodological nationalism' – the 'givenness' of the nation-state in question. In the case of the Mithila region, for instance, the question of language and identity of Maithili-speaking people on both sides of the border is mired in the politics of caste and ethnicity. The inhabitants of the *Terai* (*Madheshi*[29]) – who constitute a large part of the Maithili-speaking population in Nepal – have been fighting for the recognition of their identity, in fact their existence, with the inhabitants of the hills (*Parbatiya*), who control almost all domains of public life in Nepal. The *Madheshi* movement has been articulating and demanding the rights of the Maithili-speaking, non-hill (*Madhesh*) people, since they want to retain their Maithil identity, as well as want to be considered as legitimate citizens of the Nepalese nation-state. Simultaneously, the demand for a separate Mithilanchal state to be carved out of Bihar in the Indian part of Mithila continues to be articulated. However, the question that needs to be asked is: do both these movements represent the interest of *all* people? Or do they stem from the imagination solely of the caste elites, being fought along the lines of ethnicity, language, and culture, and not social justice and equality *within* those categories? Are Dusadhs and other Dalit communities – both men and women – considered 'authentic', 'legitimate' *Madheshis* by the leaders of the *Madheshi* movement? What about the space and voice of these communities within the movement for Mithilanchal? While *Dusadhs* and other communities have formed their own political parties in the Indian part of Mithila, *Madheshi Dusadhs* are still struggling to seek accountability from leaders of the *Madheshi* movement that claim to represent them.

As my scholarship and research developed beyond my Master's in Social Work, and I continued to engage as a Hindi-speaking Maithil, upper-caste woman moving across the India–Nepal border to interrogate issues of identity and agency in the context of caste and gender hierarchies and exclusionary politics, I saw the border as an important site of analysis. In the case of the Indo-Nepal border, its relative seamlessness and fluidity allow for the questioning of the idea of a coherent, homogenous nation, city, and community. *Who* belongs to a nation? Who represents a community?

Bangladeshi Women in India (Rimple Mehta)

I am not scared of saying anything. I have not done anything. I came to India just to feed my stomach. This is my only crime, that I came to India. Here, in the prison, everyone says only one thing – these are Bangladeshi women. They always stereotype Bangladeshis. They don't know our names so they just say Bangladeshi. So I am now here. Eating food of the prison. They refer to us as Bangladeshis all the time. I can't bear it any longer. I feel like dying. But my desire to see my child again keeps me alive. I now understand I have committed a crime, but I have also served a sentence for the same. Four months (including 1 Month 3 days in the State Home in Bangalore) since I was first rescued and then arrested. How much more time am I supposed to serve in the prison? It had been just a month and a half since I had arrived in India and I was arrested. I hoped to work in India and send some money back home. But as soon as I reached India I was unwell and could not work. I could not send any money home. I have some issues in my stomach. Other women used to work and feed me. (Kakoli, twenty-two year old, married, and a mother of a six-year-old child)

My work with Bangladeshi women in prisons began as a student social worker from Tata Institute of Social Sciences in a prison for women under trial[30] in Mumbai. My interventions were focussed on facilitating legal aid for the women in the undertrial prison but gradually my interest kept narrowing down to the issues faced by the Bangladeshi women within the prison. Though Marwari by birth, I had grown up in Kolkata and was familiar with Bengali, a language that the Bangladeshi women also spoke, albeit often in varying dialects. The familiarity with language worked as a bond between the Bangladeshi women and me, as most of the prison officials and social workers could not speak the language. I became the obvious choice for the Bangladeshi women to come and speak with. This was a drastic change from my location in Kolkata, where my Bengali would often be corrected due to my inability to match up to the vernacular finesse. I identified myself as hailing from Kolkata and felt a strong sense of belongingness to the place. A diasporic upbringing at home kept me grounded to the traditions and customs in Rajasthan as well. Though a visit to Rajasthan during the summer vacations in school was enough to make me realise how I was not Rajasthani enough. This sense of belongingness to the two places resulted in me being perceived as not 'enough' for either of the places. This constant need to assert a sense of belongingness in two places is what probably drew me to the lives of the Bangladeshi women. For it is not by chance that my ability to speak Bengali immediately becomes a point of connect for both the Bangladeshi women and me.[31] Later, when I went on to pursue Women's Studies, it gave me the theoretical apparatus to understand the social constructions of the 'self' and belongingness.

My assignment in the prison as a student social worker was spread across two semesters from 2008 to 2009. In this time, I was able to gather some insights on the experiences of Bangladeshi women in a prison in India, the way they make their way to India, and such other details of their life in Bangladesh. Thereafter, I decided to pursue my doctoral studies on the lives of Bangladeshi women in prisons in India, and locate it in Women's Studies. Three broad objectives guided my doctoral research – first, to explore the trajectories of violence in their lives; second, to unravel the role of the notion of 'honour' and the way it shapes their experiences; third, to understand their experiences in the criminal justice system in India. I interviewed forty Bangladeshi women in two prisons in Kolkata between December 2010 and December 2011.

My initial visits to the prison were seen with much suspicion and curiosity by the prison warders and they would attempt to monitor the interviews and be around while the women spoke with me. They also played a role in selecting the women who would come and speak with me. But their apprehensions about my presence fizzled out soon enough as they did not find much interest nor sense any danger in my discussions with the women. The Bangladeshi women and I were left to talk on our own. Commonly, I would begin by telling the women to tell me something about themselves. Almost all the women began by talking about the moment when they crossed the border. The narratives would then move back and forth in time and I would get an insight into their experiences and vulnerabilities. The ruptures in the narrative actually marked the moments and experiences that shape their everyday life in prison. Often, there were long periods of silence and long periods of what may have passed off as 'ramblings'. These had to be interpreted not merely for the content but for its temporality in their life.

It is important to note that though they began their narratives by talking about the moment of crossing the border, they were still not sure of what constituted the idea of a nation-state. That the border was responsible for them being in prison was understood but the nature of their crime and the 'victim' of the crime eluded them. The idea of a nation-state eluded them. As a result, while in prison, they kept going back to the memory of crossing borders to look for an explanation for their incarceration. They placed their act of crossing the border on a continuum of *bhool* (mistake) or *aporadh* (crime) and made meaning of their everyday life in prison.

> Everyone goes to India. I thought this is the right thing to do. There are so many socio-economic problems in Bangladesh. While crossing the border I didn't even know what a visa or passport is. I had never heard those words. But now I know everything. I have made a *bhool* once, it will not happen again. Human beings commit a mistake without knowing but intentionally commit a crime. The way I have come here was a *bhool*. (Aalia, thirty year old, married, worked in a hospital in Bangalore for a year before the prison)

Saleha, a twenty-four-year-old widow, was aware of parts of the shared history of India and Bangladesh. She said:

> My father was a freedom fighter and he used to tell me that India had really helped Bangladesh at the time it was trying to gain freedom and become independent. I think it was Indira Gandhi who really helped us. If India supported us so much that time then why can it not think about us now? We are citizens from the same Bangladesh. We really respect India and want to continue to do so.

In this way borders began to take a central position in my arguments and conjectures with regard to the everyday lives of Bangladeshi women in prisons in India. The emergence of borders necessitated a view of the everyday life in the prison in terms of national identity, apart from other intersecting identities of class, caste, and gender. This was a conceptual shift in the research which took the research from one located broadly within sociology to one located in an emerging field of study referred to as 'criminology of mobility'.[32]

After my doctoral research, I carried out a small research study to understand the experiences of Bangladeshi brides in India. I was exploring the phenomenon of cross-border child marriages across the Bangladesh–India border. This research revealed the extended kinship ties that families on the two sides tried to maintain by way of marriage.[33] Brides from Bangladesh were often brought across the border clandestinely. Much to the dismay of the brides, soon after, they realise that they may never see their natal family again due to the presence of the border. Some of these women shared daring stories such as how they crossed a river with their child in a vessel on their head to go and see their parents or how they called their parents to their fields, which were on the other side of the barbed wire. The women relied on their marital family for their citizenship documents. This uncertainty and fear around their 'illegal' status compelled them to perform the duties expected of them as well as remain faithful to their marital relationships. The women bear the burden of the shared history between Bangladesh and India. They become the fulcrum of the ties between the families on the two sides divided by a border.

My work in the prison as well as in a few villages along the India–Bangladesh border highlights the seamlessness of the political and geographical borders for those who inhabit it or move across it. In both cases the women had crossed the border of the home as well as the nation-state, only to find themselves in the confining space of the prison or their marital home. While they could hold the 'border' responsible for their confinement, they could not fully comprehend the cartographic collage of nation-states, in which borders were the central organising principle.

These narratives counter the dominant contemporary political debates and legislations around citizenship in India. The newly elected BJP government in 2014 gave a clarion call to oust all 'illegal' Bangladeshi from India, send them back to Bangladesh. The Citizenship Amendment Bill first introduced in parliament in 2016, subsequently lapsed but was revived and finally became an Act in December 2019 after both the houses of parliament approved it. It proposes to give refuge to all Hindus, Sikhs, Buddhists, Jains, Parsis, and Christians who have fled to India from Pakistan, Afghanistan, and Bangladesh – without valid travel documents or whose valid documents have expired in recent years – by providing them with an option of acquiring Indian citizenship through naturalization. Rohingyas from Myanmar, Ahmadis of Pakistan, Muslims from Bangladesh, Tamils from Sri Lanka, and Uyghurs from China were conspicuous by their absence from the Act. Further, the Assam National Register of Citizens (NRC) which declared a little over nineteen lakh people 'illegal' in August 2019 has shaken identity and sense of belongingness among those residing there for generations. Making it to the register depended not only on the identity documents one has but also the procedural lapses that may take place in proving belongingness in a socio-geographical context where identities often seem to merge seamlessly for those who inhabit or move across the Indo-Bangladesh border. In a notification issued by the Ministry of Home Affairs on 31 July 2019, the Registrar General of Citizen Registration stated:

> In pursuance of sub-rule (4) of rule 3 of the Citizenship (Registration of Citizens and Issue of National Identity Cards) Rules, 2003, the Central Government hereby decides to prepare and update the Population Register and the field work for house to house enumeration throughout the country except Assam for collection of information relating to all persons who are usually residing within the jurisdiction of Local Registrar shall be undertaken between 1st day of April, 2020 to 30th September, 2020.

There are apprehensions that the preparation and updation of the nation-wide population register in the present context will result in a similar fate as NRC in Assam. All these developments mark the beginning of what may be a tumultuous struggle of claiming belongingness for those at the margins of caste, class, and gender hierarchies.

IN LIEU OF A CONCLUSION: INTERROGATING THE BORDER

Mithilesh Kumar Jha writes that the 'the idea of India as a secular nation enters a phase of crisis in contemporary times with the majoritarian turn in

Indian politics, which should prompt academics to probe a series of issues on the formation of the Indian nation and nationalism and its various fault-lines based on language, religion, caste, peasants, tribe, gender, and regional or sub-national politics'.[34] Therefore, this stumbling upon the border and its meaning in the work we do is of much significance. To understand the work that borders do for exclusionary politics, we need to understand the borders established under colonialism in the Asian subcontinent. Here rendered visible and invisible simultaneously on different scales are the everyday exclusions and inclusions. The experiences of India/Nepal and India/Bangladesh borders outline and serve as examples for a global understanding of post-colonial border-making and their continued problematics.

Our initial work, though located within the realm of feminist understandings of criminology of mobility and cultural studies, respectively, had assumed the 'space' of data collection. Only later did the presence of the border in everyday practices emerged as a concept central to understanding much of the institutions and spaces we traversed while doing fieldwork. Any act of decolonisation needs to weave in an understanding of the practices that bring the border from the margins of the country to the centre of our analysis. There are various similarities in language and culture across the two borders – Bangladesh and Nepal, and people residing on the two sides define their everyday life through this fluidity. We as researchers got immersed in this fluidity and did not interrogate the border and how central it is to everyday practices of the communities we were researching.

In our research, the questions of border and national identity eventually played a crucial role, in direct and indirect ways, in understanding the lives of the people we engaged with. This chapter has discussed the centrality of the border and national identity in communities in India, especially those close to the border. South Asia has been seen as being continuously constructed through the interplay of larger socio-cultural, political, economic, colonial forces but not necessarily through the everyday practices. In this chapter, we argue that to understand the 'field' in the context of Asia, it is important to look at 'border' narratives. Interrogation of the border leads us to question the premises of nationalism as well as provides us one of the ways in which to imagine decolonisation of knowledge systems.

In both the research processes, the border emerged in a way that it necessitated a conceptual re-positioning of our initial objectives. This led us to make connections with contemporary political developments despite our individual work being niche. While Rimple's work could have remained limited to the prison, Sandali's work could be limited to art. The intersectional feminist and critical lens adopted by both the researchers has not only enabled an understanding of the intersectional gendered politics of the prison and art, but has also provided a standpoint to view the nation-state and its borders from an alternative position.

What has emerged in both our research is a definitive understanding that political boundaries do not necessarily coincide with linguistic-cultural territorialisation. Further, that nationalism cannot be made sense of without considering the simultaneous processes of centring and marginalisation *within* nation-states. 'Whose nation?' is a question that needs to be asked each time the idea of the nation is being interrogated.[35] Further, this interrogation, which moves beyond territories and other official markers of borders and nationhood into the realm of people and human relations, has to bring into its fold another set of contentious questions related to social identity – gender, caste, class, and so on. Which social, economic groups are part of the normative framework of the nation, and which are not?

The other methodological insight that often eludes researchers when engaging with questions of identity, as witnessed in Sandali's research, is that struggles around identity spring from the need to claim recognition, dignity, and social worth and at the same time demand for equitable distribution of material resources. It is never one or the other, but always both.

As discussed earlier, both of us have moved across different states in the country either to pursue higher education or to work. It may not be an overestimation to suggest that this mobility did allow us to seamlessly cross the borders of the country in our conceptual journeys. Our individual search for a sense of belongingness and rootedness did not limit us or restrict us, rather it expanded our horizons to see these struggles in the communities we met, as part of fieldwork for research. We argue that our search for social issues and solutions is not only driven by what may seem like external interests, which have developed over a period of time; instead our search is an extension of ourselves and our own search.

We have carried the values, principles, as well as strategies integral to Social Work and Women's Studies into the field while doing research. Some of these are upholding people's right to self-determination, recognising intersectionalities and power relations, belief in social justice, dignity and worth of the individual, understanding the link between research and intervention, using 'self' as a resource in engagement with people, and so on. This dimension in reflexivity becomes of epistemological importance and consequently impacts methodology adopted in research or for that matter social work practice. The voice that is then presented in the form of writing or intervention is a collective one of both the researcher and the research participants and their quest to be heard, though it is laden with the awareness of the difference in power between those voices.

According to Scott,[36] it is important to change the focus and philosophy of our history 'from one bent on naturalising "experience" through a belief in the unmediated relationship between words and things, to one that takes all categories of analysis as contextual, contested and contingent'. Decentring is essential for a process of decolonisation and Indigenisation of knowledge systems. The self-reflexive research process will also enable the researcher in the representation of the field, the way we view socio-cultural relationships in the field. In the context of not having sufficient literature on this kind of a research process, Rao[37] has pointed out that 'writing' is an important step towards indigenisation of knowledge. However, indigenisation of knowledge should in no way lay undue emphasis on local cultures, beliefs, values, and practices as they may further perpetuate already existing patriarchal and other hierarchical and discriminatory structures.

According to feminists such as Narayan,[38] 'Nonwestern feminists will no doubt be sensitive to the fact that positivism is not our only enemy . . . [m]any problems they confront arise in non positivist contexts'. This puts the cultural anthropologist in a dilemma, and works such as those of Sandali will have to carve out the passages through which cultures, beliefs, values, and practices may be used for the project of indigenisation, which is cognisant of inherent hierarchies.

Chen and Huat[39] state that, '[w]ithout collective re-thinking, it is difficult to break away with the vicious circle of domination and retaliation'. We contend that the collective re-thinking needs to be aware of and prepared to take on the arduous task that lies ahead: of deepening democracy in spaces of knowledge production. Niranjana[40] emphasises on working together under the 'third world' subjectivity and not just get swayed by the celebratory process of 'rise of Asia'; instead work towards comparative research. The question often is and keeps recurring – Can the subaltern speak?[41] In addition, we call on Haraway's[42] work on 'situated knowledges' to concur that knowledge production involves partiality, positionality, and accountability. Therefore, even in the context of 'Asia as a Method', one needs to acknowledge that there are only partial views and partial representation of voices. While comparing societies geographically closer that share similar historical experiences is an urgent political endeavour,[43] the question of situatedness of this knowledge is of equal, if not of more importance. Along with partiality and positionality, the process of accountability is a complex one. Epistemological standpoints of multiple, intersectional marginalisations[44] can help create new frameworks and perspectives that demolish hegemonic understandings and generate new insights for a transformative politics ahead. In this regard, an intersectional feminist, critical perspective on 'Asia as a Method' can be particularly important to contribute towards deepening an understanding of colonial subjectivity and the need for intellectual collaborations between ex-colonisers and ex-colonies for rewriting imperial histories.

* * *

NOTES

1. Veena Das, *Life and Words: Violence and the Descent into the Ordinary* (Berkeley: University of California Press, 2006); David Gilmartin, "Partition, Pakistan, and South Asian History: In Search of a Narrative," *The Journal of Asian Studies* 57, no. 4 (November 1998): 1068–1095; Rimple Mehta, "Borders: A View from 'Nowhere'," *Criminology and Criminal Justice* 16, no. 3 (July 2016): 286–300.

2. India was partitioned into India and Pakistan (West and East) in 1947. The political boundaries that were drawn by the British colonialists often ran through people's houses, communities, and neighbourhoods. In 1971, East Pakistan separated from Pakistan and emerged as the new state of Bangladesh. For a detailed discussion on cartography and boundary making in post-colonial states, please refer to footnote 15 of Willem ven Schendel, "Stateless in South Asia: The Making of the India-Bangladesh Enclaves," *The Journal of Asian Studies* 61, no. 1 (February 2002): 120. Also, for a discussion on the Radcliffe Line and how it finally took shape, refer to Joya Chatterji, "The Fashioning of a Frontier: The Radcliffe Line and Bengal's Border Landscape, 1947–52," *Modern Asian Studies* 33, no. 1 (Feb 1999): 185–242. Sahana Ghosh, "Relative Intimacies: Belonging and Difference in Transnational Families across the Bengal Borderland," *Economic and Political Weekly* LII, no. 15 (April 2017); Sahana Ghosh, "Security Socialities: Gender, Surveillance and Civil-Military Relations in India's Eastern Borderlands," *Comparative Studies in South Asia, Africa and the Middle East* 39, no. 3 (December 2019): 439–450; and Malini Sur, "Through Metal Fences: Material Mobility and the Politics of Transnationality at Borders," *Mobilities* 8, no. 1 (2013): 70–89; Malini Sur, "Danger and Difference: Teatime at the Northeast India-Bangladesh Border," *Modern Asia Studies* 53, no. 3 (May 2019): 846–873 have done extensive work along the porous India–Bangladesh border, interspersed with riverine and land stretches, to understand the ways in which people continue to acknowledge a shared past in their everyday lives. However, among the many legal provisions in India, the Foreigners Act 1946 disrupts the sense of shared history. According to the Foreigners Act 1946, a foreigner is a person, who is not a citizen of India. The category of citizen defines the framework for exclusion of a person, who is 'not citizen'. Further, the provisions of section 14 (b) of the Foreigners Act 1946 indicate that a person arrested in contravention of this Act could be sentenced to imprisonment for two to eight years and are also liable to pay a fine. It was observed during the research that the fine imposed on the Bangladeshi women was usually close to INR 10,000 (approximately US $165). None of the women had the resources to pay the fine amount and in turn served another two or three months in prison as a penalty for not paying the fine. Very often these women continued to languish in prison long after their terms in prison were over (see Rimple Mehta, *Women, Mobility and Incarceration: Love and Recasting of Self across the Bangladesh-India Border* [New York and London: Routledge, 2018]). The international India–Nepal border is an open one; it came into existence in its present form after the Treaty of Sugauli that was signed between Nepal and the British Raj in 1816.

3. The researchers have chosen to write in first person while referring to their fieldwork experiences and at times in third person. This is in keeping with feminist research methodology that acknowledges researchers are both subject and object individuals who are at once personal and social.

4. Kuan-Hsing Chen. *Asia as a Method: Toward Deimperialisation* (Durham and London: Duke University Press, 2010).

5. Donna Haraway, "Situated Knowledges: The Science Question in Feminism and the Privilege of Partial Perspectives," *Feminist Studies* 14, no. 3 (Autumn 1988): 575–599; Sandra Harding, "Introduction: Standpoint Theory as a Site of Political, Philosophical and Scientific Debate," in *The Feminist Standpoint Reader*, ed. Sandra Harding (New York and London, Routledge, 2004), 1–15; Nancy Harstock, "The Feminist Standpoint: Developing the Ground for a Specifically Feminist Historical Materialism," in *The Feminist Standpoint Theory Reader*, ed. Sandra Harding (New York and London: Routledge, 2004), 35–54.

6. Kimberlie Crenshaw, "Mapping the Margins: Intersectionality, Identity Politics and Violence Against Women of Color," *Stanford Law Review* 43, no. 6 (July 1991): 1241–1299; Gopal Guru, "Dalit Women Talk Differently," *Economic and Political Weekly* 30, no. 41–42 (October 1995): 2548-2550; Patricia Hill Collins, *Black Feminist Thought: Knowledge, Consciousness and the Politics of Empowerment* (New York: Routledge, 2009); Sharmila Rege, "Dalit Women Talk Differently: A Critique of 'Difference and Towards a Dalit Feminist Standpoint Position," *Economic and Political Weekly* 33, no. 44 (Oct–Nov 1998): WS39–WS46.

7. I carried out the research on cross-border child marriages as a part of a project titled 'Love, Law and Labour: Child Marriage in West Bengal' conducted by the School of Women's Studies, Jadavpur University, and funded by the American Jewish World Service.

8. *Dusadh* is an ex-Untouchable community, traditionally agricultural labourers, whose men have been village watchmen, and were also recruited in the British army. They are part of a pan-India social group that has taken on the adjective-noun 'Dalit' (meaning 'oppressed'), which seeks to re-define a stigmatised identity into a political, powerful one through resistance in the domain of culture, politics, economy, and knowledge production.

9. Pankaj Kumar Jha, "The Politics of Mono-Linguism and Identity-Formation: Interpreting Maithili-Hindi Tangle," *Proceedings of the Indian History Congress* 65 (2004): 852–862; Mithilesh Kumar Jha, *Language Politics and Public Sphere in North India: Making of the Maithili Movement* (New Delhi: Oxford University Press, 2017).

10. Those who belong to Bihar, as distinct from Bengalis and others who were part of the Bengal Presidency.

11. It is only after a long and concerted struggle that Maithili has recently been included in the Eighth Schedule of the Indian Constitution, and recognised as a language in its own right and not a dialect of Hindi.

12. Dorinne K. Kondo, *Crafting Selves: Power, Gender, and Discourses of Identity in a Japanese Workplace* (Chicago: University of Chicago Press, 1990);

Kirin Narayan, "How Native Is a 'Native' Anthropologist?" *American Anthropologist* 95, no. 3. New Series (September 1993): 671–686; Nayantara Sheoran Appleton, "Once an Insider, Always an Outsider: (re)Negotiating Boundaries when Researchers Return 'Home'," *Anthropology News* 53, no. 2 (February 2012).

13. Several artists have travelled across the country and abroad to showcase their work and interact regularly with tourists, buyers who visit the area as well as communicate via electronic and digital media.

14. A category of ancient Sanskrit texts.

15. Upendra Thakur, *History of Mithila: From the Earliest Times to 1556* (Mithila Institute: Bihar, 1988).

16. The epic Valmiki's Ramayana, available in several translations.

17. The town of Madhubani is considered to be the 'epicentre' of the evolution of the commoditised form of the art, as the state-sponsored livelihood programme was initiated in its surrounding villages; it however does not imply that this art is practiced only in and around Madhubani. 'Mithila painting' is a more comprehensive label, as the art is practiced in the entire region.

18. A pan-Indian community considered to be at the top of the caste hierarchy, men have traditionally been priests; have historically controlled knowledge production

19. An 'upper' caste group, men have traditionally been scribes, accountants, record-keepers in Courts, British bureaucracy, and so on.

20. W.G. Archer, "Maithil Painting," *Marg* 3, no. 3 (1949): 24–23; Jagdish Chandra Mathur, "The Domestic Arts of Mithila," *Marg* 20, no. 1 (1966): 43–55; Upendra Thakur, *Madhubani Painting* (New Delhi: Abhinav Publications, 1982).

21. Sandali P. Sharma, "Imagining Traditions: The Contested Canvas of Mithila Paintings," in *Colonial and Contemporary Bihar and Jharkhand*, ed. Lata Singh, and Biswamoy Pati (Delhi: Primus Books, 2014), 181–198 (Sandali Thakur and Sandali P. Sharma is the same person).

22. Ranajit Guha, *Elementary Aspects of Peasant Insurgency in Colonial India* (New York: Duke University Press, 1999).

23. Women of *mali* (gardener) caste whose traditional occupation is to grow and sell flowers; for the folklore of Raja Salhesa, see George. A. Grierson, Hetukar Jha, and Vedanath Jha, *Maithil Chrestomathy and Vocabulary* (Darbhanga: Kalyani Foundation, 2009).

24. It is speculated that Modi's aggressive embracement of Nepal is an attempt to wean away from the Chinese influence. For more on this, see http://www.mainstrea mweekly.net/article8021.html.

25. http://pib.gov.in/PressReleaseDetail.aspx?PRID=1531923.

26. Nepal was part of the kingdom of Videha during the Late Vedic era. It signed a treaty with the British empire in 1923 that acknowledged it as an independent nation.

27. Aloysius Irudayam, Jayshree Mangubhai, and Joel G. Lee, *Dalit Women Speak Out: Violence against Dalit Women in India* (Chennai: National Campaign on Dalit Human Rights, National Federation of Dalit Women, and Institute of Development Education, Action and Studies, 2006).

28. David Gellner, *The Idea of Nepal, The Mahesh Chandra Regmi Lecture* (Kathmandu: Social Science Baha, 2016).

29. The term is used for people of Indian ancestry residing in the foothills (Terai region) of Nepal.

30. An undertrial prisoner is one whose case is under trial in a court of law and no conclusion has been drawn on their offence.

31. Dorina Damsa, and Thomas Ugelvik, "One of Us or One of Them? Researcher Positionality, Language, and Belonging in an All-Foreign Prison," in *Criminal Justice Research in an Era of Mass Mobility*, ed. Andriani Fili, Synnøve Jahnsen, and Rebecca Powell (London: Routledge, 2018), 201–212.

32. Katja Franco Aas, and Mary Bosworth, ed., *The Borders of Punishment: Migration, Citizenship, and Social Exclusion* (UK: Oxford University Press, 2013); Mary Bosworth, and Emma Kaufman, "Foreigners in a Carceral Age: Immigration and Imprisonment in the United States," *Stanford Law & Policy Review* 22, no. 2 (June 2011): 429–454; Jude McCulloch, and Sharon Pickering, "Introduction," in *Borders and Crime: Pre-Crime, Mobility and Serious Harm in an Age of Globalization*, ed. Jude McCulloch and Sharon Pickering (UK: Palgrave Macmillan, 2012), 1–14.

33. Rimple Mehta, "Barbed Affect: Bangladeshi Child Brides in India Negotiate Borders and Citizenship," *Journal of Gender-Based Violence* 3, no. 1 (February 2019): 67–82. Also see Ghosh, "Relative Intimacies".

34. Mithilesh Kumar Jha, *Language Politics and Public Sphere in North India: Making of the Maithili Movement* (New Delhi: Oxford University Press, 2017).

35. G. Aloysius, *Nationalism without a Nation in India* (Delhi: Oxford University Press, 1997).

36. Joan Scott, "The Evidence of Experience," *Critical Enquiry* 17, no. 4 (Summer 1991): 796.

37. Vidya Rao, "Decolonising Social Work: An Indian Viewpoint," in *Decolonising Social Work*, ed. Mel Gray, John Coates, Michael Yellow Bird, and Tiani Hetherington (Burlington: Ashgate Publishing Company, 2013), 43–61.

38. Uma Narayan, "The project of Feminist Epistemology: Perspectives from a Non-Western Feminist," in *Feminist Theory Reader*, ed. Carole McCann, and Seung-Kyung Kim (New York: Routledge, 2003), 312.

39. Kuan-Hsing Chen, and Chua Beng Huat, "An Introduction," *Inter-Asia Cultural Studies* 1, no. 1 (2010): 11.

40. Tejaswini Niranjana, "Alternative Frames? Questions for Comparative Research in the Third World," *Inter-Asia Cultural Studies* 1, no. 1 (2010): 97–108.

41. Gayatri Chakraborty Spivak, *Can the Subaltern Speak?* (Basingstoke: Macmillan, 1988).

42. Haraway, "Situated Knowledges".

43. Chen, *Asia as a Method*.

44. Hill Collins, *Black Feminist Thought: Knowledge, Consciousness and the Politics of Empowerment*; Guru, "Dalit Women Talk Differently"; Rege, "Dalit Women Talk Differently".

REFERENCES

Aas, Katja Franco, and Bosworth, Mary. ed. *The Borders of Punishment: Migration, Citizenship, and Social Exclusion.* UK: Oxford University Press, 2013.

Aloysius, G. *Nationalism without a Nation in India.* Delhi: Oxford University Press, 1997.

Appleton, Nayantara Sheoran. "Once an Insider, Always an Outsider: (re)Negotiating Boundaries when Researchers Return 'Home'." *Anthropology News* 53, no. 2 (February 2012): 1–6.

Archer, W.G. "Maithil Painting." *Marg* 3, no. 3 (1949): 24–33.

Bosworth, Mary, and Kaufman, Emma. "Foreigners in a Carceral Age: Immigration and Imprisonment in the United States." *Stanford Law & Policy Review* 22, no. 2 (June 2011): 429–454.

Chatterji, Joya. "The Fashioning of a Frontier: The Radcliffe Line and Bengal's Border Landscape, 1947–52." *Modern Asian Studies* 33, no. 1 (Feb 1999): 185–242.

Chen, Kuan-Hsing. *Asia as a Method: Toward Deimperialisation.* Durham and London: Duke University Press, 2010.

Chen, Kuan Hsing, and Chua Beng Huat. "An Introduction." *Inter-Asia Cultural Studies* 1, no. 1 (2010): 9–12.

Crenshaw, Kimberlie. "Mapping the Margins: Intersectionality, Identity Politics and Violence Against Women of Color." *Stanford Law Review* 43, no. 6 (July 1991): 1241–1299.

Damsa, Dorina, and Thomas Ugelvik. "One of Us or One of Them? Researcher Positionality, Language, and Belonging in an All-Foreign Prison." In *Criminal Justice Research in an Era of Mass Mobility*, edited by Andriani Fili, Synnøve Jahnsen, and Rebecca Powell, 201–212. London: Routledge, 2018.

Das, Veena. *Life and Words: Violence and the Descent into the Ordinary.* Berkeley: University of California Press, 2006.

Gellner, David. *The Idea of Nepal, Mahesh The Mahesh Chandra Regmi Lecture, 2016.* Social Science Baha, Kathmandu, 2016. Available at: https://soscbaha.org /mc-regmi-lecture/.

Ghosh, Sahana. "Relative Intimacies: Belonging and Difference in Transnational Families across the Bengal Borderland." *Economic and Political Weekly* LII, no. 15 (April 2017): 45–52.

Ghosh, Sahana. "Security Socialities: Gender, Surveillance and Civil-Military Relations in India's Eastern Borderlands." *Comparative Studies in South Asia, Africa and the Middle East* 39, no. 3 (December 2019): 439–450.

Gilmartin, David. "Partition, Pakistan, and South Asian History: In Search of a Narrative." *The Journal of Asian Studies* 57, no. 4 (November 1998): 1068–1095.

Guha, Ranajit. *Elementary Aspects of Peasant Insurgency in Colonial India.* New York: Duke University Press, 1999.

Guru, Gopal. "Dalit Women Talk Differently." *Economic and Political Weekly* 30, no. 41–42 (October 1995): 2548–2550.

Haraway, Donna. "Situated Knowledges: The Science Question in Feminism and the Privilege of Partial Perspectives." *Feminist Studies* 14, no. 3 (Autumn 1988): 575–599.

Harding, Sandra. "Introduction: Standpoint Theory as a Site of Political, Philosophical and Scientific Debate." In *The Feminist Standpoint Reader*, edited by Sandra Harding, 1–15. New York and London: Routledge, 2004.

Harstock, Nancy. "The Feminist Standpoint: Developing the Ground for a Specifically Feminist Historical Materialism." In *The Feminist Standpoint Theory Reader*, edited by Sandra Harding, 35–54. New York and London: Routledge, 2004.

Hill Collins, Patricia. *Black Feminist Thought: Knowledge, Consciousness and the Politics of Empowerment*. New York: Routledge, 2009.

Irudayam, Aloysius S.J., Mangubhai, Jayshree P., and Lee, Joel G. *Dalit Women Speak Out: Violence against Dalit Women in India*. Chennai: National Campaign on Dalit Human Rights, National Federation of Dalit Women, and Institute of Development Education, Action and Studies, 2006.

Jha, Mithilesh Kumar *Language Politics and Public Sphere in North India: Making of the Maithili Movement*. New Delhi: Oxford University Press, 2017.

Jha, Pankaj Kumar. "The Politics of Mono-Linguism and Identity-Formation: Interpreting Maithili-Hindi Tangle." *Proceedings of the Indian History Congress* 65 (2004): 852–862.

Jha, Hetukar, and Vedanath Jha, ed. *Maithil Chrestomathy and Vocabulary*, by George A. Grierson. Kalyani Foundation, 2009.

Kondo, Dorinne K. *Crafting Selves: Power, Gender, and Discourses of Identity in a Japanese Workplace*. Chicago: University of Chicago Press, 1990.

Mathur, Jagdish Chandra. "The Domestic Arts of Mithila." *Marg* 20, no. 1 (1966): 43–55.

McCulloch, Jude, and Pickering, Sharon. "Introduction." In *Borders and Crime: Pre-Crime, Mobility and Serious Harm in an Age of Globalization*, edited by Jude McCulloch, and Sharon Pickering, 1–14. UK: Palgrave Macmillan, 2012.

Mehta, Rimple. "Borders: A View from 'Nowhere'." *Criminology and Criminal Justice* 16, no. 3 (July 2016): 286–300.

Mehta, Rimple. *Women, Mobility and Incarceration: Love and Recasting of Self across the Bangladesh-India Border*. New York and London: Routledge, 2018.

Mehta, Rimple. "Barbed Affect: Bangladeshi Child Brides in India Negotiate Borders and Citizenship." *Journal of Gender-Based Violence* 3, no. 1 (February 2019): 67–82.

Narayan, Kirin. "How Native Is a 'Native' Anthropologist?" *American Anthropologist* 95, no. 3. New Series (September 1993): 671–686.

Narayan, Uma. "The Project of Feminist Epistemology: Perspectives from a Non-Western Feminist." In *Feminist Theory Reader*, edited by Carole McCann, and Seung-Kyung Kim, 308–331. New York: Routledge, 2003.

Niranjana, Tejaswini. "Alternative Frames? Questions for Comparative Research in the Third World." *Inter-Asia Cultural Studies* 1, no. 1 (2010): 97–108.

Rao, Vidya. "Decolonising Social Work: An Indian Viewpoint." In *Decolonising Social Work*, edited by Mel Gray, John Coates, Michael Yellow Bird, and Tiani Hetherington, 43–61. Burlington: Ashgate Publishing Company, 2013.

Rege, Sharmila. "Dalit Women Talk Differently: A Critique of 'Difference and Towards a Dalit Feminist Standpoint Position." *Economic and Political Weekly* 33, no. 44 (Oct–Nov 1998): WS39–WS46.

ven Schendel, Willem. "Stateless in South Asia: The Making of the India-Bangladesh Enclaves." *The Journal of Asian Studies* 61, no. 1 (February 2002): 115–147.

Scott, Joan. "The Evidence of Experience." *Critical Enquiry* 17, no. 4 (Summer 1991): 773–797.

Sharma, Sandali P. "Imagining Traditions: The Contested Canvas of Mithila Paintings." In *Colonial and Contemporary Bihar and Jharkhand*, edited by Lata Singh, and Biswamoy Pati, 181–198. Delhi: Primus Books, 2014.

Spivak, Gayatri Chakraborty. *Can the Subaltern Speak?* Basingstoke: Macmillan, 1988.

Sur, Malini. "Through Metal Fences: Material Mobility and the Politics of Transnationality at Borders." *Mobilities* 8, no. 1 (2013): 70–89.

Sur, Malini. "Danger and Difference: Teatime at the Northeast India-Bangladesh Border." *Modern Asia Studies* 53, no. 3 (May 2019): 846–873.

Thakur, Upendra. *Madhubani Painting*. New Delhi: Abhinav Publications, 1982.

Thakur, Upendra. *History of Mithila: From the Earliest Times to 1556*. Bihar: Mithila Institute, 1988.

Chapter 3

Violence from Another Angle

The Cold War and Contemporary Cambodia

Caroline Bennett

ABSTRACT

Even in 2021, in Southeast Asia the ongoing effects of the Cold War are inescapable. Wars fought in the East as part of the ideological conflict against communism, caused mass death across many countries, and the ongoing consequences continue to affect understandings of kin, religion, politics, and sociality in many areas. In Cambodia, the Cold War contributed to the rise of the Khmer Rouge, a millenary Maoist regime that between 1975 and 1979 caused the death of an estimated 1.7 million people, through starvation, exhaustion, disease, and execution. The ongoing effects of that genocide are still felt today, not least in the political sphere, where impunity and a hybrid, or illiberal, democracy, have enabled an autocratic rule by the current ruling party and the Prime Minister Hun Sen.

Drawing on moments in my research when political violence became evident, and later considering the way I altered my practice in response to the same challenges, I consider how one of the ongoing legacies of the Cold War in Cambodia is a political sphere of distrust and insecurity, of violence and repression. Using Kuan-Hsing Chen's urge to re-centre stories of the Cold War as part of the deimperialisation project in Asia, I consider how this legacy is a result of both internal and external influences that have yet to be fully untangled. Thus, they continue to have an influence on contemporary Cambodia. As researchers in Asia, it is our duty to bring these entanglements to the fore and show how the wounds of the Cold War are still open in some areas.

* * *

Even in 2021, in Southeast Asia the ongoing effects of the Cold War are inescapable. Wars fought in the East as part of the ideological conflict against communism in the West, caused mass death across many countries, and the ongoing consequences continue to affect understandings of kin, religion, politics, and sociality in many areas. In Cambodia, the Cold War contributed to the rise of the Khmer Rouge, a millenary Maoist regime that between 1975 and 1979 effected a genocide that caused the death of an estimated 1.7 million people, through starvation, exhaustion, disease, and execution. The ongoing effects of that genocide are still felt today, not least in the political sphere, where impunity and a hybrid, or illiberal, democracy[1] have enabled an autocratic rule by the current ruling party, the Cambodian People's Party (CPP), and the Prime Minister Hun Sen.

While a 'local' political force, the Khmer Rouge could not have come to power, or maintained its rule, without influence from the global geopolitical sphere. Immense diplomatic support even after their deposal continued to provide the regime with influence both in Cambodia and internationally. It has helped shape the realm of politics in to one that has seen the same regime, albeit with different names and in slightly different forms, in power since 1979. Today, relations with external nations, particularly the United States and China, continue to influence politics in Cambodia, contributing to the maintenance of the impunity that has allowed the current regime to become increasingly violent, and Hun Sen, to consolidate his autocratic rule. The Cold War never ended in Cambodia. Its influence, as well as the geopolitical machinations it enabled, is lived and embodied in everyday life. The effects of the Cold War are ongoing.

Interestingly, despite the external influence in the rise of the Khmer Rouge regime, the maintenance of its rule, and the ongoing political violence, many people at my fieldsites saw the international community as potential saviours. Hope for change was put at the feet of external powers, particularly the West, while Cambodia was seen as a country in need of development and aid. This chapter considers this paradox, through the lens of 'Asia as method', by placing the Cold War, and its ongoing effects, at the centre of analysis. By doing so, it contributes to the growing literature that challenges the dominant discourse of the Cold War as an ideological war between two Western superpowers, fought without casualties, that ended after the fall of the Berlin wall. Instead, I position Asian (here Cambodian) knowledge and experience at the centre of the story in and of itself, to show how the Cold War was very real, very bloody, not at all cold, and has not yet ended in places like Cambodia, even as the 'West' believes and perpetuates its own myths about the conflict.

RESEARCHING THE KHMER ROUGE

In 2012, I set out to start my PhD fieldwork researching relationships to, and understandings of, mass graves from the Khmer Rouge regime. I wanted to see from the ground how people think about the genocide, how they use the spaces of killing and burial, and how they relate to the dead from that regime. My research had emerged from experience as a forensic anthropologist in Iraq, where I worked for a short time on a capacity building project funded by USAID and the UN, training Iraqi and Kurdish officials on how to investigate mass graves. While there, I became interested in the political influence on mass grave investigation and the identification of human remains, and the Western/Eurocentric assumptions related to trauma, healing, and justice that accompanied them. For my PhD, I chose to work in Cambodia specifically because they did not seek to exhume all the mass graves from the Cambodian genocide, and because there appeared to be no drive, politically or from the ground, to seek individual identification of the remains. My work spans across topics such as grave-looting and excavation, rituals for the mass dead, haunting after the regime, political campaigning, tourism, and museums and memorialisations of the genocide and its dead.[2]

As part of my consideration of how conflict and genocide are manifested locally, one of my areas of interest was the treatment of human remains following the Khmer Rouge. I was particularly interested in their display at memorial sites across Cambodia, but most strikingly at Choeung Ek Genocidal Center – the killing site of Tuol Sleng prison – now a national memorial and popular tourist site. During the regime over 14,000 people had been brought to Choeung Ek, executed, and then buried in mass graves.[3] In the early 1980s, many of the graves had been excavated: by local people looting them searching for valuables, and then under the orders of the government, in order to provide material evidence of the violence of the regime as part of their political legitimation.[4] These remains are now housed in a massive stupa at the centre of the site, in which the skeletal remains of almost 9,000 people are displayed.

One of the people who helped me understand Choeung Ek was Om Chann.[5] An elderly man, born sometime in the 1940s, he had lived through the horrors of the regime, and had lived in one of the villages close to the site both before and after the regime. He had returned in early 1979, just after the Khmer Rouge were deposed, and had lived there ever since, seeing the site change from one where only journalists and officials were brought by government representatives in the early 1980s, to a busy tourist site that (pre-Covid times) in the high season sees up to 1,000 international tourists a day come through its gates.[6] Like most Cambodians I encountered, he had lost family, friends, and colleagues during the genocide, some of whom potentially could be displayed at the site. He had participated in the looting of graves at Choeung Ek as people searched for valuables to trade in their efforts to rebuild life.

The display of human remains has caused some debates over the years, but like many other Cambodians I interviewed, Om Chann thought the displays were important. There were a number of reasons for that, including caring for the dead; however, the reason he considered most pertinent was the need for foreigners to see the physical evidence. He said:

> It's important. It's better that we keep them, so that Khmer and foreigners know
> . . . . We need to let foreigners know. So many people were killed because
> foreigners didn't know.

I felt an inherited guilt hearing these words. The Khmer Rouge took power in April 1975, and stories of the horrors occurring in Cambodia were heard internationally in that year, as international personnel were expelled from the country, and Cambodians fled the work camps to Thailand and Vietnam. These stories, however, were ignored or dismissed. Not only had the international community known about the genocide, but also they had been integral to its rise, and active in ensuring its continuance, primarily because of the Cold War. And yet, in Om Chann's imaginary, memorials such as Choeung Ek were a way of keeping the international community informed of the horrors – horrors that they had known about, and ignored, at the time.

While a multitude of circumstances led to the rise of the Khmer Rouge, the Cold War was central.[7] As part of its offensive against the rise of communism in Southeast Asia, a US bombing campaign in the late 1960s and early 1970s killed unknown numbers of Cambodians, 'setting in motion the expansion of the Vietnam War deeper into Cambodia, a coup d'état in 1970, the rapid rise of the Khmer Rouge, and ultimately the Cambodian genocide'.[8] Killings and purges during the genocide escalated with the intensification of the Vietnamese War. Thailand provided aid to the Khmer Rouge throughout their rule.[9] Although the bombing in the 1970s had been to try and prevent the advance of the Khmer Rouge (as part of their support to the Lon Nol regime that preceded the Khmer Rouge, during which an estimated 200,000 and 300,000 people died[10]), once they took power, the United States viewed North Vietnam as the greater threat. As early as 1975, they were willing to ignore the killings and support the Khmer Rouge, while encouraging an alliance with China,[11] who provided immense support to the Khmer Rouge in the form of equipment, provisions, and consultancy.[12] China was also the primary market for the export of rice grown during the regime, which was killing people in Cambodia as they starved to death and died from exhaustion.[13]

The Khmer Rouge regime was deposed in 1979 by Vietnam who, tired of border skirmishes into their country, invaded with a small group of Khmer Rouge defectors who were put into government as the People's Republic of Kampuchea (PRK). However, because Vietnam was still viewed as an enemy of the West, its invasion, and subsequent governance, of Cambodia, although ending the genocide, was viewed by many as an illegal occupation.[14] The UN embargoed Cambodia, refusing trade, aid, and diplomatic relations, and the Khmer Rouge was supported to become part of a government in exile, which continued to occupy Cambodia's seat in the UN until the early 1990s.[15] They ran refugee camps across the border in Thailand, where beatings, and even murder, were frequent.[16] Meanwhile, from their remaining strongholds in Northwest and Southern Cambodia, they continued to wage a civil war against the Cambodian government, raiding villages, kidnapping people, and sometimes committing murder. These raids were so frequent in the 1980s and early 1990s, that in one of my research sites – Phnom Voar – people chose to move to a new village being created with cadre to try and encourage their defection, because they considered it safer to live with the Khmer Rouge, than in a village that could be raided by them. And yet, Om Chann thought that 'so many people were killed because foreigners didn't know'.

This belief in external powers extended beyond its past and into Cambodia's future. The 2013 general elections occurred during my first period of fieldwork. It was interesting to note how the government and the opposition mobilised the Khmer Rouge regime in their campaigning – using it as a continued threat through both rhetorics of conflict and political campaigning.[17] I also began to notice how the contemporary political sphere re-enacts its mechanisms of rule and violence – ruling through an opaque political practice of insecurity and distrust.[18] The lead up to, and events that followed, the elections provoked (guarded) conversations about politics, and the opportunity to see, and feel, first-hand how the political sphere functions in contemporary Cambodia.

The elections raised tension around the country. After a shock result in which the opposition party – the Cambodian National Rescue Party – dramatically increased their seats in the National Assembly (taking twenty-two from the ruling party), concerns about violence rose. While the opposition had made massive gains, the ruling party still announced their victory, and the opposition party contested the result. A series of protests occurred in the capital, becoming increasingly violent, and eventually resulting in protestors' deaths.[19] Interviewing a government employee shortly after the elections, we got to talking about Cambodia's future:

If we base our hope on the Khmer, there's no hope at all. We can only depend on the International community. . . . The Khmer are all oppressed now.

The conversation continued, and after asking for clarification, he responded:

> The election organized by UNTAC was just and fair. The King won, we can say so. FUNCINPEC[20] won. But after that, in elections without international monitors, [they] never won again.

This was an interesting comment, because while some commentators do consider the elections to have been free and fair,[21] the outcome certainly was not. The 1993 elections were managed by the United Nations Transitional Authority in Cambodia (UNTAC), which, following the 1991 Paris Peace Accords, aimed to oversee Cambodia's transition from civil war to a liberal democracy, bringing peace and stability to the country.[22] As part of this transitional project, UN soldiers were based in Cambodia and helped negotiate peace settlements, as well as oversee the elections. Many of my participants saw this period as pivotal in the transformation of Cambodia from a warring state to one of relative stability and security. '1993 was the turning point', Om Chann told me.

In the 1993 elections FUNCINPEC won the most votes. This was a royalist party established by former king Norodom Sihanouk in opposition to the Vietnamese backed PRK, and part of the coalition government in exile, along with the Khmer Rouge. Although officially winning the election, the CPP, with Hun Sen at the helm, forced a coalition, and then took sole control of Cambodia in a bloody coup in 1997.[23] They won the 1998 elections in extremely dubious circumstances and have never lost an election since. International monitors have been present at each election, but have not been able to stop the corruption, intimidation, and violence that have shaped each one. Meanwhile, as violence has escalated in the kingdom, international funding has continued to flow and investment to grow.

JUXTAPOSING VIOLENCE AND REALITY

As an anthropologist who works on violence, and in particular having studied violence in Cambodia, I am intrigued by the way local and global forces make sense of violence, its prevention, or its end. Given the ways foreign powers were important contributors to the rise of the Khmer Rouge, the success of their regime, and their continued influence well in to the 1990s, why do some of my participants see the international community as the only hope for the future of Cambodia? How do people come to view the West as their saviour, despite the evidence that they were integral to the rise, and impact, of the Khmer Rouge, and actively ignore the pervasive impunity that enables an escalating sphere of violence in politics today? The answers lie both in contemporary Cambodia, and in the way Cold War structures still influence knowledge creation in the country.

Cambodia is officially a democratic, constitutional monarchy; however, the contemporary *real politik* is a one-party state under the authoritarian rule of Prime Minister Hun Sen, head of the CPP. This party has been in power in one form or another since the Khmer Rouge was deposed in 1979. At the core of the CPP is a group of former Khmer Rouge who defected to Vietnam in 1977 and 1978, when internal purges were occurring of the regime.

Hun Sen has the worst human rights record of any democratically elected leader,[24] and his influence on the governance sphere of Cambodia is profound. In recent years, the political sphere has become increasingly violent, with beatings, assassinations, and threats of conflict and war increasingly occurring in the open. Hun Sen's personal bodyguard is implicated in much of this public violence.[25] In addition to the direct violence, political repression has escalated: in the eighteen months running up to the 2018 elections, the opposition party was dissolved, its leader imprisoned on charges of treason, other party members banned from politics for five years (eliminating them from the 2023 elections), media outlets closed, and political commentators and opposition lawmakers beaten and imprisoned.

The political violence enacted by the current regime is not only directed at public figures. Bureaucratic and other violence against the population is rife, and impunity extends across politics and into the public sphere, particularly for the elite. The Khmer Rouge is raised as a threat to anyone opposing the prime minister, using both euphemisms (returning to the forest) and outright threats. He is rumoured to have a network of spies across Cambodia, discouraging trust from building between people, and adding to the conception of a controlling government under which there is an ever-present pervasive surveillance. The Khmer Rouge was said to have 'the eyes of a pineapple', that is, eyes everywhere seeing in all directions from which there was no escape.[26] Thus, people learned silence, speaking neither of their own pain and suffering, nor of anything they witnessed against others. This silence remains today, as does the distrust. When one of the men at one of my research sites – a small island in the Bassac River I call Koh Sap – was brutally beaten by another, the people of the village refused to talk to the police, preferring to claim they had seen and heard nothing. On several occasions people I was talking to or interviewing called the current government *Ångkar* – the organisation. This was the name given to the Khmer Rouge during Democratic Kampuchea, and it functioned as a mode of perpetual insecurity by being an amorphous, unknowable, untraceable organisation,[27] whose rules were changeable and whose ire was deadly. The use of this term for the current regime highlights the insecurity that people feel under its rule, and creates linkages between the Khmer Rouge mode of governance and the political sphere today.

This suspicion and surveillance extended to my research. When I first arrived in Koh Sap, many people were suspicious of my motives. It was only a couple of months before the general election, and some refused to talk to me, thinking I must be collecting information for the government. The day after visiting one of the Buddhist pagodas that houses remains from the island, the head monk sent two novices to the village to ask around about why I was there and why I was really interested in the pagoda.[28] When my partner of the time and I worked in Chamcar Bei, a new village created in the 1990s by bringing ex-Khmer Rouge cadre, government soldiers, and other people from across Kep province together, the village chiefs received regular phone calls from the provincial office asking what we were doing, and one of them appeared mysteriously wherever we went.

While I never felt directly threatened, the low-level surveillance kept me on edge, and I became increasingly cautious in my topics of conversation and with whom I had them. This extended once I left Cambodia. Shortly after arriving in Aotearoa-New Zealand in 2016, I was due to present a working paper on political violence in the anthropology seminar series. Discovering around 45 minutes before the seminar that six government officials from Cambodia would be attending my talk (in New Zealand on a NZAID funded scheme, bringing officials from Southeast Asia to New Zealand for training in English), I hastily changed the topic to one 'less political'. I do not know what the consequences of presenting a paper highlighting Cambodia's violent politics to members of the ruling party would be. Perhaps nothing. As far as I am aware, no one has been denied entry in to the country for publishing critiques of the government, or people within it, and at the time (2016), I had not heard about foreign scholars or journalists being imprisoned inside the country, although that has now changed.[29] Colleagues in Cambodia have, however, been harassed, their participants threatened, and had to leave fieldsites because their research was on politically sensitive matters.[30] I did not want to take the risk. To protect my research space, therefore, I too contributed to the political impunity that pervades the political sphere of Cambodia.

THE EFFECTS OF THE COLD WAR

In the book *Asia as Method: Toward Deimperialization*, Kuan-Hsing Chen questions understandings of the Cold War that position it as an ideological conflict between political and economic systems, fought without casualties, between two superpowers in the West.[31] He argues that this story is part of the marginalisation of Asia as a centre of experience and knowledge creation, because for many in Asia, the Cold War never ended. Through an analysis of the colonial and Cold War legacies in Taiwan, Chen shows that for many people in many places, it is not yet the post-Cold War era. Rather the effects of this conflict have been embedded in national, personal, and family histories, and the structures created during the era have been weakened but not dismantled. Subjectivities formed during the era remain, including political and institutional forms, and systems of popular knowledge. Thus, 'the Cold War is still alive'[32] for many people.

Chen argues that global colonial structures of power were replaced by Cold War structures, which remain in place today. Thus, in order to reposition Asian subjectivities at the centre of knowledge production and experience, Chen argues that 'the imperial question must be brought back to centre stage'.[33] To de-cold war, as he names it – that is, to dismantle the structures of knowledge production and allow meaningful reconciliation – there must first be space made for honest and reflexive stories to be told, that allow critical reflection on the historical trajectories that have created the current systems of knowledge creation and governance.[34] This includes within Asia as well as outside.

In the same year that *Asia as Method* was published, Heonik Kwon published *The Other Cold War*,[35] which similarly questioned understandings of the Cold War and its effects. Not only does Kwon show how the Cold War was an active conflict for many nations but he also challenges the rhetoric that has positioned it as a 'single globally identical phenomenon'.[36] For Kwon, the Cold War is multiple, because its effects, consequences, and temporality are variable and contextually dependent. Even in the West, the Cold War was never purely symbolic – the bipolar politics of Germany, for example, was brought to the fore through everyday activities such as consumption,[37] and McCarthyism in the United States was hugely damaging for social unity, political solidarity, academic and cultural freedom, education, and much more.[38] For many nations in Asia, the Cold War was a radicalising force that resulted in violent civil conflicts killing millions. As Kwon points out, this was not a conflict without casualties, nor 'cold' in any way.

Both Chen and Kwon invite us to reposition Asia and its experiences at the centre of our analysis. In Cambodia, this means bringing the story of the Cold War back to the fore, and continuing to interrogate how it is positioned in relation to the Cambodian genocide, and the state today, as well as critically reflecting on our own research on the matter. Deimperialisation must be undertaken from the direction of the imperial powers and the colonisers, not by the colonised locale. By 'confronting historically constituted structures of sentiments on the psychoanalytic terrain of the social and the cultural',[39] new possibilities are opened: for reconciliation within nations, but also throughout Asia and beyond.

CONTEMPORARY GEOPOLITICS AND CAMBODIA

In the 1990s, as part of its transition towards a liberalising democracy, Cambodia was opened to international markets. This has seen a massive amount of investment and development in the country. Since the early 1990s, Cambodia has received over $20 billion in international aid,[40] and it has the second highest number of NGOs per capita in the world, after Rwanda.[41] While a few existed before the Khmer Rouge, and a handful worked there in the 1980s, most entered after the UNTAC elections in 1993, when Cambodia opened its gates to international trade, investment, and development, and the UN lifted the aid embargo put in place during the PRK. Today the NGO sector brings in more than US $1 billion to Cambodia's economy, and their presence is noticeable around Cambodia, particularly in cities such as Phnom Penh and Siem Reap, where NGOs run cafes, restaurants, educational facilities, and much more. International and local NGOs further the rhetoric and perpetuate the idea that Cambodia is a nation that cannot survive without external support.

Meanwhile, the current regime continues to be supported both implicitly and explicitly by international powers. Although they suspended funding for the 2018 elections, the United States and the EU continue to trade and provide aid to Cambodia. China, Cambodia's biggest investor, has remained silent on the increasing violence in the country. The China–US trade war has impacted tourism and investment to the kingdom, but in 2010, China and Cambodia signed a strategic partnership which ensured ongoing ties for years to come,[42] and when in 2013 the Belt and Road Initiative (BRI) was unveiled in China, Cambodia was one of the countries its new silk road would connect.[43] Of the 6.2 million tourists who arrived in the country in 2018, 4.3 million of them came from Asia, with two million of those being Chinese.[44] While the EU trade deals for the garment industry are important, Cambodia's largest sector is agriculture (accounting for 22% of GDP in 2019[45]), with the majority of its exports from this going to Asia – primarily Vietnam and China.[46]

The increasing ties between China and Cambodia have enabled Cambodia to step free from some of the restrictions placed on funding from other donors, such as the United States and the EU. Like Norodom Sihanouk before him, Hun Sen practices political polygamy. He is willing to open Cambodia to investment from whichever direction it comes. But China's increasing invest-ment gives him confidence to reject other funding and the pressures that come with it. While the United States and the EU suspended funding for the 2018 elections, Russia, Japan, South Korea, and China all continued to support them.[47] The US disapproval of Cambodia did not last long. In January 2020, at an event celebrating seventy years of diplomatic ties between the United States and Cambodia, a spokesman for the ruling party praised the US ambassador for his non-interventionist stance, stating that ties between the two countries were based on non-interference and mutual respect.[48] While some people in Cambodia see the international community as vital to freeing Cambodia's future, most of it has, instead, continued to support Hun Sen and the ruling party. Meanwhile, the ruling dynasty have amassed millions, kept in international banks and property abroad,[49] while the minimum wage in Cambodia was US $190 pcm in 2020, and many people in the rural areas live on less than that.

However, people such as Om Chann, and others who I interviewed, still hold a firm belief in the benevolent powers of external intervention. This appears to be an internalisation of a combination of different narratives: first, of the deposition of the Khmer Rouge by Vietnam in 1979; secondly of the subsequent management by the UN of the 1993 elections, which were seen as a key turning point by many people I interviewed; and thirdly of development narratives in post-genocide and contemporary Cambodia that position it as a state in need of intervention at all levels of society. In addition, it reflects a notion that still pervades in the country, that Western knowledge and expertise is superior to Cambodian. Many wealthy Khmers travel abroad for higher education, and others are sent by employers to 'improve the human capital of Cambodia'. In the last few years numerous international schools have opened in Phnom Penh, where teachers from abroad teach Cambodian children in English, in the hope of improving job opportunities.[50]

The current impunity has its roots in a political system that emerged from the Khmer Rouge. It also has its roots in the governing and justice systems. The 1993 elections, overseen by the UN, removed the term genocide from the lexicon, replacing it with the 'practices and policies of the past', because it was deemed unfair for one party to be able to accuse another of genocide.[51] This allowed the obscuring of the genocide, as well as the geopolitical circumstances leading to its rise. The establishment of the international tribunal currently trying the leaders of the Khmer Rouge, the Extraordinary Chambers in the Courts of Cambodia, was actively blocked during the 1980s and into the 1990s by the current regime, but also by the United States and China.[52] When it was eventually established in 2003, its remit was to prosecute those 'most responsible' for the crimes of the regime (the top five leaders), within the period of its rule – April 1975–January 1979: a temporal and personnel limitation conveniently obscuring not only the culpability of hundreds of other Cambodians, including members of the current government, but also the wider causes and effects of the regime, including the geopolitical context that influenced and supported it.[53]

Like all regimes, Cambodia's is the result of interactions of internal and external factors, and a complex interplay of geopolitical circumstances of the past few decades. A myriad of geopolitical realities over preceding decades have helped support, and even bolster, Hun Sen's position today. Erik Kuhonta notes that the stability of ASEAN as a region actually rests on its inclusion of illiberal states, because they hold a vested interest in protecting their sovereignty and control against external influences, particularly from the West.[54] This is reflected in the impunity Hun Sen extends to other countries in the region. In 2017, his opinion of the Rohingya genocide, for example, was that it was Myanmar's internal affair.[55] China's investment in many of the ASEAN countries helps enable this illiberalism.[56] In many countries this has led to 'benign neglect towards democratic movements', which 'in the process has strengthened authoritarianism'.[57] This also reflects a global shift, both in power balances and the dynamics of international trade relations. Around the world we are seeing a rise of authoritarian regimes and illiberal democracies.

Many people living in Cambodia today lived through the Khmer Rouge regime. In the years following the regime, they experienced civil conflict, and despite peace being brokered in the 1990s, an increasingly repressive political sphere. Many younger people I interviewed felt anger and frustration at the current ruling party: its corruption and the violence it engenders through impunity of the elite. They have only lived with this ruling party, and have seen an escalation of its violence and repression in recent years. It is unsurprising, given this background, that despite all other evidence, many people thought change could only come from abroad.

In fact, limits to Hun Sen's rule have primarily been Cambodian. As Jonathan Sutton shows, it was not external pressure that limited Hun Sen's grasp and his violence prior to 2015, rather it was internal opposition within the party.[58] It was only after the death of the party president, Chea Sim, that Hun Sen was able to consolidate his rule – by eliminating internal opposition through a cabinet reshuffle that removed those loyal to Sim and replacing them with people with whom he has ties of patronage. Thus, the barrier to violence and political autocracy was within Cambodia, and even within the ruling party. It was never external.

In reflecting on my respondents' articulations of Cambodian violence and benevolent saviours, what is noteworthy is the continued articulation of local political 'lack', mirroring the international rhetoric of both the development and the political sphere. While some may see the solution in global forces, and others in local resistance, the fact that gets highlighted in accounts that I heard is that an intervention is necessary, and that the violence cannot be re-lived in Cambodia. When Om Chann talked about the need to keep skeletal remains from the genocide so that foreigners could see them, it was as a reminder to international audiences of what they 'turned away from' years ago. It is also a material intervention into contemporary politics to not forget the legacy of the genocide, and to never let this happen again. The elections serve as sites to see the re-enactment of Khmer Rouge violence through an opaque political sphere in which people have no trust: of each other, or of the governance of Cambodia as a whole, which therefore needs external intervention to fix. These moments that appeared in my research highlighted the dissonance between stories on the ground, and the geopolitical realities- in the past and in the present - that were shaped by the Cold War. As such, they provide important reflections from the everyday about the nature of violence itself.

CONCLUSION: VIOLENCE FROM ANOTHER ANGLE

The Cold War continues to effect Cambodia today, not least in the ongoing affects caused by the loss of over 1.7 million people in a devastating genocide that dismantled the nation. The current regime is violent, repressive, and becoming more so. While hope was bright in the run up to the 2013 elections, nowadays people are less hopeful. The prime minister is a powerful man and seems unlikely to let go of his hold on the nation. He uses the Khmer Rouge in his political campaigning, both directly and symbolically. It is also recreated in the way politics operates as a sphere of insecurity, surveillance, and distrust. Looking at this, it is easy to lay the blame at the feet of Cambodia, and forget the influence international powers have both on the rise of the Khmer Rouge, but also on the political impunity that enables Hun Sen to openly increase his violence and dictatorial hold on Cambodia today. But foreign relations that helped create and maintain the regime have also helped create the current political system, including the impunity that enables an autocratic rule by the current prime minister and his party.

In 2010, both Kuan-Hsing Chen and Heonik Kwon published books reconsidering global understandings of the Cold War. By positioning Asian experience and realities as the centre point of their analysis, they showed that the Cold War has not ended, and its effects are still felt and lived in localities across Asia today. Through their cultural and ethnographic explorations, both ask us to question knowledge creation, and its implications, using Asia as a reference point. By centring lived experiences of the Cold War, both show how Western systems of knowledge not only fail to comprehend everyday realities in Asia, but also actively dismiss them by forgetting, or rendering invisible, the realities of the conflict and its ongoing impacts. In this chapter I have attempted to illustrate what this looks like in Cambodia.

The violence, corruption, and political impunity that run rife across Cambodia are positioned as a legacy of its decades of conflict, which has left a deficit in good governance and mechanisms of reconciliation and restoration. The Khmer Rouge is blamed for contemporary issues as far reaching as the crumbling of trust in communities,[59] sex trafficking and other human rights abuses,[60] the endemic corruption across Cambodia,[61] and the poor educational attainment in the nation.[62] But these deficits are also viewed as being the fault of Cambodia and its structures of governance, with often little consideration of the geopolitical legacies that have enabled this contemporary reality, including, and in particular, the Cold War. The Cambodian genocide shaped the country's history, but it also continues to shape the contemporary and the future(s) of Cambodia. As researchers, it is our responsibility to go further into the history of Asia and Cambodia to lay bare the geopolitical machinations (both locally and globally) that have implications on the daily lives of our interlocutors.

Through this Chen and Kwon inspired re-reading of Cold War influence on Cambodia I do not position Cambodia, its government, or its people as weak, non-agentive, or helpless victims of external circumstance – to do so would continue paternalistic narratives of Cambodia as a developing nation incapable of self-governance and in need of external oversight. Rather, by considering the international influence on the rise of the Khmer Rouge, and in enabling the current government to come to power, I want to show that the current situation is both internally and externally influenced – now and historically. My aim for this chapter is small – the argument I make here is that the current regime could not be, and remain, in power, were it not for the legacy of the Khmer Rouge, which enacted a genocide, which was, in part, a result of the Cold War. Thus, I bring the Cold War back to the fore, and add to other literature that continues to question the dominant narrative of an ideological war fought without casualties between two powers in the West. The lack of trust and security in the political sphere, and the deficit felt by my participants, reflects the way people in Cambodia are still living with the Cold War. The display of human remains, the tension within which elections occur, and the everyday violence of politics in Cambodia keep the Cold War alive. It was never, and it has not yet become, cold.

* * *

ACKNOWLEDGEMENT

The fieldwork for this research was supported by the ESRC (grant number ES/J500148/1) and VUW Faculty of Humanities and Social Sciences. Thanks to everyone in Cambodia who generously participated in this research and to my research assistants in particular. I do not name them due to the political nature of this chapter and my research. Thanks to Nayantara for her generous reading and comments on this chapter, and to others including my colleagues at VUW, and colleagues at the Nordic Institute of Asian Studies, University of Copenhagen, where I was a guest researcher from March to June 2019, and who have helped develop my thinking on my Cambodian research.

NOTES

1. Un Kheang, "Patronage Politics and Hybrid Democracy: Political Change in Cambodia, 1993–2003," *Asian Perspectives* 29, no. 2 (2005): 203–230.

2. Caroline Bennett, "Human Remains from the Khmer Rouge Regime, Cambodia," in *Ethical Approaches to Human Remains: A Global Challenge in Bioarchaeology and Forensic Anthropology*, ed. Kirsty Squires, David Errickson, and Nicholas Márquez-Grant (New York: Springer, 2020), 567–582; Caroline Bennett, "Karma after Democratic Kampuchea: Justice Outside the Khmer Rouge Tribunal," *Genocide Studies and Prevention: An International Journal* 12, no. 3 (December 2018): 68–82; Caroline Bennett, "Living with the Dead in the Killing Fields of Cambodia," *Journal of Southeast Asian Studies* 49, no. 2 (June 2018): 184–203.

3. See David Chandler, *Voices from S-21: Terror and History in Pol Pot's Secret Prison* (Berkley: University of California Press, 1999) for a comprehensive narration of the creation and work of Tuol Sleng, and Caroline Bennett, "To Live Amongst the Dead: An Ethnographic Exploration of Mass Graves in Contemporary Cambodia," (PhD diss. University of Kent, UK, 2015), for a discussion of Choeung Ek.

4. Bennett, "To Live Amongst the Dead".

5. All names given are pseudonyms.

6. These numbers are given directly from statistics collected by the management of Choeung Ek Genocidal Centre.

7. For further discussion of the rise of the Khmer Rouge, see Ben Kiernan, *How Pol Pot Came to Power: Colonialism, Nationalism, and Communism in Cambodia, 1930–1975*, Second Edition (New Haven: Yale University Press, 2004). James Tyner also discusses the legacy of the Cold War on Democratic Kampuchea in his book *Landscape, Memory, and Post-Violence in Cambodia* (London: Rowman and Littlefield, 2016), 171–198.

8. Taylor Owen, and Ben Kiernan, "Bombs Over Cambodia," *The Walrus*, October 12, 2006. So powerful was the lived memory of the fear and disruption caused by the bombing, that when the national front and Vietnam invaded to depose the regime in late 1978, some of my research participants fled with the Khmer Rouge: 'we weren't sure who were good or bad [of the Vietnamese and Khmer Rouge], so we kept following them [the Khmer Rouge]', one person told me. 'They told us the Vietnamese would kill us, so we kept running'.

9. Elizabeth Becker, *When the War was Over: Cambodia and the Khmer Rouge Revolution*, Revised Edition (New York: PublicAffairs, 1998).

10. Marek Sliwinski, *Le Génocide Khmer Rouge: Une Analyse Démographique* (L'Harmattan, 1995).

11. In a meeting between Thai foreign minister Chatichai Choonhavan and US secretary of state, Henry Kissinger, in November 1975, Kissinger asked Choonhavan what the Cambodians thought about the United States, before commenting 'You should tell them that we bear no hostility towards them. We would like them to be independent as a counter-weight to North Vietnam [. . .] We would prefer to have Laos and Cambodia aligned with China rather than with North Vietnam'. Later in the conversation, despite hearing that they had already killed thousands of people, he said 'tell the Cambodians that we will be friends with them. They are murderous thugs, but we won't let that stand in our way. We are prepared to improve relations with them'. (The entire transcript of the meeting is available at: https://www.mekong.net/cambodi a/download/cambodia_chatchai_kissinger_19751126.pdf.)

12. Andrew Mertha, *Brothers in Arms: Chinese Aid to the Khmer Rouge, 1975– 1979* (Ithaca: Cornell University Press, 2014).

13. Stian Rice, and James Tyner, "The Rice Cities of the Khmer Rouge: An Urban Political Ecology of Rural Mass Violence," *Transactions of the Institute of British Geographers* 42, no. 2 (December 2017): 559–571.

14. Edwin A. Martini, *Invisible Enemies: The American War on Vietnam, 1975– 2000* (Amherst, MA: University of Massachusetts Press, 2007).

15. Ben Kiernan, "The Cambodian Crisis, 1990–1992: the UN Plan, the Khmer Rouge, and the State of Cambodia," *Bulletin of Concerned Asian Scholars* 24, no. 2 (1992): 3–23.

16. Becker, "When the War was Over".

17. Caroline Bennett, "To Live Amongst the Dead," 270–307.

18. Ibid.

19. Prak Chan Thul, "Cambodian Opposition Rallies for Second Day after Protest Death," *Reuters*, September 16, 2013. https://www.reuters.com/article/us-cambo dia-politics/cambodian-opposition-rallies-for-second-day-after-protest-death-idU SBRE98E07G20130916.

20. Front uni national pour un Cambodge indépendant, neutre, pacifique et coopératif.

21. Duncan McCargo, "Cambodia: Getting Away with Authoritarianism?" *Journal of Democracy* 16, no. 4 (October 2005): 98–112.

22. Michael Sullivan provides an excellent overview of the elections in Cambodia in his book, *Cambodia Votes: Democracy, Authority, and International Support for Elections 1993–2013* (Copenhagen: NIAS Press, 2016).

23. Brad Adams, "July 1997: Shock and Aftermath," *The Phnom Penh Post*, July 27, 2007.

24. Human Rights Watch, "30 Years of Hun Sen: Violence, Repression, and Corruption in Cambodia," [online report], 2015. https://www.hrw.org/report/201 5/01/12/30-years-hun-sen/violence-repression-and-corruption-cambodia, accessed January 18, 2020.

25. Neang Ieng, and Sel San, *Cambodian Prime Minister Promotes Body Guards Who Beat Lawmakers*. Trans Nareth Muong. *Radio Free Asia*, December 28, 2018.

https://www.rfa.org/english/news/cambodia/cambodian-prime-minister-promotes-body-12282016133914.html.

26. Henri Locard, *Pol Pot's Little Red Book: The Sayings of Angkar* (Chiang Mai: Silkworm Books, 2004), 112.

27. Alexander Laban Hinton, *Why did they Kill? Cambodia in the Shadow of Genocide*. California Series in Public Anthropology (London: University of California Press Limited, 2005).

28. Luckily, these monks did not take their job too seriously – they stopped at at a relative's house and spent the afternoon drinking, and when I happened to walk past, called me in and told me of their orders.

29. Washington Post Editorial Board, "In Cambodia, Journalism has Become a Crime," *Washington Post*, August 24, 2019. https://www.washingtonpost.com/opinions/global-opinions/in-cambodia-journalism-has-become-a-crime/2019/08/23/52e57b0c-afb9-11e9-bc5c-e73b603e7f38_story.html; Len Leng, "Cambodia Pardons Australian Filmmaker Jailed for Espionage," *Phnom Penh Post*, September 21, 2019.

30. Laura Schoenberger, and Alice Beban, "They Turn Us into Criminals": Embodiments of Fear in Cambodian Land Grabbing," *Annals of the American Association of Geographers* 108, no. 5 (2018): 1338–1353.

31. Chen, Kuan-Hsing *Asia as Method: Toward Deimperialization*. Durham: Duke University Press, 2010.

32. Ibid., 117–120.

33. Chen, *Asia as Method*, xiii.

34. Heonik Kwon, *The Other Cold War* (West Sussex: Columbia University Press, 2010), 150–159.

35. Kwon, *The Other Cold War* .

36. Ibid., 28.

37. Ibid., 29.

38. Ellen W. Schrecker, *No Ivory Tower: McCarthyism and the Universities* (New York: Oxford University Press, 1986); Thomas Doherty, *Cold War, Cool Medium: Television, McCarthyism, and American Culture* (New York: Columbia University Press, 2003); James L. Gibson, "Political Intolerance and Political Repression During the McCarthy Red Scare," *American Political Science Review* 82, no. 2 (June 1988): 511–529; to name but a few.

39. Chen, *Asia as Method*, xiv.

40. Takehiko Koyanagi, "Hun Sen's Cambodia: Aid to Cambodia Tops $20bn, But 'Democratic Society' Still Far Off," *Nikkei Asia Review*, August 14, 2018. https://asia.nikkei.com/Spotlight/Hun-Sen-s-Cambodia/Aid-to-Cambodia-tops-20bn-but-democratic-society-still-far-off.

41. Cooperation Committee for Cambodia, 2017. https://www.ccc-cambodia.org/kh.

42. Sigfrido Burgos, and Sophal Ear, "China's Strategic Interests in Cambodia: Influence and Resources," *Asian Survey* 50, no. 3 (May/June 2010): 615–639.

43. Sarwat Viqar in this volume discusses the impact of the BRI in Pakistan.

44. Ministry of Tourism, "Tourism Statistics Report 2018," PDF. Phnom Penh: Ministry of Tourism Statistics and Tourism Information Department.

45. World Bank, "Cambodia Economic Update, May 2019," http://documents .worldbank.org/curated/en/843251556908260855/pdf/Cambodia-Economic-Update-Recent-Economic-Developments-and-Outlook.pdf, accessed January 20, 2020.

46. Ibid.

47. Aun Chenngpor, "Former Opposition MP Calls for Japan Boycott of General Election," *Voice of America Khmer*, June 1, 2018. https://www.voacambodia.c om/a/former-opposition-mp-calls-for-japan-boycott-of-general-election/4419577 .html.

48. Mech Dara, "US Ambassador Marks 70 Years of Diplomatic Relations with the Kingdom," *Phnom Penh Post*, January 9, 2020.

49. Claire Baldwin, and Andrew RC Marshall, "Khmer Riche: How Relatives and Allies of Cambodia's Leader Amassed Wealth Overseas," *Reuters Investigates*, October 16, 2019. https://www.reuters.com/investigates/special-report/cambodia-h unsen-wealth/.

50. Jose Rodriguez T. Senase, "Cambodia Lagging in English Proficiency: Index," *Khmer Times*, November 14, 2019. https://www.khmertimeskh.com/659171/camb odia-lagging-in-english-proficiency-index/.

51. Tom Fawthope, and Helen Jarvis, *Getting Away with Genocide? Elusive Justice and the Khmer Rouge Tribunal* (London: Pluto Press, 2004).

52. Ibid.

53. Rebecca Gidley gives a good discussion on the establishment of the courts in her book *Illiberal Transitional Justice and the Extraordinary Chambers in the Courts of Cambodia* [Palgrave Studies in the History of Genocide] (Basel: Springer Nature Switzerland 2019).

54. Erik Martinez Kuhonta, "Walking a Tightrope: Democracy Versus Sovereignty in ASEAN's Illiberal Peace," *The Pacific Review* 19, no. 3 (2006): 337–358.

55. Sao Phal Niseiy, "Cambodia's Prime Minister is Wrong about Myanmar's Rohingya Issue," *The Diplomat*, February 9, 2017.

56. Kuhonta, "Walking a Tightrope".

57. Ibid., 340.

58. Jonathan Sutton, "Hun Sen's Consolidation of Personal Rule and the Closure of Political Space in Cambodia," *Contemporary Southeast Asia* 40, no. 2 (2018): 173-195.

59. May Ebihara, and Judy Ledgerwood, J., "Aftermaths of Genocide: Cambodian Villagers," in *Annihilating Difference: The Anthropology of Genocide*, ed. Alexander Hinton (California Series in Public Anthropology. Berkley and London: University of California Press, 2002), 272–291.

60. Leakhena, Nou, "Prosecuting the Perpetrators (the Khmer Rouge Genocide Part 3)," *Engaging Peace* [Online], October 15, 2012. http://engagingpeace.com/?p =5162, accessed January 19, 2020.

61. Joel Brinkley, *Cambodia's Curse: The Modern History of a Troubled Land* (New York: Public Affairs, 2011).

62. Damien de Walque, "The Long-Term Legacy of the Khmer Rouge Period in Cambodia," PDF. *World Bank Policy Research Working Paper*, Washington DC: The World Bank. Report number: 3446 (2004).

REFERENCES

Adams, Brad. "July 1997: Shock and Aftermath." *The Phnom Penh Post*, July 27, 2007.

Baldwin, Claire, and Andrew RC Marshall. "Khmer Riche: How Relatives and Allies of Cambodia's Leader Amassed Wealth Overseas." *Reuters Investigates*, October 16, 2019. https://www.reuters.com/investigates/special-report/cambodia-hunsen-wealth/.

Becker, Elizabeth. *When the War was Over: Cambodia and the Khmer Rouge Revolution*. Revised Edition. New York: PublicAffairs, 1998.

Bennett, Caroline. "Human Remains from the Khmer Rouge Regime, Cambodia." In *Ethical Approaches to Human Remains: A Global Challenge in Bioarchaeology and Forensic Anthropology*, edited by Kirsty Squires, David Errickson, and Nicholas Márquez-Grant, 567–582. New York: Springer, 2020.

———. "Karma after Democratic Kampuchea: Justice Outside the Khmer Rouge Tribunal." *Genocide Studies and Prevention: An International Journal* 12, no. 3 (December 2018): 68–82.

———. "Living with the Dead in the Killing Fields of Cambodia." *Journal of Southeast Asian Studies* 49, no. 2 (June 2018): 184–203.

———. "To Live Amongst the Dead: An Ethnographic Exploration of Mass Graves in Contemporary Cambodia." PhD dissertation, University of Kent, UK, 2015.

Brinkley, Joel. *Cambodia's Curse: The Modern History of a Troubled Land*. New York: Public Affairs, 2011.

Burgos, Sigfrido, and Sophal Ear. "China's Strategic Interests in Cambodia: Influence and Resources." *Asian Survey* 50, no. 3 (May/June 2010): 615–639.

Cambodian Genocide Studies Program. "US Involvement in the Cambodian War and Genocide." Interactive Map [online]. 2020. https://gsp.yale.edu/case-studies/cambodian-genocide-program/us-involvement-cambodian-war-and-genocide, accessed January 19, 2020.

Chandler, David. *A History of Cambodia*. Fourth Edition. London: Routledge, 2007[1983].

———. "Cambodia Deals with Its Past: Collective Memory, Demonisation, and Induced Amnesia." *Totalitarian Movements and Political Religions* 9, no. 2–3 (2008): 355–369.

———. *Voices from S-21: Terror and History in Pol Pot's Secret Prison*. Berkley: University of California Press, 1999.

Chen, Kuan-Hsing. *Asia as Method: Towards Deimperialization*. Durham and London: Duke University Press, 2010.

Chhengpor, Aun. "Former Opposition MP Calls for Japan Boycott of General Election." *Voice of America Khmer*, June 1, 2018. https://www.voacambodia.c om/a/former-opposition-mp-calls-for-japan-boycott-of-general-election/4419577 .html.

Cooperation Committee for Cambodia, 2017. https://www.ccc-cambodia.org/kh.

Department of State Transcript—discussion Kissinger and Chunhawan. https://ns archive2.gwu.edu//NSAEBB/NSAEBB193/HAK-11-26-75.pdf, accessed January 17, 2020.

Doherty, Thomas. *Cold War, Cool Medium: Television, McCarthyism, and American Culture.* New York: Columbia University Press, 2003.

Dorsch, Jörn. "ASEAN's Reluctant Liberal Turn and the Thorny Road to Democracy Promotion." *The Pacific Review* 21, no. 4 (2008): 527–545.

Ebihara, May, and Ledgerwood, Judy. "Aftermaths of Genocide: Cambodian Villagers." In *Annihilating Difference: The Anthropology of Genocide*, edited by Alexander Hinton, 272–291. California Series in Public Anthropology. Berkley and London: University of California Press, 2002.

Fawthrope, Tom, and Jarvis, Helen. *Getting Away with Genocide: Elusive Justice and the Khmer Rouge Tribunal.* London: Pluto Press, 2004.

Fein, Helen. "Genocide by Attrition 1939–1993: The Warsaw Ghetto, Cambodia, and Sudan." *Health and Human Rights* 2, no. 2 (1997): 10–45.

Gibson, James L. "Political Intolerance and Political Repression during the McCarthy Red Scare." *American Political Science Review* 82, no. 2 (June 1988): 511–529.

Gidley, Rebecca Ann. *Illiberal Transitional Justice and the Extraordinary Chambers in the Courts of Cambodia.* London: Palgrave Macmillan (Palgrave Studies in the History of Genocide), 2019.

Human Rights Watch. "30 Years of Hun Sen: Violence, Repression, and Corruption in Cambodia." [Online report], 2015. https://www.hrw.org/report/2015/01/12/30 -years-hun-sen/violence-repression-and-corruption-cambodia, accessed January 18, 2020.

International Monetary Fund. "Regional Economic Outlook, Asia and Pacific 2019." https://www.imf.org/en/Publications/REO/APAC/Issues/2019/10/03/areo1023, accessed January 19, 2020.

Kiernan, Ben. *Blood and Soil: A World History of Genocide and Extermination from Sparta to Darfur.* New Haven: Yale University Press, 2007.

———. "External and Indigenous Sources of Khmer Rouge Ideology." In *The Third Indochina War: Conflict between China, Vietnam and Cambodia, 1972–1979*, edited by Arne Westad Odd, and Sophie Quinn–Judge, 187–206. New York: Routledge, 2006.

———. *How Pol Pot Came to Power: Colonialism, Nationalism, and Communism in Cambodia, 1930–1975.* Second Edition. New Haven: Yale University Press, 2004.

———. "The Cambodian Crisis, 1990–1992: the UN Plan, the Khmer Rouge, and the State of Cambodia." *Bulletin of Concerned Asian Scholars* 24, no. 2 (1992): 3–23.

Koyanagi, Takehiko. "Hun Sen's Cambodia: Aid to Cambodia tops $20bn, but 'Democratic Society' Still Far Off." *Nikkei Asia Review*, August 14, 2018. https:/

/asia.nikkei.com/Spotlight/Hun-Sen-s-Cambodia/Aid-to-Cambodia-tops-20bn-but -democratic-society-still-far-off.

Kuhonta, Erik Martinez. "Walking a Tightrope: Democracy Versus Sovereignty in ASEAN's Illiberal Peace." *The Pacific Review* 19, no. 3 (2006): 337–358.

Kwon, Heonik. *The Other Cold War*. West Sussex: Columbia University Press, 2010.

Leakhena, Nou. "Prosecuting the Perpetrators (the Khmer Rouge Genocide Part 3)." *Engaging Peace* [Online], October 15, 2012. http://engagingpeace.com/?p=5162, accessed January 19, 2020.

Leng, Len. "Cambodia Pardons Australian Filmmaker Jailed for Espionage." *Phnom Penh Post*, September 21, 2019.

Locard, Henri. *Pol Pot's Little Red Book: The Sayings of Angkar*. Chiang Mai: Silkworm Books, 2004.

Martini, Edwin, A. *Invisible Enemies: The American War on Vietnam, 1975–2000*. Amherst, MA: University of Massachusetts Press, 2007.

McCargo, Duncan. "Cambodia: Getting Away with Authoritarianism?" *Journal of Democracy* 16, no. 4 (October 2005): 98–112.

Mech, Dara. "US Ambassador Marks 70 Years of Diplomatic Relations with the Kingdom." *Phnom Penh Post*, January 9, 2020.

Mertha, Andrew. *Brothers in Arms: Chinese Aid to the Khmer Rouge, 1975–1979*. Ithaca, NY: Cornell University Press, 2014.

Ministry of Tourism. "Tourism Statistics Report 2018." PDF. Phnom Penh: Ministry of Tourism Statistics and Tourism Information Department, Royal Government of Cambodia.

Neang Ieng, and Sel San. "Cambodian Prime Minister Promotes Body Guards Who Beat Lawmakers." Trans Nareth Muong. *Radio Free Asia*, December 28, 2018. https://www.rfa.org/english/news/cambodia/cambodian-prime-minister-promotes -body-12282016133914.html.

Niseiy, Sao Phal. "Cambodia's Prime Minister is Wrong about Myanmar's Rohingya Issue." *The Diplomat*, February 9, 2017.

Owen, Taylor. "Bombs over Cambodia." *The Walrus*, October 12, 2006 (updated October 17, 2019). https://thewalrus.ca/2006-10-history/, accessed January 17, 2020.

Rice, Stian, and James Tyner. "The Rice Cities of the Khmer Rouge: An Urban Political Ecology of Rural Mass Violence." *Transactions of the Institute of British Geographers* 42, no. 2 (December 2017): 559–571.

Senase Jose Rodriguez T. "Cambodia lagging in English proficiency: index." *Khmer Times*, November 14, 2019. https://www.khmertimeskh.com/659171/cambodia- lagging-in-english-proficiency-index/.

Schoenberger, Laura, and Alice Beban. "They Turn Us into Criminals": Embodiments of Fear in Cambodian Land Grabbing." *Annals of the American Association of Geographers* 108, no. 5 (2018): 1338–1353.

Schrecker, Ellen W. *No Ivory Tower: McCarthyism and the Universities*. New York: Oxford University Press, 1986.

Sullivan, Michael. *Cambodia Votes: Democracy, Authority, and International Support for Elections 1993–2013*. Copenhagen: NIAS Press, 2016.

Sutton, Jonathan. "Hun Sen's Consolidation of Personal Rule and the Closure of Political Space in Cambodia." *Contemporary Southeast Asia* 40, no. 2 (2018): 173–195.

Thul, Prak Chan. "Cambodian Opposition Rallies for Second Day after Protest Death." *Reuters*, September 16, 2013. https://www.reuters.com/article/us-cambo dia-politics/cambodian-opposition-rallies-for-second-day-after-protest-death-idU SBRE98E07G20130916.

Tyner, James. *Landscape, Memory, and Post-Violence in Cambodia*. London: Rowman and Littlefield, 2016.

Un Kheang. "Patronage Politics and Hybrid Democracy: Political Change in Cambodia 1993–2003." *Asian Perspective* 29, no. 2 (2005): 203–230.

de Walque, Damien. "The Long-Term Legacy of the Khmer Rouge Period in Cambodia." PDF. World Bank Policy Research Working Paper, Washington DC: The World Bank. Report number: 3446 (2004).

Washington Post Editorial Board. "In Cambodia, Journalism has Become a Crime." *Washington Post*, August 24, 2019. https://www.washingtonpost.com/opinions/ global-opinions/in-cambodia-journalism-has-become-a-crime/2019/08/23/52e57b 0c-afb9-11e9-bc5c-e73b603e7f38_story.html.

World Bank. "Cambodia Economic Update, May 2019." http://documents.worldbank. org/curated/en/843251556908260855/pdf/Cambodia-Economic-Update-Recent -Economic-Developments-and-Outlook.pdf, accessed January 20, 2020.

Chapter 4

Researching Karachi's Spatial Politics

Processes and Practices of Ethnography in Urbanity

Sarwat Viqar

ABSTRACT

In this chapter I analyse the dialectic between the methods employed for ethnographic work and the urban context of Karachi that is undergoing urban transformations that echo larger changes in Asia. Privatisation, informality, and state fragmentation are key aspects of these processes within which urban ethnographers seek to make sense of everyday urban life and practices. As urban researchers in Asian contexts, we also have to negotiate the tension between Western-centric urban orientations and local practices that never quite seem to fit or come up to global aspirations and ambitions for city building. These aspirations are also predicated upon reified categories of state and nationhood as well as history which are often unsettled during ethnographic work. In order to understand the challenges posed by such a field, I examine the processes and practices of ethnographic fieldwork in terms of what they reveal about the nature of the present urban conjuncture in Karachi and its relation to the wider region that is Asia. Central to this examination are questions of positionality, identity, reflexivity, and orientation. I examine these aspects of field research as constantly shifting concepts that are interrogated and challenged during the process of fieldwork and that are related to the social and economic pressures that are driving Asian urbanisms at large.

* * *

This chapter is an attempt to examine 'questioning' moments in ethnographic fieldwork in urban environments, in order to raise key issues related to the challenges of doing anthropological work in Pakistan, in conversation with the larger Asian region. As a diasporic scholar who is originally from Pakistan but now living in Canada, undertaking extensive fieldwork in Karachi, Pakistan's largest urban conglomeration led me to critically evaluate the ways in which we engage with the field. In this chapter I foreground three kinds of encounters to make my point: field encounters that brought to the fore my identity and positionality as a researcher, field interactions with respect to urban informality, and encounters with bureaucracy. I elucidate how ethnographic work in a dense, and Asian urban environment like Karachi, Pakistan's largest city, created questionings around the role of the anthropologist, the role and function of the state, and the effects of the larger historical structures and narratives of colonialism and imperialism in the postcolonial Third World. I thus bring attention to the linkages that bind urban regions in the Asian and Global South regions, as a way to contribute towards efforts to re-orient the epistemologies and methods used to study locations in Asia today.

Roy and Ong argue that Asian urban centres are sites of a wide array of urban processes and projects that tend to unsettle the established norms of global modernity, especially as it applies to the future of urban regions.[1] From this perspective, these urban regions can be seen as sites of experimentation with urban processes that offer new and diverging ways in which Asia engages with modernity. These ways come up against universalist assumptions that see the state as a reified and only legitimate site of social production, of development as a linear process of technological improvement and prosperity, and the urban as a natural and unproblematic progression on the trajectory of development. As scholars have argued, most urban regions in Asia and in the Global South at large tend to unsettle linear trajectories of development because they do not fit neatly into binary framings of state/civil society, public/private, religious/secular.[2] Indeed, these unsettlings do not only have implications for the divergent experiences of Asian cities, but for understandings of the urban everywhere. The question is, how does the category of 'Asia' emerge and/or is relevant when engaging in ethnographic studies of cities that broadly reside in the Asian region?

The largest metropolitan regions of the world are now located in the Global South – Djakarta, Mumbai, Shanghai, Mexico City, Sao Paolo – urban regions whose trajectories of urban development and state formation with the resultant political economies are quite distinct from Western cities. Increasingly, while manifesting very distinct local political and economic trends, city regions in the Global South show some common patterns, which have to do with their entanglements in regional and global histories of colonialism, decolonisation, and post-colonial conditions. Therefore, as Chen suggests, the Third World, and substantial parts of Asia as part of it, 'provide an imaginary horizon of comparison, or a method' for what Chen calls 'inter-referencing'.[3] I interpret this 'inter-referencing' process as a theoretical, historical, and methodological re-orienting and re-positioning towards regions, peoples, and histories that have been marginal in the discourse of social sciences. This methodological re-orientation is particularly salient for urban anthropology, as urban marginality and rising economic disparity is a defining feature of urban regions across the Global South and Asia.

While political and economic conditions can vary widely across the region, ubiquitous features include large-scale displacements of urban populations as a result of evictions, unequal access to basic services and infrastructure, and uneven development leading to spatial inequalities, as has been revealed through a rich body of work across the region, but particularly South Asia.[4] Inter-urban comparisons across South Asia thus provide a rich field of urban processes and practices that, while manifesting local particularities, also point towards a shared condition of post-coloniality. These comparisons are important because they allow an examination of how local particularities and variations scale up in terms of revealing national, regional, and universal patterns. These patterns need to be read, as Chari and Verdery propose, not as hostage to the overarching power of "capitalism', 'colonialism', or 'socialism' qua fixed entities'[5] but as the fragmented and dispersed histories of colonialism and modernity.

IDENTITY AND POSITIONALITY IN THE FIELD

What does it mean to come to the field with a post-colonial as well as a diasporic subjectivity? It would mean, while embedded in local histories of post-colonial angst, also recognising the privileges accorded by diasporic lives. As scholars practicing 'engaged' anthropology have argued, we cannot ignore our own implication and responsibilities in the social lives we study. This requires becoming aware of the power relations at work in the field, particularly when studying urban marginality. It means to actively work to create collaborative relationships in the field rather than function within existing hierarchical ones.[6] But, also, in the current political and economic conjunctures that urban Asian regions find themselves, there are particular challenging moments that prompt a fundamental re-evaluation of our roles and responsibilities as anthropologists. It means being interrogated by interlocutors about not just our intentions, but also our own investment in improving local lives and national futures. During fieldwork, a recurring question is the responsibility of using our diasporic privilege to improve local lives as a way of fulfilling a national obligation. For me, such interactions provoked a critical questioning of our 'objective' stance as anthropologists/ethnographers.

When considering issues around methodology and fieldwork conduct, while there is an acknowledgement of the subjective nature of anthropological work and responsibility towards individuals, there is less engagement with reflexivity around questions of collective social responsibility. Such questions become particularly pertinent when working in the context of urban marginality in terms of class, gender, and race. The question then becomes how to situate ourselves as anthropologists and ethnographers in the process of deimperialisation and decolonisation.

The relevance of these questions became apparent to me during significant moments in field research in Karachi. One of my key interlocutors, Razia Bano, was a dynamic female ex-councillor who also had an active affiliation with the Muttahida Qaumi Movement (MQM), which was then Karachi's most powerful political party. While I learned about the political dynamics of the neighbourhood from her, she posed very pertinent questions back to me about my role and objective in conducting my research. Recognising me also as a fellow Pakistani and the member of the same ethnicity (Mohajir),[7] she was particularly concerned about what I intended to do with my professional future. Would I come back to Pakistan and make myself useful there? And if so, would I pledge to better the conditions of those I was now in the process of studying? While Razia's questions were posed in a context of an ongoing friendly relationship, I would encounter these questions in brief encounters with users of public spaces and streets during participant observation of these areas, as well. Fundamentally, these questions forced me to view myself as a national subject – a Pakistani – with responsibilities towards the collectivity at a time of scarcity, struggle, and want. These reminders of my own post-colonial subjectivity precipitated questionings around my social responsibility and commitment to developing an anti-imperialist and decolonising practice.

Other ways in which my subjectivity shaped my encounters were related to my gender and ethnic identity, which, as perceived by my interlocutors, led to questions about the role of gendered and ethnic subjectivities in the current political conjunctures defining urban politics and struggles around the control of space. A close rumination on my field encounters revealed to me the contingent nature of these identities, their performative aspects, and their relation to larger post-colonial concerns about belonging and identity in the nation.[8] As a diasporic female scholar of Muslim origin I was acutely aware of both the privileges and marginalities embedded within the multiple social locations I inhabited, and certain elements of my social identity made me acutely aware of both the local and global power relations linked to those identities. Firstly, carrying out research in Pakistan, often defined by the tropes of underdevelopment and terrorism linked to its Islamic identity, created a heightened awareness and a sense of responsibility in terms of how my research would be read and perceived in the West. For example, while in Pakistan studying the dialectic of socio-spatial practices in public, I was acutely aware and critical of the assumption of Muslim women in public spaces being perceived primarily as a threat to patriarchy in spaces controlled by Muslim men, an assumption that has been critiqued by scholars like Lila Abu-Lughod.[9] While I listened to male anxieties about family, sexuality, and masculinity that surfaced in contestations around public space, I was attentive to all the ways in which both men and women were present in these spaces and how both periodically participated in the destabilisation of norms and accepted practices. Living in Quebec, Canada and having encountered a very one-dimensional and stereotypical perspective around the veiling practices of Muslim women pushed me to be deeply critical of the limitations of those perspectives while observing the everyday public activities of women in Karachi's neighbourhoods. As I observed the range of social practices undertaken by women unfolding in the old mohallas of Karachi, I concluded that women were constantly in a state of exercising their agency. Often these practices exist in the interstices between what is conventionally deemed as public or private space, straddling the domains of religion, and politics, the domestic and the public.[10] These ways of inhabiting space, while rooted in older traditions of participation in the collective life of the community, also reflect women in the urban economy, as more and more women step out of the home for employment as well as education. When I was conducting interviews in the public spaces of the old city area of Karachi, I was thus placed, in either praiseworthy or censorious ways, by both my male and female interlocutors, in this space of changing gender norms where diasporic female academics are seen as engaging in social service to the nation, and also represent female empowerment.

Therefore, this diasporic orientation created a productive bias that allowed me to be attentive to forms of life and practices that often go unnoticed and are often deemed as non-agentive and unfree. I understand this coming together of personal experience and social positionality to create a particular epistemic focus, as a confluence of the global and post-colonial forces at work, particularly among scholars of colour. Such an analysis is attentive to the ways in which race and positionality has been shaped in the aftermath of what Chari and Verdery term 'post-cold war effects'.[11] Thus, our positionalities have been generated in a post-Cold War environment of othering and demonisation facilitated by a biopolitics of othering practices that deem specific groups of people as enemies based on race, gender, and class. These biases permeate the fields of theoretical and practical engagement between the West and the 'rest'. In the context of urbanism, this means the positioning of Western urban regions as the 'norm' against which the 'rest' are measured, and legitimacy and authority given to expertise based on the identity of who speaks. Remaining attentive to these tensions, the following sections high-light the way local practices converse with the wider socio-economic trends in Asia by foregrounding the influence of rising regional hegemonies as well as shared features that define state–society relations.

URBAN COMPETITION AND REGIONAL LINKAGES

One aspect of regional processes driving urban development is city branding and marketing. In Karachi, these processes are increasingly oriented not to Western cities but to cities within Asian and, in the case of Pakistan, the Middle-Eastern region. While cities like London and New York provided the aspirational focus in the early years of post-colonial development, today, economically peripheral urban regions within Asia, like those of Pakistan, look towards Hong Kong, Singapore, and Kuala Lumpur as models of urban growth. In fact, the 'Singapore model' – 'a set of normative and technical urban plans' – is actively invoked as the ideal of urban development in cities across South Asia.[12] It is a model that is invoked differently in different Asian urban contexts, to fulfil widely diverging objectives, from principles of 'urban sustainability' to modes of spatial privatisation and corporatisation in the name of urban efficiency. The invocation of such speculative models has been critiqued as leading to large-scale dispossessions and exclusion of the poor, stripping ordinary citizens of their human rights.[13] The permeation of the Singapore model through the region is also a two-way process. For example, part of an ongoing bilateral free trade agreement between Singapore and Pakistan is an offer by the Singapore government to build five million low-cost houses and its 'expertise in urban planning'.[14] These regional orientations are increasingly significant drivers of urban development and the politics of urban infrastructure provision.

In Asia, the new power arrangements are centred more on the geo-economic rivalries between China, Japan, India, and Russia to invest in and exploit the vast pools of labour and resources in the less developed regions. This is a shift, particularly in the case of Pakistan, for example, from being a subject of US influence, largely as a result of Cold War rivalries which came to a head in the war in Afghanistan in 1979, and Pakistan's subsequent entanglements in the militarisation and occupation of Afghanistan by the United States in the post-9/11 era of the war on terror. In fact Pakistan's most significant Asian connection is its insertion into the Chinese BRI. The aim of the BRI is to find new export markets for Chinese goods and destinations for Chinese investments, and this initiative includes sixty-four countries that cover various projects in the entire Eurasian zone, with an approximate value of $900 billion.[15] As Golley and Ingle note, it, calls for a multi-dimensional infrastructure network including a number of 'economic corridors' (such as China Pakistan Economic Corridor, China-Mongolia-Russia Economic Corridor, and the New Eurasian Continental Bridge). It will upgrade land, sea and air transportation routes through major railway, port and pipeline projects. The initiative will also create mechanisms for the Five Connectivities: policy dialogue, infrastructure connectivity, tariff reductions, financial support, and people-to-people exchanges through the participating countries.[16]

In Pakistan, BRI's investment, in the form of the China Pakistan Economic Corridor (CPEC), is significant – US $60 billion. The Corridor runs for 2000 kilometres, connecting Kashgar, a Chinese city to the north-west, to the Pakistani port of Gwadar on the Arabian Sea, and gives China access to Central Asian energy sources, as well as the Arabian Gulf, fulfilling military objectives as a safe harbour for the Chinese navy. In return, Pakistan receives infrastructure and energy supply through a network that charts a terrain of multiple infrastructure projects from roads, railways, and pipelines, to energy grids and agricultural projects.

Critics have argued that the BRI represents a new kind of development model, one that is built on state-centric and 'pluralist' ideas – a divergence from the traditional market-oriented privatisation models. Although there is no doubt that privatisation underpins the model, there is heavy state regulation, creating a model of economic governance that is a kind of state capitalism.[17]

This new orientation begs attention when considering the direction of urban development in Pakistan, as currently, when local urban practices scale up, they will encounter and dialogue most significantly with this model. A significant example of this is the Karachi Central Railway (KCR) project that is part of the Mass Transit component of CPEC. While plans for the project have existed since the early 2000s, under CPEC it is now being fast-tracked and is slated to service over half a million commuters daily. The project will be constructed on land that is currently inhabited by twenty-eight informal settlements with a population of 45,000 who will be removed, through a process of eviction and relocations.[18] Resistance to the KCR has emerged in the form of protests and demands for alternative solutions by the 'Karachi Bachao Tehreek' (Movement to Save Karachi). Similarly, in the province of Balochistan, the site of the deep water port of Gwadar and the keystone project of CPEC, there has been rising local opposition to the project due to loss of local jobs.[19] The project is seen as benefitting China more than Pakistan as both labour and equipment are imported from China. Chinese firms contracted to work on the project have also been accused of violating local laws and transgressing social customs.[20]

The conflicts outlined above are increasingly representative of emerging forms of opposition to the new forms of economic, cultural, and security relations initiated by regional powers that are engendering new hegemonies. As such, the struggles originating in these margins are located in sites that hold the 'biopolitical debris of capitalism, colonialism and nationalism',[21] in the form of excluded and criminalised populations, redundant labour, and degraded environments. These are also sites where orders of rule and governance do not fit into conventional understandings of state, society, and law and where law and governance operate in formal and informal ways. In the next section, I raise urban informality as one such site and a key signifier of urban living in Asia and in Pakistan to examine the ways in which it shaped and informed the ethnographic encounter.

URBAN INFORMALITY AND THE FIELD

Considered one of the world's fastest growing cities in the world, Karachi's annual growth rate has hovered around 5% since 1972, with a present estimated population of 15.4 million, projected to rise to 20 million by 2030.[22] Approximately 54% of central government tax revenues are collected in Karachi, and its monopoly over sea bound trade ensures it remains a key site for the collection of customs duties. Nearly 61% of the city's residents belong to low- and middle-income groups who reside in 'unplanned' settlements where civic resources are poorly distributed. Like many other cities in the Global South, informality underpins Karachi's post-colonial urbanity. With the state's inability to provide housing and social amenities to the lower-class population, 'illegally' acquired land and privately contracted infrastructure arrangements – aided by political party strongmen, land brokers, and the lower echelons of the state – have engendered new forms of patronage and political alliances. The supply of basic infrastructure in the city is deeply embedded in networks of exchange that circulate between the legal and illegal.

Urban informal economies are expected to dominate the political economies of Asian cities in the coming decades. Urban informality is a key site of struggle in multiple urban regions across Asia and Karachi is no exception. Karachi's informal economies can most closely be paralleled with urban regions in India and the broader South Asian region. The present politics of land and infrastructure in Karachi has been shaped by the colonial and post-colonial transformations of the urban economy, with the partition of British India and the birth of two new countries as major markers of change. Karachi's demographic landscape was radically transformed in 1947 when almost one million refugees from various parts of newly established India migrated to the city in newly established Pakistan.

Roy refers to urban informality as 'a state of exception from the formal order of urbanization'.[23] This condition of informality as an exceptional state, however, as has been argued by urbanists working in diverse Global South contexts, is the way states function on a routine basis and indeed, as Simone reiterates, based on extensive work in similar contexts, the very nature of states in much of the Global South has been determined by their entanglements with and dependence on informalities and illegalities in various domains of social life.[24] As Roy argues in a summarisation of the significance of informality in defining the urban experience, states actively facilitate conditions of informality, mainly through materialising a geography of uneven development at the service of both local and global capital.[25] Thus, informality represents a state of provisionality and contingency that has become a key signifier of urban living in the Asian and Global South urban context. This view of informality is more nuanced and critical than the ways in which informality surfaces; on the one hand as a state of crisis – literally representing a crisis of the state as dysfunctional – or on the other hand when it is romanticised as 'heroic entrepreneurship'. Roy recommends considering informality as a 'mode' rather than a sector – a mode that defines 'a series of transactions that connect different economies and spaces to one another'.[26] This assessment is supported by other studies – for example, based on an examination of cross-regional informal economies in India and Vietnam, it has been argued that the state may purposefully sustain informalities through maintaining obscurity around formalisation and legalisation frameworks and making them inaccessible.[27]

However, although this ambiguity around legal processes is commonly seen in terms of state dysfunctionality, more nuanced views point out that informality is actually a constitutional force in post-colonial state formation.[28] As an illustration of this critique, much of my ethnographic work, undertaken in Karachi between 2011 and 2014 as part of my doctoral work examining informal sovereign arrangements and the politics of public spaces, involved noting the absence or presence of the state in the provision of infrastructure and the governance of public spaces in the city. These observations eventually led to a recognition of the role of the state in sustaining informal states/conditions, particularly in terms of urban infrastructure provision.

Thus, encountering informality during fieldwork became a way to interrogate the role of informality and state–society relations, and questioning the conventional and Western-centric dichotomies of public/private, work/ leisure, state, and civil society. Much of this critical approach developed as a result of engaging in 'inter-referencing' work on Third World cities, which has challenged the thresholds that define these categories.[29] Following Chatterjee's insights into the existence of a 'political society' – the realm of social actors that fits neither the category of state or civil society[30] – I was particularly attentive to the everyday practices of urban living during my research on informal occupations of public spaces and informal governance in the inner city neighbourhoods of Karachi. These constitute another aspect of the politics at work in the grey areas that inhabit the interstices of received categories of social and political domains. As Chen argues, moving away from accepting civil society as a normative category, towards interrogating it as an analytical category, helps in becoming attentive to the power relations that have always been at work in the reification of this category.[31] For the purposes of my fieldwork, this questioning opened up a space for the recognition of norms and forms of life that do not fit into the state or civil society categorisations. Further, it led to a recognition of ordinary people as political agents rather than as only cultural agents, and everyday practices as active contributions towards the making of political economies rather than just expressions of cultural norms.

A similar logic applies towards considering the state as an analytical, rather than normative category. Such a shift allows attentiveness to the ways in which state practices become dynamic and shifting as opposed to static and prescriptive, invisible and illegible, as opposed to transparent and rational. Thus, while I began my research with a focus on the ways in which the state was present on the streets and public spaces of the neighbourhood, what became more significant was the space and time in which the state was absent. Regardless of whether this absence was actual or perceived, it was foregrounded in field interactions with a range of social actors who, in expressing their frustrations with this absence, revealed their practical and ideological relationship with the state and nation. In Pakistan, in particular, the contested relationship with the state is reflected in unresolved questions about belonging and nationhood, the trauma of the violence of reconfigured borders, and the resultant displacement unleashed at partition.

STATES OF VIOLENCE, RISK, AND CONTINGENCY

In his work across urban regions in Africa and Asia, AbdouMaliq Simone has shown the contingent and provisional nature of marginal urban life.[32] During my fieldwork researching the role of informal sovereign arrangements – political groups, local gangs, religious organisations, it was brought home to me how much ethnographic work in such a context requires readiness for states of contingency and provisionality. During the course of year and a half long fieldwork in Lyari and Kharadar, two of Karachi's oldest neighbourhoods, there were dramatic changes in political dispensations and local states of governance that resulted in realignments in local ruling arrangements. As governance practices become more and more fragmented, provisional arrangements of rule become the norm as I concluded in a study of governance practices in Lyari,[33] and the threat of violent conflict became a constant feature of everyday life, for both me, and my interlocutors. This was a context of clashing political groups and criminal gangs in their efforts to assert territorial control over the neighbourhood as well as state crackdowns using paramilitary forces. Fieldwork became a fundamentally disorienting experience as contacts disappeared, organisations went underground, and new actors emerged to take their place within a period of months. While this experience is similar to fieldwork in any conflict environment, it has been noted as an increasingly ubiquitous feature of urban ethnographic fieldwork in many Global South urban contexts.[34] Fieldwork in such a context required a major questioning of not only the state as a normative category, but also a re-evaluation of field methodology.

I thus experienced significant 'questioning' moments regarding the nature of state–society relations and the rule of law versus disorder and violence. In a previous article, on the question of risk and violence in fieldwork, I have shown how perceptions and dominant narratives about violence and states of urban marginality distort the reality of violence in everyday life.[35] Such perceptions, dominated by fear, obscure the rational and practical role of the violence enacted by both state and non-state actors. In addition it is possible to better navigate the field through a critical awareness of this contradiction with close attention to the ways in which ordinary residents living in marginality negotiate this violence on an everyday basis. For example, working in Lyari required witnessing and moving through an urban terrain that was regularly represented in the media and by the state as a 'no-go area' and a danger zone, infested with criminal gang warfare and terrorist activities. Understanding and deconstructing these narratives was crucial in order to continue working in the field and key to this understanding was the critique, insights, and experiences of local residents who inhabit a zone of extreme urban marginality. Further, this understanding was also informed by my own experiences of growing up and witnessing the pervasive state and non-state violence, albeit with privilege, in the city. The larger methodological question posed by this insight is about the role of 'order and disorder' in the postcolony, as posited by Comaroff and Comaroff.[36] The dilemma is how democratisation in many Global South contexts has been accompanied with rising violence particularly in urban regions, which begs the question of the kind of democratic subjectivities and new citizenship categories that are arising in these contexts.[37]

Studying the informalities of land use, the contestations around public spaces and the political economy of public spaces also required forging relationships with non-state sovereign arrangements. It required insertion in circuits of movement and mobility that were managed by non-state actors who were involved in informal service provisions as well as informal governance. This led to ethical dilemmas, largely emerging from seeing myself linked with the various illegalities that sustained urban informality. As non-state governance overlapped with criminal networks, my embeddedness in the context of informal governance raised many ethical questions due to associating with social actors who breached social norms and legalities. Participant observation thus became a process fraught with risks, not just for myself, but for my associates and interlocutors in the field. In encounters with the young, male political workers of MQM, I became aware of the performative aspects of participant observation as I had to negotiate threat and risk. When interacting with these workers in public spaces I was often questioned about my intentions as well as my ethnic identity. The intersection of political and ethnic affiliation speaks to Karachi's fraught post-independence history in which ethnic divisions have become key faultlines in the competition for resources and the right to belong to the city. The workers of the MQM (who identify as Mohajir) who I encountered in the public spaces wanted me to prove my right to be in these spaces. While being a Mohajir myself and growing up in Karachi, I had not only never affiliated myself with the movement, but I had been deeply critical of its militant methods and ideology. When interacting with these young, male, and armed, workers though, I had to adopt a language of shared ethnic affinity in order to ensure my safety. This is something that many city residents learn to do, on a routine basis, to negotiate the social and political geography of the city. In the process, these engagements also precipitated questions about my own relationship with Pakistan as a national and post-colonial subject, as questions of identity and belonging, national and regional affiliations, were always present as an undercurrent in field encounters.

ENCOUNTERS WITH BUREAUCRACY

Pakistan shares the legacy of British colonial bureaucracy[38] with much of the Asian region. The colonial period brought new regimes of documentation, new infrastructures (both physical and social), and new modes of governance. The current state of bureaucracy in Pakistan is a result of a dialectic between colonial history and the political and economic developments in the early post-independence decades. The bureaucracy occupies a central role in the political processes of the country and is strongly imbued with colonial continuities, especially with regard to administrative regimes ruling infrastructure design and provision that includes urban planning.[39] One way in which urban planning carries the afterlives of colonialism is through the colonial nostalgia expressed by local bureaucrats of the best practices of British colonial rule. Colonial planning practices are often the reference point for future imaginings of the urban. Municipal officials, as well as residents in Karachi, often make references to British practices as the model for planning, diversion from which is supposed to have caused most of the problems besetting the city today. In interviews with the director of the Karachi Master Plan department, references to colonial governance surfaced in interesting ways. The director still refers to the colonial regime as the British Crown (Taj-e-Bartania in Urdu). When I asked him for access to current plans of city neighbourhoods he referred me to the maps made during the British era – 'their plans are still the best plans ever made of the city – they are much more reliable than the plans we make today'. His answer is emblematic of the way the deimperialised present still engages with colonial sovereignty. During this process, accessing and researching archives also revealed how maps and planning documents, such as land ownership documents, leases, and transfers, are invested with power and acquire political currency. Indeed the intense politics of accessing and viewing city maps and census data posed one of the most difficult challenges in fieldwork, and eventually led to a major re-orientation of research goals and objectives. It also led to larger questions about the afterlives of colonialism in the use of documentation for the purposes of governance.

Matthew Hull, in his ethnography of bureaucratic practices around land and property allotment practices in Pakistan, argues that the opacities and ambiguities that are pervasive in access to data and documentation can be productive at times, not only for the state but for citizens as well. The other side of the stringent governmentalities that manage data access is the lack of archiving and documentation, that is, the absence of any data. There are two ways in which issues around spatial data emerged in Karachi – the lack of any existing data, and ambiguity around the process of accessing data. Critics have labelled this ambiguity as a lack of accountability and a protection against legal recourse by citizens as: 'state control can be extended not only through specification, but through ambiguity, by leaving matters undocumented'.[40] The absence of data, such as land titles and accurate maps, can sustain the informal occupation of urban land by those who inhabit the margins of citizenship, who are subject to its disciplines, but not beneficiaries of its entitlements. On the other hand, when suppression of data and lack of documentation is used by the state to appropriate land for development through mass evictions, transparency and legibility in documentation has been used to assert rights of occupancy by those who are dispossessed.[41]

Therefore, beyond seeing this absence as a dysfunction of bureaucracy, it begins to make sense when looked at through the lens of post-colonial awareness of the way colonial modes of governance created paradoxes around the role of documents and governance, and the power relations behind colonial mapping and cartography. Ultimately, understanding planning bureaucracies in a city like Karachi requires considering them as sites of both colonial and post-colonial knowledge production, where documents are more than just a record of facts, rather they are artefacts of mediation between state and society.

CONCLUSION: INFRASTRUCTURES OF ETHNOGRAPHY

It is obvious that ethnographic work in Asia needs to be attentive to the historical and present conjunctures that have defined regional pasts and the present. Increasingly, the processes that are driving urbanisation in a city like Karachi begin to make sense when considered in dialogue with the broader South Asian and Global South context rather than the Western context and discourse of urbanisation. What is needed, therefore, is an understanding of capitalism and colonialism, not as fixed totalising categories, but as processes that are constantly being re-worked in the twenty-first-century context and that are translated in local contexts in ways that give rise to diverse and distinct modernities. This includes attention to the rise of regional hegemonies, for example, the BRI – in both their physical and discursive effects. These emerging configurations of power are also creating sites of opposition, conflict, and reaction that call into question the promises of development and that need to be understood through a questioning of received and normative understandings of statehood and citizenship.

An urban context like that of Pakistan requires understanding how marginality is constructed in the interstices of state and society with an interrogation of the binaries of state and civil society, public and private, and a reflexive awareness of researcher positionality. In this context, the significance of social and collective responsibility to social and political futures, particularly of marginalised subjects, challenges us to think of the ethics of doing anthropology in a more expansive way. The contested nature of national identities, the implications of ethnic affiliations, and the changing norms around gender provide a field of social relations that constantly challenges static and essentialist notions of identity. Finally, the opacity and ambiguity of bureaucratic processes of documentation reveal the fractures and fragmentation of governance processes that speak to colonial pasts as well as to the contested state of contemporary post-colonial nationhood that Pakistan shares with much of the post-colonial Third World across and beyond Asia.

* * *

NOTES

1. Ananya Roy, and Aihwa Ong, ed., *Worlding Cities: Asian Experiments and the Art of Being Global* (Oxford: Wiley-Blackwell, 2011).

2. Asef Bayat, *Life as Politics: How Ordinary People Change the Middle East* (Stanford, CA: Stanford University Press, 2009); Partha Chatterjee, *Lineages of Political Society: Studies in Postcolonial Democracy* (New York: Columbia University Press, 2011); Ayona Datta, *The Illegal City: Space, Law and Gender in a Delhi Squatter Settlement* (Farnham: Ashgate, 2012); Diane Singerman, *Cairo Contested: Governance, Urban Space and Global Modernity* (Cairo: American University in Cairo Press, 2009).

3. Chen Kuan-Hsing, *Asia as Method: Towards Deimperialization* (Duke University Press, 2010).

4. Soloman Benjamin, "Occupancy Urbanism: Radicalizing Politics Beyond Policy and Programs," *International Journal of Urban and Regional Research* 32, no. 3 (September 2008): 719–729; Partha Chatterjee, *The Politics of the Governed: Reflections on Popular Politics in Most of the World* (New York: Columbia University Press, 2004); Datta, *The Illegal City*; Akhil Gupta, *Red Tape, Bureaucracy, Structural Violence and Poverty in India* (Durham: Duke University Press, 2012); Thomas Blom Hansen, *Violence in Urban India: Identity Politics, 'Mumbai' and the Postcolonial City* (New Delhi: Princeton University Press, 2005); Ranjana Padhi, "Forced Evictions and Factory Closures; Rethinking Citizenships and Rights of Working Class Women across Delhi," *Indian Journal of Gender Studies* 14, no. 1 (January 2007): 73–92; Ananya Roy, "Slumdog Cities: Rethinking Sublatern Urbanism," *International Journal of Urban and Regional Research* 35, no. 2 (March 2011): 223–238.

5. Sharad Chari, and Katherine Verdery, "Thinking Between the Posts: Postcolonialism, Postsocialism and Ethnography after the Cold War," *Comparative Studies in Society and History* 51, no. 1 (January 2009): 30.

6. Setha M. Low, and Sally Engle Merry, "Engaged Anthropology: Diversity and Dilemmas," *Current Anthropology* 51, no. S2 (October 2010): S203–S226.

7. 'Mohajir' meaning migrant is the identity claimed by the Muslims who migrated from different parts of India, mostly Uttar Pradesh and Andhra Pradesh at partition in 1947. The largest population of Mohajirs in Pakistan resides in Karachi, which is majority Mohajir with other pockets in the urban areas of Sindh province.

8. Sarwat Viqar, "Women's Public Lives and Sovereign Arrangements in Karachi's Inner City," *Gender, Place and Culture: A Journal of Feminist Geography* 25, no. 3 (2018): 416–433.

9. Lila Abu-Lughod, "Do Muslim Women Need Saving? Anthropological Reflections on Cultural Relativism and its Others," *American Anthropologist* 104, no. 3 (2008): 783–790.

10. Viqar, "Women's Public Lives".

11. Chari, and Verdery, "Thinking Between the Posts".

12. Roy, and Ong, *Worlding Cities*.

13. Ibid.

14. Pervaiz Ashfaq Rana, "Singapore Offers Help in Building 5m Low-Cost Houses," *Dawn*, February 26, 2019. https://www.dawn.com/news/1466078.

15. Jane Golley, and Adam Ingle, "The Belt and Road Initiative: How to Win Friends and Influence People," in *Prosperity*, ed. Jane Golley, and Linda Jaivin (Canberra: ANU Press, 2018), 45–60.

16. Golley, and Ingle, "The Belt and Road Initiative," 52–53.

17. Matteo Dian, and Silvia Mengazzi, "Belt and Road, State Capitalism and China's Economic Interests," in *New Regional Initiatives in China's Foreign Policy: The Incoming Pluralism of Global Governance*, ed. Matteo Dian, and Silvia Mengazzi (Basel: Springer International Publishing Switzerland, 2018), 67–94.

18. Soha Makhtoum, "Life Along KCR: Between Aspirations for Mobility and Threat of Eviction," *Dawn*, May 29, 2019. https://www.dawn.com/news/1456242.

19. Ismail Sasoli, "Gwadar Fishermen Protest Against Construction of CPEC's Project Enters 12th Day," *Dawn*, December 29, 2018, https://www.dawn.com/news/1454126.

20. Dian, and Mengazzi, "Belt and Road."

21. Chari, and Verdery, "Thinking Between the Posts," 28.

22. Development Advocate Pakistan, "Sustainable Urbanization," *Development Advocate Pakistan* 5 no. 4 (Islamabad: United Nations Development Program Pakistan, 2019), https://www.pk.undp.org/content/pakistan/en/home/library/development_policy/dap-vol5-iss4-sustainable-urbanization.html.

23. Roy, and Ong, *Worlding Cities*, 147.

24. AbdouMaliq Simone, "'The Urban Majority and Provisional Recompositions in Yangon.' The 2016 *Antipode* RGS-IBC Lecture," *Antipode* 50, no. 1 (January 2018): 23–40; Hansen, *Violence in Urban India*; Oskar Verkaaik, *Migrants and Militants: Fun and Urban Violence in Pakistan* (New Jersey: Princeton University Press, 2004); Ananya Roy, "Urban Informality: Towards an Epistemology of Planning," *Journal of the American Planning Association* 71, no. 2 (June 2005): 147–158; Diane Singerman, *Cairo Contested: Governance, Urban Space and Global Modernity* (Cairo: American University in Cairo Press, 2009).

25. Ananya Roy, "The 21st Century Metropolis: New Geographies of Theory," *Regional Studies* 43, no. 6 (2009): 819–830.

26. Roy, "Urban Informality".

27. Jean-Pierre Cling, Mireille Razafindrakoto, and Francois Roubaud, "The Informal Economy in Asia: Introduction to the Issue," *Journal of the Asia Pacific Economy* 17, no. 4 (2012): 553–559.

28. Chatterjee, *Lineages of Political Society*; Matthew Hull, *Government of Paper: the Materiality of Bureaucracy in Pakistan* (Berkeley, CA: University of California Press, 2012).

29. Chatterjee, *Lineages of Political Society*; Bayat, *Life as Politics*; AbdouMaliq Simone, "Assembling Douala: Imagining Forms of Urban Sociality," in *Locating the City: Urban Imaginaries and the Practices of Modernity*, ed. Alev Cinar, and Thomas Bender (Minneapolis; London: University of Minnesota Press, 2007), 79–99; Singerman, *Cairo Contested*.

30. Chatterjee, *Politics of the Governed*.

31. Chen, *Asia as Method*, 233

32. Simone, "Assembling Douala"; "The Urban Majority".

33. Sarwat Viqar, "Constructing Lyari: Place, Governance and Identity in a Karachi Neighbourhood," *South Asian History and Culture* 5, no. 3 (April 2014): 365–383.

34. Teresa PR Caldeira, and James Holston, "Democracy and Violence in Brazil," *Comparative Studies in Society and History* 41, no. 4 (October 1999): 691–729; Hansen, *Violence in Urban India*.

35. Sarwat Viqar, "'We Are Your Brothers, We Will Know Where You Are At All Times': Risk, Violence and Positionality in Karachi," *Contemporary Social Science* 13, no. 1 (2018): 386–396.

36. Jean Comaroff, and John Comaroff, *Law and Disorder in the Postcolony* (Chicago: University of Chicago Press, 2006).

37. James Holston, *Insurgent Citizenship: Disjunctures of Democracy and Modernity in Brazil* (Princeton: Princeton University Press, 2008); Hansen, *Violence in Urban India*.

38. Direct British colonial rule in India, also known as Crown rule, began in 1858 and lasted till the partition of the subcontinent into the independent nation-states of India and Pakistan in 1947.

39. Hull, *Government of Paper*.

40. Ibid., 248.

41. Nausheen Anwar, "Mapping Politics in/of the Modern City: Cartography as Representation," in *Exhausted Geographies: An Experimental Art Publication Mapping the City of Karachi*, ed. Zahra Malkani, and Shahana Rajani (Karachi: Karachi Press, 2015), 1–17.

REFERENCES

Abu-Lughod, Lila. "Do Muslim Women Need Saving? Anthropological Reflections on Cultural Relativism and its Others." *American Anthropologist* 104, no. 3 (September 2002): 783–790.

Anwar, Nausheen. "Mapping Politics in/of the Modern City: Cartography as Representation." In *Exhausted Geographies: An Experimental Art Publication Mapping the City of Karachi*, edited by Zahra Malkani, and Shahana Rajani, 1–17. Karachi: Karachi Press, 2015.

Anwar, Nausheen, and Sarwat Viqar. "Research Assistants, Reflexivity and the Politics of Fieldwork in Urban Pakistan." *AREA* 49, no. 1 (March 2017): 114–121.

Bayat, Asef. *Life as Politics: How Ordinary People Change the Middle East.* Stanford, CA: Stanford University Press, 2009.

Benjamin, Soloman. "Occupancy Urbanism: Radicalizing Politics Beyond Policy and Programs." *International Journal of Urban and Regional Research* 32, no. 3 (September 2008): 719–729.

Caldeira, Teresa P. R., and James Holston. "Democracy and Violence in Brazil." *Comparative Studies in Society and History* 41, no. 4 (October 1999): 691–729.

Chari, Sharad, and Katherine Verdery. "Thinking Between the Posts: Postcolonialism, Postsocialism and Ethnography after the Cold War." *Comparative Studies in Society and History* 51, no. 1 (January 2009): 6–34.

Chatterjee, Partha. *The Politics of the Governed: Reflections on Popular Politics in Most of the World*. New York: Columbia University Press, 2004.

———. *Lineages of Political Society: Studies in Postcolonial Democracy*. New York: Columbia University Press, 2011.

Chen, Kuan-Hsing. *Asia as Method: Towards Deimperialization*. Durham, NC: Duke University Press, 2010.

Cling Jean-Pierre, Mireille Razafindrakoto, and Francois Roubaud. "The Informal Economy in Asia: Introduction to the Issue." *Journal of the Asia Pacific Economy* 17, no. 4 (2012): 553–559.

Comaroff, Jean, and John Comaroff. *Law and Disorder in the Postcolony*. Chicago: University of Chicago Press, 2006.

Datta, Ayona. *The Illegal City: Space, Law and Gender in a Delhi Squatter Settlement*. Farnham: Ashgate, 2012.

Development Advocate Pakistan. "Sustainable Urbanization." *Development Advocate Pakistan* 5 no. 4. Islamabad: United Nations Development Program Pakistan, 2019.

Dian, Matteo, and Silvia Mengazzi. "Belt and Road, State Capitalism and China's Economic Interests." In *New Regional Initiatives in China's Foreign Policy: The Incoming Pluralism of Global Governance*, edited by Matteo Dian and Silvia Mengazzi, 67–94. Basel: Springer International Publishing Switzerland, 2018.

Finney, Suzanne S., Mary Mostafanezhad, Guido Carlo Pigliasco, and Forrest Wade Young. *At Home and In the Field: Ethnographic Encounters in Asia and the Pacific Islands*. Honolulu: University of Hawaii Press, 2015.

Gayer, Laurent. *Karachi: Ordered Disorder and the Struggle for the City*. New York: Oxford University Press, 2014.

Golley, Jane, and Adam Ingle. "The Belt and Road Initiative: How to Win Friends and Influence People." In *Prosperity*, edited by Jane Golley and Linda Jaivin, 45–60. Canberra: ANU Press, 2018.

Gupta, Akhil. *Red Tape, Bureaucracy, Structural Violence and Poverty in India*. Durham: Duke University Press, 2012.

Hansen, Thomas Blom. *Violence in Urban India: Identity Politics, 'Mumbai' and the Postcolonial City*. New Delhi: Princeton University Press, 2005.

Holston, James. *Insurgent Citizenship: Disjunctures of Democracy and Modernity in Brazil*. Princeton: Princeton University Press, 2008.

Hull, Matthew. *Government of Paper: the Materiality of Bureaucracy in Pakistan*. Berkeley, CA: University of California Press, 2012.

Low, Setha M., and Sally Engle Merry. "Engaged Anthropology: Diversity and Dilemmas." *Current Anthropology* 51, no. S2 (October 2010): S203–S226.

Makhtoum, Soha. "Life Along KCR: Between Aspirations for Mobility and Threat of Eviction." *Dawn*, May 29, 2019. https://www.dawn.com/news/1456242.

Padhi, Ranjana. "Forced Evictions and Factory Closures; Rethinking Citizenships and Rights of Working Class Women across Delhi." *Indian Journal of Gender Studies* 14, no. 1 (January 2007): 73–92.

Pereira, Nihal, and Wing-Shing Tang, eds. *Transforming Asian Cities: Intellectual Impasse, Asianizing Space, and Emerging Translocalities*. 1st Edition. London: Routledge, 2012.

Rana, Pervaiz Ashfaq. "Singapore Offers Help in Building 5m Low-Cost Houses." *Dawn*, February 26, 2019. https://www.dawn.com/news/1466078.

Roy, Ananya. "Urban Informality: Towards an Epistemology of Planning." *Journal of the American Planning Association* 71, no. 2 (June 2005): 147–158.

———. "The 21st Century Metropolis: New Geographies of Theory." *Regional Studies* 43, no. 6 (2009): 819–830.

———. "Slumdog Cities: Rethinking Sublatern Urbanism." *International Journal of Urban and Regional Research* 35, no. 2 (March 2011): 223–238.

Roy, Ananya, and Aihwa Ong, eds. *Worlding Cities: Asian Experiments and the Art of Being Global*. Oxford: Wiley-Blackwell, 2011.

Sasoli, Ismail. "Gwadar Fishermen Protest Against Construction of CPEC's Project Enters 12th Day." *Dawn*, December 29, 2018. https://www.dawn.com/news/1454126.

Simone, AbdouMaliq. "Assembling Douala: Imagining Forms of Urban Sociality." In *Locating the City: Urban Imaginaries and the Practices of Modernity*, edited by Alev Cinar, and Thomas Bender, 79–99. Minneapolis; London: University of Minnesota Press, 2007.

———. "'The Urban Majority and Provisional Recompositions in Yangon.' The 2016 *Antipode* RGS-IBC Lecture." *Antipode* 50, no. 1 (January 2018): 23–40.

Singerman, Diane. *Cairo Contested: Governance, Urban Space and Global Modernity*. Cairo: American University in Cairo Press, 2009.

Verkaaik, Oskar. *Migrants and Militants: Fun and Urban Violence in Pakistan*. New Jersey: Princeton University Press, 2004.

Viqar, Sarwat. "Constructing Lyari: Place, Governance and Identity in a Karachi Neighbourhood." *South Asian History and Culture* 5, no. 3 (April 2014): 365–383.

———. "Sovereignty, Modernity and Urban Space: Everyday Socio-Spatial Practices in Karachi." PhD dissertation, 2016.

———. "'We are Your Brothers, We Will Know Where You Are At All Times': Risk, Violence and Positionality in Karachi." *Contemporary Social Science* 13, no.1 (2018): 386–396. https://doi.org/10.1080/21582041.2017.141852.

———. "Women's Public Lives and Sovereign Arrangements in Karachi's Inner City." *Gender, Place and Culture: A Journal of Feminist Geography* 25, no. 3 (2018): 416–433. https://doi.org/10.1080/0966369X.2018.1450730.

Section II

THINKING ACROSS
SPACE AND TIME

Chapter 5

'The Child as Method'?

Paradigm Shifts, Positionality, and Participatory Methods for Researching Children in Asia

Kathie Carpenter

ABSTRACT

In research, in transnational adoption, in work, and in parenting practices, the global 'coming of age' of Asia has had complicated effects on children. While Asia asserts its right to its children, its 'most precious resource', its 'future', modernist, globalised constructions of childhood maintain that children are rights-bearing human beings, and as such, they can not 'belong' to anyone. The paradigm which privileges the best interests of the child would seem to provide a simple rubric for simplifying researchers' responsibilities to children, yet this simplicity recedes quickly; in vanishingly few situations is there any consensus on what the child's best interest is.

In this chapter, I provide an overview of changing methodological approaches to research with children in Asia, in particular the innovative participatory methods that have been developed in response to these trends. I will also discuss the challenges inherent in the fact that while children as research subjects are considered inherently powerless and therefore require special research protections, local assertions of cultural autonomy may reinforce children's status as more empowered, and as bearing more responsibilities, at an earlier age than the strict dividing line of eighteen years would suggest. The discussion is based on my three decades of conducting research with children in Thailand, Indonesia, and Cambodia. Through this discussion, I provide a space for considering how Asia's relationship to the West influences not only the physical spaces of research, but also the conception of what research is and does for those of us working there.

* * *

In 1983, I stepped off the Bangkok to Chiang Mai overnight bus, and almost immediately walked through the gates of a children's preschool and started interviewing children. Getting permission was simple: after a brief introduction, I received verbal consent from the office staff (as I recall I didn't even show any ID), who lined the children up and sent them to play a game with me and my puppets while I audio taped them. Along with a promise to send my dissertation to Thailand's National Research Council, that was it, and I was able to interview 247 children, all under the age of thirteen.[1]

Many things have changed in the intervening three decades. The economic, political, and academic profiles of many Asian countries have risen enormously, just as those countries also work towards ensuring particular rights for their citizens – including children. The Convention on the Rights of the Child (CRC) was adopted in 1989. The Cold War ended right after that, followed by the 'rights pivot' among NGOs and the founding of Childhood Studies as an academic discipline. Today a young foreign graduate student 'straight off the bus' would not, and should not, walk into a preschool and expect to be granted unrestricted access to the children. In research, in transnational adoption, in work, and in parenting practices, the global 'coming of age' of Asia has had complicated implications for the wellbeing of children. While Asia's children are now its 'most precious resources',[2] modernist globalised constructions of childhood maintain that children are rights-bearing and autonomous human beings, and as such, they don't 'belong' to anyone. The CRC-inspired paradigm which privileges the best interests of the child would seem to provide a basic rubric for simplifying researchers' responsibilities to children, yet this simplicity recedes quickly; in vanishingly few situations is there any consensus on what the child's best interests are.

Things have changed for me as well of course, and in many ways my own career trajectory has paralleled the trajectory of the nascent field of Childhood Studies. Originally my youth and incompetence cast me in the role of an honorary or quasi-child; I was called 'Big Sister' by the children I studied and my research took a very developmentalist position, analysing the deficits of children's developing language against the assumed final and correct adult version. A fascination with the whole child came later, with parenthood. When I brought my four-year-old daughter with me to Thailand and enrolled her in a Thai preschool, my commitment to cultural immersion and captivation with local models of child rearing collided with my assumptions about children's rights when one of the Thai teachers used corporal punishment on her. While the 'participation' part of participant-observation entailed for me the full immersion of my daughter in local children's worlds, the discordance I experienced between popular local practices, such as spanking, and the universalised rights-based norms I personally embraced mirrors a broader zone of contention in Childhood Studies. Yes, she got spanked, just as most of the other children in her class did, and yes, she turned out fine, just as most of the other children in her class did. And yes, I still don't practice corporal punishment myself, but I can't deny that it worked out okay, there, then, for her. My tolerance for the ambiguity inherent in maintaining these contradictory beliefs without reconciling them is perhaps the hallmark of the most recent role I have been assigned, that of fictive grandparent, now called *yeay* ('Grandma') by the Cambodian children I work with. Even as I remain sympathetic to rights-based approaches to childhood, I have come to increasingly appreciate how they can feel like just another imposition of alien norms. I may appreciate the enterprise of empowering children, but I also appreciate how critical it is to empower adults to be the parents of their own children, particularly in former colonies with a legacy of empowering neither child nor parent.

In this paper, I will use Chen's *Asia as Method*[3] as a point of departure for an exploration of how research with children in Asia has changed. Chen's call to 'reverse Eurocentric flows of knowledge' can be taken in two distinct senses when applied to children, one literal and concrete, and the other more abstract and philosophical. The first interpretation of Chen's phrase insists that we take Asian childhoods on their own terms rather than comparing them, implicitly or explicitly, to childhoods as lived and conceptualised in the West. This reading suggests that Asian models and experiences of childhood have much to offer the West, in terms of new understandings and new practices. The second, more abstract sense of reversing flows of knowledge recognises that just as knowledge, power, and permission to participate tend to flow in one direction, from the coloniser to the colonised, they tend also to flow in one direction from adults towards children. Much of the current field of Childhood Studies concerns itself with reversing these flows, and recognising children as autonomous rights- and culture-bearing human beings. This approach incites tensions in contexts where children are not viewed in this way, and can even undermine adults or jeopardise children's wellbeing. It is obviously far-fetched to view childhood as colonised by adults . . . or is it?

This chapter is meant to be provocative, not prescriptive. In it, I will provide an overview of changing methodological approaches to research with children in Asia, taking into account both these ways to reverse flows of knowledge – across generations and across geopolitical divides. The focus will be on Southeast Asia, based on my three decades of conducting research in Thailand, Cambodia, and Indonesia. I will also examine the tensions that methodologies can incite, especially with respect to local constructions of childhood and notions of appropriate adult–child interactions. While children as research subjects are classified among the inherently powerless groups that require special research protections (along with pregnant women, prisoners, and people with disabilities), local assertions of cultural autonomy and modernist constructions of children as rights-bearing autonomous individuals may assign children more power and more responsibilities at an earlier age than their status as minors incapable of consent would suggest.

Children are invisible throughout most of the critique of Orientalism and Eurocentric scholarship, just as they are left out of much 'serious' scholarship in general. Lin points out, for example, that in *Asia as Method*, Chen invites 'the ex-colonized to try out the subject positions of women, of homosexuals, of transsexuals, of linguistic and ethnic minorities, of the "learning disabled", of the poor and so on'.[4] Conspicuously missing are the subject positions of children, or indeed any mention of the young at all. Children appear only as a metaphor to be discarded. As Edward Said pointed out, racist colonial discourses explicitly label 'the Oriental' as 'childlike', with damaging repercussions that persist today. This reveals more about ideologies of childhood than anything about local peoples and cultures, and indeed it obscures much about Asian childhoods. What does it say about our constructions of childhood that we use 'childlike' as an epithet alongside 'irrational, depraved, fallen, . . . different'?[5] The delusion that colonial subjects were childlike also obscured distinctions such as age and generational status among them, justifying abuses such as child labour, substandard education, and disruption of native families, and masking these abuses with the language of benign paternalism and the 'civilising mission' as a kind of developmental process.[6]

Before discarding that discourse entirely though, it is necessary to interrogate what it actually *means* to say that someone is 'childlike'. If calling some human beings 'childlike' is insulting, to whom can the label be appropriately applied? Who is a child? What is a child? If *Asia as Method* highlights the critical importance of clarifying points of reference before we undertake to answer questions or indeed before we even decide what questions to ask, then what would it mean to take 'the child as method'?

FLOWS OF KNOWLEDGE ABOUT CHILDHOOD

Informing studies of children and childhood with the lived experiences of children in Asia as well as Indigenous Asian models of human development would not only capacitate Asian scholarship, but could also reinvigorate Western scholarship with new frames of reference, new ideas, and new approaches as well. With respect to children, it is necessary to reference two complementary but often also competing paradigms through which we tend to conceptualise childhood. First, children as juvenile, maturing humans, and second, children as 'a social, rather than developmental, category',[7] and by extension a metaphor, a symbol, and the other as contrasted with adults.

At first glance, it may be counterintuitive to view childhood as a social construct. Children seem to be different from adults in ways that are hard to attribute to cultural lenses, and it is nearly impossible to ignore the visible developmental changes that the child undergoes. It is indisputable when they grow, they mature, they become more self-sufficient and less vulnerable. However, childhood is also powerful as a source of symbolism and metaphor, and examining metaphors is one way to make socially constructed dimensions more salient. For example, the negative connotations many associate with referring to the colonised as childlike or even to children themselves as immature highlight the social dimension of the construct. By definition, children are immature, yet calling an individual child 'immature' is always a criticism. As Chen has pointed out, 'the West performs a wide range of functions',[8] serving as a point of reference from which to frame societies and knowledge structures, and thereby imposing judgements along with those framings, such as developed/underdeveloped or progressive/repressive. In much the same way, childhood also performs a wide range of functions. Children evoke and represent innocence, the future, purity, inalienable possession, and redemption; they can also signify a precious resource and an investment, as well as the easily exploited, the desirable, the malleable, the small, the weak, the abundant, and even the robust, the dangerous, the out of place, the swarming, the filthy, the pesky, the uncontrollable, the natural, the life force, and the wild.[9]

These diverse symbolic values are not just literary abstractions; they have real fallout throughout societies in terms of structuring worldviews, institutions, and relationships. For example, Fong has reported that throughout China, the singleton children born after the one-child policy was enacted are consistently referred to as the 'only hope'[10] not just for their families, but for the country as a whole; children's education is seen as the key to a moral society. In other words, children's lives show wide variability, and so too does the significance and consequence of childhood itself. While Childhood Studies emphasises the perspective that children's worlds are valuable and worthy of understanding in their own right, it is also true that children's worlds provide valuable insights into broader cultural phenomena that may be less accessible in their more covert adult manifestations. As Xu has proposed, the study of childhood 'may contribute to a finer-grained understanding of contemporary Chinese cultural dynamics'.[11]

There is value in multiplying frames of reference with respect to children and childhood. One compelling reason is pragmatic self-interest; novel ideas and deeper understandings can come from actively seeking out new frameworks and perspectives. Despite the ubiquity of children in all cultures and the universality of the experience of having been a child, not only do societies vary widely with respect to which human beings they construct as children and which human beings they construct as adults, but also they may construct a single individual as both child and adult simultaneously, as when children behave or 'feel that they are still living their previous lives' through reincarnation.[12] Not only do many societies use a different age than eighteen, the bright line dividing childhood from adulthood formalised in the *Convention on the Rights of the Child*, but not all societies even use chronological age; there are other, functionally determined milestones, such as becoming a parent, getting married, participating in a rite of passage, or performing certain kinds of work. By contrast, in Confucianism, not only is one's adulthood not achieved by crossing the threshold of eighteen years, but one's full humanity must be cultivated over a lifetime. The changes encountered when crossing the threshold from childhood to adulthood can vary widely across social contexts as well. For example, Froerer found that among the Mohanpur of central India, children remain children throughout their life span if they remain unmarried, with the consequence that they never become culpable for their own wrongdoing, regardless of their chronological age or psychological and biological maturation.[13]

To summarise thus far, the answer to the question 'What is a child?' is informed by culture, history, and circumstances, as well as by biology, and can be more deeply interrogated through other cultures, other histories, and other circumstances. For example, in Western education and psychology, the construct of 'developmental appropriateness'[14] is intended to strengthen education by ensuring that children are not expected to accomplish things of which they are not yet capable, and to protect children by ensuring that they are not 'damaged' by traumatic experiences for which they are not ready. However, strict conformity to developmental appropriateness can pose limitations on our knowledge as well as on children's lived experiences, because different societies have very different ideas of what children are capable of, and what it is appropriate for adults to expect of them.

By way of illustrating how this can be, in one Cambodian orphanage I have researched, which grouped children into smaller cottage-like residences to replicate family life, I was surprised and concerned that there seemed to be some cottages with no adults in residence.[15] Older resident girls were serving as housemothers, and they performed all of the duties, including nurturance, discipline, and education. Although this seemed, to me, to be a kind of 'double jeopardy' which deprived the younger children of a real parent figure while simultaneously depriving the older children of a carefree childhood, in my observations I was struck by the tender seriousness with which these teenaged girls undertook their caretaking responsibilities and the unmistakable pride they showed in their role. I was also amazed by how well the younger children seemed to be faring in the absence of adult caretakers. Cambodians expect children to enjoy providing care for other children, and consider it essential practice for becoming a competent parent. The objections that these girls were not developmentally ready to provide adequate care or that they were being 'robbed of their childhood' by serving as caretakers reject the validity of local Cambodian notions of developmental appropriateness, and imposing a foreign standard of age-appropriate expectations would have resulted in losses for both age groups.

Western visitors to many Asian societies are frequently struck by the level of competence children show in caring for other children, and the self-reliance of children even in extremely challenging circumstances, such as those living and working on the street.[16] While few of us would ever argue that children *should* be living or working on the street, what is striking is that they *can* do it, often performing at a level of competence that seems impossible for more protected Western children of the same age. Glimpses of the lives of children in other cultures can inform us that children are capable of living in many more ways and of accomplishing many more things than we realise from our own limited experience, opening up new understandings of child development. Child-headed households are common among children living and working on the street[17] and the decision to support them rather than pathologise them can facilitate novel but valid policy possibilities. One orphanage I have researched actually built special living quarters for child-headed families, allowing them to remain together rather than have to choose between remaining on the street or being separated. Multiplying frames of reference in this regard provides a new lens through which to see this situation, and helped me to appreciate how much more children are capable of than my assumptions about the 'irrational', 'incomplete' adolescent brain[18] had previously permitted.

The Western developmentalist perspective maintains strict dividing lines between the world of adults and the world of children, with the assumption that children's innocence and vulnerability to trauma must be protected, but my experiences in Asia have revealed ways that children's experiences can be much more integrated with the world of adults. Even very young children may be exposed to, rather than protected from, adult knowledge. One day at my daughter's Thai preschool, I was at first pleased but then stunned when the teacher began talking about the importance of gratitude to one's parents but segued quickly to a graphic description of labour pain and the dangers of childbirth, something I would never have discussed with a group of such young children. 'Especially your mother, you must be grateful to your mother', she admonished. 'When she gave birth to you, it hurt her. It hurt, hurt, hurt! It hurt a lot!' I was quite astonished at how she went on and on about it. Not only were the children apparently not traumatised by this graphic knowledge, but they participated enthusiastically. She asked 'How did it feel?' 'It hurt!' shouted all the children in unison. The point of this story is not to highlight differences in child-raising practices per se, but to suggest that from these differences can come new understandings of the process and outcomes of child development. Thai children appear to be quite capable of assimilating such graphic knowledge into a lifelong closeness with and respect for their mothers that many American parents would envy.

My surprise at how competently young children are able to perform tasks for which I assumed they are not ready is corroborated by most Western scholars who research childhoods in Asia.[19] For example, in my classes I continue to use Tobin, Wu, and Davidson's 1991 film and book *Preschool in Three Cultures*, comparing four-year-olds in China, Japan, and the United States, precisely because of scenes such as the one showing Japanese four-year-olds mediating disputes without adult assistance, and another one showing Chinese children absorbed for a longer time on a complex, solitary task than Western audiences believe possible.[20] My students typically respond that such young children can't perform such tasks. And yet, the video shows that they do, casting doubt on established assumptions about developmental capacities and opening up new understandings that would be missed if we only used ourselves as the reference point.

However, this chapter is not just about collecting interesting and counter-intuitive examples of children's potentialities, revealing though they may be. The more important point is that the problem of one-way flows of knowledge is perhaps even greater in research about children than in other domains, because it is one experience that all adults everywhere have in common, making all research on children inherently comparative (see Gibson in this volume for further discussion of comparison). We use our own childhoods as reference points, whether we realise it or not, and the effort to observe childhood through the eyes of children, while at the limit perhaps impossible, requires the same kind of conscious and deliberate intention as Chen suggests is required by the effort to put the 'intent to deimperialize before all else' if we are ever to 'overcome the limits of the postcolonial critique'.[21] However, there may be no such thing as pure unanalysed observation of children, because we have such strong internalised normative views of appropriate behaviour around children, and different observers are likely to interpret their observations very differently. For example, a newborn infant, lacking language and motor control, is likely to be seen by American adults as help-lessly dependent, reliant on adults for meeting basic needs. However, the same infant with the same limitations is likely to be seen by Japanese adults as helplessly *in*dependent because it is unable to forge the basic relationships that embed it in a web of healthy interdependency.[22] In other words, while the idea of dependency informs both observations, it informs them differently, in turn forging very different notions of appropriate adult–child interactions. American adults view it as their responsibility to help the dependent child become independent so they can one day leave home, while Japanese adults view their role as helping the child become increasingly dependent and interconnected.

Reversing Eurocentric flows means being able to construct new models and paradigms informed by the ethnotheories of other cultures, both the well-articulated worldviews embedded in rich literary and scholarly traditions, such as Confucianism, as well as less formalised, but no less consequential, implicit cultural values.[23] For example, the previously mentioned discussion of labour pain with four-year-olds helps usher them into a very important regional value, often termed the milk debt[24] which itself reveals a very different way to conceptualise children's relationships with their parents. Children are not just passive vessels to be filled with parental concern, but subjects who have accrued a debt that they must repay. Assigning this level of responsibility to children in turn empowers them, even as it makes them more obligated and therefore less autonomous.

METHODOLOGICAL APPROACHES TO ANTHROPOLOGICAL RESEARCH ON CHILDHOOD

Throughout the history of Western scholarship, there have been individuals who carefully observed young children, most often their own.[25] However, they have been outflanked by the many more who theorised *about* children but who did not base their theorising on first-hand experience *with* children. Even Jean-Jacques Rousseau, whose ideas about child development continue to inform education and parenting practices, based his philosophies of childhood on his own introspections, rather than any experience with actual children.[26] Thus, it was still relatively unusual when Franz Boas and his students, especially Margaret Mead, focused explicitly rather than incidentally on childhood, both in terms of content and in terms of methodology.[27] Mead made a real contribution to anthropological studies of childhood with her willingness to talk to children about their own lives, rather than to speak only with adults, to gather either their memories of their own childhoods, their thoughts about how they were raising their own children, or their inferences about children's worldviews based solely on observations of them.[28] However, her ethnographies contain little explicit description of how participation and observation actually took place, or whether any special strategies or challenges occurred when it came to children. For example, the methods chapter for *Coming of Age in Samoa* lists interviews, observation, questionnaires, and tests of skills such as memory and vocabulary. Mead mentions that some aspects of children's behaviour were 'baffling' and that she pursued a 'more extensive enquiry' until confident that she understood, but she does not specify what kinds of things were most baffling or how she pursued these follow-ups.[29] There is no discussion of whether her methods involving children are any different from those involving adults, nor any mention of special adjustments or accommodations she may have made for children of different ages among the nine- to twenty-year-olds that she describes.

Similarly, Ruth Benedict, also one of the first anthropologists to talk of Asian childhoods and their connections to Asian societies and cultures, delved deeply into the significance of childhood in both Thailand[30] and Japan,[31] and considered it revealing as well as important in its own right, but she based all her conclusions upon interviews with adults' recollections, rather than looking at children directly. While her work was limited by wartime circumstances, most critiques focus on her ability to make inferences about a society she had not immersed herself in; no one critiques her ability to make inferences about the world of childhood based on adult reports.

In Cambodia, the most significant and detailed village ethnography remains that of May Mayko Ebihara[32] who in her methodology described in great detail the basis for her village selection, but, similarly to Mead, tells us very little of how she interacted with children. While her work is rich in details of children's lives, she does not address how that information was obtained, for example, how much came from direct interaction, how much was reported by adults, how much came from the anthropologist's interpretation of children's behaviours. Children's worldviews are inferred; she writes, for example, that 'because of this constant attention and love, immediate fulfillment of demands and permissiveness, the child in the first year of life or so probably views the world as being warm and receptive . . . This is especially true for girls who, from a very young age, are given the responsibility of caring for younger children, and who usually assume this task with as much pleasure as the western child playing with dolls'.[33] This is not to cast doubt on Ebihara's intuitions, which were deep, nor her conclusions, which appear robust even today. Inferences may be correct, but regardless of whether they are or not, it is important to acknowledge that they are based on adult interpretations of children's observable behaviour, rather than children's own reports. The relationship of the anthropologist with the children, and how she developed a relationship that enabled her to make these inferences reliably, are entirely missing.

Even today, influential research on children in Asia often shows the same methodological lacunae with respect to the details of researchers' interactions with children. For example, Spyrou has noted that while silences are ubiquitous in all human communication, especially between adults and children, the topic of children's silences is completely neglected in childhood research.[34] In general, left undescribed in most ethnographies are the minutiae of interactions with children that make up participation and observations, and that would be critical information today. How are observations obtained by anthropologists? Do they follow children around? Do the children follow them around? Do they participate by babysitting or performing care tasks? Do they become an honorary or a functional child, or do they acquire honorary or fictive children or grandchildren? Do children gravitate towards them or run away from them? Much of the ethnography of the time seems to be based on the assumption that an outsider adult can watch a child and accurately infer that child's inner state, or that one can simply ask an adult and get accurate, complete information about their own childhood or that of their children, but the justification for this is rarely given. Many of these concerns about participant-observation research applied to children continue to be debated in the literature today. Because adults tend to assume that they understand children based on the fact that they once were children or that they have parented children, it is too easy to assume that one can gain sufficient insight simply by talking to adults *about* children, rather than talking *to* children.

Scepticism regarding positionality and the limitation it places on fully understanding another culture is instinctively suspended when it comes to children, perhaps because we assume that children and their worlds are simple. This assumption drove the mid-century's explicit focus on children as 'becoming' fully fledged persons as well as full members of their own culture (e.g., *Becoming a Kwoma*[35]) rather than the self-evident fact that a Kwoma child is already a Kwoma, a Balinese child *is* Balinese, a Japanese child *is* Japanese, and so on. Children may have only partial or erroneous knowledge of adult society, but they function as experts in their own worlds, of which adults may have only partial or erroneous knowledge.[36] The recognition that '[w]e know very little about the inner life of children, about their desires, aspirations, or fears and sorrows, the imaginative creation of their own world and how the world of adults appears to the child'[37] calls into question participant-observation as a methodology. Researchers need to admit that 'adults are unable to be full participants in children's social worlds because they can never truly be children again'.[38] Once called into question and examined, the limitations of participant-observation for revealing the richness of children's lives in children's worlds became clear. For example, in many societies, children, even fully parented ones, tend to run in bands of village children, out of sight, and immediate control of adults, and it would be odd, if not impossible, for an adult to join these groups. In some societies too, children are not believed to have anything interesting to say, and so they are unlikely to take the initiative to interact with the researcher.

Benedict and Mead were criticised for both over-interpretation as well as under-interpretation,[39] highlighting issues that pervade research on children even today. On the one hand, one's observations can be limited by appropriate roles and constraints on interactions; on the other hand, to what extent does one take at face value what one is told by children? Throughout graduate school, the paradigm in which I originally trained was informed by the 'Pop goes the weasel' effect;[40] we assumed that what children said was unreliable, and that indirect, ingenious methods needed to be devised to access children's 'true' competencies. Research protocols had to be fun and gamelike in order to keep children's attention and ensure willing participation. Rather than striving to inspire children's curiosity or invest them in our questions, we recruited children by asking them if they wanted to play a game with us. We *never* used the word 'research' in front of them. But even as I invested tremendous creative effort in creating 'games' that would elicit whatever specifically I was interested in, I found myself more and more interested by everything that I was supposed to avoid, and more and more concerned that I was missing something vital about children that I needed to focus on, rather than control for. I was not alone in these concerns, which came to be highlighted as a new intellectual movement was gathering momentum. With the rise of a new paradigm of Childhood Studies at the end of the century, reacting against the 'developmental discourse of children's incompetence, rather than competence',[41] a new approach to methodology was also seen as needed.

CHILDHOOD STUDIES: DECOLONISING CHILDHOOD, DEIMPERIALISING ADULTHOOD?

The debut of Childhood Studies as an academic discipline is usually marked at 1991, with the opening of the first academic programme in Childhood Studies at Brooklyn College. Although the socially constructed dimension of childhood had long been recognised, for example with Ariès's publication of *Centuries of Childhood*,[42] Childhood Studies was founded with a goal of unifying different disciplinary approaches to children. In addition to interdisciplinarity, other key principles were that childhood is socially and historically constructed, making it both contingent and changing; that children are rights-bearing subjects, rather than just objects of adult interest or concern; that children function as experts within their own culture, rather than simply as novices within an imperfect or incomplete replica of adult culture; and that children are motivated by forces similar to those that motivate adults, in particular that they have a right to 'mature' concerns such as dignity and self-expression. In addition, Childhood Studies considered that children are more capable than views of them as developing but only partially complete human beings would suggest; and in general that children must be viewed 'in their fullness as human beings',[43] rather than as a series of transitions between birth and adulthood or a bundle of developmental processes.

The rise of Childhood Studies joined a confluence of events that began in the early 1990s and, concomitant with the economic, political, and cultural rise of Asia, have changed the landscape for conducting research on Asian children. In particular, the end of the Cold War meant that a human rights rhetoric was no longer seen only as an instrument of superpower policy, so that more nuanced and less bipolarised rights-based discourses emerged, especially for the NGOs that flourished after the end of the Cold War.[44] The signing of the UN CRC, which became effective in 1990, bolstered this rights pivot as it pertained to children. Not only did the CRC become the most widely ratified human rights document in history,[45] but the norms it promoted became quickly widespread. Globalisation, the rise of the 'tiger economies' of East Asia and the rise of the NGOs in Southeast Asia, which all accelerated during the 1990s, increased receptivity to modernist constructions of childhood which have come to dominate global discourses on child welfare and child research, including a value placed on participatory methods.[46]

Paramount in this discourse is an idea of childhood that prioritises the affective value of protected innocence and assails the notion that children ought to be making economic contributions to adults.[47] These notions came to dominate development discourses in particular, even where this ideology of childhood is not central to the local worldview and even though this ideology often fails to align with actual patterns of behaviour and practices within families.[48] Although the emotional contributions and academic labour that children perform in wealthier countries may in fact be quite taxing,[49] foreign aid workers sacralise the ideal of responsibility flowing in one direction, from adult to child, rather than reciprocally,[50] and researchers need to be even more careful not to take an extractive approach to their research methods; they must research with, rather than on, children.[51] Furthermore, much subsequent research on childhood has been initiated by the need for regular formal reporting that the CRC requires of all states parties, an additional reason why much research on children currently has a rights-based focus.

Methodology is therefore a central concern of Childhood Studies, and methodologies have been sought that reinforce children's right to participation and respect their capabilities rather than emphasise their deficiencies, and which acknowledge the value of children's own understandings of their experiences. As Harriot Beazley and her colleagues assert, 'Children have a "right to be properly researched"'.[52] The academic movement towards participatory methodologies was complementary to a similar rise in focus on participation in NGOs and development work. Participation is primary among the methodological concerns of Childhood Studies in order to ensure that children are not exploited and that the power differential between adults and children is not exacerbated. Research reports need to explicitly detail how their methods are participatory, and ideally children should be treated as research partners rather than as objects of scrutiny.

While 'encouraging children's participation in research is in some quarters now seen as a *sine qua non* of a pro-child stance',[53] a complicated debate has arisen over what actually constitutes an authentically participatory research method.[54] While James and Prout propose that 'ethnography may be the most important methodology for studying children',[55] participant-observation methods may not allow for full expression of children's voices because children may be mobile, uninterested in talking to unfamiliar adults, or precluded from doing so by conventional norms of adult–child interaction. Minimally, researchers have been expected to be sensitive to power relations and ensure that children have a real choice over whether to participate or not, but increasingly 'participatory' has been taken to mean that children should be consulted about what aspects of their lives should be researched, that they should be empowered to conduct the research themselves, and that children's opinions must be consulted on issues other than 'children's issues'. While it is now axiomatic in Childhood Studies that children are the best experts in their own lived experiences, their expertise is increasingly assumed to extend beyond their own lives to issues in the broader society. James proposes that 'in addition to the applied potential of childhood studies, it is important that the voices of children should not be confined to childish concerns',[56] and Kesby writes that 'we must offer a broader critique of society based on the insights that studies of/with "children" gives us'.[57]

Increasingly too, the movement in the field has been towards research with demonstrable positive benefits in terms of galvanising social change, rather than just having a short term, individual benefit for children.[58] While there is no doubt that children enjoyed the fun puppet games I so assiduously designed as a graduate student, today benefits such as temporary enjoyment and entertainment have come to be seen as insufficient, and presenting research as a 'game' is seen as misleading or deceptive. Research, in order to be non-extractive, must build into it children's informed, voluntary participation, and have benefits beyond the rather abstract 'advancing knowledge'. For example, Hastadewi incorporated into her research goals not just an enhanced understanding of the conditions of child labour, but the identification of effective strategies for its elimination.[59] However, other researchers contend that it is no longer acceptable for methods to be treated 'only as a means to an end';[60] rather, the research process itself, not just the results, must have some intrinsic benefit to child participants as individuals, not just benefits to society in general. For example, Jabeen speaks of how the participatory methods she used with children living and working on the street in Lahore, Pakistan 'made the research experience useful for children'[61] because 'it was empowering for them' vis-à-vis the 'subordinate position of children in the broader Pakistani society'.[62]

While some researchers struggle with the potential or intrinsic benefits of their research, others struggle with the messages that methods send to and about children and their maturity and capabilities. Human Subjects Committees treat children as a special protected category, incapable of legally giving consent, but some researchers contend that there is no qualitative difference between child and adult subjects at all, and a tension has arisen out of the charge that on the one hand, children's participation must be voluntary, uncoerced and ideally enjoyable, but on the other hand, children's limitations vis-à-vis adults should be downplayed rather than highlighted. Thomson rejects the need to use any methodology with children that one would not also use with adults, claiming good success with more direct ones;[63] likewise, Kesby suggests that often direct or complicated protocols don't work that well with adults either, and that 'when children struggle with language, have a limited attention span, suffer social inequalities, etc., it is not by dint of the fact that they are children' but rather other factors that could also be typical of adults (e.g., preliteracy, inexperience, small size, etc.).[64]

Regardless of the desirability of participatory child-centred methodologies, they can be much more difficult to implement in reality than one might suppose from reading reports of research using them. For example, inspired by PhotoVoice and its potential to empower children as the subjects and narrators of their own stories, on one research trip I brought photo and drawing materials to the children in a Cambodian orphanage so they could document and describe their daily lives from their own points of view.

I was unprepared for how the materials became a kind of currency, increasingly concentrated in the hands of older children and staff, although I too cringed when the younger children buried theirs in the sand, threw them at each other, or otherwise used them in ways that did not fit my own schema of how they should be used. I also sympathised with the adult staff who couldn't afford such materials for their own children. Such challenges of conducting participatory research with young children are often glossed over. In an analysis of articles in the leading Childhood Studies journals, McNamee and Seymour found that while research reports referred to 'children' as a general category, in reality most research was conducted on ten- to twelve-year-olds.[65]

While not explicitly stated, one inference that can be drawn from their results, certainly consistent with my own experience, is that it's much easier to obtain interpretable results using participatory methods on ten- to twelve-year-olds than it is on younger children.

One of the biggest challenges for a Western scholar conducting research on Asian children is navigating the expectations inherent in strong age hierarchies. In many societies, children are not considered valuable sources of information, and it can be odd to ask them questions when there are adults present who could readily answer them. A decade after my graduate fieldwork in Thailand, I began a project in Indonesia on traditional stories and children's narratives with the determination not to bypass local adults this time.[66] I hired an Indonesian friend to be my research associate who was herself a mother with a great deal of experience with children, and who had been very engaged and enthusiastic when I told her about the research project. Together we explained the research to the children and let them control the session by pushing the buttons on the recording equipment. Then, she told them a story and she invited them to tell her a story – a model of participation and reciprocity, I thought. Still, my Indonesian research associate simply couldn't get children to use sustained narratives in her presence. One problem was that she was regularly interrupted by the more senior adults nearby who couldn't fathom why we were more interested in talking to children than in talking to them. She and other adults also were reluctant to allow children to be recorded making what they considered to be 'mistakes' in their stories, and adults often insisted on taking over and telling the child's story the 'right way'.

But even when no other adult was present, her prompting had the effect of decreasing rather than increasing the amount of talking each child did, until each session became a near-monolog of 'Speak up!' 'Go on!' 'Tell some more!' directed at a silent child. The basic issue was not that she was uncomfortable or unskilled in interacting with children, but that it would have been *inappropriate* for her to effectively encourage the children to take the conversational or narrative floor away from her. She knew it, the children knew it, and the adults who insisted on being a part of the storytelling sessions knew it. Ironically, given my standing as a cultural outsider and linguistic novice, it turned out not to be as inappropriate for me to elicit stories from them, and my linguistic incompetence empowered the children in a way that a fully competent cultural expert could not. But how did it affect the stories that I gathered, knowing that they were *inappropriate* within that cultural setting? Did my empowering the children to 'tell their own stories' undermine the adults' roles and responsibilities towards them by diminishing the importance of adult contributions to the interaction?

My failed research project in Indonesia illustrates how the requirement that research involving children must in some way be intrinsically empowering raises an additional issue – is it even responsible for an outsider to come in and 'empower' the children of another culture? Does empowering children undermine the adulthood of post-colonial Asian adults? Because of the transition from being slandered as 'childlike' themselves, asserting not just adulthood but the generative capacity for parenting the next generation could make methods that are 'empowering' for children disempowering for adults, and vice versa. Particularly when age hierarchies significantly determine interactions between adults and children, there is a risk of slighting adults who are already sensitised to diminishments of their adult status through colonialism and racism. The idea of 'giving children a voice' is not necessarily well received everywhere in the world. For example, Chakraborty found that her engagement of research participants as researchers themselves, using cameras she had given them, provided benefits such as 'increased peer support and amity amongst young women . . . an acknowledgment of their alternative identities by peers; and increased cultural capital by acquiring photography skills'.[67] However she also noted that it was 'not a risk-free venture'.[68] Her participants reported that their behaviour was strictly curtailed by their parents' concerns about family honour, and there was 'anxiety expressed by parents' about many of the behaviours documented in the research, which may even have entailed risks for the girls who had been encouraged to explore ways to 'resist and challenge the normative understanding of the "good girl"'.[69]

A marker of a society's rise and identification with modernity is often indicated by its increasing prioritisation, at least discursively, of children's welfare as they transition 'from workers to objects of sentimentality'.[70] This shift occurs society-wide and can also be seen in changing national attitudes about other child-related issues. Several countries in Asia have made the transition from sending countries to curtailing or halting transnational adoption of children, and the move to do so is widely perceived as a way of asserting national pride about being perceived as incapable of caring for one's own children and to be 'selling or giving away our most precious resources'.[71] A heightened sensitivity to criticism of one's ability to parent can have repercussions for rights-aligned methodologies, some of which are in fact critical of local parenting practices. For example, while corporal punishment is accepted and expected in many Asian societies, a research guide to methodologies for researching corporal punishment, widely disseminated by a prominent, very influential child welfare organisation, was explicitly designed to train researchers in methodology that 'will inform and fuel advocacy' while not being in itself 'abusive and compound the harm done by physical and emotional punishment'.[72]

CONCLUSION: THE CHILD AS METHOD?

As the economic, political, and academic profiles of many Asian societies have risen, Asian children have concomitantly become more assimilated to modernist constructions of children as vulnerable and in need of special protection. The days of foreign scholars lining up the children of Asia are long past, and today, it is unlikely that I could walk in off the street, armed only with my tape recorder and my privilege as a westerner, and interview 247 children without at least explaining more about who I was and what I was up to. It is also unlikely that anyone reviewing my work would be comfortable with the way my child participants were ordered to participate by adults in authority, convenient though that might have been. It would call into question the legitimacy of my results, the ethics of my methods, and my own standing as someone sensitive to children, and their adults, as representatives of a culture not my own.

In this chapter, I have explored two ways that the goal of reversing the directionality of knowledge flows from the coloniser to the formerly colonised may be extended to research with children. The first is in the straightforward sense that Asian childhoods need to be understood on their own terms within their own cultural contexts, and from that perspective, have much to offer to all scholars of child development. The second is that childhood itself can be viewed as a site of disempowerment dominated by one-way flows of authority and knowledge, emanating from adults and silencing children. Both ways of thinking about reversing flows of knowledge present paradoxes and provocations, inviting interesting new lines of inquiry. The first way suggests a straightforward research agenda. How do non-Western paradigms of human development analyse dominant Western constructs? For example, much of the paradigm of Western developmental psychology is shaped by attachment theory; how does this play out in Buddhist societies, where non-attachment is a desired state? Confucianism offers another perspective to erase the bright line separating children from adults: rather than singling out childhood as an unfinished state of becoming, Confucianism also describes adults as continually and unceasingly cultivating their full humanity. What does it mean to recognise the child as a human being rather than a human becoming in a worldview where we are all still on our journey to becoming fully human? More specifically, what might Confucianism have to say about critical periods and the current widespread Western conviction that the most important developments in a child's life occur before the age of two?

Asian studies of Asian childhoods have a lot to offer the West, and more importantly – they have a lot to offer Asia. Entirely new paradigms based on milestones that have local relevance could be not only ethically but intellec-tually richer than using the practices and beliefs of various cultures simply as examples or counterexamples to support or disconfirm Western-generated models of child development. Unprecedented social conditions, such as the entire generation dominated by singleton children in China due to the one-child policy, offer unforeseen windows onto the lives of children, with opportunities for theorising that extend beyond current Western thinking.[73] Still, the positionality of an adult researcher in a rising Asia is confusing. Nothing is more universalised than 'the child' as a not-yet-adult human and yet children are also the ultimate other, and the peculiar positionality of adults researching children mirrors and also compounds the tensions inherent in studying 'the other', or in studying 'the self' through foreign paradigms and lenses. It also raises provocative questions concerning whether efforts to empower children must always also serve to disempower adults. Chen's *Asia as Method* therefore provides not just a push forward towards decentring Eurocentric research paradigms, but a guide for ways to pose entirely new questions about childhood and to distil, clarify, and examine the challenges before us, if not entirely to reconcile them.

* * *

NOTES

1. Kathie Carpenter, "How Children Learn to Classify Nouns in Thai," (PhD dissertation, Stanford University, 1987); Kathie Carpenter, "Later Rather than Sooner: Extralinguistic Categories in the Acquisition of Thai Classifiers," *Journal of Child Language 19*, no. 1 (February 1991): 93–113.

2. Cary Silver, "Thailand—Conquering Polio in the 'Land of Smiles," *The Rotarian 22–27* (January 1990): 24; Elizabeth Bartholet, "International Adoption: The Human Rights Position," *Global Policy 1*, no. 1 (January 2010): 91–100.

3. Chen Kuan-Hsing, *Asia as Method: Toward Deimperialization* (Durham, NC: Duke University Press, 2010).

4. Angel M.Y. Lin, "Towards Transformation of Knowledge and Subjectivity in Curriculum Inquiry: Insights from Chen Kuan-Hsing's *Asia as Method*," *Curriculum Inquiry 42*, no. 1 (January 2012): 160.

5. Edward Said, *Orientalism* (New York: Pantheon Books, 1978), 40.

6. Sarada Balagopalan, "Childhood, Culture, History: Redeploying "Multiple Childhoods," in *Reimagining Childhood Studies*, ed. Spyros Spyrou, Rachel Rosen, and Daniel Thomas Cook (London: Bloomsbury Academic, 2019), 23–40.

7. Allison James, "Giving Voice to Children's Voices: Practices and Problems, Pitfalls and Potentials," *American Anthropologist 109* (June 2007): 263.

8. Angel Lin, "Preface: Can a Spider Weave Its Way Out of the Web that It Is Being Woven into, Just As It Weaves?" in *Asia as Method in Education Studies: a Defiant Research Imagination*, ed. Hongzhi Zhang, Philip Wing Keung Chan,

and Jane Kenway (Abingdon-on-Thames, UK: Routledge Critical Studies in Asian Education, 2012), xiii–xv.

9. David Lancy, *The Anthropology of Childhood: Cherubs, Chattel, Changelings* (Cambridge, UK: Cambridge University Press, 2008).

10. Vanessa L. Fong, *Only Hope: Coming of Age Under China's One-Child Policy* (Stanford, CA: Stanford University Press, 2006).

11. Jing Xu, "Becoming a Moral Child amidst China's Moral Crisis: Preschool Discourse and Practices of Sharing in Shanghai," *Ethos 42*, no. 2 (2014): 222.

12. Akhil Gupta, "Reliving Childhood? The Temporality of Childhood and Narratives of Reincarnation," *Ethnos 67*, no. 1 (2002): 7.

13. Peggy Froerer, "Wrongdoing and Retribution: Children's Conceptions of Illness Causality in a Central Indian Village," *Anthropology and Medicine 14*, no. 3 (2007): 321–333.

14. Kay Sanders, and Flora Farago, "Developmentally Appropriate Practice in the Twenty-First Century," in *International Handbook of Early Childhood Education*, ed. Marilyn Fleer, and Bert van Oers (Dordrecht, Netherlands: Springer, 2018), 1379–1400.

15. Kathie Carpenter, "Continuity, Complexity and Reciprocity in a Cambodian Orphanage," *Children and Society 29*, no. 2 (March 2015): 85–94.

16. Md Hasan Reza, and Nicole F. Bromfield, "Poverty, Vulnerability and Everyday Resilience: How Bangladeshi Street Children Manage Economic Challenges through Financial Transactions on the Streets," *The British Journal of Social Work 49*, no. 5 (2019): 1105–1123.

17. Leo de Haan, "Livelihoods in Development," *Canadian Journal of Development Studies/Revue canadienne d'études du développement 38*, no. 1 (2017): 22–38.

18. Robert Epstein, "The Myth of the Teen Brain," *Scientific American Special Editions 17*, no. 2s (June 2007): 68–75.

19. Harriot Beazley, "Multiple Identities, Multiple Realities: Children who Migrate Independently for Work in Southeast Asia," *Children's Geographies 13*, no. 3 (2015): 296–309.

20. Josepth Tobin, David Wu, and Dana Davidson, *Preschool in Three Cultures* (New Haven: Yale University Press, 1991).

21. Chen, *Asia as Method*, 2.

22. Alan Fogel, Alan, Sueko Toda, and Masatoshi Kawai, "Mother-infant Face-to-Face Interaction in Japan and the United States: A Laboratory Comparison Using 3-Month-Old Infants," *Developmental Psychology 24*, no. 3 (1988): 398–406.

23. Lijie Zheng, Mariëtte De Haan, and Willem Koops, "Parental Ethno Theories of Two Groups of Chinese Immigrants: A Perspective from Migration," *Migration and Development 8*, no. 2 (2019): 207–226.

24. Jonathan H.X. Lee, *Southeast Asian Diaspora in the United States: Memories and Visions, Yesterday, Today and Tomorrow* (Cambridge: Cambridge Scholars Publishing, 2015); David Lancy, "Children as a Reserve Labor Force," *Current Anthropology 56*, no. 4 (2015): 545–568.

25. Charles Darwin, "A Biographical Sketch of an Infant," *Mind 2*, no. 7 (1877): 285–294.

26. Jean-Jacques Rousseau, *Emile, or On Education* (New York: Basic Books, 1979[1762]).

27. Franz Boas, "Instability of Human Types," in *Papers on Interracial problems*, ed. Gustav Spiller (London: Kessinger Publishing, 1912), 99–103; David Lancy, "Why Anthropology of Childhood? A Brief History of an Emerging Discipline," *AnthropoChildren 1* (January 2012): 1–17.

28. Margaret Mead, and Gregory Bateson, *Character Formation in Different Cultures Film Series* (University Park, PA: Penn State Media Sales, 1951–1978); Margaret Mead, and Ken Heynman, *Famil* (New York: Macmillan Publishing Company, 1965).

29. Margaret Mead, *Coming of Age in Samoa* (New York: Morrow Quill Paperbacks, 1928), 264.

30. Ruth Benedict, *Thai Culture and Behavior: An Unpublished War-time Study* (Ithaca, NY: Cornell University Southeast Asia Program Data Paper No. 4, September, 1943).

31. Ruth Benedict, *The Chrysanthemum and the Sword* (Boston, MA: Houghton Mifflin Harcourt, 1946).

32. May Mayko Ebihara, *Svay: A Khmer Village in Cambodia*, ed. Andrew Mertha (Ithaca: Cornell University Press Southeast Asia Program Publications, 2018).

33. Ebihara, *Svay*, 451–452.

34. Spyros Spyrou, "Researching Children's Silences: Exploring the Fullness of Voice in Childhood Research," *Childhood 23*, no. 1 (February 2016): 7–21.

35. John W.M. Whiting. *Becoming a Kwoma: teaching and learning in a New Guinea tribe* (New Haven, CT: Yale University Press, 1941).

36. Iona Opie, and Peter Opie, *The Lore And Language Of Schoolchildren* (New York: New York Review Books, 1959).

37. Gertrud Lenzer, "Children's Studies: Beginnings and Purposes," *The Lion and the Unicorn 25*, no. 2 (April 2001): 185.

38. Samantha Punch, "Research with Children: The Same or Different from Research with Adults?" *Childhood 9*, no. 3 (August 2002): 322.

39. Dolores Janiewski, and Lois W. Banner, *Reading Benedict, Reading Mead* (Baltimore, MD: The Johns Hopkins University Press, 2004); Paul Shankman, *The Trashing of Margaret Mead: Anatomy of an Anthropological Controversy* (Madison, WI: The University of Wisconsin Press, 2009).

40. Roger Brown, and Ursula Bellugi, "Three Processes in the Child's Acquisition of Syntax," *Harvard Educational Review 34*, no. 2 (July 1964): 133–151.

41. James, "Giving Voice to Children's Voices," 266.

42. Philippe Ariès, *Centuries of Childhood* (London: Vintage Press, 1960).

43. Lenzer, "Children's Studies," 183.

44. Hugo Slim, "Dissolving the Difference between Humanitarianism and Development: The Mining of a Rights-based Solution," *Development in Practice 10*, no. 3 and 4 (2000): 491–494.

45. United Nations, "UN Lauds Somalia as Country Ratifies Landmark Children's Rights Treaty," *UN News*, January 20, 2015, https://news.un.org/en/story/2015 /01/488692-un-lauds-somalia-country-ratifies-landmark-childrens-rights-treaty, accessed January 27, 2020.

46. Ragnhild Lund, "At the Interface of Development Studies and Child Research: Rethinking the Participating Child," *Children's Geographies 5*, no. 1–2 (2007): 131–148.

47. Viviana Zelizer, *Pricing the Priceless Child* (Princeton, NJ: Princeton University Press, 1994).

48. Ruth Paradise, and Barbara Rogoff, "Side by Side: Learning by Observing and Pitching,' *Ethos 37*, no. 1 (2009): 102–138.

49. Elinor Ochs, and Tamar Kremer-Sadlik, "How Postindustrial Families Talk," *The Annual Review of Anthropology 44* (2015): 87–103.

50. Harriot Beazley, and Dyann Ross, "Dominant Positionings and Paradoxical Mobilities: Child Migrants in Java, Indonesia," in *Geographies of Children and Young People: Movement, Mobilities, and Journeys*, ed. Caitriona Ni Laoire, Allen White, and Tracey Skelton (Singapore: Springer, 2016), 85–109.

51. Sharon Bessell, "Rights-Based Research with Children: Principles and Practice," in *Methodological Approaches, Geographies of Children and Young People 2*, ed. Ruth Evans, Louise Holt, and Tracey Skelton (Singapore: Springer Science+Business Media, 2015), 1–18.

52. Harriot Beazley, Sharon Bessell, Judith Ennew, and Roxana Waterson, "The Right to be Properly Researched: Research with Children in a Messy, Real World," *Children's Geographies 7*, no. 4 (December 2009): 370.

53. Helen Roberts, "Listening to Children: And Hearing Them," in *Research with Children*, ed. Pia Christensen, and Allison James (London: Falmer Press, 2000), 238.

54. Lund, "At the Interface".

55. Allison James, and Alan Prout, *Constructing and Reconstructing Childhood: Contemporary Issues in the Sociological Study of Childhood* (Abingdon-on-Thames, UK: Routledge, 1997), xiv.

56. James, "Giving Voice to Children's Voices," 267.

57. Mike Kesby, "Methodological Insights on and from Children's Geographies," *Children's Geographies 5*, no. 3 (2007): 194.

58. Kesby, "Methodological Insights".

59. Yuli Hastadewi, "Participatory Action Research with Children: Notes from the Field," *Children's Geographies 7*, no. 4 (2009): 481–486.

60. Beazley et al., "The Right to be Properly Researched."

61. Tahira Jabeen, "'But I've Never been Asked!' Research with Children in Pakistan," *Children's Geographies 7*, no. 4 (2009): 418.

62. Jabeen, "But I've Never been Asked," 409.

63. Thomson, "Are Methodologies for Children".

64. Kesby, "Methodological Insights".

65. Sally McNamee, and Julie Seymour, "Towards a Sociology of 10–12 Year Olds? Emerging Methodological Issues in the 'New' Social Studies of Childhood," *Childhood 20*, no. 2 (May 2013): 156–168.

66. Kathie Carpenter, "Implicit and Explicit Feedback to Young Children Learning Indonesian," Paper presented at Symposium on Malay Dialects, Sixth International Conference on Austronesian Languages (Honolulu: Hawai'i, 1991).

67. Kabita Chakraborty, "'The Good Muslim Girl': Conducting Qualitative Participatory Research to Understand the Lives of Young Muslim Women in the Bustees of Kolkata," *Children's Geographies 7*, no. 4 (2009): 432.

68. Chakraborty, "The Good Muslim Girl," 430.

69. Chakraborty, "The Good Muslim Girl," 421.

70. Linda Gordon, "The Perils of Innocence, or What's Wrong with Putting Children First?" *The Journal of the History of Childhood and Youth 1*, no. 3 (January 2008): 331.

71. Elizabeth Bartholet, "International Adoption: The Human Rights Position," *Global Policy 1*, no. 1 (2010): 92.

72. Judith Ennew, and Dominique Plateau, *How to Research the Physical and Emotional Punishment of Children* (Bangkok: International Save the Children Alliance, 2004), ix, xii.

73. Vanessa L. Fong, "Filial Nationalism among Chinese Teenagers with Global Identities," *American Ethnologist 31*, no. 4 (November 2004): 631–648; Sungwon Kim, and Vanessa L. Fong, "How Parents Help Children with Homework in China: Narratives across the Life Span," *Asia Pacific Education Review 14* (October 2013): 581–592.

REFERENCES

Ariès, Philippe. *Centuries of Childhood*. London: Vintage Press, 1960.

Balagopalan, Sarada. "Childhood, Culture, History: Redeploying "Multiple Childhoods." In *Reimagining Childhood Studies*, edited by Spyros Spyrou, Rachel Rosen, and Daniel Thomas Cook, 23–40. London: Bloomsbury Academic, 2019.

Bartholet, Elizabeth. "International Adoption: The Human Rights Position." *Global Policy 1*, no. 1 (January 2010): 91–100.

Beazley, Harriot. "Multiple Identities, Multiple Realities: Children who Migrate Independently for Work in Southeast Asia." *Children's Geographies 13*, no. 3 (2015): 296–309.

Beazley, Harriot, and Dyann Ross. "Dominant Positionings and Paradoxical Mobilities: Child Migrants in Java, Indonesia." In *Geographies of Children and Young People: Movement, Mobilities, and Journeys*, edited by Caitriona Ni Laoire, Allen White, and Tracey Skelton, 85–109. Singapore: Springer, 2016.

Beazley, Harriot, Sharon Bessell, Judith Ennew, and Roxana Waterson. "The Right to be Properly Researched: Research with Children in a Messy, Real World." *Children's Geographies 7*, no. 4 (December 2009): 365–378.

Benedict, Ruth. *Thai Culture and Behavior: An Unpublished War-Time Study.* Data Paper No.4. Ithaca, NY: Cornell University Southeast Asia Program, September, 1943.

———. *The Chrysanthemum and the Sword.* Boston, MA: Houghton Mifflin Harcourt, 1946.

Bessell, Sharon. "Rights-Based Research with Children: Principles and Practice." In *Methodological Approaches, Geographies of Children and Young People 2,* edited by Ruth Evans, Louise Holt, and Tracey Skelton, 1–18. Singapore: Springer Science+Business Media, 2015.

Boas, Franz. "Instability of Human Types." In *Papers on Interracial Problems,* edited by Gustav Spiller, 99–103. London: Kessinger Publishing, 1912.

Brown, Roger, and Ursula Bellugi. "Three Processes in the Child's Acquisition of Syntax." *Harvard Educational Review 34,* no. 2 (July 1964): 133–151.

Carpenter, Kathie. "How Children Learn to Classify Nouns in Thai." PhD dissertation, Stanford University, 1987.

———. "Later Rather than Sooner: Extralinguistic Categories in the Acquisition of Thai Classifiers." *Journal of Child Language 19,* no. 1 (February 1991): 93–113.

———. "Implicit and Explicit Feedback to Young Children Learning Indonesian." Paper presented at Symposium on Malay Dialects, Sixth International Conference on Austronesian Languages, Honolulu: Hawai'i, 1991.

———. "Continuity, Complexity and Reciprocity in a Cambodian Orphanage." *Children and Society 29,* no. 2 (March 2015): 85–94.

Chakraborty, Kabita. "'The Good Muslim Girl': Conducting Qualitative Participatory Research to Understand the Lives of Young Muslim Women in the Bustees of Kolkata." *Children's Geographies 7,* no. 4 (2009): 421–434.

Chen, Kuan-Hsing. *Asia as Method: Toward Deimperialization.* Durham, NC: Duke University Press, 2010.

Darwin, Charles. "A Biographical Sketch of an Infant." *Mind 2,* no. 7 (1877): 285–294.

de Haan, Leo. "Livelihoods in Development." *Canadian Journal of Development Studies/Revue canadienne d'études du développement 38,* no. 1 (2017): 22–38.

Ebihara, May Mayko. *Svay: A Khmer Village in Cambodia.* Edited by Andrew Mertha. Ithaca: Cornell University Press Southeast Asia Program Publications, 2018.

Ennew, Judith, and Dominique Plateau. *How to Research the Physical and Emotional Punishment of Children.* Bangkok: International Save the Children Alliance, 2004.

Epstein, Robert. "The Myth of the Teen Brain." *Scientific American Special Editions 17,* no. 2s (June 2007): 68–75.

Fogel, Alan, Sueko Toda, and Masatoshi Kawai. "Mother-infant Face-to-face Interaction in Japan and the United States: A Laboratory Comparison Using 3-Month-Old Infants." *Developmental Psychology 24,* no. 3 (1988): 398–406.

Fong, Vanessa L. "Filial Nationalism among Chinese Teenagers with Global Identities." *American Ethnologist 31,* no. 4 (November 2004): 631–648.

———. *Only Hope: Coming of Age Under China's One-Child Policy.* Stanford, CA: Stanford University Press, 2006.

Froerer, Peggy. "Wrongdoing and Retribution: Children's Conceptions of Illness Causality in a Central Indian Village." *Anthropology and Medicine 14*, no. 3 (2007): 321–333.

Gordon, Linda. "The Perils of Innocence, or What's Wrong with Putting Children First?" *The Journal of the History of Childhood and Youth 1*, no. 3 (January 2008): 331–350.

Gupta, Akhil. "Reliving Childhood? The Temporality of Childhood and Narratives of Reincarnation." *Ethnos 67*, no. 1 (2002): 1–23.

Hastadewi, Yuli. "Participatory Action Research with Children: Notes from the Field." *Children's Geographies 7*, no. 4 (2009): 481–486.

i-learning Asia. https://www.facebook.com/ilearningasia828/, 2016, accessed March 29, 2017.

Jabeen, Tahira. "'But I've Never been Asked!' Research with Children in Pakistan." *Children's Geographies 7*, no. 4 (2009): 405–419.

James, Allison. "Giving Voice to Children's Voices: Practices and Problems, Pitfalls and Potentials." *American Anthropologist 109* (June 2007): 261–272.

James, Allison, and Alan Prout. *Constructing and Reconstructing Childhood: Contemporary Issues in the Sociological Study of Childhood.* Abingdon-on-Thames, UK: Routledge, 1997.

Janiewski, Dolores, and Lois W. Banner. *Reading Benedict, Reading Mead.* Baltimore, MD: The Johns Hopkins University Press, 2004.

Kesby, Mike. "Methodological Insights on and from Children's Geographies." *Children's Geographies 5*, no. 3 (2007): 193–205.

Kim, Sungwon, and Vanessa L. Fong. "How Parents Help Children with Homework in China: Narratives across the Life Span." *Asia Pacific Education Review 14* (October 2013): 581–592.

Lancy, David. *The Anthropology of Childhood: Cherubs, Chattel, Changelings.* Cambridge, UK: Cambridge University Press, 2008.

———. "Why Anthropology of Childhood? A Brief History of an Emerging Discipline." *AnthropoChildren 1* (January 2012): 1–17.

———. "Children as a Reserve Labor Force." *Current Anthropology 56*, no. 4 (2015): 545–568.

Lareau, Annette. *Unequal Childhoods: Class, Race and Family Life.* Berkeley, CA: University of California Press, 2003.

Lee, Jonathan H.X. *Southeast Asian Diaspora in the United States: Memories and Visions, Yesterday, Today and Tomorrow.* Cambridge, UK: Cambridge Scholars Publishing, 2015.

Lenzer, Gertrud. "Children's Studies: Beginnings and Purposes." *The Lion and the Unicorn 25*, no. 2 (April 2001):181–186.

Lin, Angel. "Preface: Can a Spider Weave Its Way Out of the Web that It Is Being Woven into, Just As It Weaves?" In *Asia as Method in Education Studies: A Defiant Research Imagination*, edited by Hongzhi Zhang, Philip Wing Keung Chan, and Jane Kenway, xiii–xv. Abingdon-on-Thames, UK: Routledge Critical Studies in Asian Education, 2012.

Lin, Angel M.Y. "Towards Transformation of Knowledge and Subjectivity in Curriculum Inquiry: Insights from Chen Kuan-Hsing's *Asia as Method*." *Curriculum Inquiry 42*, no. 1 (January 2012): 153–178.

Lund, Ragnhild. "At the Interface of Development Studies and Child Research: Rethinking the Participating Child." *Children's Geographies 5*, no. 1–2 (2007): 131–148.

McNamee, Sally, and Julie Seymour. "Towards a Sociology of 10–12 Year Olds? Emerging Methodological Issues in the 'New' Social Studies of Childhood." *Childhood 20*, no. 2 (May 2013): 156–168.

Mead, Margaret. *Coming of Age in Samoa*. New York: Morrow Quill Paperbacks, 1928.

———. *Growing up in New Guinea*. New York: Doubleday, 1930.

Mead, Margaret, and Gregory Bateson. *Character Formation in Different Cultures Film Series*. University Park, PA: Penn State Media Sales, 1951–1978.

Mead, Margaret, and Ken Heynman. *Family*. New York: Macmillan Publishing Company, 1965.

Ochs, Elinor, and Tamar Kremer-Sadlik. "How Postindustrial Families Talk." *The Annual Review of Anthropology 44* (2015): 87–103.

Opie, Iona, and Peter Opie. *The Lore and Language of Schoolchildren*. New York: New York Review Books, 1959.

Paradise, Ruth, and Barbara Rogoff. "Side by Side: Learning by Observing and Pitching." *Ethos 37*, no. 1 (2009): 102–138.

Punch, Samantha. "Research with Children: The Same or Different from Research with Adults?" *Childhood 9*, no. 3 (August 2002): 321–341.

Reza, Md Hasan, and Nicole F. Bromfield. "Poverty, Vulnerability and Everyday Resilience: How Bangladeshi Street Children Manage Economic Challenges through Financial Transactions on the Streets." *The British Journal of Social Work 49*, no. 5 (2019): 1105–1123.

Roberts, Helen. "Listening to Children: And Hearing Them." In *Research with Children*, edited by Pia Christensen, and Allison James, 225–241. London: Falmer Press, 2000.

Rousseau, Jean-Jacques. *Emile, or On Education*. New York: Basic Books, 1979[1762].

Said, Edward. *Orientalism*. New York: Pantheon Books, 1978.

Sanders Kay, and Flora Farago. "Developmentally Appropriate Practice in the Twenty-First Century." In *International Handbook of Early Childhood Education*, edited by Marilyn Fleer, and Bert van Oers, 1379–1400. Dordrecht, Netherlands: Springer, 2018.

Shankman, Paul. *The Trashing of Margaret Mead: Anatomy of an Anthropological Controversy*. Madison, WI: The University of Wisconsin Press, 2009.

Silver, Cary. "Thailand—Conquering Polio in the 'Land of Smiles." *The Rotarian* (January 1990): 22–27.

Slim, Hugo. "Dissolving the Difference between Humanitarianism and Development: The Mining of a Rights-based Solution." *Development in Practice 10*, no. 3 and 4 (2000): 491–494.

Spyrou, Spyros. "Researching Children's Silences: Exploring the Fullness of Voice in Childhood Research." *Childhood 23*, no. 1 (February 2016): 7–21.

Thomson, Fionagh. "Are Methodologies for Children Keeping them in their Place?" *Children's Geographies 5*, no. 3 (2007): 207–218.

Tobin, Joseph, David Wu, and Dana Davidson. *Preschool in Three Cultures*. New Haven: Yale University Press, 1991.

United Nations. "UN Lauds Somalia as Country Ratifies Landmark Children's Rights Treaty." *UN News*, January 20, 2015. https://news.un.org/en/story/2015/01/488 692-un-lauds-somalia-country-ratifies-landmark-childrens-rights-treaty, accessed January 27, 2020.

Whiting, John W.M. *Becoming a Kwoma: Teaching and Learning in a New Guinea Tribe*. New Haven, CT: Yale University Press, 1941.

Xu, Jing. "Becoming a Moral Child amidst China's Moral Crisis: Preschool Discourse and Practices of Sharing in Shanghai." *Ethos 42*, no. 2 (2014): 222–242.

Zelizer, Viviana. *Pricing the Priceless Child*. Princeton, NJ: Princeton University Press, 1994.

Zheng, Lijie, Mariëtte De Haan, and Willem Koops. "Parental Ethno Theories of Two Groups of Chinese Immigrants: A Perspective from Migration." *Migration and Development 8*, no. 2 (2019): 207–226.

Chapter 6

Comparison as Method in India and Papua New Guinea

Lorena Gibson

ABSTRACT

Comparison has always been integral to anthropological epistemology. It can make valuable contributions to knowledge by destabilising our perspectives and framing issues 'in a way that do not accord with disciplinary common sense' (Robbins et al., 2014: 563). However the ways in which 'the comparative method' has been conceptualised and practiced has changed considerably over the past sixty years. This chapter discusses how comparison foregrounds relations of power, the politics of representation, epistemology, and methodology. Drawing on Chen Kuan-Hsing's *Asia as Method*, and Marilyn Strathern's comparative ethnography, I propose 'comparison as method', and suggest that through intra-referencing between sites, people, places, and experience, mutually acceptable goals and methods for comparison can be negotiated with interlocutors and others when doing fieldwork.

The reflections and theoretical considerations of this chapter are based on questions about why and how I wanted to take a comparative approach that arose during my first major research project – a comparative ethnographic study of grassroots women's organisations working for social change in India and Papua New Guinea. Overall I show how research methods and relationships can be developed in multiple sites by privileging ongoing epistemological conversations with interlocutors about how we can know one another across difference. Considering the praxis of comparison enables the shifting localities emerging from this work to be considered as methodological discourse: a means of reconceptualising place as well as practice within the contemporary global sphere, with particular reference, in my research, to Asia and Oceania.

* * *

115

In this chapter I discuss 'comparison as method' by reflecting on my first major research project, a comparative study of women organising collectively for development through community-based non-governmental organisations (NGOs) in India and Papua New Guinea. Inspired by Chen Kuang-Hsing's concept of inter-referencing, and drawing on Marilyn Strathern's comparative anthropology, I explore how comparison is a form of 'practical ontological work'[1] that enables us to create knowledge attuned to our social worlds so we can 'live sanely'[2] while working to effect change, that is, so we can create sustainable transformations without compromising our relationships and ability to live in our worlds. For my participants, this involved creating practical knowledge about how to operate a community-based NGO and develop meaningful interventions in their own, and others' lives. My practical knowledge as an anthropologist was concerned with how to undertake a comparative ethnographic study of NGOs in India and Papua New Guinea that would foreground local issues and practices.

Comparison has always been integral to anthropological epistemology, although there have been considerable changes to how it has been conceptualised and practiced over the past sixty years.[3] Comparison can make valuable contributions to anthropological knowledge by destabilising our perspectives, creating 'new categories of common sense and comparabilities that are never immediate "givens"',[4] and opening up new possibilities for understanding difference. Comparison is also an inherent component of NGO knowledge practices. NGOs reference themselves against other NGOs to articulate their form (e.g., whether they are community based, grassroots, international, faith based, etc.), their point of difference (what they will focus on, how they will operate, and where they will work), and their eligibility for donor funding. They align their goals with those of other institutions, such as the UN Sustainable Development Goals, so they are comparable to donor priorities and ideas of development. Monitoring and evaluation processes include comparing the outcomes of NGO interventions against their goals in order to generate knowledge about success and failure. Their comparative practices also have a temporal dimension, with interventions aimed at addressing context-specific issues in the present in order to achieve future-oriented goals. Thus, in both anthropology and NGOs, comparison opens spaces for knowledge production and for creating alternative ways of being in the world, through negotiated understandings of contemporary realities.

This chapter is informed by methodological debates that have emerged from NGO anthropology.[5] In particular, I am interested in the challenges and opportunities that arise from engaging with NGOs as 'inherently multisited phenomena' that are already 'producers of knowledge, information, and representation'.[6] Anthropologists working with NGOs are often drawn to do so because we share similar objectives: we want to effect change and improve people's lives.[7] This creates a methodological challenge for those of us who want to engage in transformative research: as Amanda Woomer, who sought to combine her conservation activism with anthropological research by volunteering for a conservation NGO in Tanzania, expressed it, how do we 'do good' while also 'doing good research'?[8]

ETHNOGRAPHIC MOMENTS IN INDIA AND PAPUA NEW GUINEA

Our challenge for this edited collection was to reflect on what was unique about our experiences in contemporary Asia that required us to think, work, and move differently as anthropologists. Several of the chapters in this volume discuss how the specifics of place shape our research methodologies, and mine adds to that conversation by reflecting on what Strathern calls 'the ethnographic moment',[9] or the connections between our fieldwork experiences and the concepts we use to analyse them. My point of difference is comparison, which takes me beyond Asia.

My interest in comparison arose during my first trip to India in 2004. I spent six weeks there as research assistant for Sita Venkateswar, another anthropologist from Massey University in Aotearoa New Zealand, who was conducting participatory research into the activities of grassroots women's organisations working in neglected bastis[10] of Kolkata and Howrah.[11] Howrah and Kolkata are twin cities separated by the river Hooghly. Howrah city lies along the river's western bank and has a population of around one million, and Kolkata city to the east has a population of around 4.4 million according to the most recent (2011) Census of India.[12] Both cities are encompassed within the wider metropolis known as the Kolkata Metropolitan Area, often referred to simply as 'Kolkata'. During this visit, Sita introduced me to two community-based NGOs that are led by, and primarily work with, Muslim women in different bastis. I spent much of my time during that six weeks visiting each NGO, ascertaining whether the women involved would be interested in participating in a future research project with me, developing relationships with key participants, learning about the issues they considered important in the different bastis (including poverty, the low social status of women, and access to education and employment opportunities), and observing how they sought to improve the lives of women – and by extension their families and communities – through initiatives in education and income generation.

Conversations with women from the NGOs in India made me think of similar groups I had met in Lae, Papua New Guinea, a few years earlier. NGOs in various forms have played important roles in women's lives in both India and Papua New Guinea long before NGOs were officially named as such in the 1945 United Nations charter.[13] In nineteenth-century Bengal, for example, movements to educate women and campaigns to abolish sati (widow immolation) – both of which involved collective organisation – had enduring effects on women's lives.[14] In nineteenth-century Papua New Guinea, female missionaries and wives of male missionaries encouraged women's fellowships and offered domestic training, literacy classes, and religious instruction.[15] NGOs became key actors in international development in the late 1980s for a number of reasons, including the rise of neoliberal public policy, the increasing interest in 'good governance' among international development agencies such as the World Bank, and the renewed interest in 'civil society' in the post-Cold War era.[16] Many at the time turned their attention to questions of women's welfare and empowerment.[17] Today there are hundreds[18] of international, national, and local NGOs offering various forms of development aid and humanitarian assistance in metropolitan Kolkata, many of them targeting women. Likewise, Papua New Guinea receives significant amounts of international aid and gender inequality is a key concern of the many NGOs working there.

Lae, which had an official population of 148,934 in the 2011 census,[19] is the capital of Morobe Province. I visited Lae in 2001 with my father, who had been invited to look after a friend's saw-sharpening and timber-mill business while he and his wife travelled overseas. Wanting to keep myself occupied, I asked our hostess about opportunities to become involved in local community groups. She arranged for me to continue her numerous charitable activities in her absence, thus introducing me to Lae's vast network of women's organisations engaging with development. I found myself vividly recollecting some of these encounters while talking with the coordinators of the NGOs in India and was struck by what appeared to be some interesting similarities in their efforts to organise collectively in these otherwise disparate contexts.

I returned to Lae in 2005 with a research project on community-based NGOs in mind and met with several NGOs running education and income generation development initiatives for women in urban settlements. The issues they identified as important, along with the activities they ran to address them, had parallels with those of the women I had met in India. The connections I could envisage, sparked by my movements between India and Papua New Guinea, and informed by my anthropological knowledge of development and NGOs, led me to consider comparison as method for understanding how women-led, community-based NGOs in India and Papua New Guinea work to effect social change.

BEYOND ASIA AS METHOD: INTRA-REFERENCING ASIA AND MELANESIA

The research project discussed here involved four community-based NGOs: two led by Muslim women in bastis in Howrah and Kolkata cities in West Bengal (India), and two led by Christian women in urban areas of Lae (Papua New Guinea).[20] While comparison felt like an appropriate method for this project, I soon discovered that the way anthropologists understand comparison was at odds with how others view it. I was not interested in assessing India against Papua New Guinea in terms of progress towards development goals, nor did I want to evaluate or rank the NGOs based on their achievements. Instead, I wanted to draw out similarities and differences in my participant's efforts to organise collectively through NGOs. I had three aims in using comparison as method: (1) to discover the diversity of women's experiences in organising community-based NGOs, (2) to consider how social change is conceptualised and pursued in India and Papua New Guinea with my ethnographic knowledge of these NGOs, and (3) to gain a better understanding of what sustains collective action in adverse situations. In this section I discuss, via 'Asia as method', how an ethnographic moment concerning my comparative intent led me to an approach that recognises shared points of reference (or 'intra-referencing') between Asia and Melanesia.

This ethnographic moment arose from my inability to communicate why and how I wanted to use a comparative approach to my university's Human Ethics Committee. At a review meeting, Committee members expressed 'serious concerns' about the comparative nature of my research, in particular about whether I would make unfavourable cultural comparisons that might position one group as 'better' than another. When I finally received ethics approval it came with the stipulation that 'the activities and processes of the NGOs could be compared, but that comparative evaluations of cultural practices that reflect badly on any community should be avoided'.[21] The discrepancy between understandings of comparison as method prompted me to think carefully about how comparison has been mobilised in anthropological (and other Western social scientific) knowledge production about societies in Asia and Melanesia.

In his 1960 lecture on 'Asia as Method', Takeuchi Yoshima advanced the idea that Asia, and not just the West, can be a site of knowledge production.[22] Reflecting on his efforts to understand Japanese modernisation after World War II, Takeuchi critiqued the prevailing practices of the time, which involved holding up the West as an ideal standard against which Japan was compared, and argued that such comparisons 'were inadequate to the task of grasping our own position'.[23] Instead, he called on Japanese scholars to pursue a trilateral approach, looking to China to see what could be learnt about different processes of modernisation, and critically engaging with, rather than discarding, Western theories and concepts:

> the Orient must re-embrace the West, it must change the West itself in order to realize the latter's outstanding cultural values on a greater scale. Such a rollback of culture or values would create universality. The Orient must change the West in order to further elevate those universal values that the West itself produced. . . . When this rollback takes place, we must have our own cultural values. And yet perhaps these values do not already exist, in substantive form. Rather I suspect that they are possible as method, that is to say, as the process of the subject's self-formation. This I have called 'Asia as method', and yet it is impossible to definitively state what this might mean.[24]

Chen Kuan-Hsing expanded Takeuchi's ideas in his book *Asia as Method: Toward Deimperialization* (2010), problematising the kinds of comparisons often made between Asia and the West:

> the real problem is that Euro-American theory is simply not all that helpful in our attempts to understand our own conditions and practices. There is something wrong with the frame of reference. It makes more sense and is more productive to compare the formation of the society of consumption in Taiwan with that in Korea, the condition of the peasantry in India with that in China, or the form of the city-state in Hong Kong with that in Singapore, because their experiences of being colonised societies, routes of modernisation, geographical sizes, and structural locations in the current global capitalist system are more similar, making these comparisons more useful than any with the West.[25]

For Chen, 'the potential of Asia as method is this: using the idea of Asia as an imaginary starting point, societies in Asia can become each other's points of reference, so that the understanding of the self may be transformed, and subjectivity rebuilt'.[26] This concept of 'inter-referencing' – a key contribution from Chen – can be a decolonising method for Asian intellectuals to situate the West as 'one cultural resource among many others' and reorient their frames of reference to Asia and other formerly colonised spaces.[27] In this chapter, India and Papua New Guinea offer an 'imaginary horizon for comparison'[28] whereby local concerns are viewed as the starting point for understanding the knowledge practices of these NGOs, rather than the concerns of Western social sciences.

Scholars in Oceania have engaged in similar debates about whose knowledge counts in social theory. For example, Linda Tuhiwai Smith critiques the way Western academia 'claims theory as thoroughly Western', excluding Indigenous voices from knowledge production while constructing analytical frameworks by which Indigenous worlds are theorised.[29] Like Takeuchi and Chen, Smith notes the need for dialogue with Western theory, knowledge, and methodologies in devising decolonising approaches to research that centre Indigenous concerns and values.[30] Drawing on work by scholars from Africa, Latin America, Iran, and India, Raewyn Connell shows that contrary to the Northern bias, theory *does* come from the South – although those in the North might not be able to recognise it as such – and argues for a multi-centred social science that respects such knowledge.[31]

It is no exaggeration to say that Melanesia has played a vital role in the development of anthropological thought, and in turn anthropology as a discipline 'pioneered scholarly descriptions of Melanesian places, peoples, and cultures'.[32] Both aspects have come under scrutiny in recent times,[33] with some people taking an outright stance against anthropology as a practice in the area.[34] Epeli Hau'ofa provides a sharp critique of early anthropological work in the area:

> after decades of anthropological field research in Melanesia we have come up only with pictures of people who fight, compete, trade, pay bride-price, engage in rituals, invent cargo cults, copulate, and sorcerise each other. There is hardly anything in our literature to indicate whether these people have any such sentiments as love, kindness, consideration, altruism, and so on . . . By presenting incomplete and distorted representations of Melanesians we have bastardised our discipline, we have denied people important aspects of their humanity in our literature, and we have thereby unwittingly contributed to the perpetuation of the outrageous stereotypes of them made by ignorant outsiders who lived in their midst.[35]

Nevertheless, Hau'ofa saw value in anthropology as a discipline and called for local knowledge and interests to be placed at the centre of its research. For Hau'ofa, as for Takeuchi and Chen, the scale of comparison should be firmly grounded in the cases compared rather than the interests of the social scientist. This sentiment is shared by Marilyn Strathern, whose ethnographic work in Papua New Guinea formed the basis for her influential approach to comparison in anthropology.[36]

Strathern puts social relations at the centre of her comparative work, using the different ways they manifest in Melanesia and the West as a method for demonstrating analogies within and between contexts.[37] Unlike Chen, Strathern stresses the binary divide between Melanesia and the West, and by doing so, 'aims to reveal the foundations of Western conceptions and destabilise them by making connections with Melanesian perspectives'.[38] This includes drawing an analogy between anthropological knowledge practices (including our efforts to derive scales for comparison) and those of our participants in order to inform, and potentially transform, the former.[39] If I were to recast Strathern's comparative anthropology as 'Melanesia as method', it might look something like this: using the ideas of Melanesia and the West as imaginary starting points, knowledge practices in both places can become each other's self-scaling points of reference, so that understandings of social relations may be transformed and mechanisms of power illuminated. Informed by 'Asia as method' and Strathern's comparative anthropology, this chapter further multiplies my points of reference – moving beyond inter-referencing to intra-referencing – to encompass the knowledge practices of community-based NGOs in India and Papua New Guinea, and my own.

A short reflection on the politics of 'Asia as method' is warranted before I move on. As well as offering an Asian-centred way to think critically about Asia, 'Asia as method' has had important institutional effects. Both Chen and Takeuchi emphasise Asian subjectivities, Asian self-transformations, and inter-Asian collaboration.[40] Over the past two decades a number of academic, publishing, and activist networking activities throughout Asia (such as the Inter-Asia Cultural Studies project, the National University of Singapore's Asia Research Institute, and the journal *East Asian Science, Technology and Society*) have 'provided an avenue for critical exchanges and convictions on issues that are of concern to the region even if they may not be of concern to those outside the region', enabling 'scholars to band together to struggle against nationalist and other dominations within and between countries'.[41] In this chapter, I mobilise the concept of intra-referencing to make connections between the knowledge practices of women organising development initiatives through community-based NGOs in India and Papua New Guinea. I do so as a Pākehā[42] anthropologist studying NGOs in South Asia and Oceania, situated in the Cultural Anthropology Programme at Te Herenga Waka – Victoria University of Wellington, Aotearoa New Zealand. Like other 'world anthropologies',[43] anthropology in Aotearoa has its own history and trajectories,[44] and our Programme's curriculum includes Māori scholars Sir Āpirana Ngata, Makereti Papakura, and Te Rangihīroa alongside other internationally well-known anthropological ancestors. My university is one of many academic institutions and journals intellectually oriented to the Asia-Pacific region; one of Te Herenga Waka-Victoria University of Wellington's 'distinctive attributes' according to its strategic plan is 'being Asia-Pacific globally minded'.[45] I have long-standing interests in efforts to unsettle and transform anthropology from the 'antipodes' and share an intellectual affinity with the scholars above. In this chapter, I attend to my participant's knowledge practices in their own terms in the belief that they provide valuable ways of opening up new potentials for understanding how people pursue social change through NGOs. However, I am neither Asian nor Melanesian. Accordingly, comparison as method requires continuously reflecting on how my non-Asian, non-Melanesian practices intrude upon my participants. Here I am inspired by Morita's work[46] which, following Strathern, laterally examines the relationship between the analytical device and the practice being studied, which I turn to next.

LATERAL COMPARISON

After gaining ethics approval, comparison continued to be a point of contention throughout the course of my research. The question of scale, in particular, was raised on more than one occasion, and again my inability to explain how I conceptualised this to a non-anthropological audience facilitated important ethnographic moments. For example, in the ethics review process mentioned above, a Committee member commented: 'There is a very big difference in population size and ethnicity [between Kolkata and Lae]. I don't see how you are possibly going to compare these two very different sites'.[47] This sentiment was echoed during a public seminar I gave in Kolkata in 2006. 'How can you compare India with Papua New Guinea?' one audience member demanded to know. 'Kolkata is a megacity. That place [Lae] doesn't even have electricity or proper roads!' (Lae does, in fact, have both electricity and roads.) Recent work on lateral comparison by Morita[48] and Christopher Gad and Casper Bruun Jensen[49] offers a way to conceptualise scale that I believe is in keeping with the spirit of intra-referencing.

Lateral comparison recognises that comparative acts – which are already present in any ethnographic fieldsite – are diverse, move in multiple directions, and can take 'material-technological forms as often as linguistic-discursive ones'.[50] As Morita explains, his analysis is lateral because it 'mostly draws on the juxtaposition of the journeys and comparisons of the Japanese engineers and the Thai mechanics rather than appealing to analytical concepts external to their practices'.[51] This aligns with the goals of intra-referencing as I have outlined it, where the scale of comparison is derived from within the cases compared.

Lateral comparison is also informed by Strathern's efforts to juxtapose anthropological knowledge practices with those of our participants by examining the internal connections among all perspectives, including the analyst.[52] Morita makes this lateral move when he places his anthropological comparison alongside the comparative practices of his participants, discussing how his ethnographic travel generated a space for comparison that was induced by his participant's comparative interests.[53] Gad and Jensen adopt a similar lateral approach in their analysis of comparative technologies onboard a Danish fishery inspection vehicle by treating comparison simultaneously as an empirical finding and an analytic tool.[54] By adopting a lateral comparative approach in this chapter, I show how my ethnographic inquiry into the knowledge practices of my participants became an extension of their interests, opening a space for comparison that stimulated their comparative imaginations and transformed my own.

AGENCY, BY COMPARISON

Led by women who would normally be the target populations of development interventions, the NGOs I worked with in both India and PNG coordinate grassroots development initiatives that aim to 'do something good' for themselves, their families, and their wider communities. Knowledge practices about the best way to pursue their goals became the starting point for acts of comparison that led to an analytical interest in agency – understood as the intention to act and our capacity to take action, both of which are influenced by cultural, historical, and social conditions – in my ethnographic work.

The first NGO is Rehnuma-e-Niswaan,[55] which provided vocational training for girls and women from bastis in Narkeldanga, Raja Bazaar, and Park Circus in Kolkata city. Rehnuma-e-Niswaan began in 1997 when Tabassum, who grew up in Kasai Basti in Narkeldanga and was then headmistress of a school in the area, decided to utilise the classrooms after school hours by offering sewing classes to local Muslim girls who had dropped out of school. After obtaining permission to use the school, Tabassum recruited young female school-leavers from the basti by visiting their parents.

> 'At first their parents refused', she told me. 'They didn't want to send their ado-
> lescent girls. They had this idea that if girls go to school, maybe they'll get to
> know about the world and argue or fight for their rights. They didn't want that.
> But I convinced them. I said, "I am a girl from your area, you have known me
> since my childhood, do you see anything bad in me?" They came then because
> I am a local girl and they saw that I wanted to do something good.'

Conservative attitudes towards girls' and women's mobility in India's Muslim communities are well documented.[56] It is likely that this is one of the reasons why Kolkata's leading development agency, the Kolkata Metropolitan Development Authority, promoted home-centred work 'as a major component of economic development programmes targeting women'.[57] Many women from the poorest households in Narkeldanga[58] are compelled to work in order to survive, especially if their husbands have deserted them or died. They do so by taking on home-centred work and, in some cases, work in other households (as maidservants, for example). In this way, poverty overrides some of the restrictions on female movement to which more affluent households might adhere. Nevertheless, girls and women face more restrictions than boys and men, and are usually confined to their immediate neighbourhoods.

Attuned to such constraints, Tabassum pitched her vocational training pro-gramme as a women's activity so it could be 'justified in the patriarchal climate' in which she operated (personal communication). Her efforts were successful and Rehnuma-e-Niswaan became quite well known within Narkeldanga by the year 2000. She was not as successful in avoiding community resistance, however. 'Most of the negative attitudes I get are from the men in our society', she said, reflecting on the tensions that arose after she found employment in a nearby boutique for some of the girls who completed Rehnuma-e-Niswaan's first sewing course. As the girls became financially independent, some com-munity members started 'making things difficult' for Tabassum. She felt particularly targeted by one of her male relatives who publicly humiliated and shamed her. He would make snide comments about her and twist the name of her organisation, referring to it as something that 'led girls astray' rather than guided them. Following a long period of subtle harassment and opposition, she felt compelled to leave. She had married her husband and moved away from Narkeldanga to Park Circus by the time I met her in 2004.

Although classes stopped for a few months, Tabassum soon resumed them in her family's home in Kasai Basti, where her mother still lived. Over the course of my fieldwork, I became interested in her efforts to negotiate con-servative gender norms regarding mobility in Narkeldanga, where Muslim girls and women were not often permitted to move outside the basti (e.g., to attend school or work) unaccompanied by male relatives. We discussed how she invited sceptical families to compare their knowledge of her – a 'good' Muslim woman, educated and married with two children – against the problems they imagined would occur in allowing their daughters to engage in vocational training and pursue financial independence. During a group interview with fifteen Rehnuma-e-Niswaan students in 2007, I listened as Tabassum advised them about how to discuss their desire to work, outside of Narkeldanga if the opportunity arose, with their hesitant families. She turned to me as a comparative example: 'Look, she has spent thousands of rupees to come here to learn', she said, pointing at me. 'She came all the way from New Zealand to India for her education. And you're telling me you cannot go outside of Narkeldanga?'

During the interview, Tabassum commented on how much her students were enjoying themselves. 'Lorena, we must plan a picnic with them', she

said between bouts of laughter. I immediately agreed, seeing an opportunity to help Tabassum pursue her goals while simultaneously gaining
ethnographic knowledge for my project. Tabassum's students responded
enthusiastically to the idea, exclaiming 'We can go anywhere with you!' We
began planning the picnic, which would involve a trip outside the basti for
all thirty-one women enrolled in the course, and agreed to meet again once
they had asked their families for permission. At the next meeting Tabassum
discussed venues (the favoured option being the zoological gardens), transport, and calculated how much the picnic would cost. Fewer than half of the
thirty-one women said they could go. Some did not get permission from their
husbands or fathers while money was an issue for others. 'Money isn't the
problem here', Tabassum told me afterwards. 'It's because the men don't
want the women to go out of Narkeldanga and experience a picnic'. In the
end we compromised and held the picnic at Tabassum's family home in
Kasai Basti.

Later, Tabassum compared the picnic with her efforts to run sewing
courses through Rehnuma-e-Niswaan. 'It's the same', she said. 'They didn't
go to the picnic because their families didn't allow it. But I know that
after three or four times their families will allow them to go on picnics'.
Tabassum's knowledge practices, drawn from comparisons with past experience and informed by her attunement to her social world, sustain her investment in Rehnuma-e-Niswaan in the face of adversity. Agency here is aimed at
perseverance – what Spinoza called *conatus* and what Jarett Zigon (drawing
on Talal Asad) calls living sanely:

> To live sanely in the world is to practically know and to be known practically
> in the world. To live sanely in the world is not to have agency in the sense
> of resisting the social order or actively working for an ideal future. Rather,
> it is the attempt to live acceptably both for oneself and others, and to do so
> within the world in which one finds oneself. (See also Mahmood 2005; Zigon
> 2011)[59]

Tabassum is actively working for an imagined future where Muslim girls
and women can improve their education and employment opportunities and
increase their social and spatial mobility. Her knowledge practices allowed
me to see how NGOs like Rehnuma-e-Niswaan are deeply embedded in
social relations, and that their development initiatives inherently compare
possibilities (in the form of future goals) with probabilities in the present.

Travelling now to Papua New Guinea, the second NGO I discuss is
Butibam Women's Flower Group. This grassroots NGO operated in Butibam
village, which is one of the original Ahi villages around which the city of

Lae grew. Butibam Women's Flower Group was founded in early 2007 by Rachael, a keen gardener and nurse from the village. The idea for the group was planted shortly after the 2003 Morobe Agricultural Show, where Rachael had displayed some of her flowers and developed networks with people from the agricultural industry. By 2007, floriculture – a branch of ornamental horticulture concerned with cultivating flowers and ornamental plants – was frequently promoted in local newspaper articles and blogs as a promising new 'road to development' for women in Papua New Guinea.[60] Enthused by the potential to generate income from an activity she and many Butibam women enjoyed, Rachael formed the group in order to engage with PNG's emerging floriculture industry.

In August 2007, Butibam Women's Flower Group had sixty-three members. As the group was still in its early planning stages, the women had formed an executive committee but had not yet started to grow flowers as a collective. They had, however, initiated some fundraising activities, including 'bring-and-buy' food meetings on Fridays and senisim basket – 'basket exchange', where women exchange baskets of food and other store-bought products before contributing money – both common fundraising methods among women's groups and church fellowships in Papua New Guinea. They had liaised with two other local floriculture NGOs to form a larger organisation, the Morobe Floriculture Group, and run a food and flower sale at a hall in Bubia, just outside Lae. In July 2007 they had attended a meeting in Lae that simultaneously served as the opening of a six-month scoping study into the potential of floriculture to contribute to economic development,[61] and as the third planning meeting of another newly established organisation, the Papua New Guinea Women in Agriculture Development Foundation (PNGWiADF). Their enthusiasm for floriculture was apparent during my visits, but lack of resources and technical knowledge hindered their efforts.

> Basically, we've started our group but it's come to halt as we don't have the money or resources to take it any further," explained Rachael. "We need pots to grow plants in, a nursery, a garden for our plants, and land for the nursery and garden. We need someone to show us how to do floral arrangements. We also need someone to train us in how to grow, market, and export our flowers. We need someone to come in and help us with all of this. We don't see how we can do it ourselves. It's hard to raise money. When we do manage to save any, we need to spend it on our families and on food.

Seeing an opportunity to 'do good' while also 'doing good research',[62] I developed an informal needs assessment workshop with my research assistant, Bing, for the women at Butibam. One of the biggest obstacles for community-based NGOs in Lae stems from lack of material resources, so I was interested to see if we could collectively identify potential issues and discuss strategies that would enable them to pursue their goals. Bing facilitated the workshop, which we ran over two group meetings in Butibam. During the workshop, the women identified a need for more training and networking, so I organised a garden and nursery tour of Lae as a way of addressing one of their needs. I later prepared a report for the group summarising their achievements to date and the needs they identified.

The nursery tour became an important knowledge-making practice for me and the nine women (including Bing) who came with me. We visited two women Bing identified as successful floriculturists, one in Bubia and the other near Markham Valley. The Butibam women said they enjoyed the trip (which they called an 'awareness-raising experience') and I was intrigued by the comparisons generated from within the plant nurseries and gardens. As we walked around the various sites, the Butibam women discussed differences in the materials used to build greenhouses; the quality of soil; the pros and cons of nurseries compared with outdoor gardens for large plants; whether they should grow flowers in a communal garden (and which clan might be approached to provide communal land) or individually next to their houses; the different security requirements necessitated by being located in Butibam; how the flowers they could grow would differ from those already on the market; whether to specialise in one flower or grow multiple varieties; what quantity of flowers to grow; and, most importantly, how they might access the networks of NGOs and financial support necessary to achieve their goals.

The Butibam women came away from the nursery tour with a clearer idea of the practical actions they would need to take in order to turn their collective hope for a successful floriculture enterprise into knowledge. Despite the material discussion inspired by the nursery tour, the next step was to join the newly established PNGWiADF rather than immediately grow flowers. When I asked the executive committee members why they wanted to join the PNGWiADF's Morobe branch, I was told that it would help 'to make this organisation actually viable'. Other replies all shared a common theme: they saw it as a road, a way to access training, knowledge, advice, support, markets, and other social actors who would acknowledge their organisation and potentially provide further opportunities to achieve their goals. For my part, the nursery tour attuned me to the agentive power of networking and the importance of growing relationships – with other NGOs and social actors as well as with their own sense of how their NGO should operate – along with flowers.

CONCLUSION: COMPARISON AS METHOD

One of the criticisms levelled at the inter-Asian dialogues opened up by Asia as method is that they can reify cultural difference – especially the Asia-West binary that Chen sought to move away from – and reinforce cultural relativism.[63] Writing that 'inter-Asia discourses risk reinventing Asia as the new place of power', Beng-Lan Goh argues that Asian scholars need to engage with critical theoretical advancements beyond Asia: 'Only by also engaging with other critical imaginaries emanating from outside the region can Asian scholars bring their alternative regional convictions to rectify knowledge hierarchies and force a rethinking of the region, and also the world, and of the mutual interrogation and interrelationship of their converging and contrasting political projects, as well as projects of self and of living'.[64] This chapter has contributed to this call by offering a way of expanding Asia as method to Melanesia.

In both India and Papua New Guinea, the knowledge practices of women involved in these NGOs create a mutually referring relationship that mobilised some form of agency, although this is not necessarily a term my participants would use. Attuned to their social worlds, they make decisions and embark upon action in ways that enable them to negotiate difficulties arising from social and economic norms that influence everyday action. Comparison as method illustrates how my participants oscillate between their knowledge of probabilities and their comparative imaginings of what might be possible in the future to create action and knowledge that slowly influences the lives of the people they work with. Agency is not solely about resistance to power, as Saba Mahmood has discussed,[65] and these case studies demonstrate how women navigate their social worlds in ways that reflect their interests and their understandings of what they can achieve from their social locations. This is not to say they do not imagine possibilities beyond their current circumstances; instead, they employ strategies that enable them to "live sanely" [66] in the world.

At the same time as changing practice and knowledge at the NGOs I worked with, comparison expanded my understanding of agency by allowing me to see that it is not just about the intentional pursuit of 'culturally constructed projects',[67] but that it is also aimed at perseverance, and encompasses material, as well as social, aspects of life. Women organise collectively through NGOs for reasons that are not always easily comparable with measurable development outcomes. The women I worked with all gained a sense of purpose through these NGOs, or what Bourdieu has described as *illusio*: 'being occupied, projected towards goals, and feeling oneself objectively, and therefore subjectively, endowed with a social mission'.[68] Their social investment helped them sustain motivation in the face of challenges and makes organising collectively through NGOs valuable of itself, regardless of outcomes (although a successful outcome helps, of course).

Importantly, while I received resistance from my university (a Western-based academic institute), the women involved in this research were quite open to the comparative nature of my project. They frequently asked about the other NGOs I worked with and the kinds of initiatives they ran, which opened up discussions about the reasons behind the initiatives as well as gendered and structural inequalities, and facilitated what Mohásci and Morita have called the comparative travel of ideas[69] – a space for discussion and comparison about development interventions opened up by my own ethnographic travel. They were especially interested in what obstacles the other NGOs faced, how they negotiated them, and successful strategies for gaining funding, which inspired much conversation at various group meetings. Strathern argues that comparison is about relations; while eager to know about the practices of the other NGOs I worked with, many of the women concentrated on stories of the people within them, asking about marriage, children, work. Comparing their lives and experiences with mine and with the women in the other NGOs, imaginary connections were drawn across the sites. This became what I view as an ongoing epistemological conversation where we worked out how we could come to know one another across difference.

Comparison as method provides a generative way of understanding agency and the various relationships navigated by women running community-based NGOs in India and Papua New Guinea as they work towards transformative development-related goals. As this chapter has shown, by foregrounding issues of concern to our participants, attending to the diverse comparative acts already present in our fieldsites, and reflecting on the space for comparison that our ethnographic practices generate, comparison as method offers new insights into the knowledge practices of anthropologists and our participants alike.

* * *

ACKNOWLEDGEMENT

Support for this research was provided by doctoral scholarships from Massey University and the Tertiary Education Commission, and a travel award from the Asia New Zealand Foundation. Many thanks to the research participants who gave their time and energy to this project; to Atsuro Morita for his generous feedback on an earlier version of this chapter; to Caroline Bennett and Nayantara Sheoran Appleton for their useful guidance; and to Aaron, Ivy, and Reed.

NOTES

1. Christopher Gad, and Casper Bruun Jensen, "Lateral Comparisons," in *Practising Comparison: Logics Relations Collaborations*, ed. Joe Deville, Michael Guggenheim, and Zuzana Hrdličková (Manchester: Mattering Press, 2016), 69.

2. Talal Asad, "Agency and Pain: An Exploration," *Culture and Religion* 1 (2000); Jarrett Zigon, "Hope and Waiting in Post-Soviet Moscow," in *Ethnographies of Waiting: Doubt, Hope and Uncertainty*, ed. Manpreet K Janeja, and Andreas Bandak (London: Bloomsbury Publishers, 2018).

3. See Matei Candea, *Comparison in Anthropology: The Impossible Method* (Cambridge and New York: Cambridge University Press, 2019); Richard G. Fox, and Andre Gingrich, "Introduction," in *Anthropology, By Comparison*, ed. Richard G. Fox, and Andre Gingrich (London: Routledge, 2002); Thomas A. Gregor, and Donald Tuzin, "Comparing Gender in Amazonia and Melanesia: A Theoretical Orientation," in *Gender in Amazonia and Melanesia: An Exploration of the Comparative Method*, ed. Thomas A. Gregor, and Donald Tuzin (Berkeley: University of California Press, 2001); Gad, and Jensen, "Lateral Comparisons"; Gergely Mohácsi, and Atsuro Morita, "Traveling Comparisons: Ethnographic Reflections on Science and Technology," *East Asian Science, Technology and Society* 7, no. 2 (June 2013); Joel Robbins, Bambi B. Schieffelin, and Aparecida Vilaça, "Evangelical Conversion and the Transformation of the Self in Amazonia and Melanesia: Christianity and the Revival of Anthropological Comparison," *Comparative Studies in Society and History* 56, no. 3 (July 2014); Michael Schnegg, "Anthropology and Comparison: Methodological Challenges and Tentative Solutions," *Zeitschrift für Ethnologie* 139 (2014); Michael Schnegg, and Edward D Lowe, eds. *Comparing Cultures: Innovations in Comparative Ethnography* (Cambridge: Cambridge University Press, 2020); Marilyn Strathern, *Partial Connections* (Walnut Creek, CA: AltaMira Press, 2004).

4. Marcel Detienne, *Comparing the Incomparable* (Stanford, CA: Stanford University Press, 2008), xi.

5. See David Lewis, and Mark Schuller, "Engagements With a Productively Unstable Category: Anthropologists and Nongovernmental Organizations," *Current Anthropology* 58, no. 5 (October 2017); Erica Bornstein, "Introduction to Part III: How to Study NGOs Ethically," in *Cultures of Doing Good: Anthropologists and NGOs*, ed. Amanda Lashaw, Christian Vannier, and Steven Sampson (Alabama: University of Alabama Press, 2017); Katherine Lemons, "The Ethics and Politics of NGO-Dependent Anthropology," in *Cultures of Doing Good: Anthropologists and NGOs*, ed. Amanda Lashaw, Christian Vannier, and Steven Sampson (Alabama: University of Alabama Press, 2017); Amanda Woomer, "The Anthropologist and the Conservation NGO: Dilemmas of and Opportunities for Engagement," in *Cultures of*

Doing Good: Anthropologists and NGOs, ed. Amanda Lashaw, Christian Vannier, and Steven Sampson (Alabama: University of Alabama Press, 2017).

6. Lewis and Schuller, "Engagements with a Productively Unstable Category," 639–640.

7. Steven Sampson, "Introduction: Engagements and Entanglements," in *Cultures of Doing Good: Anthropologists and NGOs*, ed. Amanda Lashaw, Christian Vannier, and Steven Sampson (Alabama: University of Alabama Press, 2017), 1–18.

8. Woomer, "The Anthropologist and the Conservation NGO," 213.

9. Marilyn Strathern, *Property, Substance, and Effect: Anthropological Essays on Persons and Things* (New Brunswick, NJ: Athlone Press, 1999), 6.

10. Basti, which means settlement in Bengali and Hindi, is a word currently used to refer to areas of low-quality housing and urban degradation.

11. Sita Venkateswar, "Poverty, Empowerment and Grass-Roots Democracy: Defining Participatory Approaches," in *Working Women: Stories of Strife, Struggle and Survival*, ed. Kogi Naidoo, and Fay Patel (New Delhi, India: Sage Publications, 2009), 210–219.

12. https://www.census2011.co.in/census/metropolitan/184-kolkata.html.

13. Lewis and Schuller, "Engagements with a Productively Unstable Category," 635.

14. Radha Kumar, *The History of Doing: An Illustrated Account of Movements for Women's Rights and Feminism in India 1800–1990* (New Delhi: Kali for Women, 1993); Lata Mani, *Contentious Traditions: The Debate on Sati in Colonial India* (Berkeley: University of California Press, 1998).

15. Anne Dickson-Waiko, "The Missing Rib: Mobilizing Church Women for Change in Papua New Guinea," *Oceania* 74 (September–December 2003): 98–119; Bronwen Douglas, "Christianity, Tradition, and Everyday Modernity: Towards an Anatomy of Women's Groupings in Melanesia," *Oceania* 74 (September–December 2003): 6–23.

16. Lewis and Schuller, "Engagements With a Productively Unstable Category," 635–636.

17. Victoria Bernal, and Inderpal Grewal, "Introduction—the NGO Form: Feminist Struggles, States, and Neoliberalism," in *Theorizing NGOs: States, Feminisms, and Neoliberalism*, ed. Victoria Bernal, and Inderpal Grewal (Durham: Duke University Press, 2014), 1.

18. This is a conservative estimate; in 2014 the *Times of India* reported that India had 1 NGO for every 600 people, or approximately 2 million NGOs (Dhananjay Mahapatra, "India Witnessing Ngo Boom, There is 1 for Every 600 People," *Times of India* 23 (2014)).

19. Roko Koloma, and Hajily Kele, *2011 National Population and Housing Census of Papua New Guinea—Final Figures* (Port Moresby, Papua New Guinea: National Statistical Office, 2013), 25.

20. Research for this project was carried out between 2004 and 2011, including ten months of participant-observer fieldwork in Lae, Howrah, and Kolkata, where I worked closely with local research assistants. Adopting a longitudinal approach, I travelled from Aotearoa New Zealand to each country three times between 2004 and 2007,

spending 7–8 weeks per visit in India and Papua New Guinea. I returned to Papua New Guinea in 2011 and use social media to keep in contact with the organisations from India. My main participants were the people who lived in bastis and settlements: women and men who volunteered for the four NGOs, their family members, and children and adults who participated in their development initiatives. I also interviewed activists and academics working on issues related to development, city renewal, and social justice; long-term residents of each city; development extension workers; and members of other regional, national, and international development organisations.

21. Lorena Gibson, "Institutional Ethics Requirements and Anthropological Research Techniques, or, Why I Want to Join a University Ethics Committee," *Ex Plus Ultra: The Postgraduate Ejournal of the WUN International Network in Colonial and Postcolonial Studies* 1 (2009): 81–86.

22. See Naoki Sakai, "*Theory and Asian Humanity: On the Question of Humanitas and Anthropos*," *Postcolonial Studies* 13, no. 4 (2010): 441–464, for a critical discussion of how and why theory is usually associated with the West in the humanities.

23. Yoshimi Takeuchi, *What is Modernity? Writings of Takeuchi Yoshimi*, trans. Richard F Calichman (Columbia University Press, 2005), 156; see also Atsuro Morita, "Encounters, Trajectories, and the Ethnographic Moment: Why "Asia as Method" Still Matters," *East Asian Science, Technology and Society* 11, no. 2 (June 2017): 245; and Shu-mei Shih, "Theory, Asia and the Sinophone," *Postcolonial Studies* 13, no. 4 (2010): 471.

24. Takeuchi, *What is Modernity?*, 165.

25. Kuan-Hsing Chen, *Asia as Method: Toward Deimperialization* (Durham and London: Duke University Press, 2010), 226.

26. Chen, *Asia as Method*, 212.

27. Chen, *Asia as Method*, 223, 224; see also Beng-Lan Goh, "The Question of Cultural Incommensurability: An Intercultural Interpretation Arising Out of Southeast Asia," *American Anthropologist* 121, no. 2 (May 2019): 500.

28. Chen, *Asia as Method*, 223.

29. Linda Tuhiwai Smith, *Decolonizing Methodologies: Research and Indigenous Peoples*, 2nd Edition (London and New York: Zed Books, 2012), 30.

30. Smith, *Decolonizing Methodologies*, 40.

31. Connell, Raewyn, *Southern Theory: The Global Dynamics of Knowledge in Social Science* (Cambridge: Polity Press, 2007).

32. Tarcisius Kabutaulaka, "Re-Presenting Melanesia: Ignoble Savages and Melanesian Alter-Natives," *The Contemporary Pacific* 27, no. 1 (2015): 116.

33. Epeli Hau'ofa, "Anthropology and Pacific Islanders," *Oceania* 45, no. 4 (June 1975): 283–289; Kabutaulaka "Re-Presenting Melanesia: Ignoble Savages and Melanesian Alter-Natives," *The Contemporary Pacific* 27, no. 1 (2015): 110–145; Stephanie Lawson, "'Melanesia'," *The Journal of Pacific History* 48, no. 1 (2013): 1–22; Serge Tcherkézoff, "A Long and Unfortunate Voyage Towards the 'Invention' of the Melanesia/Polynesia Distinction 1595–1832 (trans. Isabel Ollivier)," *The Journal of Pacific History* 38, no. 2 (2003): 175–196.

34. For example, Warilea Iamo has discussed how anthropologists in the 1980s were monitored, controlled, and even banned from doing social research in the Trobriand Islands, Manus, Morobe, and West Sepik (Warilea Iamo, "The Stigma of New Guinea: Reflections on Anthropology and Anthropologists," in *Confronting the Margaret Mead Legacy: Scholarship, Empire, and the South Pacific*, ed. Lenora Foerstel, and Angela Gilliam (Philadelphia: Temple University Press, 1992), 91).

35. Epeli Hauʻofa, *We Are the Ocean: Selected Works* (Honolulu, HI: University of Hawaiʻi Press, 2008), 6.

36. Marilyn Strathern, *The Gender of the Gift: Problems With Women and Problems With Society in Melanesia* (Berkeley: University of California Press, 1988); Marilyn Strathern, "The Nice Thing About Culture is That Everyone Has it," in *Shifting Contexts*, ed. Marilyn Strathern (London and New York: Routledge, 1995), 153–176; Strathern, *Property, Substance, and Effect: Anthropological Essays on Persons and Things* (New Brunswick, NJ: Athlone Press, 1999); Marilyn Strathern, *Partial Connections* (Walnut Creek, CA: AltaMira Press, 2004).

37. Eric Hirsch, "Melanesian Ethnography and the Comparative Project of Anthropology: Reflection on Strathern's Analogical Approach," *Theory, Culture & Society* 31, no. 2–3 (March/May 2014): 42, 60; Martin Holbraad and Morten Axel Pedersen, "Planet M: The Intense Abstraction of Marilyn Strathern," *Anthropological Theory* 9, no. 4 (December 2009): 371–394; Atsuro Morita, "The Ethnographic Machine: Experimenting With Context and Comparison in Strathernian Ethnography," *Science, Technology, & Human Values* 39, no. 2 (March 2014): 214–235.

38. Morita, "The Ethnographic Machine," 228–229.

39. Hirsch, "Melanesian Ethnography"; Holbraad and Pedersen, "Planet M"; Morita, "The Ethnographic Machine." Hirsch makes the point that Strathern emphasises the Melanesia/West distinction 'so that we do not lose sight of the differences of relations that inform regimes of power and economy that both increasingly connect us in the world but also fundamentally separate us, sustaining the advantages of a few at the expense of many' (Hirsch, "Melanesian Ethnography," 59).

40. Morita, "Encounters, Trajectories, and the Ethnographic Moment."

41. Goh, "The Question of Cultural Incommensurability," 499.

42. A term given by Māori to early non-Māori settlers in Aotearoa New Zealand, which has come to refer to white settler New Zealanders.

43. Gustavo Lins Ribeiro, "World Anthropologies: Anthropological Cosmopolitanisms and Cosmopolitics," *Annual Review of Anthropology* 43, no. 1 (2014): 483–498; Junji Koizumi, "Notes on the Globalization of Japanese Anthropology," *Japanese Review of Cultural Anthropology* 16 (2016): 105–112.

44. Jade Gifford, "Double Visions: Māori and Anthropology in Aotearoa New Zealand," (2018): https://www.asaanz.org/timatanga.

45. Victoria University of Wellington, "Strategic Plan 2020–2024." https://www.wgtn.ac.nz/__data/assets/pdf_file/0005/1791824/strategic-plan-2020-2024.pdf, 15.

46. Atsuro Morita, "Traveling Engineers, Machines, and Comparisons: Intersecting Imaginations and Journeys in the Thai Local Engineering Industry," *East Asian Science, Technology and Society* 7, no. 2 (June 2013): 221–241; Morita, "The Ethnographic Machine."

47. Gibson, "Institutional Ethics Requirements," 83.

48. Morita, "Traveling Engineers, Machines, and Comparisons,"; "The Ethnographic Machine."

49. Gad and Jensen, "Lateral Comparisons." This understanding of lateral comparison differs from the lateral comparison described by Candea (Candea, *Comparison in Anthropology*).

50. Gad and Jensen, "Lateral Comparisons," 190; Morita, "Traveling Engineers, Machines, and Comparisons," 235–236.

51. Morita, "Traveling Engineers, Machines, and Comparisons," 239.

52. Hirsch, "Melanesian Ethnography,"; Morita, "The Ethnographic Machine."

53. Morita, "Traveling Engineers, Machines, and Comparisons," 239.

54. Gad and Jensen, "Lateral Comparisons," 210.

55. Rehnuma-e-Niswaan means 'guiding the girls' in Urdu. I have not disguised the locations of the organisations I worked with, and make no distinction between real names (used with permission) and pseudonyms in the text.

56. See Kabita Chakraborty, "'The Good Muslim Girl': Conducting Qualitative Participatory Research to Understand the Lives of Young Muslim Women in the *Bustees* of Kolkata," *Children's Geographies* 7, no. 4 (2009): 421–434; Zoya Hasan, and Ritu Menon, *Unequal Citizens: A Study of Muslim Women in India* (New Delhi: Oxford University Press, 2004); Zoya Hasan, and Ritu Menon, "Introduction," in *The Diversity of Muslim Women's Lives in India* (New Brunswick: Rutgers University Press, 2005), 1–17.

57. Mallika Bose, "Women's Home-Centred Work in India: The Gendered Politics of Space," *International Development Planning Review* 29, no. 3 (2007): 272.

58. 98.8% of Narkeldanga's population of 46,814 reside in bastis (Census of India 2001, *Data on Religion*: http://www.censusindia.net/religiondata/index.html ; Census of India 2001, *Provisional Population Totals, West Bengal*; Sohel Firdos, "Encountering Socio-Spatial Exclusion: The Experiences of Muslims in Kolkata," *Working paper presented at the School of People, Environment and Planning* (2007). Elsewhere I have argued that Howrah and Kolkata's bastis are "forgotten places", historically and politically constructed enclaves that are neglected, yet nevertheless deeply inhabited, by the state (Lorena Gibson, "Bastis as "Forgotten Places" in Howrah, West Bengal," in *Globalisation and the Challenges of Development in Contemporary India: Dynamics of Asian Development*, ed. Sekhar Bandyopadhyay, and Sita Venkateswar (Singapore: Springer Singapore, 2016), 187–207; see also Yong-Sook Lee, and Brenda S A Yeoh, "Introduction: Globalisation and the Politics of Forgetting," in *Globalisation and the Politics of Forgetting* (Oxon: Routledge, 2006), 1–7, and Leela Fernandes, "The Violence of Forgetting: Poverty and Change in Post-Liberalization India," *Critical Asian Studies* 42, no. 2 (2010): 265–272). In such bastis, people have limited access to basic civic amenities such as water, education, and health services, resulting in uneven development and the growth of NGOs.

59. Zigon, "Hope and Waiting in Post-Soviet Moscow," 72.

60. The Post-Courier, "Flowers have big potential to help PNG economy" (29 April 2004); The Post-Courier, "PNG climate, soils suit flower business" (23 August 2007); Veronica Manuk, "Making Money From Your Flowers" (24 February 2009).

61. See Australian Centre for International Agricultural Research, *Strategies for using floriculture to improve livelihoods in indigenous Australian and Pacific Island communities* (26 November 2010): https://www.aciar.gov.au/project/HORT/2008/011; Andrew M McGregor, et al., "Developing the Ornamentals Industry in the Pacific: An Opportunity for Income Generation (Final Report)" (2008); Sherrie Wei, and Darryl Joyce, "Floricultural Value Chain Case Studies in Fiji, Solomon Islands and Papua New Guinea," (2013); and Sherrie Wei, et al., "Developing Floricultural Supply-Chain Strategies—Papua New Guinea Case Study," (2013).

62. Woomer, "The Anthropologist and the Conservation Ngo," 213.

63. Goh, "The Question of Cultural Incommensurability," 501.

64. Goh, "The Question of Cultural Incommensurability," 503–504. Warwick Anderson has expressed a similar sentiment, suggesting that 'deterritorializing' Asia to include the Middle East, Australasia, and the Pacific would offer an effective means of sharpening Asia as method (Warwick Anderson, "Asia as Method in Science and Technology Studies," *East Asian Science, Technology and Society* 6, no. 4 (November 2012): 448). Hyang Jin Jung agrees, calling for "more explicitly intra-Asia work to contribute to critical intercultural awareness and translations beyond Asia" (Hyang Jin Jung, "Inter-Asia, Intra-Asia, and Asian Anthropologies," *American Anthropologist* 121, no. 2 (May 2019): 506).

65. Saba Mahmood, "Feminist Theory, Embodiment, and the Docile Agent: Some Reflections on the Egyptian Islamic Revival," *Cultural Anthropology* 16, no. 2 (May 2001): 202–236.

66. Asad, "Agency and Pain," 43.

67. Sherry B Ortner, *Anthropology and Social Theory: Culture, Power, and the Acting Subject* (Durham: Duke University Press, 2006), 145.

68. Pierre Bourdieu, *Pascalian Meditations*, trans. Richard Nice (Cambridge: Polity Press, 2000), 240.

69. Mohácsi and Morita, "Traveling Comparisons."

REFERENCES

Anderson, Warwick. "Asia as Method in Science and Technology Studies." *East Asian Science, Technology and Society* 6, no. 4 (November 2012): 445–451.

Asad, Talal. "Agency and Pain: An Exploration." *Culture and Religion* 1 (2000): 29–60.

Bernal, Victoria, and Inderpal Grewal. "Introduction—the NGO Form: Feminist Struggles, States, and Neoliberalism." In *Theorizing NGOs: States, Feminisms, and Neoliberalism,* edited by Victoria Bernal, and Inderpal Grewal, 1–18. Durham: Duke University Press, 2014.

Bornstein, Erica. "Introduction to Part III: How to Study NGOs Ethically." In *Cultures of Doing Good: Anthropologists and Ngos,* edited by Amanda Lashaw,

Christian Vannier, and Steven Sampson, 183–193. Alabama: University of Alabama Press, 2017.

Bose, Mallika. "Women's Home-Centred Work in India: The Gendered Politics of Space." *International Development Planning Review* 29, no. 3 (2007): 271–298.

Bourdieu, Pierre. *Pascalian Meditations*. Translated by Richard Nice. Cambridge: Polity Press, 2000.

Candea, Matei. *Comparison in Anthropology: The Impossible Method*. Cambridge and New York: Cambridge University Press, 2019.

2001 Census of India. *Data on Religion* (2001): http://www.censusindia.net/religion data/index.html.

2001 Census of India. *Provisional Population Totals, West Bengal* (2001).

Chakraborty, Kabita. "'The Good Muslim Girl': Conducting Qualitative Participatory Research to Understand the Lives of Young Muslim Women in the *Bustees* of Kolkata." *Children's Geographies* 7, no. 4 (2009): 421–434.

Chen, Kuan-Hsing. *Asia as Method: Toward Deimperialization*. Durham and London: Duke University Press, 2010.

Connell, Raewyn. *Southern Theory: The Global Dynamics of Knowledge in Social Science*. Cambridge: Polity Press, 2007.

Detienne, Marcel. *Comparing the Incomparable*. Stanford, CA: Stanford University Press, 2008.

Dickson-Waiko, Anne. "The Missing Rib: Mobilizing Church Women for Change in Papua New Guinea." *Oceania* 74 (September–December 2003): 98–119.

Douglas, Bronwen. "Christianity, Tradition, and Everyday Modernity: Towards an Anatomy of Women's Groupings in Melanesia." *Oceania* 74 (September–December 2003): 6–23.

Fernandes, Leela. "The Violence of Forgetting: Poverty and Change in Post-Liberalization India." *Critical Asian Studies* 42, no. 2 (2010): 265–272.

Firdos, Sohel. "Encountering Socio-Spatial Exclusion: The Experiences of Muslims in Kolkata." Working Paper Presented at the School of People, Environment and Planning (2007).

Fox, Richard G., and Andre Gingrich. "Introduction." In *Anthropology, By Comparison*, edited by Richard G. Fox, and Andre Gingrich, 1–24. London: Routledge, 2002.

Gad, Christopher, and Casper Bruun Jensen. "Lateral Comparisons." In *Practising Comparison: Logics Relations Collaborations*, edited by Joe Deville, Michael Guggenheim, and Zuzana Hrdličková, 189–219. Manchester: Mattering Press, 2016.

Gibson, Lorena. "Institutional Ethics Requirements and Anthropological Research Techniques, or, Why I Want to Join a University Ethics Committee." *Ex Plus Ultra: The Postgraduate Ejournal of the WUN International Network in Colonial and Postcolonial Studies* 1 (2009): 81–86.

———. "Bastis as 'Forgotten Places' in Howrah, West Bengal." In *Globalisation and the Challenges of Development in Contemporary India: Dynamics of Asian Development*, edited by Sekhar Bandyopadhyay, and Sita Venkateswar, 187–207. Singapore: Springer Singapore, 2016.

Gifford, Jade. "Double Visions: Māori and Anthropology in Aotearoa New Zealand." (2018): https://www.asaanz.org/timatanga.

Goh, Beng-Lan. "The Question of Cultural Incommensurability: An Intercultural Interpretation Arising Out of Southeast Asia." *American Anthropologist* 121, no. 2 (May 2019): 498–505.

Gregor, Thomas A., and Donald Tuzin. "Comparing Gender in Amazonia and Melanesia: A Theoretical Orientation." In *Gender in Amazonia and Melanesia: An Exploration of the Comparative Method*, edited by Thomas A. Gregor, and Donald Tuzin, 1–15. Berkeley: University of California Press, 2001.

Hasan, Zoya, and Ritu Menon. *Unequal Citizens: A Study of Muslim Women in India.* New Delhi: Oxford University Press, 2004.

———. "Introduction." In *The Diversity of Muslim Women's Lives in India*, 1–17. New Brunswick: Rutgers University Press, 2005.

Hauʻofa, Epeli. "Anthropology and Pacific Islanders." *Oceania* 45, no. 4 (June 1975): 283–289.

———. *We Are the Ocean: Selected Works.* Honolulu, HI: University of Hawaiʻi Press, 2008.

Hirsch, Eric. "Melanesian Ethnography and the Comparative Project of Anthropology: Reflection on Strathern's Analogical Approach." *Theory, Culture & Society* 31, no. 2–3 (March/May 2014): 39–64.

Holbraad, Martin, and Morten Axel Pedersen. "Planet M: The Intense Abstraction of Marilyn Strathern." *Anthropological Theory* 9, no. 4 (December 2009): 371–394.

Iamo, Warilea. "The Stigma of New Guinea: Reflections on Anthropology and Anthropologists." In *Confronting the Margaret Mead Legacy: Scholarship, Empire, and the South Pacific*, edited by Lenora Foerstel, and Angela Gilliam, 75–99. Philadelphia: Temple University Press, 1992.

Jung, Hyang Jin. "Inter-Asia, Intra-Asia, and Asian Anthropologies." *American Anthropologist* 121, no. 2 (May 2019): 506–506.

Kabutaulaka, Tarcisius. "Re-Presenting Melanesia: Ignoble Savages and Melanesian Alter-Natives." *The Contemporary Pacific* 27, no. 1 (2015): 110–145.

Koizumi, Junji. "Notes on the Globalization of Japanese Anthropology." *Japanese Review of Cultural Anthropology* 16 (2016): 105–112.

Koloma, Roko, and Hajily Kele. *2011 National Population and Housing Census of Papua New Guinea—Final Figures.* Port Moresby, Papua New Guinea: National Statistical Office, 2013.

Kumar, Radha. *The History of Doing: An Illustrated Account of Movements for Women's Rights and Feminism in India 1800–1990.* New Delhi: Kali for Women, 1993.

Lawson, Stephanie. "'Melanesia'." *The Journal of Pacific History* 48, no. 1 (2013): 1–22.

Lee, Yong-Sook, and Brenda S. A. Yeoh. "Introduction: Globalisation and the Politics of Forgetting." In *Globalisation and the Politics of Forgetting*, 1–7. Oxon: Routledge, 2006.

Lemons, Katherine. "The Ethics and Politics of NGO-Dependent Anthropology." In *Cultures of Doing Good: Anthropologists and NGOs*, edited by Amanda Lashaw,

Christian Vannier, and Steven Sampson, 183–193. Alabama: University of Alabama Press, 2017.

Lewis, David, and Mark Schuller. "Engagements with a Productively Unstable Category: Anthropologists and Nongovernmental Organizations." *Current Anthropology* 58, no. 5 (October 2017): 634–651.

Mahapatra, Dhananjay. "India Witnessing NGO Boom, There is 1 for Every 600 People." *Times of India* 23 (2014): https://timesofindia.indiatimes.com/india/Ind ia-witnessing-NGO-boom-there-is-1-for-every-600-people/articleshow/30871406 .cms.

Mahmood, Saba. "Feminist Theory, Embodiment, and the Docile Agent: Some Reflections on the Egyptian Islamic Revival." *Cultural Anthropology* 16, no. 2 (May 2001): 202–236.

Mahmood, Saba. *Politics of Piety: The Islamic Revival and the Feminist Subject.* Princeton, New Jersey: Princeton University Press, 2005.

Mani, Lata. *Contentions Traditions: The Debate on Sati in Colonial India.* Berkeley: University of California Press, 1998.

Manuk, Veronica. "'Making Money from Your Flowers'." (24 February 2009): https://malumnalu.blogspot.com/2009/02/making-money-from-your-flowers. html.

McGregor, Andrew M., Kyle Stice, Aileen Burness, and Mary Taylor. "Developing the Ornamentals Industry in the Pacific: An Opportunity for Income Generation (Final Report)." (2008).

Mohácsi, Gergely, and Atsuro Morita. "Traveling Comparisons: Ethnographic Reflections on Science and Technology." *East Asian Science, Technology and Society* 7, no. 2 (June 2013): 175–183.

Morita, Atsuro. "Traveling Engineers, Machines, and Comparisons: Intersecting Imaginations and Journeys in the Thai Local Engineering Industry." *East Asian Science, Technology and Society* 7, no. 2 (June 2013): 221–241.

———. "The Ethnographic Machine: Experimenting With Context and Comparison in Strathernian Ethnography." *Science, Technology, & Human Values* 39, no. 2 (March 2014): 214–235.

———. "Encounters, Trajectories, and the Ethnographic Moment: Why "Asia as Method" Still Matters." *East Asian Science, Technology and Society* 11, no. 2 (June 2017): 239–250.

Ortner, Sherry B. *Anthropology and Social Theory: Culture, Power, and the Acting Subject.* Durham: Duke University Press, 2006.

Post-Courier, The. "Flowers Have Big Potential to Help PNG Economy." (29 April 2004): http://www.postcourier.com.pg/20040429/rural04.htm.

———. "PNG Climate, Soils Suit Flower Business." (23 August 2007).

Research, Australian Centre for International Agricultural. "Strategies for Using Floriculture to Improve Livelihoods in Indigenous Australian and Pacific Island Communities (26 November 2010): https://www.aciar.gov.au/project/HORT/20 08/011.

Ribeiro, Gustavo Lins. "World Anthropologies: Anthropological Cosmopolitanisms and Cosmopolitics." *Annual Review of Anthropology* 43, no. 1 (2014): 483–498.

Robbins, Joel, Bambi B. Schieffelin, and Aparecida Vilaça. "Evangelical Conversion and the Transformation of the Self in Amazonia and Melanesia: Christianity and the Revival of Anthropological Comparison." *Comparative Studies in Society and History* 56, no. 3 (July 2014): 559–590.

Sakai, Naoki. "Theory and Asian Humanity: On the Question of Humanitas and Anthropos." *Postcolonial Studies* 13, no. 4 (2010): 441–464.

Sampson, Steven. "Introduction: Engagements and Entanglements." In *Cultures of Doing Good: Anthropologists and NGOs*, edited by Amanda Lashaw, Christian Vannier, and Steven Sampson, 1–18. Alabama: University of Alabama Press, 2017.

Schnegg, Michael. "Anthropology and Comparison: Methodological Challenges and Tentative Solutions." *Zeitschrift für Ethnologie* 139 (2014): 55–72.

Schnegg, Michael, and Edward D. Lowe, eds. *Comparing Cultures: Innovations in Comparative Ethnography*. Cambridge: Cambridge University Press, 2020.

Shih, Shu-mei. "Theory, Asia and the Sinophone." *Postcolonial Studies* 13, no. 4 (2010): 465–484.

Smith, Linda Tuhiwai. *Decolonizing Methodologies: Research and Indigenous Peoples*. 2nd Edition. London and New York: Zed Books, 2012.

Strathern, Marilyn. *The Gender of the Gift: Problems With Women and Problems With Society in Melanesia*. Berkeley: University of California Press, 1988.

———. "The Nice Thing About Culture is That Everyone Has it." In *Shifting Contexts*, edited by Marilyn Strathern, 153–176. London and New York: Routledge, 1995.

———. *Property, Substance, and Effect: Anthropological Essays on Persons and Things*. New Brunswick, NJ: Athlone Press, 1999.

———. *Partial Connections*. Walnut Creek, CA: AltaMira Press, 2004.

Takeuchi, Yoshimi. *What is Modernity? Writings of Takeuchi Yoshimi*. Edited by Richard F. Calichman, Translated by Richard F. Calichman. New York: Columbia University Press, 2005.

Tcherkézoff, Serge. "A Long and Unfortunate Voyage Towards the 'Invention' of the Melanesia/Polynesia Distinction 1595–1832 (Translated by Isabel Ollivier)." *The Journal of Pacific History* 38, no. 2 (2003): 175–196.

Venkateswar, Sita. "Poverty, Empowerment and Grass-Roots Democracy: Defining Participatory Approaches." In *Working Women: Stories of Strife, Struggle and Survival*, edited by Kogi Naidoo, and Fay Patel, 210–219. New Delhi, India: Sage Publications, 2009.

Victoria University of Wellington. "Strategic Plan 2020–2024." https://www.wgtn.ac.nz/__data/assets/pdf_file/0005/1791824/strategic-plan-2020-2024.pdf.

Wei, Sherrie, and Darryl Joyce. "Floricultural Value Chain Case Studies in Fiji, Solomon Islands and Papua New Guinea." (2013): http://www.pacificfarmers.com/wp-content/uploads/2014/06/Floricultural-Value-Chain-Case-Studies-in-Fiji-Solomon-Islands-and-Papua-New-Guinea.pdf.

Wei, Sherrie, Darryl Joyce, Sim Sar, and Noah Boas-Singomat. "Developing Floricultural Supply-Chain Strategies—Papua New Guinea Case Study." (2013):

https://pdfs.semanticscholar.org/48fb/208417ea9ae5c6de985fe25310a6de353482.pdf?_ga=2.164239612.2119075386.1548705445-2002112634.1548705445.

Woomer, Amanda. "The Anthropologist and the Conservation NGO: Dilemmas of and Opportunities for Engagement." In *Cultures of Doing Good: Anthropologists and NGOs*, edited by Amanda Lashaw, Christian Vannier, and Steven Sampson, 212–229. Alabama: University of Alabama Press, 2017.

Zigon, Jarrett. "Hope and Waiting in Post-Soviet Moscow." In *Ethnographies of Waiting: Doubt, Hope and Uncertainty*, edited by Manpreet K Janeja, and Andreas Bandak, 65–86. London: Bloomsbury Publishers, 2018.

Chapter 7

The Bali of Anthropology and the Anthropology of Bali

Research in a Fast-Moving Part of Asia

Graeme MacRae and Lee Wilson

ABSTRACT

We both discovered the imaginary region 'Asia' as young travellers in India, a decade or more apart – Graeme in the 1970s, and Lee in the early 1990s. We rediscovered it another decade on in Bali as anthropologists. The classic ethnography of Bali, written in the 1930s, is entitled simply 'Island of Bali' (Covarrubias 1937). The cultural map of this island was presumed to coincide with its geographical boundaries. This island remained the assumed unit of analysis for over half a century, until the unavoidable realities of globalisation forced a rethinking. Since then Bali has kept changing and we keep running to keep up. This is the story of our ongoing dances, similar but different, with the methodological challenges presented by an island and ethnographic methods that are both works in progress.

The challenge for the anthropology of Bali is to comprehend and analyse this dynamic and complex landscape of multiple factors and constant change. A new generation of scholars (many anthropologists, and Indonesian as well as foreign) are finding new ways of working this landscape, mostly by focusing on relatively limited parts of it. What has been lost in the process is an overview and sense of the island as a whole. It might be argued, given the transnational flows of people and money, goods and services, images and information that constitute contemporary Bali, that the geo-cultural unit of the island has lost whatever utility it had as a unit of analysis. But it remains relevant for (at least) two reasons: (1) Bali remains for most Balinese people, a meaningful locus of cultural and religious identity, notwithstanding significant internal cleavages and conflicts; (2) if we reconceptualise 'Bali' less as an island, but as a node in a network of trans-local processes, it is a node of particular intensity, in which the process of globalisation can be seen in particularly concentrated form, on a scale feasible for integrated analysis.

* * *

When we were young, we went travelling – to discover somewhere we thought was Asia. Later, we became anthropologists, ethnographers of Bali, a very particular corner of Asia – atypical in some ways, but typical in others. Our Asias, and our ideas of them, became more complicated and working out how to work them out is an ongoing process. Here are our stories of how it happened and our provisional understandings of Bali, Asia and ethnographic method.

GRAEME'S ASIA

I heard about somewhere called 'Asia' in the mid-1970s, from veterans of the overland trail between Europe and Australasia. It sounded like the opposite and antidote to all the things I thought were wrong with my own society, so I went to look for myself, travelling for months, through Indonesia, India, Nepal, Afghanistan, moving from town to city to village, walking all day (that was my method) meeting people, looking, listening, and recording it in my diaries. I imagined that I learnt something about Asia and I fancied myself an anthropologist. Fifteen years later I became one. India would have been my first choice as a research site, but the logistics of extended ethnographic research there, with a family in tow, seemed daunting, so I found myself drawn back to Bali, my first stop in Asia. The idea was to revisit and interrogate a sepia-tinted memory of a village/town called Ubud – the penumbral gloom of huge lychee trees along the main street, cool, damp, brown earth underfoot, women drifting past carrying something on their heads, the scent of frangipani and clove cigarettes, the creaking of tall, ancient, black Dutch bicycles, cocks crowing, and the fading notes of a distant gamelan. What had happened in the intervening years and how did it all work now?

I was fortunate to enjoy a glorious year and a half of what was already seen as an old-fashioned style of ethnographic fieldwork. I was guided by what local people told me was important – which was essentially ritual, so much of my time was spent in apprenticeship in local temples, then in a widening circle around Ubud. This became my window into everything else – religion, cultural geography, history, political economy – eventually even the banalities of tourism.

The 1980s and 1990s were something of a golden age for research in Bali, with a cohort of brilliant researchers, mostly anthropologists, working in the reflected glow of Clifford Geertz's celebrated essays based on his experiences there.[1] They went beyond Geertz, critiquing and overturning many of his evocative, provocative, and sometimes ethnographically questionable generalisations about Bali. I arrived in their wake, learnt my trade from them, and worked in their shadow. Now, two decades on, most are gone – retired or moved elsewhere and now I am left, one of a handful of anthropologists still working there and even fewer with extended ethnographic experience of a local community.

LEE'S ASIA

Like Graeme, my Asia began with Bali, albeit more than a decade later. Similarly, my appetite whet from this first encounter, I headed to India, and spent a year in the early 1990s trying to avoid the 'muesli trail', a tourist route across the subcontinent for the new breed of backpackers. I tried earnestly to immerse myself in a world that seemed profoundly different from that in which I had grown up in the UK. A desire for difference that somewhat ironically drew me back to London to study anthropology at the School of Oriental and African Studies (SOAS). SOAS at that time had a thriving Indonesian Studies department, somewhat philological in bent, but which offered captivating insight into Indonesia through the study of the classical literature of the archipelago. Taking a degree in anthropology with a minor in Indonesian Studies, I became aware of differences between the static worlds of the *hikayat* and other historical texts, and the dynamism and fluidity of contemporary realities that were the stuff of anthropological discussions and debates. I was drawn to the latter while the former, although never losing its fascination, seemed to me to perpetuate a somewhat faded image of Asian antiquity perpetuated largely by Western scholars.

I continued to return to Bali in connection with my doctoral research on Indonesian martial arts, which segued into subsequent work on informal security, and longer periods of fieldwork on the island. While I am not an anthropologist of Bali per se, as an ethnographer I have known and worked with some people and groups on the island for over sixteen years. Like Graeme, my understanding of social and economic transformation in Asia is framed by my experience of change in Bali. It is our respective experiences of Asia as itinerant tourists, and later as (relatively) disciplined social observers, that foreshadow some of the concerns we share with ways of doing anthropology in Bali today. The aim of this chapter is first to provide a rough sketch of the complex landscape of this new Bali, and second to outline the way each of us, half a generation apart, have developed methodological approaches, different but complementary, to anthropological analysis of this landscape.

BALI AND ANTHROPOLOGY

The classic ethnography of Bali, written in the 1930s, but still widely read, is entitled simply 'Island of Bali'.[2] The cultural map of this island was presumed to coincide with its geographical boundaries, notwithstanding significant historical flows of people, goods and services, and cultural/religious ideas across its borders. It appeared to foreigners as '. . .a thing apart. . . . [from] . . . the rest of the Indies'.[3] This geo-cultural island remained the assumed unit of analysis for over half a century, until the unavoidable realities of globalisation forced some rethinking.[4]

Bali was changing, but so was our view of it. We began to discover political-economic realities obscured by the 'anthropological romance' of spectacular cultural performance.[5] We also reminded ourselves that behind the appearance of 'timeless' culture surviving even the onslaught of tourism was a century of profound and often violent change.[6] Since the 1990s the speed and scale of change has accelerated, and the Bali of that time is now almost unrecognisable – transformed by tourism and investment-driven economic growth leading to an overloaded raft of social and environmental consequences. The primary challenge for a renewed anthropology of Bali is to comprehend and analyse this dynamic and complex landscape of multiple factors and constant change.

A new generation of scholars, Indonesian as well as foreign, are finding new ways of exploring this landscape, but most are doing it piecemeal, by focusing on relatively limited parts of it.[7] In the process we have begun to lose sight of the island as a whole. Is it too 'complicated'? Is the overview too hard to grasp?

It might be argued, given the transnational flows that constitute contemporary Bali, that the geo-cultural unit of the island has lost whatever utility it once had as a unit of analysis. But we believe it remains relevant for (at least) two reasons. The first is that Bali remains, for most Balinese people, a meaningful locus of cultural and religious identity, notwithstanding significant internal cleavages and conflicts – an existential anchor in the turbulent ocean of change in which they find themselves. The second reason is that, if we reconceptualise 'Bali' less as a geographical island, than as a node in a network of trans-local processes, it is a node of particular intensity, in which processes of globalisation can be seen in heightened form, on a scale feasible for integrated analysis.

The aim of this chapter is firstly to provide a rough sketch of the complex landscape of this new Bali and secondly to outline the way each of us, half a generation apart, have developed methodological approaches, different but complementary, to anthropological analysis of this landscape.

THE NEW BALI

Here is a minimal checklist of critical issues in contemporary Bali:

Demographics
  Tourism
  Expatriates and migrants
  Visas + Land sales
  Migration and Islam
Social Problems
  Unemployment,
  Drug use and addiction
  Gangs, violence, and organised crime
Money
  Investment
  Money laundering
  Local economies
  Land
    Prices
    Foreign ownership
    Conversion
Environment/Resources
Construction
Agriculture
Environment
Water
Transport
Marine Reclamation
Mining (sand/gravel/rock)
Cultural Heritage
Hindu Religion
[break]

This raw list could be more helpfully arranged into either a centre-and-periphery mandala form or a sequential flow chart, to reflect the processual and causal logics involved (figures 7.1 and 7.2).

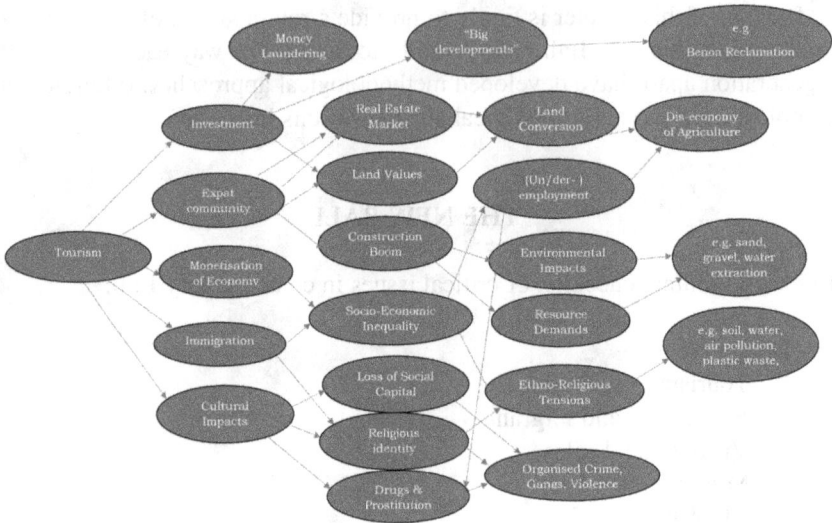

Figure 7.1   Current Issues in Bali: view 1

Or, as a linear sequence of words . . .

For the past forty-five years tourism has brought into Bali an increasing flow of people from all over the world. Tourists spend large amounts of outside money (of the order of 4,000 million dollars a year).[8] Some of this money flows straight back out to international tourism operators and suppliers, but some flows into the local economy. Many visitors now stay for extended periods (months or years rather than days or weeks) while others have established more or less permanent homes in Bali.[9] They too bring substantial flows into (and through) the local economy. These flows of money have gradually become the basis of the entire economy of the island.

The flows of people and money attract investment capital, which goes mainly into construction of hotels and other tourism infrastructure, but also into real estate. This has the further effects of inflating property values and driving a building boom. The building boom creates a demand for resources, some of which are imported, but others are local raw materials such as sand and gravel (for concrete), wood, bamboo, and water. These demands create new mini-frontiers where these resources are available and consequent short-term booms in local economies.[10] These booms (and subsequent busts) create new patterns of wealth and poverty as well as significant environmental side effects.

The building boom and economic growth, in general, also create a demand for labour that local people are either unable or unwilling to meet, so it attracts migration of unskilled labour from other less affluent parts of Indonesia, especially East Java. These migrants are economically poorer, linguistically and

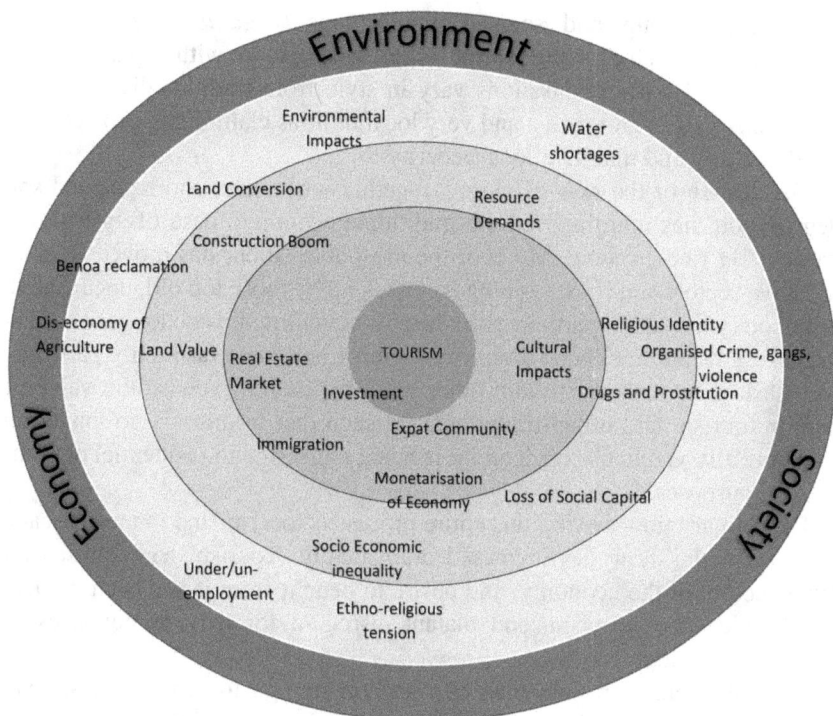

Figure 7.2 Current Issues in Bali: view 2

culturally different from Balinese, and most significantly, Muslim, rather than Hindu. Balinese communities are not structured to accommodate this kind of diversity and consequently newcomers of different cultural background are not easily integrated.[11] These tensions are exacerbated by widespread Balinese fears of expansionist and hostile Islamic colonisation.[12]

The combined influx of well-heeled expatriates (Indonesian as well as foreign) and unskilled labour migration has had the effect of colonising both the top and bottom ends of the economy. A growing share of especially the larger hospitality sector is owned by foreign and Jakarta-based companies, while the majority of unskilled manual work is performed by immigrants from other parts of Indonesia, especially East Java.[13] Indigenous Balinese now occupy a shrinking middle ground of precarious employment in tourism-related service industries and even more precarious participation in the agricultural economy.[14]

The inflation of real estate values, the speculative building boom, the coastal tourism zone of supercharged hedonistic consumption, and the booming transport sector together have created fertile soil for the growth of organised crime. Networks of criminality often overlap with the membership of local security groups and 'societal organisations' (*organisasi kemasyarakatan, Ormas*) as well as some foreign gangs, who operate with apparent impunity in Bali. These organisations vary in style from traditionally economic mafia-like ones to nationalist and very local militias claiming to protect Bali-Hindu culture and maintain local security.[15]

The growth of the new economy, together with water shortages and soil degradation, has marginalised the traditional economic base of agriculture, particularly rice-growing. Much of the most able labour has moved to more lucrative sectors and most farming is now done by those too old, uneducated, or remotely located to participate in the new economy. It is no longer possible to make a viable livelihood from rice-farming and most farm only part-time for subsistence, combined with other work for cash. Likewise the value of land in tourism and urban-fringe areas is such that farming is no longer an economically viable use for it and it is being converted to residential or commercial purposes.[16]

The primary flow driving this entire process is tourism and in recent years, the size of this flow has increased dramatically. Tourism has eclipsed all other sectors of the economy, and desire to benefit from it has been marked by chronic short termism, and blatant disregard for the consequences of unbridled development.

In 2008, there were less than two million foreign tourists and less than three million domestic ones. By 2019 this had increased to over six million.[17] This process is qualitatively complex, multidimensional, and numbers are increasing at an ever-accelerating rate. The overall effects are growing economic inequality, social fragmentation, loss of cultural confidence, an escalating burden on resources, and significant environmental degradation. Concerns over these transformations in Bali are not new. In 2000, the satirical comic, Bog Bog, presciently depicted globalisation as a bomb, several years before the island became a target for terrorist attacks.

In the cartoon (figure 7.3) the Balinese passively watch the bomb's fuse burn while protecting their ears in anticipation of the blast caused by globalisation as it detonates on the island, seemingly oblivious to the fact that they are standing on the bomb. The cartoon suggests inaction in the face of threat, and a failure to appreciate the implications of global connections. Globalisation is understood in this sense by Balinese commentators as a confluence of social, cultural, and economic flows, the effects of which on Balinese society are greatly disruptive. Bali has become in many ways iconographic of the troubles that accompany greater connectivity to the world. This notoriety had profound consequences for the island when tourist hotspots became the target of terrorist attacks in 2002 and 2005.

This roughly sketched overview is obviously simplified, generalised, and incomplete. It is impossible to study holistically but it begs for

Figure 7.3 "Globalism", courtesy of Jango Paramartha

ethnographic-level exploration and filling of gaps at every point. Some of this work is being done, much of it very well, by the new generation of researchers, but at the price of losing sight of the overview. The question is whether an overview is really necessary or even relevant in this multidimensional landscape of shifting trans-local flows. And if it is useful, what is the appropriate scale of such an overview? The natural boundaries of the island are no longer barriers to any of these flows, nor is Balinese culture heterogeneously contained within them. Is the notion of a culture, let alone a geographically bounded one, a defensible unit of analysis, let alone methodological point of departure? Such models were thoroughly critiqued a couple of decades ago, most convincingly and eloquently by Gupta and Ferguson[18] and have been all but abandoned since. 'Asia' may have its value as 'method',[19] but what about

'Bali as method'? We believe that both levels of study are necessary and possible but also compatible and complementary.

BALI AS METHOD

Despite this deep globalisation, Bali remains an appropriate scale of analysis for two reasons – one grounded in anthropological method, the other in Indigenous understandings, respect for which is part of anthropological method. For most Balinese we know, 'Bali' is a self-evident unit defined by an integrated whole of language, culture, and especially religion, expressed explicitly in an 'invented tradition' known as Tri Hita Karana.[20] The daily experience of economic survival, multicultural encounter, and media exposure contradicts and challenges this, and foreign observers routinely lament the 'loss of traditional culture', but 'Balineseness' is reinforced strongly and regularly – daily at the level of household ritual, and almost weekly in the customs and celebrations of local communities and temples. The level of this cultural resilience is not a function of distance from the influences of tourism and urbanisation – some of the strongholds of ritual and community are actually in the most intensively touristed and urbanised areas.[21] These are social facts of some significance, which need to be taken seriously in any anthropological analysis.

The more directly anthropological and methodological reason is that, while neither the wholeness of the island nor its geographical boundaries any longer define a self-evident unit of study, what happens within its boundaries becomes distinctive and worthy of study, when viewed from a more global perspective. The network of processes and flows outlined above, when seen from within Bali, appears to fragment any sense of wholeness and violate any sense of boundedness. However, when seen from a global perspective, Bali appears as a site in which flows of people, money, resources, and images intersect in an extraordinarily concentrated way. This, we argue, is what constitutes the anthropological subject that we might call 'the new Bali'. How then can we make sense of this new Bali?

This is a specific instance of the disciplinary methodological challenge Gupta and Ferguson identified two decades ago (1997). They argued that ethnographic methods were still part of the answer, but they had little to say about larger overviews, let alone how these levels might be integrated. Anna Tsing (2005) addresses this challenge more comprehensively. She begins with the problem of how to understand a complex local scenario of social and environmental collapse. The causes and driving factors are multiple and located at various distances and scales from the local, but linked to it by 'chains of global connection'. Her method is firstly to identify and map these chains across scale and culture, then to intervene ethnographically at key points along those chains. The most productive points for ethnographic exploration are the 'gaps' between understandings or 'zones of awkward engagement, where words mean something different across a divide' (2005: xi) where the 'friction' between global/universal ambitions and projects meets the reality of local cultures, economies, and ecosystems.

The lists, diagrams, and description above provide a rough sketch of the main chains of connection across various scales. We (and others) have made ethnographic interventions into various points on this network.[22] The methodological challenge now is to integrate them in such a way that overview and ethnographic interventions mutually inform each other. The result might be a book of many chapters which we imagine below, then consider two of them in more detail:

> Economic Development versus the environment: mining the sacred mountains to build sacred hotels.
> New Tourisms and New Expatriates.
> Island of Waste: the culture and political-economy of plastics, recycling and composting.
> Where will our rice come from when all the farmers and land are gone? A broken food-system.
> Tourism/infrastructure development: Reklamasi Benoa.
> Migration, Islam and ethnic tensions.
> Water.
> The transformation of upland economies and ecologies.
> Whose security? The rise of paramilitary organisations.
> World Cultural Heritage: global imaginings meet local

This list implies a less than optimistic picture. The reality is a familiar one of increased economic growth with undeniable economic benefits for many people, but at the price of significant costs in terms of economic equality, social harmony, cultural coherence, and environmental sustainability. Clear-eyed analysis is needed to understand these problems, but equally important is focus on resistance to destructive change as well as creative and innovative initiatives to effect beneficial change. What follows are brief sketches of our modes of ethnographic intervention into the last two imaginary chapters listed above.

Methods: Lee

In my postgraduate work, I studied contemporary manifestations of tradition by researching martial arts as an aspect of the nation-building project in Indonesia. My conceptual focus was cultural hegemony and forms of power. Empirically, my work centred on the institutional transformation of the pedagogy and practice of Indonesian martial art of Pencak Silat as an object of national culture. It was the practice and management of the art, rather than geographical boundaries, that circumscribed my fieldsite. This was not exactly 'multi-sited ethnography' in the sense proposed by George Marcus.[23] I simply followed the connections between people, places, ideas, practices and events, adumbrating congeries of interests and the distribution of resources to describe the trajectory of my encounter with Pencak Silat. This was less a methodological response to perceived shortcomings of localised ethnography, than an attempt to come to terms with the complexity of studying Pencak Silat as an aspect of the national cultural project in Indonesia. Fifteen years later, it is more obvious to me how this approach was implicitly framed by broader disciplinary concerns with global trends and transformations, and indeed, could only have been conceived subsequent to these anxieties being aired.

A central concern of anthropology in the 1990s was with the limitations of the 'bounded' fieldsite[24] as the basis for production of ethnographic knowledge capable of articulating the growing complexities of an increasingly connected world. Marcus's argument for methodological engagement with a globalised world epitomised these concerns and became a reference point in the anthropological literature. While, despite the elisions of European historical narratives, the world has always been connected,[25] the sheer scale of contemporary global connections and flows is unprecedented in human history.

Concerns with the relevance of locality in an increasingly interconnected global ecumene gave rise to attempts to trace these flows and their social and cultural relevance. Global assemblages,[26] translocality and flexible citizenship,[27] and 'friction' between connections[28] were all attempts to fashion conceptual models adequate for an ethnography of globalisation. What seems common sense today required considerable theoretical innovation to broaden the horizons of a discipline accustomed to the study of the particular. Modern Asian realities in particular seemed ever more dynamic in light of the timeless portrayal of tradition perpetuated in some anthropological accounts, especially in Indonesian and Southeast Asian ethnography prior to the 1990s[29] (e.g., Geertz 1980, Errington1989, Tambiah 1976). It is no surprise that many innovations in the production of anthropological knowledge arose from ethnographic encounters with Southeast Asia given the intensity and pace of globalisation in the region.

Some years later I returned to Indonesia, interested in the growth of citizen militia groups since the fall of Soeharto. Particularly prolific in Bali, these militia developed in a post-bomb security space marked by the perceived need for greater vigilance and security on the island. Response to the terrorist threat in Bali provided a focal point for anti-immigrant sentiment, and concerns with the erosion of Balinese culture too found new voice in an exclusionary assertion of Balinese identity in the face of perceived threats to Balinese lives and livelihoods. A cultural revitalisation movement, *Ajeg Bali* ('let Bali stand strong'), resonating with the heightened anxiety over threats to Balinese ways of life, found increasing traction in the aftermath of the Kuta bombing in 2002. Ajeg Bali and its discriminatory message of 'Bali for the Balinese'[30] became increasingly prominent in public discourse. Preserving Balinese ways of life was no longer just about cultural preservation in the face of the onslaught of globalisation, and the threat of terrorism galvanised local efforts to promote increasing vigilance in the wake of these attacks.

Prior to the first terrorist attack in Bali in 2002, efforts to safeguard Balinese values and ideals had given rise to the revival of *pecalang*, customary security guards answerable to village-level authority. A term derived from the root *calang*, or 'vigilant', *pecalang* are charged with safeguarding the ritual practices important to all aspects of social life in Bali. They are sanctioned through appeal to custom, and legitimised by 'local regulation' (*Peraturan Daerah* 3/2001) passed by provincial government in 2001 that underwrites their role as customary guardians.[31] A dual system of administration cedes authority on customary matters to the *desa adat*, or customary village, while formal administrative matters are dealt with by the civil administration, or *desa dinas*. At local level, lines between these jurisdictions become blurred,[32] especially in matters of communal security. The role of *pecalang* often overlaps with that of the Community Protection Groups (*Perlindungan Masyarakat*, or *Linmas*), civilian security officers under the authority of the local civil service. In many villages the same people fulfil both roles, changing uniforms according to the situation.

More recently, *pecalang* have become involved in more mundane aspects of security, checking the identity cards of migrants from other areas of Indonesia, particularly from Java. This has taken a somewhat sinister turn, resulting at times in overt harassment of Indonesian migrants to the island. Bali, as Henk Schulte Nordholt put it, has become an 'open fortress' in which boundary marking and the suspicion of non-Balinese outsiders are in part justified by the continuing threat of terrorist attacks.[33]

While non-Indonesian outsiders, as the main source of revenue, are treated with greater deference than Indonesian migrants, the constant exposure to Western values and ideals is seen to present an insidious threat to Balinese ways of life. One of the largest militant *ormas* on the island, Baladika Bali, refers to the need to preserve Balinese identity in the face of the influx of visitors to the island, and to harness Bali's youth to protect from the threat of terrorism and the corrupting influences of Western culture. The popularity of *ormas* has grown at the same time as an increasing alienation of youth from political parties. They have become political actors in their own right, fielding candidates for local parliamentary elections, and consolidating their electoral footprint. The authority of the charismatic strong men who lead these groups, backed by extremely loyal memberships, has capitalised on popular conceptions of power as a highly gendered ideal in which capacity for violence is an index of agency and efficacy.[34]

Baladika Bali has its roots in a large martial art school, Bakti Negara, which I knew from earlier trips to Bali. It was founded by influential head of Bakti Negara, who leveraged membership of Baladika from the ranks of the martial art school. Baladika now claims an active membership of over 20,000 young men throughout Bali. Ethnographic opportunity came knocking when I discovered the relationship between the two organisations. Existing friendships and relationships thus opened up new possibilities for research.

Clifford Geertz described the practice of ethnography as professional 'hanging out'.[35] It is more than this, though. My earlier visits demonstrate the importance of relationship building as a fundamental aspect of ethnographic enquiry, and the value of a methodological commitment to open-ended enquiry over time. Hanging out in Bali today one cannot be anything but aware of the global processes and flows that are transforming the island. Whether the threat to the island's water supplies,[36] waste management problems,[37] or the ways in which concerns with security assume such prominence in social and political life,[38] the obvious effects of globalisation are a stark reminder of these connections. Insight into the ways in which people negotiate familiar problems in sites where the confluence of global flows is particularly intense and turbulent contributes to our comprehension of the diverse ways in which people conceptualise and respond to change and social transformation. While the commonality of the modern experience of globalisation cannot be taken for granted, it does provide a conceptual and methodological point of departure for our ethnographic peregrinations. From a loftier vantage point, bounded social imaginaries appear to be inundated by global flows. At a local level, however, these imaginaries are not washed away, but assume new prominence in transformed social, economic, and cultural landscapes. Sensitivity to the power relations that frame the production of ethnographic knowledge is heightened by accountability thrust on us by greater awareness of the interconnectedness of human lives and actions, easier access to global knowledge by those with whom our lives intersect, and ethnographic sensibilities agitated by the increasing precariousness of human existence on this planet. It is not just hanging out in Bali today that is a very different kind of exercise. Those doing the hanging out are themselves different.

In many ways the production of ethnographic knowledge has been transformed by the anthropology of the interconnected. Whether for analytical or heuristic purposes, both difference and distance can no longer be easily assumed, and as a consequence, we are more accountable to our ethnographic interlocutors. An example from Bali to illustrate this point, I was recently introduced to I Made Muliawan, the head of Pemuda Bali Bersatu (PBB, 'United Bali Youth'). Our meeting was at a communal *otonan* celebration (ceremonial birthday). I arrived after the ceremony proper, when twenty or so members of the group were eating and drinking together. PBB are one of the smaller *ormas* in Bali, with some 1,000–1,500 active members, mostly in Denpasar, the capital city. Muliawan, known as 'De Gajah' (the elephant) on account of his imposing physique, is a charismatic figure, well liked by the members of PBB. His easy manner, quick wit, and physical presence contribute to his popularity, and more recently his political success. De Gajah sits in the provincial parliament of Bali as member of Gerindra (*Partai Gerakkan Indonesia Raya* – the Greater Indonesia Movement Party) led by current presidential candidate (April 2019) Prabowo Subianto. As we began to talk about PBB, De Gajah brought up the matter of a newspaper article published in Australia that was highly critical of the activities of *ormas* like PBB in Bali. The article had reported cases of the extortion of expatriate home owners living in Bali by local militia members. As far as I knew this had nothing to do with PBB, but the article painted all these groups in a bad light and gave the impression that Bali had become a gangster's paradise. Needless to say, this had not been well received by militia members in Bali.

As a researcher working on security groups and militia in Indonesia, I had been interviewed for the article. I had given what I thought were fair and objective statements about the prominence of charismatic strong men in Balinese political life. While I had not been directly critical of Balinese militia or their activities, De Gajah and other PBB members called my motives for the current research into question. What were my reasons for interviewing members of PBB? Did I intend to write another article condemning the members of these groups as gangsters and thugs? I justified my position as well as I could, explaining that I had not written the piece, and while I was interviewed by the author, it did not necessarily reflect my views. I explained that as a social scientist I was interested in the widespread presence of groups such as PBB in Bali and throughout Indonesia. The question I wished to answer was why, in arguably the most democratic country in Southeast Asia, these highly militaristic civil organisations continued to grow in popularity? De Gajah took me at my word that my aim was not to defame PBB and their like, but to better understand their place in Balinese society. He was, and PBB remain, open to my questions about their activities, organisation, and political motivation, and this has been the case for the majority of militia that I have worked with in Indonesia.

For my part, being held accountable for what I say publicly about these groups is a good thing, and demands a more open and critical engagement with my interlocutors. Being publicly accountable goes some way to mitigate the skewed power relationships that allow me to write about the people that I hang out with, and often provokes open discussion and debate, and a more politicised ethnographic intervention. Certainly, this approach prevents some things from being said, but arguably no more so than one would expect when working on any sensitive topic.

The accounts I produce of Balinese social and political life, of security groups and their place in Balinese society, contribute in some small way to the discursive production of multiple and discordant representations of Bali in Indonesian and English language media. In these, Bali is constituted as, among other things, a paradisiacal tourist destination, a site of protectionism and extortion, an impending ecological disaster zone, an island under siege from jihadist *fanatik*, and a bastion of Balinese identity and culture. While hanging out in Balinese security spaces, it is these representations of Bali that form the backdrop to ethnographic encounter. Groups such as PBB and Baladika Bali articulate conceptions of Balinese community and values against this backdrop. Part of the appeal of charismatic leaders such as De Gajah and Gus Bota and the organisations they lead is the reference point they offer in shifting social, cultural, and economic landscapes – a normative militancy that strives to secure Bali from the many threats that it faces at the confluence of global flows.

Methods: Graeme

My early research was an ethnographic study of the small town of Ubud and its constitution, ritually and historically in terms of cultural landscape. My plan was to extend this to tracking Balinese cultural/religious expansion into the wider landscape of Indonesia, but the circumstances of my employment and funding provided little opportunity for a project of this scale. Instead I developed a strategy of (more or less) annual visits of five to seven weeks, on a shoestring budget but with few other strings attached. Because I had neither time nor resources for systematic, let alone extended research, I simply 'hung out' in my familiar neighbourhood, more in the mode Geertz refers to than with Lee's enforced reflexivity, until something interesting or important emerged and then followed it as far as I could. Subsequent visits involved a combination of following existing interests and developing new ones. This led to a series of articles and chapters on topics including architecture, electoral politics, rice-farming, legacy of Clifford Geertz, waste management, climate change, disaster recovery, illegal mining, tourism, and cultural heritage.[39] Occasional trips to central Java and India provided material for comparative perspectives on some of these topics as well as others. Twenty years later, some of these interests have faded while others continue. This modus operandi, born of limitations of circumstance and pragmatic or opportunistic depending on one's point of view, reminds us that anthropological method has never been independent of the material circumstances of its production. Mine is not an approach I would recommend as a path to career advancement, but it has proved to have other advantages. While it is grounded primarily in extended engagement with site rather than topic, the accumulated 'ethnographic capital'[40] has (as for Lee) enabled relatively quick and easy shifting between apparently disparate topics. The resulting pattern of generalisation rather than specialisation has also provided a basis for attention to both the big picture outlined above and to some of its parts.

One of these parts is a UNESCO World Heritage (WH) listing of 'The Cultural Landscape of Bali Province: the *subak* system as a manifestation of the Tri Hita Karana Philosophy'. It was listed in 2012, but barely a year later, the WH committee was sufficiently concerned about reported problems, that it advised the Government of Indonesia (GoI) of these concerns. An underlying concern was that the statutory body supposed to manage the heritage estate had not been properly convened. In the event of this not being addressed in an adequate and timely manner, it could conceivably lead to the national embarrassment of delisting. A couple of years later, at the urging of the WH Committee, the GoI invited an 'Advisory Mission' to report on unresolved issues. I became interested, partly through my ongoing research on rice-farming, but also because of discussions with disillusioned members of the team who wrote the application for WH listing, but who had been excluded from the subsequent process.

The best known part of the listing is Jatiluwih, a highland basin of spectacular terraced ricefields, still planted with traditional varieties using traditional methods. Other parts of the listing include highland lakes, irrigation systems, and temples, but the real heart of the listing is the intangible cultural heritage embodied in the bottom-up system of management of water, and the even more intangible set of cultural ideas underlying it. This intangible heritage is what the listing was most seeking to protect.

Jatiluwih has long been a tourist attraction, but after listing, visitor numbers increased dramatically, as did the interest of outside investors, leading to a raft of consequences including rapid inflation of land values, sales of land for hotels and restaurants, and increased traffic flows and parking problems. The district (*kabupaten*) government established a management body, which levies fees on visitors, the proceeds of which are split between government and local community. The community share is divided between multiple local organisations but the farmers' organisations (*subak*) – the very institution the listing seeks to protect – receive only a very small proportion of the proceeds. Farmers see themselves as having created the attraction and carrying most of the costs, but enjoying few of the benefits. These problems, very visible and widely reported in the media, prompted the concern of the WH committee.

The story is complicated, but a key element is the failure of the GoI to establish the system of governance outlined in its application, which was designed to keep the balance of decision-making power in the hands of local communities and especially farmers, rather than government officials. More broadly, the problem is of the kind described by Anna Tsing as 'friction', 'gaps', or 'awkward engagements' between different levels and scales along the spectrum of global process. In this case, the conceptual worlds of WH officials in Paris and farmers in the ricefields are so far apart as to be mutually virtually unintelligible. The application process and subsequent evaluations are intended to bridge this gap, but in practice, the people doing the actual bridging on the ground are relatively low-level officials of local government departments, whose grasp of the values and processes of the WH system are imperfect at best. Their worlds are in fact closer to those of the farmers, despite significant gaps here also.[41]

My main ethnographic intervention into these gaps and frictions was in a distant and lesser known part of the WH listing – also a set of ricefields, whose irrigation waters flow from important temples. Here the problems manifested more subtly, in a set of conflicts within and between *subak*, not really caused by the WH listing, but exacerbated by it and threatening to derail it. These problems have been discussed in detail elsewhere,[42] but in terms of method it was my accumulated ethnographic capital that enabled me to understand and access, fairly quickly and easily, the three *subak* involved, the district government department primarily responsible for managing the WH site, an academic expert advising government, communities and media, as well as other parties involved. In the process I found myself becoming a middleman, trying to help the parties involved articulate their understandings of the problem, but also carrying mediating messages between them. This became an exercise in responsibly engaged ethnographic intervention, both similar and different to that which Lee discusses above.

But this story also illustrates the way global processes, in this case the WH part of the UNESCO system, come home to roost in faraway ricefields they purport to protect, only to encounter the frictions and awkward engagement with local communities with priorities and processes of which they have little if any understanding. Likewise local communities find themselves awkwardly engaged with processes emanating from places unimaginable to them, which appear to promise much but, when they arrive deliver unexpected consequences. In between, are a complex cast of players, but especially various tiers and agencies of government, poorly equipped but struggling to fill the gaps and lubricate the friction. These specific sites of engagement are variously and often awkwardly engaged with other parts of the picture described by Lee and listed above – they are all parts of the same meta-processes which manifest variously at local, national, regional, and global levels. To understand any of this, we need to simultaneously map the larger pattern of flows and make strategic ethnographic interventions into selected points on the 'chains of global connection'[43] between such disparate locations as the WH offices in Paris and the ricefields of Tampaksiring.

CONCLUSION: BALI AS METHOD

The new Bali is, like the new Asia, indeed 'complicated' and the challenges for a new anthropology of Bali are primarily methodological ones, which until now, nobody has really tried to get to grips with. While our own ethnographic experiences, empirical foci, and methodological developments are different, they both respond to the challenges of globalisation and delocalisation of culture first identified in the 1990s. These challenges have not gone away and in Bali they remain largely unresolved, either in practice or in analysis. What we have tried to present here is a model, following Anna Tsing especially, of articulation between different scales of larger process and selective ethnographic focus on specific loci at different levels of scale. Our brief sketches of ethnographic method have identified some of the more specific complications that arise, including challenges of practical engagement, accountability, and communication across gaps of scale and culture.

In an increasingly complex and interconnected world, we can no longer maintain the myth of ethnographic enquiry as a primarily descriptive project. Rather, there is a need for greater sensitivity to the real and produced nature of the social realities that we report on,[44] and the part we play in contributing to the discursive production and perpetuation of these realities. Increased emphasis on intervention as part of any ethnographic engagement does not resolve the problem of representation, but it does bring it more readily to the fore in analysis. Our role then as ethnographers is to trace relations, make sense of global connections and flows, and indeed incommensurabilities between levels of scale as we encounter them. This we have learnt from working in Bali.

* * *

NOTES

1. Major works of this period include Fredrik Barth's *Balinese Worlds* (1993), Henk Schulte-Nordholt's *Spell of Power* (1996), Michel Picard's *Cultural Tourism*

and Touristic Culture (1996), Stephen Lansing's *Priests and Programmers* (1991), Adrian Vickers' *Bali: A Paradise Created* (1989), Margaret Wiener's *Visible and Invisible Realms* (1995), Carol Warren's *Adat and Dinas* (1993), Unni Wikan's *Managing Turbulent Hearts* (1990), as well as collections edited by Hildred Geertz (1991), Adrian Vickers (1996), Rachaelle Rubinstein, and Linda Connor (1999). Other prominent researchers of this period include Mark Hobart, Angela Hobart, Leo Howe, Jean-Francois Guermonprez, Arlette Ottino, Urs Ramseyer.

2. Miguel Covarrubias, *Island of Bali* (New York: Alfred Knopf, 1937).

3. Victor Emanuel Korn, *Het Adatrech van Bali* (s'Gravenhage: G. Naeff, 1932).

4. Raechelle Rubinstein, and Linda Connor, ed., *Staying Local in the Global Village: Bali in the Twentieth Century* (Honolulu: University of Hawaii Press, 1999).

5. Boon, James, *The Anthropological Romance of Bali 1597–1972: Dynamic Perspectives in Marriage & Caste, Politics & Religion* (Cambridge; London; New York; Melbourne: Cambridge University Press, 1977).

6. Geoffrey Robinson, *The Dark Side of Paradise: Political Violence in Bali* (Ithaca: Cornell University Press, 1990).

7. For example, Stroma Cole, and Mina Browne, "Tourism and Water Inequity in Bali: A Social-Ecological Systems Analysis," *Human Ecology* 43, no. 3 (2015): 439–450; Darma Putra, *A Literary Mirror* (Leiden: Brill, 2011); Lorenzen, Rachel, and Dik Roth, "Paradise Contested: Culture, Politics and Changing Land and Water Use in Bali," *The Asia Pacific Journal of Anthropology* 16, no. 2 (2015): 99–105; and MacDonald, Matt, and Wilson, Lee, "Trouble in Paradise: Contesting Security in Bali," *Security Dialogue* 48, no. 3 (2017): 241–258.

8. There were 4.2 million foreign tourist arrivals in 2016 (Republika 2017). The average spend per visit in 2015 was estimated as US $1,200 (Wall Street Journal 2015).

9. Graeme MacRae, "Community and Cosmopolitanism in the New Ubud," *Annals of Tourism Research* 59, issue C (2016): 16–29.

10. Graeme MacRae, "Frontier Bali: Local Scales and Levels of Global Processes," in *Transnational Frontiers of Asia and Latin America since 1800*, ed. Jaime Morena Tejada, and Bradley Tatar (London; New York: Routledge, 2016), 179–192.

11. The basis of membership in Balinese neighbourhoods (*banjar*) and especially villages (*desa*) is obligations of participation in Hindu ritual. While most communities have provisions for non-Hindu residents, this does not happen automatically and it is seen as exceptional rather than normal.

12. Pamela Allen, and Palermo Carmencita, "Ajeg Bali: Multiple Meanings, Diverse Agendas," *Indonesia and the Malay World* 33, no. 97 (November 2005): 239–255.

13. I have not yet seen any official statistical evidence of this, but it is fairly general common knowledge (e.g., Bali Discovery 2015) as well as being qualitatively apparent in my own ethnographic field of Ubud.

14. This precarity became painfully obvious during the tourism downturn after the bombings in 2002 and 2005. At the time of writing the possibility of an eruption of Mt. Agung threatens to dramatically reveal this again.

15. Lee Wilson, and Ery Nugroho, "For the Good of the People: Governing Societal Organisations in Indonesia," *Inside Indonesia*, 09 Jul–Sep 2012.

16. Graeme MacRae, "The Value of Land in Bali: Land Tenure, Land Reform and Commodification," in *Inequality, Crisis and Social Change in Indonesia: The Muted Worlds of Bali*, ed. Thomas Reuter (London: Routledge/Curzon, 2003).

17. Bali Government Tourism Office, "Buku Statistik Pariwisata Bali Tahun," 2019. https://disparda.baliprov.go.id/buku-statistik-pariwisata-bali-tahun-2019/.

18. Akhil Gupta, and James Ferguson, ed., *Culture, Power, Place: Explorations in Critical Anthropology* (Durham; London: Duke University Press, 1997).

19. Kuan-Hsing Chen, *Asia as Method: Toward Deimperialization* (Durham; London: Duke University Press, 2010), also introduction to this volume.

20. Tri Hita Karana refers to a triad of supposedly harmonious relationships between humans, the natural environment, and the supernatural world, much celebrated in recent years and oft-cited by politicians, officials, and the media but also increasingly embedded into everyday Balinese discourse. Its status as a neo-traditional ideology has been insightfully analysed by Dik Roth, "Reframing Tri Hita Karana: From 'Balinese Culture' to Politics," *The Asia Pacific Journal of Anthropology* 16, no. 2 (February 2015): 157–175.

21. The late, lamented Made Wijaya made this point consistently, insightfully, and amusingly, mostly on Facebook and YouTube.

22. Recent examples include Birgit Brauchler, *Diverging Ecologies on Bali* (2018); Birgit Brauchler, *Bali Tolak Reklamsi* (2018); Stroma Cole, and Mia Browne, *Tourism and Water Inequity in Bali* (2015); Darma Putra, *A Literary Mirror* (2011); Paul Green, *Biomedicine and 'Risky' Retirement Destinations* (2016); Graeme MacRae, *Frontier Bali* (2016), Graeme MacRae, *Community and Cosmopolitanism in the New Ubud* (2016), Michel Picard, *The Appropriation of Religion in Southeast Asia and Beyond* (2017); Thomas Reuter, *Understanding Food System Resilience in Bali* (2018); Agung Wardana, *Debating Spatial Governance in the Pluralistic Institutional and Legal Setting of Bali* (2015); Carol Warren, *Leadership, Social Capital and Coastal Community Resource Governance* (2016); Thomas Wright, *Water, Tourism, and Social Change* (2015).

23. George Marcus, "Ethnography In/Of the World System: The Emergence of Multi-Sited Ethnography," *Annual Review of Anthropology* 24 (1995): 95–117.

24. Matei Candea, "Arbitrary Locations: In Defence of the Bounded Fieldsite," *Journal of the Royal Anthropological Institute* 13, no. 1 (2007): 167–184.

25. Eric Wolf, *Europe and the People Without History* (Berkeley: University of California Press, 1982).

26. Stephen J. Collier, and Aihwa Ong, "Global Assemblages, Anthropological Problems," in *Global Assemblages: Technology, Politics, and Ethics as Anthropological Problems*, ed. Stephen J. Collier, and Aihwa Ong (Oxford: Blackwell Publishing, 2005), 3–21.

27. Aihwa Ong, "Graduated Sovereignty in South-East Asia," *Theory, Culture & Society* 17, no. 4 (2005): 55–75.

28. Anna Lowenhaupt Tsing, *Friction: An Ethnography of Global Connection* (Princeton; Oxford: Princeton University, 2005).

29. For example, Clifford Geertz, *Negara: The Theatre State in Nineteenth Century Bali* (Princeton: Princeton University Press, 1980), Shelley Errington, *Meaning and Power in a Southeast Asian Realm* (Princeton: Princeton University

Press, 1989), and Stanley Tambiah, *World Conqueror and World Renouncer: A Study of Buddhism and Polity in Thailand Against a Historical Background* (Cambridge: Cambridge University Press, 1976).

30. Pamela Allen, and Palermo Carmencita, Ajeg Bali (2005).

31. Henk Schulte Nordholt, *Bali: An Open Fortress, 1995–2005* (Leiden: KITLV, 2007), 31.

32. Carol Warren, "Indonesian Development Policy and Community Organization in Bali," *Contemporary Southeast Asia* 8, no. 3 (1986): 213–230.

33. Henk Schulte Nordholt, *Bali: An Open Fortress 1995–2005: Regional Autonomy, Electoral Democracy and Entrenched Identities* (Singapore: National University of Singapore Press, 2007).

34. Lee Wilson, *Martial Arts and the Body Politic in Indonesia* (Leiden: Brill, 2015).

35. Clifford Geertz, "Deep Hanging Out," *The New York Review of Books* 45 no. 16 (1998): 69.

36. Stroma Cole, and Mia Browne, "Tourism and Water Inequity in Bali: A Social-Ecological systems Analysis," *Human Ecology* 43, no. 3 (2015): 439–450.

37. Graeme MacRae, and Liljana Rodic, "The Weak Link in Waste Management in Tropical Asia? Solid Waste Collection in Bali," *Habitat International* 50 (2015): 310–316.

38. Matt MacDonald, and Lee Wilson, "Trouble in Paradise: Contesting Security in Bali," *Security Dialogue* 48, no. 3 (2017): 241–258.

39. Some of these have been published in other disciplinary contexts, the challenges of which are another methodological story.

40. 'Ethnographic capital' is my term, drawing on Bourdieu's metaphor of different kinds of capital and especially their exchangeability (1991: 230) to refer to the body of experience, cultural/linguistic knowledge, relationships and networks accumulated over the course of extended ethnographic research and which can be used strategically in other related contexts.

41. The structural impediment to bureaucratic effectiveness created by the cross-cutting of departmental divisions and hierarchical levels of administration is essentially similar to the one identified in India (and discussed in more detail by Akhil Gupta in *Red Tape: Bureaucracy, Structural Violence and Poverty in India* (Durham; London: Duke University Press, 2012)).

42. Graeme MacRae, "Universal Heritage and Local Livelihoods: 'Friction' at the World Cultural Heritage Listing in Bali," *International Journal of Heritage Studies* 23, no. 9 (2017): 846–859.

43. Tsing, *Friction.*

44. John Law, and John Urry, "Enacting the Social," *Economy and Society* 33, no. 3 (2004): 390–410.

REFERENCES

Allen, Pamela, and Carmencita, Palermo. "Ajeg Bali: Multiple Meanings, Diverse Agendas." *Indonesia and the Malay World* 33, no. 97 (November 2005): 239–255.

Bali Government Tourism Office. "Buku Statistik Pariwisata Bali Tahun." 2019. https://disparda.baliprov.go.id/buku-statistik-pariwisata-bali-tahun-2019/

Barth, Fredrik. *Balinese Worlds*. Chicago; London: University of Chicago Press, 1993.

Boon, James. *The Anthropological Romance of Bali 1597–1972: Dynamic Perspectives in Marriage & Caste, Politics & Religion*. Cambridge; London; New York; Melbourne: Cambridge University Press, 1977.

Bourdieu, Pierre. *Language and Symbolic Power* (ed. J. Thompson). Cambridge: Polity Press, 1991.

Brauchler, Birgit. "Diverging Ecologies on Bali." *Sojourn: Journal of Social Issues in Southeast Asia* 33, no. 2 (July 2018): 362–396.

———. "Bali Tolak Reklamasi: The Local Adoption of Global Protest." *Convergence: The International Journal of Research Into New Media Technologies* 26, no. 3 (October 2018): 620-638.

Candea, Matei. "Arbitrary Locations: In Defence of the Bounded Field-Site." *Journal of the Royal Anthropological Institute* 13, no. 1 (2007): 167–184.

Chen, Kuan-Hsing. *Asia as Method: Toward Deimperialization*. Durham; London: Duke University Press, 2010.

Cole, Stroma, and Browne, Mia. "Tourism and Water Inequity in Bali: A Social-Ecological Systems Analysis." *Human Ecology* 43, no. 3 (2015): 439–450.

Collier, Stephen J., and Ong, Aihwa. 2005. "Global Assemblages, Anthropological Problems." In *Global Assemblages: Technology, Politics, and Ethics as Anthropological Problems*, edited by Stephen J. Collier, and Aihwa Ong, 3–21. Oxford: Blackwell Publishing, 2005.

Covarrubias, Miguel. *Island of Bali*. New York: Alfred Knopf, 1937.

Darma Putra, I Nyoman. *A Literary Mirror; Balinese Reflections on Modernity and Identity in the Twentieth Century*. Leiden, Boston: Brill, 2011.

Errington, Shelley. *Meaning and Power in a Southeast Asian Realm*. Princeton: Princeton University Press, 1989.

Geertz, Clifford. *Negara: The Theatre State in Nineteenth Century Bali*. Princeton: Princeton University Press, 1980.

———. "Deep Hanging Out." *The New York Review of Books* 45, no. 16 (1988): 69.

Geertz, Hildred, ed. *State and Society in Bali: Historical, Textual and Anthropological Approaches*. Leiden: KITLV Press, 1991.

Green, Paul. "Biomedicine and 'Risky' Retirement Destinations: Older Western Residents in Ubud, Bali." *Medical Anthropology: Cross-Cultural Studies in Health and Illness* 35, no. 2 (2016): 147–160.

Gupta, Akhil. *Red Tape: Bureaucracy, Structural Violence and Poverty in India*. Durham; London: Duke University Press, 2012.

Gupta Akhil, and Ferguson, James, ed. *Culture, Power, Place: Explorations in Critical Anthropology*. Durham; London: Duke University Press, 1997.

Hitchcock Michael, and I. N. Darma Putra. *Tourism, Development and Terrorism in Bali*. Aldershot, UK: Ashgate, 2007.

Korn, V.E. *Het Adatrech van Bali*. s'Gravenhage: G. Naeff, 1932.

Law, John, and Urry, John. "Enacting the Social." *Economy and Society* 33 no. 3 (2004): 390–410.

Lewis Jeff, and Belinda Lewis. *Bali's Silent Crisis: Desire, Tragedy and Transition.* Lanham, USA; Plymouth, UK: Lexington Books, 2009.

Lorenzen, Rachel, and Dik Roth. "Paradise Contested: Culture, Politics and Changing Land and Water Use in Bali." *The Asia Pacific Journal of Anthropology* 16, no. 2 (2015): 99–105.

MacDonald, Matt, and Wilson, Lee. "Trouble in Paradise: Contesting Security in Bali." *Security Dialogue* 48, no. 3 (2017): 241–258.

MacRae. Graeme. "The Value of Land in Bali: Land Tenure, Land Reform and Commodification." In *Inequality, Crisis and Social Change in Indonesia: The Muted Worlds of Bali*, edited by Thomas Reuter, 172–194. London: Routledge/ Curzon, 2003.

———. "Rice Farming in Bali: Organic Production and Marketing Challenges." *Critical Asian Studies* 43, no. 1 (2011): 69–92.

———. "Frontier Bali: Local Scales and Levels of Global Processes." In *Transnational Frontiers of Asia and Latin America since 1800*, edited by Jaime Morena Tejada and Bradley Tatar, 179–192. London; New York: Routledge, 2016a.

———. "Community and Cosmopolitanism in the New Ubud." *Annals of Tourism Research* 59, issue C (2016b): 16–29.

———. "Universal Heritage and Local Livelihoods: "friction" at the World Cultural Heritage listing in Bali." *International Journal of Heritage Studies* 23, no. 9 (2017): 846–859.

MacRae, Graeme, and Rodic, Liljana. "The Weak Link in Waste Management in Tropical Asia? Solid Waste Collection in Bali." *Habitat International* 50 (2015): 310–316.

Marcus, George. "Ethnography In/Of the World System: The Emergence of Multi-Sited Ethnography." *Annual Review of Anthropology* 24 (1995): 95–117.

Ong, Aihwa. "Graduated Sovereignty in South-East Asia." *Theory, Culture & Society* 17, no. 4 (2000): 55–75.

Picard, Michel. *Bali: Cultural Tourism and Touristic Culture.* Singapore: Archipelago Press, 1996.

———. ed. *The Appropriation of Religion in Southeast Asia and Beyond.* London: Palgrave Macmillan, 2017.

Republika. "Kunjungan Wisatawan ke Bali Naik 23 Persen." 5 September 2017. http://nasional.republika.co.id/berita/nasional/daerah/17/09/05/ovs96r328-kunjungan-wisatawan-ke-bali-naik-23-persen.

Reuter, Thomas. *Custodians of the Sacred Mountains: Culture and Society in the Highlands of Bali.* Honolulu: University of Hawai'i Press, 2002.

———. "Understanding Food System Resilience in Bali: A Moral Economy Approach." *Culture, Agriculture, Food and Environment* 41, no. 1 (2019): 4–14.

Robinson, Geoffrey. *The Dark Side of Paradise: Political Violence in Bali.* Ithaca: Cornell University Press, 1995.

Roth, Dik. "Reframing Tri Hita Karana: from 'Balinese Culture' to Politics." *The Asia Pacific Journal of Anthropology* 16, no. 2 (February 2015): 157–175.

Rubinstein, Rachaelle, and Connor, Linda. ed. *Staying Local in the Global Village: Bali in the Twentieth Century.* Honolulu: University of Hawai'i Press, 1999.

Schulte Nordholt, Henk. *The Spell of Power: A History of Balinese Politics, 1650–1940.* Leiden: KITLV Press, 1996.

———. *Bali: An Open Fortress, 1995–2005: Regional Autonomy, Electoral Democracy and Entrenched Identities.* Leiden: KITLV, 2007.

Tambiah, Stanley Jeyaraja. *World Conqueror and World Renouncer: A Study of Buddhism and Polity in Thailand Against a Historical Background.* Cambridge: Cambridge University Press, 1976.

Tsing, Anna Lowenhaupt. *Friction: An Ethnography of Global Connection.* Princeton; Oxford: Princeton University Press, 2005.

Vickers, Adrian. *Bali: A Paradise Created.* Hong Kong: Periplus Editions, 1989.

———. ed. *Being Modern in Bali: Image and Change.* New Haven: Yale University Southeast Asia Studies, 1996.

Wall Street Journal. "The Numbers: Indonesia's Tourism Industry." 1 June 2015. https://blogs.wsj.com/briefly/2015/06/01/indonesias-tourism-industry-the-numbers/.

Wardana, Agung. "Debating Spatial Governance in the Pluralistic Institutional and Legal Setting of Bali." *The Asia Pacific Journal of Anthropology* 16, no. 2 (2015): 106–122.

Warren, Carol. "Indonesian Development Policy and Community Organization in Bali." *Contemporary Southeast Asia* 8, no. 3 (1986): 213–230.

———. *Adat and Dinas: Balinese Communities in the Indonesian State.* Kuala Lumpur; Oxford: Oxford University Press, 1995.

———. "Leadership, Social Capital and Coastal Community Resource Governance: The Case of the Destructive Seaweed Harvest in West Bali." *Human Ecology* 44, no. 3 (June 2016): 329–339.

Wiener, Margaret. *Visible and Invisible Realms: Power, Magic, and Colonial Conquest in Bali.* Chicago; London: University of Chicago Press, 1995.

Wikan, Unni. *Managing Turbulent Hearts: A Balinese Formula for Living.* Chicago; London: University of Chicago Press, 1990.

Wilson, Lee. *Martial Arts and the Body Politic in Indonesia.* Leiden: Brill, 2015.

Wilson, Lee, and Nugroho, Ery. For the Good of the People: Governing Societal Organisations in Indonesia. *Inside Indonesia,* 9 Jul–Sep 2012. http://www.insideindonesia.org/for-the-good-of-the-people

Wolf, Eric. *Europe and the People Without History.* Berkeley: University of California Press, 1982.

Wright, Thomas. "Water, Tourism, and Social Change: A Discussion of Environmental Perceptions in Bali." *Journal Kajian Bali/Journal of Balinese Studies* 5, no. 1 (2015): 1–22.

Section III

NOTES ON POSITIONALITY

Chapter 8

'We Have Always Been Cosmopolitan'

*Towards Anthropologies of
Contemporary Complexity in Japan*

Paul Hansen

ABSTRACT

This chapter is an attempt to reflexively examine an anthropological life in, and now I daresay of, Japan. The analysis, clearly micro in scope, attempts to dodge the critique of being 'narcissistic' through situating its discussion within what German Sociologist Ulrich Beck has called our 'Cosmopolitan Moment'; the point in history where dwelling with 'the Other', human or non-human, are conditions that are forced upon us regardless of choice. Broadening this notion of cosmopolitan thinking, to be, as Donna Haraway recently notes, is to always to 'be with' and who or what with has been an ever-widening concern for social scientists, perhaps especially so for those with epistemological practices rooted in ethnographic research and writing both of which are by necessity idiosyncratic and personal. Yet, anthropology has been constructed around the notion of us and them, etic and emic, researcher and informant. And perhaps nowhere is this theme more prominent than the classic anthropology of Japan, *The Chrysanthemum and the Sword: Patterns of Japanese Culture*. But as Clifford Geertz once questioned, what is a fieldworker do when 'the Zande are no longer themselves'? In other words, what to do when the taken-for-granted ethnographic wisdom of the Other no longer fits with the reality of how the Other lives today or how a researcher encounters and recounts the lives of their interlocutors. Often, lives with whom they are now deeply entwined?

When one is married into the field, has children whose native tongue is Japanese, makes a living as a part of the local economy with all the complexity that entails, can one be an objective outsider? Can one help

171

not to 'go native' confounding the hallmark of what was once responsible anthropology? In such conditions of cosmopolitan precarity and irony, one lives and researchers in a liminal state that impacts how research is conducted and how findings are interpreted and presented. Daily, one must 'do', one must exist at a confluence of research and cosmopolitics.

* * *

We Have Never Been Modern is the title of Bruno Latour's oft-cited analysis of contemporary techno-cratic society.[1] Its central claim is that self-proclaimed moderns exist in socio-politically constructed 'lifeworlds',[2] wherein nature and culture have been artificially separated and ordered largely through European Enlightenment ideas and ideals.[3] Though theoretical and practiced boundaries separating both human and non-human subjects clearly predate modernity – from religious origin stories to Aristotle's Scale of Nature – by the seventeenth century, scientific classification systems were increasingly used to separate species, and indeed *homo sapiens*, in absolute and paradigmatic terms. Life was 'progressively' segregated through defining and cataloguing *being* as a static state of *belonging*: that is to say, living subjects ascribed to a specific and definitive genus. From the eighteenth century, Romanticism further extended such ordering logic to *anthropos* and its cultures viewing subjects as belonging, or being of, one folk grouping or another (e.g., *volkskunde* or *völkerkunde*).[4] These modes of thinking about human specificity became particularly prevalent in late nineteenth and mid-twentieth centuries through a Victorian and Social Darwinian emphasis on spaces, races, and eugenics, creating both evolutionary hierarchies of perceived complexity (biological and intellectual) and linking demarcated places (nations and later nation-states) to everyday socio-cultural practices like language, arts, or marriage customs: for example, being a product of high culture, East Asia, or antiquity.[5] Thus, thinking in terms of modernity, from Linnaeus to Kant and on to contemporary anthropology, constructing categories (*the ordering and bordering of life as it were*) is what moderns, and specifically modern social scientists, have done, are trained to do, and largely continue to do.

However, this chapter queries if bordering and ordering beings is what contemporary social scientists, but especially anthropologists as ethnographers (and more specifically those permanently based in Japan), ought to be doing. In sum, are ethnographers in Japan – and keeping with the theme of this book, surely those in other parts of Asia – doing justice or violence to the diversity that long-term fieldwork as an epistemological practice affords? Or, do anthropological ethnographers tend to reify given macro-level interpretations through ignoring, and indeed being enticed to ignore, the everyday existential and phenomenological contingencies and anomalies that make up the experience of both their own lives and those they study?[6] Put another way, how often do long-term ethnographers cast aside common experiences of classificatory conflict and confusion – encounters with the 'liminal'[7] or with 'betweenness'[8] that are inherent in the prolonged micro level, existential dis-order of ethnographic encounter – to retire from the field and 'purify',[9] 'invent',[10] 'confirm, or even conform to',[11] neat and orderly, pre-conceived, macro-level categories and systems of classification? I contend that they do it too often and unquestioningly. They do it just as easily as I use the word 'Japan' above as though it were some trouble-free rubric, an unquestioned and accepted 'social fact' and not a lived and experiential 'concern'.[12]

My title is intended to be a non-hostile rejoinder to Latour. *We Have Never Been Modern*. Indeed, this is the case. But I agree with him on terms he might disapprove of. It is because *we*, both humans and non-humans, have always been multispecies cosmopolitans, category disruptions that modernist thinking would clearly eschew.[13] We are a mobile and messy (indeed, *meshy*)[14] muddle of beings who are ever-becoming. That is to say, each sentient creature emerges through a unique history of individuated and entwined experiences and intersections. Life, and its day-to-day vitality, has always, overtly or subversively, defied the *episteme du jour*, the carefully crafted order of things.[15]

This chapter focuses on how anthropological research has changed and how it seems, to me at least, to be changing. It reflexively examines my experience as an anthropologist of, and I daresay within, Japanese cosmo-politics.[16] I have lived in Japan on and off for fifteen years, steadily residing and working in the country since 2011. My research has ranged in focus from dairy farm industrialisation in rural Hokkaido, to dog–human compan-ionship in urban areas, to young Japanese tourists in Jamaica. I will discuss the dog–human aspects of this fieldwork as a way to underscore cosmo-litical connections and conditions in which contemporary anthropologists live and work. Moreover, my wife is Japanese and my Hokkaido-born son is Japanese Canadian. Obviously, the notion of a distant and disconnected observer *of* Japan is far surpassed by my role of a day in, day out partici-pant *in* Japan. While such an analysis is clearly micro in scope, I attempt to dodge the critique of being overly narrow or narcissistic through situating its discussion within recent realisations of our posthuman interconnections and what the late German Sociologist Ulrich Beck called our 'cosmopolitan moment', a period of 'forced cosmopolitanism' (however unequally being a whole other important issue).[17] The essential point here is that anthropologist or not, we increasingly find ourselves thrust into relations – with humans, other animals, and technologies – regardless of our individual actions or desires. And in this sense, we are less cosmopolitans by choice, a decidedly Kantian notion, but more 'akin' to what Donna Haraway extends beyond the human: our 'becoming is always becoming with' both sentient others,[18] alongside the environment and its 'things'.[19] This has been an ever-widening and phenomenologically catholic concern for individuals conducting ethnographic research and writing, both of which are necessarily idiosyncratic and personal practices whether one is focusing on relations with humans or more-than-humans.[20] In short, beyond any individual researcher, there is a growing acceptance of cosmopolitical conditions that exceed the aforementioned regimes of closed classification. More to the point at hand, such conditions and connections undermine Area Studies as a meaningful moniker, certainly if 'area' is taken to mean, as it commonly is, a bounded ethnic, social, political, economic, cultural totality and not 'merely' localised or individuated present-tense practices and relations.[21]

Thus, bumping up against anthropology's already suspect individualised embodied and affective methodology, 'being there' and 'participant observation', the discipline has in many ways been historically, and at present detrimentally, constructed around notions of classificatory segregation and distancing. Ethnography is an epistemic practice with deep immunological drives, with Othering, despite the proximity of encounter, being an attempt to clearly segregate kind and kin, us and them, etic and emic, researcher and informant. And perhaps nowhere in the record of modern anthropology is this theme of us vis-à-vis them more prominently showcased than in the classic anthropology of Japan, or better of Japaneseness, than *The Chrysanthemum and the Sword: Patterns of Japanese Culture*.[22] But as Clifford Geertz queried, what is a researcher to do when, even with the venerable Evans-Prichard as a textual guide, an anthropologist finds that 'the Zande are no longer themselves'? [23] What happens when in the contemporary ethnographic encounter 'they' don't act in concert with how we are led to believe they should given past anthropological accounts? What does the participant observer do when the taken-for-granted ethnographic wisdom of the 'Other-as-known' and 'Other-in-place' no longer fits with the reality of how the Other-lives-today, or indeed, how a researcher lives with them?

THE EASE OF *-ESE*: THE MANUFACTURE
AND MANAGEMENT OF OTHERNESS

To start, if we can (a) agree that we have long lived cosmopolitan lives, with life, human, or otherwise, disrespectful of a carefully crafted boxed and bordered world, and if we can also agree, along with Latour, that (b) the separation of nature and culture has been a false dichotomy, then (c) ethnographic 'Area Studies' as a paradigm originally rooted in the play of classification and cultural relativism becomes a deeply problematic proposition.[24]

First, such research is generally predicated on modern bounds and borders such as China or Cambodia, down to subregions, such as rural Yunnan or a given district of Phnom Penh. Yet, in many cases this modernist, or nation-state oriented, partitioning represents a contemporary historical conundrum more than a solid foundation for an inquiry into shared socio-cultural relations and practices, a point James Scott brilliantly outlines in the context of South and Southeast Asia as a 'shatter zone' and an idea Deirdre McKay extends to the nodal-global networks of Filipino migrants.[25] In short, it is becoming apparent in a mounting number of contemporary cases that the classic spaces of Area Studies are often not organic delineations but find root in nineteenth-century political and economic categories and constructions. These clearly demarcated areas often either defy the existence of any known origin point or alternatively rely on a specific date, a national independence or confederation day, to announce their presence. Moreover, borders are ever-shifting and seldom impermeable. Thus, for 'the people' that Area Studies scholars might refer to as a unified 'they' under study, the 'space' defined as a nation is often not viewed as synonymous with the everyday and experiential 'place' these people know and experience. Indeed, the lion's share of contemporary nation-states is macro-level constructions rooted in the typification of values. On paper these spaces are inhabited by abstracted averages not living individuals. In other words, the 'they' of the state is a statistically 'made up' people.[26] In sum, East Asia and beyond, modern states are cobbled together through a confluence of economics and politics with traditions and customs often ignored, invented, or imagined to reify homogeneity.[27] These conceptualisations of people and place are often imposed from the top down and tied to spatially concrete locations in retrospect, such as Japan's four main islands viewed as receptacle for 'the' Japanese people who share values and ways of being from some immutable (though ever unknown) origin point. This Romantic Herder inspired view of the nation or *ethnie* as a container of socio-cultural dominant practices is widely accepted, yet in actuality this is a confluence of myth and manufactured memory.[28] But why do these ideas of uniting people and place persist and how has this happened?

First, it could be argued (though I would not) that this notion of 'politicised space-as-container' is a sufficient foundation for academic disciplines that primarily focus on macro analysis such as political science, economics, or even sociology. In this sense, anthropology's focus on ethnographic field-work – interactive and individuated everyday existential processes – makes the discipline an epistemic outlier in the social sciences. This is not to say that other social sciences have got things wrong and anthropology or psychology is right. But it is a matter of scale and perspective that begs consideration. In any mappable space one can take opinion polls to derive percentages of localised public opinion and action. Indeed, this sort of study underpins much social science, for instance, Pierre Bourdieu's influential and omnipresent sociological work and the sort of statistical or composite focused data that such research produces.[29] Getting back to Asia, for example, there certainly exists a recognised area called Taiwan with defined (if constantly negotiable) borders and policies. There is a *legal* identity related to that country, concretised with documents such as a passport claiming that the entitled holder is Taiwanese. This designation differs from one marked Korea or Kyrgyzstan alongside enforceable rights and privileges availed by the owner. Japan and China have GDP values that can be cautiously compared. And one could continue on. Agriculture differs region to region, as mangos cannot be farmed in Hokkaido and cows produce less milk in tropical climates like Okinawa. All of these points are accurate enough bird's-eye observations and generalisations. There are regional and national differences and such differences can be mapped, averaged out, and attributed sober numeric values. In other words, people and places have a history open to typification and median making. However, we often find conflicting and plural histories of population and place – heterotopic interpretations of a single location. And this fluidity, this lack of a shared experience despite macro-level narratives of unification, is one reason why utilising area as a standard linked to social structure or cultural identity has always been problematic from a micro level perspective. Even leaving out contemporary mobility, in ethnographic fieldwork, personality, contingency, and anomaly ascend as particularities of idiosyncratic encounter. Sound ethnographic research is never produced through abstracted generalities but via experienced specifics.

Consequently, there is a second, linked, and more pressing problem for anthropology of an Area Studies ilk rooted in an uncritical acceptance and transference of these common macro-oriented definitions, methods, and findings. Given the above predominance of research focus on physical locations and the concomitant conventional assumption that socio-cultural ethnicities and identities are tied to (or more damning contained within) them, there is a popular acceptance, and common academic credence, extended to a dangerous form of classificatory shorthand. I call it the 'the ease of -*ese*'. In sum, the ease of -*ese* is an overly simplistic and pervasive common-sense notion of *be-longing*. That is, the aforementioned modern logic of *being* as something clearly classifiable joined with a desire, the romantic notion of *longing* – whether researcher or researched – for subjects to be *of* a bound and identifiable location or grouping of people. Its discursive ubiquity can be observed, for example, in the idea that there exists a particular and shared way of knowing, doing, feeling, (and the verbs could continue) tied to a specific geography and extended to an equally shared ethnicity: Japan*ese* notions of intimacy, Taiwan*ese* food ways, or Vietnam*ese* hospitality. Of course, there are cases where location – the land or environment itself – is intimately related to identity whether imposed or self-proclaimed as found in Indigenous ways of knowing or land claims issues from the Amazon to Australia.[30] But the influence of the ease of *-ese* in anthropology I am referring to is more generalisable. For example, it can be clearly viewed in the historical record of regional kinship structures.

Kinship remains a disciplinary lingua franca in anthropology. Yet the reason kinship study is always under duress, yet nevertheless unlikely to fade away, is because at the level of experiential encounter, the core of ethnographic accounting, familial relations vary and shift depending on a given interlocutor. For example, researchers must contend with divorce, remarriage, adoption, fictive kinship, affairs, same-sex partnerships, relations with technologies and augmentations like robotics, and in my own ethnographic examples to follow, cross-cultural marriages and cross-species family members. In short, cosmopolitical relations are often messy and boundary-frustrating connections. Moreover, there are day-to-day disagreements that surround these relationships, further complicating attempts at earnest generalised and systematic classifications of them. Yet, from the classic openness of Hawai'ian kinship, to Sudanese kin complexity, and on to the presumed hierarchy of Japanese *ie*, space linked to people and then further linked to agency remains a commonly shared anthropological tri-part imaginary. Yet, as outlined in the examples that follow, given our forced cosmopolitan and posthuman times, kinship tied to a particular place, ideology, ethnicity, or activities is a descriptive and explanatory device nearing its sell by date. Times, people, and places change and ethnographers need to shift with them and adapt to them. But it is not a simple matter of discarding the ease of *-ese*. It remains a useful shorthand. For anthropologists though, it is a matter of micro level awareness, of ever-reminding ourselves that we need to see past the equation of area = people = culture = social structure. We need to put such 'common'-sense linkages aside even to capture the 'trans-local' themes of current mainstream social science, let alone to get anywhere novel.[31]

How have anthropologists, researchers with their proverbial feet-on-the-ground, been so easily co-opted into discussing their findings in such essentialist language? The problem, as I see it, is that many ethnographers, rather than taking time in the field, trusting their interlocutors and accounting for individual differences find it easier to assume there is a shared social fact, an omnipresent, unifying, and explanatory '-ese'. In so doing, and perhaps unwittingly, they often presume a neocolonial stance. A presumption that 'their' Others do not house the intelligence, creativity, and individuality to avoid conventions or to 'objectively' observe and express themselves. However, what this amounts to is a way of not encountering interlocutors as fellow human beings, as individuals as complex and intersectional as a given researcher is in terms of ideology or biology.[32] The greatest ease in utilising -*ese* is that its deployment acts as a glue that can pervade place and social relations (not to mention singular minds) past, present, and presumable future. Indeed, assuming a shared -*ese* can trump micro level confusions and anomalies. Attributing an act to, or interaction with, an affirming '-*ese*' feels like the satisfying 'click' of pushing plastic tabs together on a child's toy: 'ahh, the Japanese are group centred, humble, love nature, (add stereotype)'. Thus, 'my Japanese', of whatever chosen intersection, ought to fit this mould. Or alternatively, 'my Japanese' exist as an intersectional group counterbalancing these hegemonic norms as a unified sub- or counterculture. And, comparable to plastic building blocks, the ease of -*ese* allows standardisation: one can erect elaborate general theories rooted in a presumed conformity of place and uniformity of people that is, simply, not there without its manufacture.

To be clear, all of this is to say one thing and not say another. First, given these conventional Area Studies presumptions – space as bounded place alongside persons as stand-in examples for 'a' people – anthropology of such ilk seems a mode of scholarship with a burgeoning identity crisis rooted in the precarious nature and maintenance of its modernist categories. It is bound by its own classification strategies; strategies – as outlined below – that often fit poorly with contemporary conditions found during the process of ethnographic fieldwork or prolonged time spent living there. In short, Area Studies (be it Japanese Studies, Korean Studies, and perhaps most absurdly given the clear breadth and diversity of presumption, Chinese Studies) is an outdated 'multicultural' project and as such it is opposed to engaging with cosmopolitical realities.[33]

Second, obviously and importantly, none of this should be read as a claim that location and identity do not matter. Quite the opposite, the point forwarded here is that they actually *matter even more* than we often give credit. When over inclusive categories like -*ese* are deployed, living places are sealed shut and identities are attributed and frozen in time. But an individual's identity is often highly idiosyncratic in our cosmopolitical times. Identity emerges from a host of intersections both ascribed and/or chosen (gender, class, ethnicity, physical or mental ability, even aesthetic interests or ideological proclivity, etc.). As such, being and belonging need to be under more careful and individuated scrutiny beyond assuming location equates with character. Moreover, interactions, even those enabling ethnographic participation and observation, are always of a place (even if cyberspace or a seascape) and connections over the *longue durée* need not be dependent on static places or identities. They can shift, from rural to urban, institution to private life, and country to country. Even, memories of places change in their re-collection and circulation.[34]

Therefore, I suggest that contemporary existential conditions hail ethnographers to ask the questions begged in conventional Area Studies in reverse order. How and to whom things matter should come before where they happen. And where things happen should not be bound to a static location or a presumption that invariable social relations persist among a growing and interconnected plurality of agents, human and non-human. More to the point, given its experiential way-to-knowledge, the questions of 'how' and 'to whom' are what ethnographic fieldwork should be focused on anyway. What drives and divides we humans (and indeed many non-humans) are our particular and singular histories and embodiments or entanglements of 'life lines' as Tim Ingold might say.[35] Again, sentient beings have always been boundary and border crossing cosmopolitans despite high modern enclosures.[36] What we ought to be focused on engaging with, surely as *contemporary* ethnographers (i.e., in coming to terms with our shared cosmopolitan and posthuman being and becoming), are concepts, even classic anthropological concepts like exchange, and daily interactions and practices not geographic coordinates and their relation to sociologically abstracted ideal types or generalisations.

Of course, this is much easier 'written' than done. One habitually slips into static notions of being and belonging – deploying the ease of -*ese* – in routine communication. First, we think and theorise in terms of metaphor and generality.[37] And second, there is economy and persuasiveness in using agreed-upon categories and labels what Noam Chomsky and Edward Herman call 'the violence of concision'.[38] But we need to recall that this simplicity comes at the cost of specificity. While Japanese or Taiwanese society, Chinese or Korean culture, and similar shorthand constructions and conceptualisations effortlessly roll of our tongues and seldom raise an eyebrow, as ethnographers we should not be so compliant and conformist when we research notions of place, identity, and practice. Moreover, there is a sizable cache of research to buttress such a focus on contemporary particularity. Numerous examples where the 'invention' and 'imagination' of shared identities and practices emerge in a long and well-argued list from the 1980s on spearheaded by the work of Benedict Anderson, Eric Hobsbawm, and Terence Ranger.[39] And specifically, in the case of Japan, one can look at the work of a range of scholars who question the ease of -*ese* from anthropologists to historians to literary critics.[40] While the ease of -*ese* disrupts the presumed subject of Area Studies projects, in the following section I discuss how it is also easy to overgeneralise a related category: 'the anthropologist of Japan'.

ETHNOGRAPHIC ENGAGEMENTS:
DOING ONE'S HOMEWORK

Contemporary anthropologists obviously do ethnographic research in conditions different from our disciplinary ancestors. There is the post-postmodern embracing of multi- or inter-disciplinarity of course, but the complexity of doing and defending contemporary ethnographic research as an affective and embodied way of knowing goes beyond this. Much as every Japanese informant does not fit a mould, every anthropologist of Japan and their research experience is particular and dependent upon physical, social, and intellectual capabilities alongside the contingency of experiences. Disciplinary differences between more macro-oriented studies and socio-cultural anthropology are particularly palpable in encounters when the researcher and researched are deeply entwined. And this is especially the case when one finds that they are more an involved participant than an aloof observer. Though this may happen in numerous additional ways, I suggest three are essential: fieldwork, work place, and personal life.

First, there is the act of fieldwork itself. Today 'would be' ethnographers seldom wash upon a distant and unknown shore, demand or command local acceptance, and start questioning 'the natives'. To start, even neophyte eth-nographers are expected to read any previous accounts of 'people and place' and notably anthropological work if it exists. This is usually done with an eye to comparison: how do these people and this place compare with others. Each anthropologist houses views on this prior research, alongside hypotheses about what they expect to encounter during their time in the field. The first real rite of passage for most professional anthropologists is a doctoral degree, whereby an extensive literature review is expected, often before entering the field at all. The steps described above are one key form of disciplinary gate-keeping, and, for better or worse, they also tend to reify existing accounts. It is easy to agree with accepted knowledge offering little more than a footnote, while disagreeing, even with overwhelming experience-based evidence, is always a far more onerous prospect. It is also common to make contact with local anthropologists and institutions, often being hosted or sponsored by them. Anthropologists are thus exposed to another set of perspectives before any ethnographic research is done. Elsewhere I have discussed the formative influence these experiences can take positively or negatively.[41]

In short, anthropologists do not enter a given fieldsite tabula rasa waiting to have informants inscribe worldviews on their open minds. And while debates (and disciplinary policing) over the interpretation and dissemina-tion of results are common, there are also dominant expectations regarding what anthropologists *ought to* be doing, observing, and writing. As a case in point, when I mention that I conduct fieldwork in Hokkaido, Japan, especially to 'Japanese Studies' scholars, the usual first assumption, until I set the record straight, is that I work on Indigenous Ainu issues. This sort of expectation is not a 'Japan' issue however. Surely this kind of Area Studies pigeonholing is similar for anthropologists in other parts of Asia, and it is also the case when I do research in rural Jamaica. I am seen (whether positively or negatively – I am often unsure) as being in cahoots with the government or a development agency. Thus, perhaps more so than in the past, local academics or interlocutors in the field itself have their own perspectives and agendas and are not waiting to be discovered or given voice by an ethnographer.

Second, the place of training and work divide anthropology past and present. Taking the conditions of employment that I know best (and begging the reader to consider their own) many Japanese-born anthropologists of Japan are foreign trained, and/or work and live outside of Japan.[42] And the reverse also holds true. Many non-Japanese anthropologists now work, live, and do research as long-term residents in Japan. In fact, an increasing number of these neolocal anthropologists are trained in Japan. For a host of reasons, from the local limitations on language to the seeming insatiable curiosity found in discussing and deconstructing 'Japaneseness' inside and outside Japan, most foreign anthropologists working in Japan do research on Japan. In sum, it is rare to find a foreign-born anthropological ethnographer working for a Japanese institution who does not focus on Japan as a research topic. But whatever the individual case, one can no longer assume an unvarying 'distant researcher–local informant' relationship in terms of study. This also importantly includes the politics of both knowledge production and career development – points I have detailed elsewhere from the perspective of a Japan-based anthropologist.[43] But briefly put, just as an anthropologist in America, Argentina, or Australia cannot be detached from local regimes of power and control, anthropologists based in Japan must function in a system that is often myopically at odds with global trends. Access to research funds, tenured positions, and certainly positions of institutional power are nearly completely dominated by Japanese middle-aged men. There are always outliers, indeed a key point in this chapter, but compared to institutions in the UK or Canada (locations I have also lived and worked in) the insularity of influences, whether ethnic or gender, and the parochial flow of power and gatekeeping, predominantly in the hands of bureaucrats not academics, is arresting.

Finally, when an anthropologist is married to 'a local', as I am, has children whose native tongue is Japanese, as I do, and moreover makes a living as a part of the local economy with all the aforementioned complexity that entails and more, can one be an objective outsider? Can one help but to 'go native', confounding the hallmark of what was once responsible anthropology?

Indeed, what would the alternative be – to somehow monkishly remain outside the socio-cultural milieu one now permanently resides in? At any rate, given the ease of *-ese* and the extremes of 'common'-sense ideology in Japan, even if one wanted to truly go native, to become Japanese, that route is an option open to very few. Hence, most foreign anthropologists live betwixt and between in Japan; they are partially accepted yet kept in their place with an ever-expanding mix of excludable Others who do not fit within the confines of a monolithic and waning 'proper' Japaneseness. In such conditions of cosmopolitan displacement and precarity, anthropology itself becomes an ironic calling, a liminal state that impacts how research is conducted and how findings are interpreted and presented. Daily, one must 'do' anthropology existing at a confluence of research and cosmopolitics. The following section highlights my own engagement in such a project.

LIVING IN POST-FAMILIAL JAPAN: CONTEMPORARY COSMOPOLITICS OF PERSON AND PLACE

Japan's post-1990s demographic disequilibrium is common knowledge and frequently analysed: underemployed youth and rapidly declining marriage and birth rates. Japan's population is ageing and the nation's largest demographic, the baby boom generation, are retiring and slowly expiring. These trends influence everything from childcare and education policies to pension spending, and one could list a sizeable amount of research into these areas. But what is less commonly discussed is the fact that baby boomers, specifically adults whose adult children have left home, are the number one consumers of companion animals in Japan. In fact, with the nation's declining birth rate, it is estimated that pets will double the number of children under the age of fifteen, dogs are the most popular companion animal with 18–20% of Japanese households being home to one or more, and there are an estimated 24,000 pet stores across the nation to provide companion animals and related products.[44]

'Post' as I use it in my research is not meant to suggest that family life in Japan has ended. I use it much in the way 'post' is used as a prefix in posthuman, not meaning the end of the human but to mark a confluence of social shifts unsettling the category of human.[45] Thus, post-familial is meant to underscore a series of sweeping, rapid, and recent changes to what is perceived as the 'traditional' experience of family life and expectations including the acceptance of dogs. That is to say, Japan's *nihonjinron* national-ethnic-family myth aside, it is clear that the 'typical' (or better put statistical) Japanese family has moved from a rural, extended, patriarchy to urban, nuclear, and increasingly egalitarian structure. It is also clear that dogs have started to transgress bounds both physically and affectively in Japan as elsewhere: and, I underscore, as elsewhere. Domesticated dogs are increasingly globally accepted social *Others*. These companion canines are post-familial cosmopolitans, what Dafna Shir-Vertesh in her anthropological study of Israeli families calls 'flexible persons'.[46] Moreover, outside of any given family they influence public space and policy and are clearly developing into what Canadian medical researchers define as a more-than-human public.[47] If the ease of -*ese* leaves you unaffected, still comfortably settled in high modern spatial and ethnic categories, then perhaps ethnographic research focused on the notion of dogs as an emergent, trans-species, cosmopolitan public might raise an eyebrow or two.

Companion canines are cosmopolites in their own specific ways of course. Yet, like their human compatriots one can trace their genealogical pedigree: German shepherds, French bulldogs, and Irish Setters. As noted above, much in the way Area Studies seeks to define a people, doggie demarcations can even filter down to a regional and often legal register: the *shih tzu* of central Tibet or the Akita *ken* with papers to prove their ancestry alongside generalised data about health concerns and breed temperament (their presumed collective 'culture and personality' as it were). However, domesticated dogs, like their companion humans, are a mobile and messy cosmopolitan collection. *Zashyū*, or mixed bred dogs, are increasingly common in Japan (as elsewhere) with lines of descent that are complicated or untraceable. Their familial ties, like humans, should be conceived as lateral and not merely linear. Borderlines are crossed in knowable and unknowable ways, meaning that at some point hyphens, the mark of clear connections, simply loose meaning. Being part X-Y-Z crossed with part A-B-Z, eventually becomes Heinz 57, mutt, or mongrel: both particular *and* cosmopolitan. Dogs are also cosmopolitan in a sense derived from recent discussions in posthuman philosophy. They are not burdened with the modernist logics of social construction. They follow their unpretentious, frequently hedonistic, doggish drives: clearly an X, Y, Z and A, B, C linage does not come from sitting on the sidelines of desire. And as a host of recent social theory and anthropology publications remind us, dogs are intelligent agents in their own right.[48] They pull their bipedal companions into novel encounters with *Others* (both dogs and humans) that people, left to themselves, might otherwise avoid. Dogs are also localised cosmopolitan citizens, in that they are legally bound to a single country and expected to follow its laws (often on pain of execution). Anyone who has tried to travel with a dog across state borders knows that they are subject to registrations and health checks. In sum, despite particular canid capabilities, they are subjects of the state much as humans are. Finally, companion dogs, in some cases, have more rights than humans who are considered stateless.[49] More to the point at hand, dogs remain steadfastly cosmopolitan in their outlook. Unaware of their state-determined status, dogs live by (and through) their own particular social relations and histories. Thus, each dog is a significant and particular subject navigating their own routes and relationships, often with smell rather that sight as a deciding factor, progressively sharing parks and homes with human and non-human inhabitants.

Given these conditions, it should be unsurprising that dogs are emerging as cosmopolitan family members. In the 1990s, anthropologist Marilyn Strathern noted how shifting technologies, such as in vitro fertilisation, altered contemporary ideas regarding kinship and nature in the UK; specifically, how notions of kin and connection are becoming divorced from relationships of blood or direct descent.[50] At the same time, there has been an increased focus on individualism, in large part fostered by state ideologies of individual responsibility alongside the breakdown of extended families. Such politics have, over decades, altered notions of responsibility and solidarity within kinship categories.[51] Similar trends of increasing individuation and individual responsibility in Japan have been commented upon by a number of researchers; from changes in pre-schools advocating personal responsibility, through to working life, among numerous other neoliberal shifts.[52] There is also the increasing recognition of numerous hybrid Japanese identities inside and outside Japan that need not be linked by or to ideology, nation, or ethnicity.[53] And in these *Japan after Japan* times, there has been an increasing stress for Japanese to rely less on assistance from extended family or even to start families.[54] So, as in other nations it ought to come as no shock that the breakdown of human affective relationships was the prominent reason offered by my informants when I asked them why they had initially decided to purchase or adopt a companion dog.

I was unambiguously told; 'my children moved away so, being lonely, we bought a dog'; 'my father passed away, the house was a quiet and sad place, so we needed to buy a dog'; 'I find my dog is a more attentive lover than a human'; 'I got divorced and the dog is my new partner'; and so on. The connection here is clear. In many cases dogs replace, though not necessarily displace, former human relationships that are clearly affective in nature. What were once 'traditional domestic roles' in Japanese society, the father, child, lover, husband have been 'outsourced' to furrier cosmopolitans. Dogs, at the least, are envisioned as stand-ins, and perhaps in some cases actual replacements, for particular and significant human others – a fuzzing of boundaries. And these cross-species cosmopolitical relations are also observable in emergent public and commercial relationships. Japan's pet industries produce and sell a stunning array of goods for dogs – specialty dog foods, dog clothing from boots to dog sunglasses, and dog baby carriages. Indeed, there are dog-oriented services such as restaurants, hotels, and spas.[55]

One extremely busy chain store called *Mother Garden* exclusively sells both children's and dog's clothes in the same space divided only by the ends of the shelves. Dogs are an increasing presence in park space. In an interview with local Osaka area city official I was told that bylaw officers and bureaucrats are struggling to adapt and police the fastest growing problem population in Japan – not errant youth or immigrants, the usual focus in sociology or criminology-oriented studies – but pet dogs. Dogs feature in a number of recent popular films, and the number one award-winning television commercial series over a decade features Softbank's White family whose stern patriarch is a celebrity dog.[56] And finally, for death is rather final, there are also an increasing number of dog–human cemeteries whereby humans and dogs can be together eternally.[57]

Thus, dogs are in Japan to stay. They have become a more-than-human-public in Japan much as they have in other affluent democratic nations. Without a *woof* of opinion they clearly influence urban public policy in Japan much as they have family life and relations, despite their species. There is growing cosmopolitan choice and force in Japan. Citizens with disposable means can enjoy Italian cars, Vietnamese pho, Brazilian movies, and find a foreign romantic partner. Alternatively, any given individual or group can be irked by this cosmopolitan moment, fretting about by the increasing use of English in the education system, vexed about their inability to stifle boisterously chatting foreigners on the train or indeed, not wanting to share park space with a dog. Far from unique, happily or hesitantly, by choice or force, Japan is increasingly becoming cosmopolitan, and humans and dogs are co-implicated in these growing cosmopolitical conditions.

CONCLUSION: ANTHROPOLOGIES OF COSMOPOLITICAL *BE-LONGING:* WHERE ARE *WE*?

'Ever-newer waters flow on those who step into the same rivers' is a statement attributed to renegade philosopher Heraclitus and it ought to be made a credo for contemporary social scientists, certainly anthropologists. I have argued that the being 'there' and being 'with' of ethnographic encounter has changed and will surely continue changing. Yet some researchers long for stasis and stability, a bracketed frame of time or space where they can account for being. Conditions whereby they can point to an article or monograph and confidently declare: 'that' is how it *is* in X or Y. There are consistencies in socio-cultural life of course, but to be trapped in such *be-longing* is a danger. It is to forget, or more actively deny, that becoming is inescapable, that change is always just another step in the river.

In many instances, Japan of 2021 is a far less bounded place physically and socially than the 'there' of 1969 or 1999. I have offered a personal migratory history and some research on human–canine relations to highlight these shifts, admittedly limited examples, but in innumerable areas the high modern boundaries separating person and place at the core of Japanese Area Studies are faltering. Moreover, what ones tenaciously remain are often contested by researchers and researched alike, negotiated by attentive and aware agents open to global flows and circulations of materials and ideas.[58] Intersectional choices are always limited and limiting to some degree, but they are nonetheless more open, more culturally, socially, ideologically, and spatially cosmopolitan than in the past. Today, many people live lives of unplanned mobility by chance or choice.[59] Moreover, the lived contingencies of the environment, perception, and embodiment 'wayfare' or entwine in an ever-creative and creating ways: stasis is death.[60] In short, 'there' as a bounded place – say Japan – alongside 'they' as a bounded people – say 'the Japanese' – are no longer clear cut, if ever they were, so what is an contemporary anthropologist to do?

In his critique of anthropology, political philosopher Kwame Appiah focuses on the non-cosmopolitan nature of a certain brand of anthropology:

> Anthropology, our source of narratives of otherness, has a professional bias towards difference. Who would want to go out for a year of fieldwork 'in the bush' in order to return with the news that 'they' do so many things just as we do? We don't hear about cross-cultural sameness for the same reason we don't hear about all those noncarcinogenic substances in our environment: sameness is a null result.[61]

Perhaps growing up on a borderland of sorts, and seeing my son growing up in similar circumstances, I have never been terribly attracted to unifying claims of collective uniqueness, or framed another way, the hegemonic denial of internal Otherness. Appiah is describing an anthropology of sorts, but it's not my anthropology. Indeed, from framing my doctoral research right up to my most recent publication, my experience as an anthropologist who focuses on marginal places and relations in Japan has been marked by Japanese Area Studies critique in line with Appiah's observations. Working in reverse, my most recent research on Japanese sojourner tourists and migrants to Jamaica has met with the criticism that these people do not reflect the values and aspirations of 'real' Japanese. Research on the industrialisation of dairy farming in Hokkaido and of dog–human companion relationships in Osaka has been met in both cases with the same, seemingly earnest, question: 'Interesting work . . . but what is particularly Japanese about these relationships?' The fact that I am talking or writing about relationships between Japanese people, dogs, and cows engaged in the production of Japanese products on Japanese farms and in Japanese companies producing services for Japanese consumers for sale almost exclusively in Japan is not Japanese enough. Despite focusing on every-day micro level encounters in detail, I cannot deliver enough essential Japan for some readers. I would argue this is because such readers are trapped in a modernist conceptualisation of 'us' and 'them', of 'self' and 'other', neglecting both the forced and chosen cosmopolitan reality that Japan has become.

* * *

NOTES

1. Bruno Latour, *We Have Never Been Modern* (Harvard: Harvard University Press, 1993).

2. For example, Martin Heidegger, *The Basic Problems of Phenomenology* (Bloomington: Indiana University Press, 1975); Jacob von Uexküll, *A Foray into the Worlds of Animals and Humans: With a Theory of Meaning* (Minneapolis: University of Minnesota Press, 2010) and more recent anthropological interpretations, Tim Ingold, *Being Alive: Essays on Movement Knowledge and Description* (Oxford: Routledge, 2011) and Michael Jackson, *Lifeworlds: Essays in Existential Anthropology* (Chicago: The University of Chicago Press, 2013).

3. Donna Haraway, *Staying with the Trouble: Making Kin in the Chthulucene* (Durham: Duke University Press, 2016); Bruno Latour, *Politics of Nature: How to Bring Sciences into Democracy* (Harvard: Harvard University Press, 2004a) and *An Inquiry into Modes of Existence: An Anthropology of the Moderns* (Harvard: Harvard University Press, 2013).

4. John Zammito, *Kant, Herder, and the Birth of Anthropology* (Chicago: University of Chicago Press, 2002).

5. George Stocking Jr, *Victorian Anthropology* (New York: The Free Press, 1991).

6. Paul Hansen, "The Anthropology of Japan's Social Saga: The Manufacture of Consent Through Descent, Dissent, and the Decent," in *Reframing Diversity in the Anthropology of Japan*, ed. John Ertl et.al. (Kanazawa: Kanazawa University, 2015), 213–245; John Ertl, and Paul Hansen, "Moving Beyond Multiculturalism as a Framework for Diversity in the Anthropology of Japan," in *Reframing Diversity in the Anthropology of Japan*, ed. John Ertl et.al (Kanazawa: Kanazawa University, 2015), 1–28; Blai Guarné, and Paul Hansen, "Introduction: Escaping Inside and Outside," in *Escaping Japan: Reflections on Estrangement and Exile in the Twenty-First Century* (London: Routledge, 2018), 1–25.

7. Victor Turner, *Forest of Symbols: Aspects of Ndembu Ritual* (Ithaca: Cornell University Press, 1967).

8. Paul Stoller, *The Power of the Between: An Anthropological Odyssey* (Chicago: University of Chicago press, 2009).

9. Latour, *We Have Never Been Modern*, 11–12.

10. Roy Wagner, *The Invention of Culture*, Second Edition (Chicago: University of Chicago Press, 2016), 10–16.

11. Hansen, "The Manufacture of Consent".

12. Bruno Latour, "Why Has Critique Run Out of Steam? From Matters of Fact to Matters of Concern," in *Critical Inquiry* 30 (Winter 2004): 225–248.

13. Alan Smart, and Josephine Smart, *Posthumanism: Anthropological Insights* (Toronto: University of Toronto Press, 2017) and Paul Hansen, "Fuzzy Bounds: Doing Ethnography at the Limits of the Network and Animal Metaphor," *Humanimalia: A Journal of Human/Animal Interface Studies* 10, no. 1 (Fall 2018), https://www.dep auw.edu/humanimalia/issue%2019/hansen.html.

14. I am borrowing from Tim Ingold's meshwork concept, see more below; Ingold, *Being Alive*, 63–94.

15. Michel Foucault, *The Order of Things: An Archaeology of the Human Sciences* (New York: Vintage Books, 1970).

16. Mario Blaser, "Is Another Cosmopolitics Possible?" *Cultural Anthropology* 31, no. 4 (November 2016): 545–570; and Isabelle Stengers, "The Cosmopolitical Proposal," in *Making Things Public: Atmospheres of Democracy*, ed. Bruno Latour, and Peter Weibel (Cambridge: MIT Press, 2005), 994–1003.

17. Ulrich Beck, 2009, *World at Risk* (Cambridge: Polity Press, 2009), 52–62.

18. This is discussed in Donna Haraway, *When Species Meet* (Minneapolis: University of Minnesota Press, 2008), 244, and *Staying with the Trouble*, 2016. For earlier if more anthropocentric versions, see Levinas, Emmanuel Levinas, *Entre Nous: On thinking-of-the-other* (New York: Columbia University Press, 1998) and Jean-Luc Nancy, *Being Singular Plural* (Stanford: Stanford University Press, 2000).

19. Key recent examples here include Ian Bogost, *Alien Phenomenology or What It's Like to be a Thing* (University of Minnesota Press, 2012); Ingold, *Being Alive*, 2011; and Annabel Wharton, *Architectural Agents: The Delusional, Abusive, Addictive Lives of Buildings* (Minneapolis: University of Minnesota Press, 2015).

20. From a human perspective see, for example, Nigel Rapport, *Anyone: The Cosmopolitan Subject of Anthropology* (Oxford: Berghahn Books, 2012), or for a more-than-human perspective, see Eduardo Kohn, *How Forests Think: Toward an Anthropology Beyond the Human* (Berkeley: University of California Press, 2013).

21. Numerous references could be deployed here but in terms of thinking through 'time' and location, see Doreen Massey, *For Space* (Los Angeles: Sage, 2005). In terms of location as diffuse, see Deirdre McKay, *An Archipelago of Care: Filipino Migrants and Global Networks* (Bloomington: Indiana University Press, 2016).

22. Ruth Benedict, *The Chrysanthemum and The Sword: Patterns of Japanese Culture* (Boston: Houghton Mifflin, 1946).

23. Clifford Geertz, *Works and Lives: The Anthropologist as Author* (Stanford University Press, 1988), 5.

24. Outside the discipline of anthropology, let alone Area Studies, contemporary posthuman theory, neo-vitalist theory, Object Oriented Ontology, and multispecies ethnography are working towards on these themes.

25. See McKay, *An Archipelago of Care*, and James Scott, *The Art of Not being Governed: An Anarchist History of Upland Southeast Asia* (New Haven: Yale University Press, 2009).

26. Ian Hacking, "Making up People," *The London Review of Books* 28, no. 16 (2006): 23–26.

27. The classic reference point here are Benedict Anderson, *Imagined Communities* (London: Verso, 1983) and Eric Hobsbawm, and Terence Ranger ed., *The Invention of Tradition* (Cambridge: Cambridge University Press, 1983).

28. Anthony Smith, *Myths and Memories of the Nation* (Oxford: Oxford University Press, 1999).

29. The tantamount example being Pierre Bourdieu, *Distinction: A Social Critique of the Judgment of Taste* (London: Routledge, 1984).

30. See Kohn, *How Forests Think*, for an Amazonian example or Elizabeth Povinelli, *Geontologies: A Requiem to Late Liberalism* (Durham: Duke University Press, 2016) for an Australian example.

31. For a summary of these trends, see Blai Guarné, and Paul Hansen, "Introduction: Escaping Japan Inside and Outside," in *Escaping Japan: Reflections on Estrangement and Exile in The Twenty-First Century*, ed. Blai Guarné, and Paul Hansen (London: Routledge, 2018), 1–25.

32. See Kimberle Crenshaw, "Demarginalizing the Intersection of Race and Sex: A Black Feminist Critique of Antidiscrimination Doctrine, Feminist Theory and Antiracist Politics," *The University of Chicago Legal Forum* 140 (1989): 139–167 for the original intersectional theory reference.

33. See John Ertl, and Paul Hansen, "Moving Beyond Multiculturalism as a Framework for Diversity in Japan," in *Reframing Diversity in the Anthropology of Japan*, ed. John Ertl et.al. (Kanazawa: Kanazawa Center for Cultural Resource Studies, 2015), 1–28.

34. Blai Guarné, "Escaping Through Words: Memory and Oblivion in the Japanese Urban Landscape," in *Escaping Japan: Reflections on Estrangement and Exile in The Twenty-First Century* (London: Routledge, 2018), 90–121.

35. Ingold, *Being Alive*, 76–94.

36. For example, see Scott, *The Art of Not Being Governed*, and Smart and Smart, *Posthumanism*.

37. See George Lakoff, and Mark Johnson, *Metaphors We Live By* (Chicago: University of Chicago Press 2003).

38. See Noam Chomsky, and Edward Herman, *Manufacturing Consent: The Political Economy of the Mass Media* (London: Vintage Books, 1988).

39. Anderson, *Imagined Communities*, and Hobsbawm, and Ranger, *Invented Traditions*.

40. The amount of work here over the past two decades is staggering; however, Harumi Befu, *The Hegemony of Homogeneity* (Melbourne: Transpacific Press, 2001) and Miyoshi Masao, *Trespasses: Selected Writings* (Durham: Duke University Press, 2010) are influential and oft-cited examples.

41. Hansen, "The Anthropology of Japan's Social Saga."

42. Kuwayama Takami, *Native Anthropology: The Japanese Challenge to Western Academic Hegemony* (Melbourne: Trans Pacific Press, 2004).

43. Paul Hansen, "Betwixt and Between JA: Japan, Jamaica, Agriculture, Education and the Will to Employment," in *The Impact of Internationalization of Japanese Higher Education: Is Japanese Education Really Changing?* ed. John Mock, Kawamura Hiroaki, and Naganuma Naeko, 159–175 (Rotterdam: Sense Publishers, 2016).

44. Paul Hansen, "Urban Japan's 'Fuzzy' New Families: Affect and Embodiment in Dog–Human Relationships," *Asian Anthropology* 12, no. 2 (November 2013): 83–103 and Paul Hansen, "Linking Cosmopolitan and Multispecies Touch in Contemporary Japan," *Japan Forum Online* (October 2018). DOI: 10.1080/09555803.2018.1504109.

45. Carry Wolfe, *What is Posthumanism?* (Minneapolis: University of Minnesota Press 2010), xi–xxxiv.

46. Hansen, "Urban Japan's Fuzzy New Families"; "Linking Cosmopolitan and Multispecies Touch"; and Dafna Shir-Vertesh, "Flexible Personhood: Loving Animals as Family Members in Israel," *American Anthropologist* 114, no. 2 (2012): 420–432.

47. Gwendolyn Blue, and Melanie Rock, "Trans-biopolitics: Complexity in Interspecies Relations," *Health* 15, no. 4 (December 2010): 353–368, and Ann Toohey et. al., "When 'Places' Include Pets: Broadening the Scope of Relational Approaches to Promoting Aging-in-Place," *The Journal of Sociology & Social Welfare* 44, no. 3 (2017): Article 7.

48. For example, Haraway, *When Species Meet*.

49. Martha Nussbaum, *Frontiers of Justice: Disability, Nationality, Species Membership* (Harvard: Harvard University Press, 2006).

50. Marylin Strathen, *After Nature: English Kinship in the Late Twentieth Century* (Cambridge: Cambridge University Press, 1992).

51. Sugita Hizuru, "The Relationship between the Presence of Children and the Degree of Attachment to Dogs in Japanese Households: Using JGSS Data," *General Social Surveys JGSS Research Series* 5, no. 2 (2005): 105–118.

52. Peter Cave, *Primary School in Japan: Self, Individuality, and Learning in Elementary Education* (London: Routledge, 2007); Kosugi Reiko, *Escape from Work: Freelancing Youth and the Challenge to Corporate Japan* (Melbourne: Trans Pacific Press, 2008); and more generally Anne Allison, *Precarious Japan* (Durham: Duke University Press, 2013) and Harry Harootunian, and Tomiko Yoda, ed. *Japan after Japan: Social and Cultural Life from the Recessionary 1990s to the Present* (Durham: Duke University Press, 2006). All focus on neoliberal shifts towards individual responsibly.

53. Including the above-mentioned texts Nelson Graburn, John Ertl, and Kenji Tierney, ed., *Multiculturalism in the New Japan: Crossing the Boundaries Within* (New York: Berghahn Books, 2010) and David Blake-Willis, and Stephen Murphy-Shigematsu, ed. *Transcultural Japan: At the Borderlands of Race, Gender, and Identity* (London: Routledge, 2008).

54. There is a breakdown of the extended family, as explored by Sunhee Lee, "Women's Lives in Family and Local Communities: The Tohoku Region," in *Gender*

and Law in Japan, ed. Tsujimura, Miyako, and Yano Emi (Sendai: Tohoku University Press, 2007), 157–169; and there is even reluctance to start new families fuelling the purchase of companion animals Roland Buerk and Ruth Evans, "Why Japan Prefers Pets to Parenthood." June 8, 2012 *The Guardian Online*, http://www.guardian.co.uk/lifeandstyle/2012/jun/08/why-japan-prefers-pets-to-parenthood.

55. For example, surrounding Tokyo's Komazawa Koen area there are literally dozens of dog friendly cafes and shops.

56. Hansen, "Linking Cosmopolitan and Multispecies Touch".

57. Barbara Ambros, *Bones of Contention: Animals and Religion in Contemporary Japan* (Honolulu: University of Hawai'i Press, 2012).

58. Guarné, and Hansen, "Introduction".

59. Rapport, *Anyone*.

60. Ingold, *Being Alive*.

61. Kwame Appiah, *The Ethics of Identity* (Princeton: Princeton University Press, 2005), 254.

REFERENCES

Allison, Anne. *Precarious Japan*. Durham: Duke University Press, 2013.

Ambros, Barbara. *Bones of Contention: Animals and Religion in Contemporary Japan*. Honolulu: University of Hawai'i Press, 2012

Anderson, Benedict. *Imagined Communities*. London: Verso, 1983.

Appiah, Kwame. *The Ethics of Identity*. Princeton: Princeton University Press, 2005.

Bauman, Zygmunt. *Liquid Times: Living in an Age of Uncertainty*. Cambridge: Polity Press, 2007.

Beck, Ulrich. *World at Risk*. Cambridge: Polity Press, 2007.

Befu, Harumi. *The Hegemony of Homogeneity*. Melbourne: Transpacific Press, 2001.

Benedict, Ruth. *The Chrysanthemum and the Sword: Patterns of Japanese Culture*. Boston: Houghton Mifflin, 1946.

Blaser, Mario. "Is Another Cosmopolitics Possible?" *Cultural Anthropology* 31, no. 4 (November 2016): 545–570.

Blue, Gwendolyn, and Melanie Rock. "Trans-Biopolitics: Complexity in Interspecies Relations." *Health* 15, no. 4 (December 2010): 353–368.

Bogost, Ian. *Alien Phenomenology or What It's Like to be a Thing*. Minneapolis: University of Minnesota Press, 2012.

Bourdieu, Pierre. *Distinction: A Social Critique of the Judgment of Taste*. Trans. Richard Nice. London: Routledge, 1984.

Buerk, Roland, and Ruth Evans. "Why Japan Prefers Pets to Parenthood." *Guardian Online*, last modified June 8, 2012. http://www.guardian.co.uk/lifeandstyle/2012/jun/08/why-japan-prefers-pets-to-parenthood.

Cave, Peter. *Primary School in Japan: Self, Individuality, and Learning in Elementary Education*. London: Routledge, 2007.

Chomsky, Noam, and Edward Herman. *Manufacturing Consent: The Political Economy of the Mass Media*. London: Vintage Books, 1988.

Crenshaw, Kimberle. "Demarginalizing the Intersection of Race and Sex: A Black Feminist Critique of Antidiscrimination Doctrine, Feminist Theory and Antiracist Politics." *The University of Chicago Legal Forum* 140 (1989): 139–167.

Ertl, John, and Paul Hansen. "Moving Beyond Multiculturalism as a Framework for Diversity in Japan." In *Reframing Diversity in the Anthropology of Japan*, edited by John Ertl, John McCrery, John Mock, and Greg Poole, 1–28. Kanazawa: Kanazawa Center for Cultural Resource Studies, 2015.

Foucault, Michel. *The Order of Things: An Archaeology of the Human Sciences.* New York: Vintage Books, 1970.

Graburn, Nelson, John Ertl, and Kenji Tierney, ed. *Multiculturalism in the New Japan: Crossing the Boundaries Within.* New York: Berghahn Books, 2010.

Guarné, Blai. "Escaping Through Words: Memory and Oblivion in the Japanese Urban Landscape." In *Escaping Japan: Reflections on Estrangement and Exile in The Twenty-First Century*, edited by Blai Guarné, and Paul Hansen, 90–121. London: Routledge, 2018.

Guarné, Blai, and Paul Hansen. "Introduction: Escaping Japan Inside and Outside." In *Escaping Japan: Reflections on Estrangement and Exile in The Twenty-First Century,* edited by Blai Guarné, and Paul Hansen, 1–25. London: Routledge, 2018.

Geertz, Clifford. *Works and Lives: The Anthropologist as Author.* Stanford: Stanford University Press, 1988.

Hacking, Ian. "Making Up People." *The London Review of Books* 28, no. 16 (2006): 23–26.

Hansen, Paul. "Urban Japan's 'Fuzzy' New Families: Affect and Embodiment in Dog–Human Relationships." *Asian Anthropology* 12, no. 2 (November 2013): 83–103.

———. "The Anthropology of Japan's Social Saga: The Manufacture of Descent, Dissent, and Decent in the Anthropology of Japan." In *Reframing Diversity in the Anthropology of Japan*, edited by John Ertl, John McCrery, John Mock, and Greg Poole, 213–245. Kanazawa: Kanazawa Center for Cultural Resource Studies, 2015.

———. "Betwixt and Between JA: Japan, Jamaica, Agriculture, Education and the Will to Employment." In *The Impact of Internationalization of Japanese Higher Education: Is Japanese Education Really Changing?*, edited by Hiroaki Kawamura, John Mock, and Naeko Naganuma, 159–175. Rotterdam: Sense Publishers, 2016.

———. "Fuzzy Bounds: Doing Ethnography at the Limits of the Network and Animal Metaphor." *Humanimalia: A Journal of Human/Animal Interface Studies* 10, no. 1 (Fall 2018): 183–212. https://www.depauw.edu/humanimalia/issue%2019/hansen.html.

———. "Linking Cosmopolitan and Multispecies Touch in Contemporary Japan." *Japan Forum Online* (October 2018), accessed April 15, 2019. DOI: 10.1080/09555803.2018.1504109.

Haraway, Donna. *When Species Meet.* Minneapolis: University of Minnesota Press, 2008.

———. *Staying with the Trouble: Making Kin in the Chthulucene.* Durham: Duke University Press, 2016.

Harootunian, H. D., and Tomiko Yoda, ed. *Japan after Japan: Social and Cultural Life from the Recessionary 1990s to the Present*. Durham: Duke University Press, 2006.

Heidegger, Martin. *The Basic Problems of Phenomenology*. Trans. Albert Hofstader. Bloomington: Indiana University Press, 1975.

Hobsbawm, Eric, and Terence Ranger. ed. *The Invention of Tradition*. Cambridge: Cambridge University Press, 1983.

Ingold, Tim. *Being Alive: Essays on Movement Knowledge and Description*. Oxford: Routledge, 2011.

Jackson, Michael. *Lifeworlds: Essays in Existential Anthropology*. Chicago: The University of Chicago Press, 2013.

Kohn, Eduardo. *How Forests Think: Toward an Anthropology Beyond the Human*. Berkeley: University of California Press, 2013.

Kosugi, Reiko. *Escape from Work: Freelancing Youth and the Challenge to Corporate Japan*. Trans. Ross Mouer. Melbourne: Trans Pacific Press, 2008.

Kuwayama, Takami. *Native Anthropology: The Japanese Challenge to Western Academic Hegemony*. Melbourne: Trans Pacific Press, 2004.

George Lakoff, and Mark Johnson. *Metaphors We Live By*. Chicago: University of Chicago Press, 2003.

Latour, Bruno. *We Have Never Been Modern*. Trans. Catherine Porter. Harvard: Harvard University Press, 1993.

———. *Politics of Nature: How to Bring Sciences into Democracy*. Trans. Catherine Porter. Harvard: Harvard University Press, 2004(a).

———. "Why Has Critique Run Out of Steam? From Matters of Fact to Matters of Concern." *Critical Inquiry* 30 (Winter 2004b): 225–248.

———. *An Inquiry into Modes of Existence: An Anthropology of the Moderns*. Trans. Catherine Porter. Harvard: Harvard University Press, 2013.

Lee, Sunhee. "Women's Lives in Family and Local Communities: The Tohoku Region." In *Gender and Law in Japan*, edited by Tsujimura Miyako, and Yano Emi, 157–169. Sendai: Tohoku University Press, 2007.

Levinas, Emmanuel. *Entre Nous: On thinking-of-the-other*. Trans. Barbara Harshav and Michael B. Smith. New York: Columbia University Press, 1998.

Massey, Doreen. *For Space*. Los Angeles: Sage, 2005.

McKay, Deirdre. *An Archipelago of Care: Filipino Migrants and Global Networks*. Bloomington: Indiana University Press, 2016.

Miyoshi Masao. *Trespasses: Selected Writings*. Durham: Duke University Press, 2010.

Nancy, Jean-Luc. *Being Singular Plural*. Trans. Anne O'Byrne, and Robert Richardson. Stanford: Stanford University Press, 2000.

Nussbaum, Martha. *Frontiers of Justice: Disability, Nationality, Species Membership*. Harvard: Harvard University Press, 2006.

Povinelli, Elizabeth. *Geontologies: A Requiem to Late Liberalism*. Durham: Duke University Press, 2016.

Rapport, Nigel. *Anyone: The Cosmopolitan Subject of Anthropology*. Oxford: Berghahn Books, 2012.

Scott, James. *The Art of Not being Governed: An Anarchist History of Upland Southeast Asia.* New Haven: Yale University Press, 2009.

Shir-Vertesh, Dafna. "Flexible Personhood: Loving Animals as Family Members in Israel." *American Anthropologist* 114, no. 2 (August 2012): 420–432.

Smart Alan, and Josephine Smart. *Posthumanism: Anthropological Insights.* Toronto: University of Toronto Press, 2017.

Smith, Anthony. *Myths and Memories of the Nation.* Oxford: Oxford University Press, 1999.

Stengers, Isabelle. "The Cosmopolitical Proposal." In *Making Things Public: Atmospheres of Democracy,* edited by Bruno Latour and Peter Weibel, 994–1003. Cambridge, MA: MIT Press, 2005.

Strathern, Marilyn. *After Nature: English Kinship in the Late Twentieth Century.* Cambridge: Cambridge University Press, 1992.

Stocking, George Jr. *Victorian Anthropology.* New York: The Free Press, 1991.

Stoller, Paul. *The Power of the Between: An Anthropological Odyssey.* Chicago: University of Chicago Press, 2009.

Sugita Hizuru. "The Relationship between the Presence of Children and the Degree of Attachment to Dogs in Japanese Households: Using JGSS Data." *General Social Surveys JGSS Research Series* 5, no. 2 (2005): 105–118.

Toohey, Ann M., Hewson, Jennifer A., Adams, Cindy L., and Rock, Melanie J. "When 'Places' Include Pets: Broadening the Scope of Relational Approaches to Promoting Aging-in-Place." *The Journal of Sociology & Social Welfare* 44, no. 3 (2017): Article 7.

Turner, Victor. *Forest of Symbols: Aspects of Ndembu Ritual.* Ithaca: Cornell University Press, 1967.

von Uexküll, Jacob. *A Foray into the Worlds of Animals and Humans: With a Theory of Meaning.* Trans. Joseph O'Neal. Minneapolis: University of Minnesota Press, 2010.

Wagner, Roy. *The Invention of Culture.* Second Edition. Chicago: University of Chicago Press, 2016.

Wharton, Annabel. *Architectural Agents: The Delusional, Abusive, Addictive Lives of Buildings.* Minneapolis: University of Minnesota Press, 2015.

Willis, David Blake, and Stephen Murphy-Shigematsu, ed. *Transcultural Japan: At the Borderlands of Race, Gender, and Identity.* London: Routledge, 2008.

Wolfe, Carry. *What is Posthumanism?* Minneapolis: University of Minnesota Press, 2010.

Zammito, John. *Kant, Herder, and the Birth of Anthropology.* Chicago: University of Chicago Press, 2002.

Chapter 9

Asia as Feminist Ethnographic Method?

Notes on Mobility, Social Media, and Studying Up

Nayantara Sheoran Appleton

ABSTRACT

Feminists often revisit the question of whether there can be a feminist ethnography, and for some the jury is still out. While some have argued it is improbable, others have started work in the 'ruins' of feminist ethnography. Drawing on fieldwork in India since 2008, in this chapter I draw on a few key ethnographic 'moments' to talk about the shifting nature of fieldwork in contemporary Asia as site from where a critical engagement on feminist ethnographic methods can emerge. Inspired by *Asia as Method*, here I utilise that critical lens to suggest that the Asian experience of feminist ethnographers may allow us to revisit the question of not only *if* there can be a feminist ethnography, but also what it can look like. I posit two insights from wherein a new feminist ethnography can emerge. First, in paying attention to our interlocutors' mobilities, and second in conceptually decentring 'studying up' in times of globally connected social media, we can make space for a feminist ethnographic project. In some sense interdisciplinary, and in another an engagement on methods, this chapter draws on, and contributes to, conversations on feminist ethnographic methods and cultural studies of/in Asia.

* * *

There is an informal acknowledgement among anthropologists that we are never really prepared for fieldwork.[1] This perhaps stems from the fact that there is often not a methods paper in graduate school, or even if you have been 'taught' methods, the fieldwork realities will require the anthropologist to adapt and 'roll with the punches'. When I started fieldwork in 2010, after a very short 'pilot study' in 2008, I was as unprepared as any other graduate student starting a new research project. However, my unpreparedness was magnified by the fact that I had been training in a cultural studies programme and not in anthropology. My advisers were anthropologists (Hugh Gusterson, Rashmi Sadana, Roger Lancaster) and one Communication Studies scholar (Tim Gibson) and I had not taken any classes on anthropological methods. Further, most of my reading in the early years of the programme had been in the (non)cannon of cultural studies. In 2010, while less prepared for anthropological fieldwork than my anthropology peers, I was also naïve enough to think I was doing a great job, and enjoyed 'working' with women, which really was often just 'hanging out' in the Delhi winter sun. Since 2010, I have gone back, and with each visit improved my research engagements (or perhaps methods), paying more focused attention to the moments of hanging out as method.

In subsequent visits to India, I got better at listening, being, and paying attention as a woman doing research with (mostly) women. My dissertation research on emergency contraception, its visual manifestations, and women's sense of reproductive 'empowerment' was greatly improved in the subsequent visits, particularly as I finished the project and started converting it into a book manuscript. My second project, on stem cell research and therapies in India, was quite different. I worked as a postdoctoral fellow with a PI (Aditya Bharadwaj) on his European Research Council (ERC) project, and while I was encouraged to develop my own fieldwork and build relationships as I had previously with my other research project, this was a much more focused and clarified method. My hanging out had to be accounted for in fieldnotes and recorded interviews that could be submitted to the group for collective data analysis. While on this second project, I also worked closely on an ethnographic team with a PhD student and we both are writing about collaborative research (explored in a short editorial here[2]). It was over the course of being in the field, not once, but multiple times – sometimes as a solo researcher and at other times as a team member – that I learned to *see* the fieldsite India, South Asia, and Asia as places from where methodological insights arose. It was here, in the field, like many ethnographers before me, that I learned how to *do* ethnography as a feminist Indian woman working with Indian women (and men) in a largely urban part of the country.

Fieldwork over the decade was never done in isolation from everyday life for me. To do research in India, where I was returning 'home' after a decade of living and studying in the United States, was to live life fully embroiled in familial obligations. It was a constant juggle, to maintain family relationships while also creating space to do the research. My research shaped my life in India, just as life shaped the process and product of my ethnographic research. To that end, in this writing, I am always visible and present – making mistakes, being surprised, and continually learning. In this chapter, by sharing of myself, I hope to make my academic authority as somebody who has done research and published on India[3] – a site of embodied vulnerability which allows for the next generation of scholars of/in India to see value in staying radically vulnerable[4] as a way to *do* fieldwork. This chapter is but the start of a conversation. Limited in scope (and word count), it is part of a larger conversation on feminist ethnographic methods in Asia – not only as an academic project, but also how this method is mobilised in activist and non-governmental worlds to enable social change for women's lives. Drawing on fieldwork in India since 2008, I draw on a few key ethnographic 'moments' to talk about the shifting nature of fieldwork in contemporary Asia as site from where a critical engagement on feminist ethnographic methods can emerge. Inspired by *Asia as Method*,[5] I suggest that the Asian experience of feminist ethnographers may allow us to revisit the question of not only if there can be a feminist ethnography, but also what it can look like in the contemporary. I suggest that visiting our interlocutor mobilities, and conceptually decentring 'studying up' in times of shared social media, might be sites from wherein a new feminist ethnography can emerge. In some sense interdisciplinary, and in another an engagement on methods, this chapter draws on, and contributes to, conversations on feminist ethnographic methods and cultural studies of/ in Asia.

ASIA AND FEMINIST ETHNOGRAPHIC METHODOLOGY

To talk of methods, as a cultural studies trained scholar doing anthropological work in Asia, requires an interdisciplinary engagement. In that spirit, this chapter draws from and contributes two scholarly conversations. The first is anthropological conversations in and about feminist ethnography. The second is feminist cultural studies as a field of study, which allows for a critical lens on ethnographic practice as well as being and researching in/from Asia. In drawing from these two spaces, I take seriously the call for interdisciplinary engagements from within Asia as ways to not only decolonise the disciplinary space, but also the way we work, live, and play in the spaces where we research and/or call home. In resisting a review essay of the moves and turns in intellectual debates, I want to closely focus on the conversations around feminist ethnographic methods and then Asia as a method with a focus on critical syncretism, in order to see the way critical engagements in these fields shape the way we re-think Asia, feminist ethnography, and our work as researchers and intellectuals with obligations to our communities.

FEMINIST ETHNOGRAPHY

It was provocative when, in 1988 Judith Stacey asked, 'Can There Be a Feminist Ethnography?'[6] Lila Abu-Lughod repeated the challenge in 1990, when she too asked 'Can There Be a Feminist Ethnography?'[7] Both these feminists were bringing to our attention the inherent power differentials in both ethnographic practice and ethnographic output between the researcher and the researched. For Stacey, it was an acknowledgement that the possibility of truly sharing authorial power was a false claim, as ethnographers eventually had to make decisions on what was written and what was not. For Abu-Lughod, the concern about feminist ethnography was epistemological; her critique was aimed at feminists that aimed to make visible 'women's experience' universally. She highlighted that this desire to research and write about other women as equals was problematic, as it erased the clear power differentials between women, and also between researchers and researched. As a graduate student, I had come to these debates by reading South Asian feminist scholars, more so than anthropologists. In *Feminism Without Borders: Decolonizing Theory, Practicing Solidarity*[8] (2003), Chandra Talpande Mohanty, while addressing how feminist scholars have treated the subject of Third World women workers, wrote:

> While number of studies provide information on the mobilization of racist and (hetero)sexist stereotypes in recruiting Third World women into this labor force, relatively few address questions of the social agency of women who are subjected to a number of levels of capitalist discipline. In other words, few studies have focused on women workers as subjects – as agents who make choices, have critical perspective on their own situations, and think and organize collectively against their oppressors.[9]

By looking at women's work as a form of agency, she argued that we create potential spaces for cross-national feminist solidarity and organising.

It was also Mohanty, who in her seminal essay 'Under Western eyes: Feminist scholarship and colonial discourse'[10] (1988), suggested that Third World women were not a monolithic subject who came to exist only in relational terms to First World women. The constructs of Third World women by First World feminists depended on assumptions of Western women as 'secular, liberated, and in control of their own lives'[11] and Third World women as a universal category of oppressed object. While Mohanty recognised the good intentions of Western feminist scholarship, her article also intended to hold up a mirror to the colonialist assumptions for First World feminists. She wrote:

> When radical and liberal feminist assumptions of women as a sex class might elucidate (however inadequately) the autonomy of particular women's struggle in the West, the application of the notion of women as a homogenous category to women in the Third World colonizes and appropriates the pluralities of the simultaneous location of different groups of women in social class and ethnic frameworks; in doing so it ultimately robs them of their historical and political agency.[12]

The late 1980s scholarship, around feminist engagements from Asia (in this case, South Asia), still bears credence.

In a chapter in *Dislocating Cultures*,[13] 'Restoring history and politics to "Third World traditions": Contrasting colonialist stance and contemporary contestations of *Sati*' Uma Narayan, another prolific Asian feminist, elucidates the problematic way in which Third World women are colonised in writings by First World feminists. Using the case of *Sati*, she problematises Western feminists' writings about Third World traditions as colonialist writing which takes this Third World tradition of *Sati* as a constant entity and does not inquire into the historical, political, and social processes that constructed this tradition. Basing her chapter on Mary Daly's analysis of '*Sati*, she posits that Daly replicates a colonialist stance by flattening this practice to tradition that is practiced by all Indians historically, when in reality *Sati* was practiced only in a few communities at particular historical moments. The lack of detail and totalising generalisations in accounts of the Third World are colonial in their very nature, and are replicated by Daly as she blurs the temporality of the practice and convolutes *Sati* with dowry-burning and other social concerns for women in contemporary India. In her attempt to talk back to the Daly mode of non-contextualised analysis, Narayan shows the readers how *Sati* was in fact constructed in its contemporary form as a Hindu tradition by the colonial powers themselves. She adds that the problem of replicating colonial moves in examining Third World traditions is problematic in and of itself; however, I also see it as further troubling when a similar trope is appropriated by fundamentalists/nationalists trying to forward their agendas based on 'authentic traditions' which lead to subjection of women and women's rights.

In another piece, Narayan draws on personal anecdotes and historic understandings of India to dislocate the dichotomy between national culture/ Third World culture and Western culture.[14] She points out that Third World feminist daughters account for their culture differently than their mothers or men in positions of power – not because they are westernised, but because they have the benefit of history and being able to look back at traditions, examining their constructed nature. She argues that cultural identities (of feminists and others within a nation) and nationalist discourse are constructed and ever evolving, thus suggesting that referring back to an authentic tradition is problematic and totalising. Instead of allowing for a polarisation of women on the basis of race and nationality, she suggests that we need to concentrate on solidarity among women across nation-states because they have been similarly afforded secondary positions compared to men. Thus, even though she critiques superficial analyses like Daly's, she urges for all feminists to be cognisant of the historical patterns that have shaped the contemporary moment. For feminists knowing and talking back to *our* own history is as important (if not more important) than always placing it in relation to spaces in the 'West'.

In addition to paying attention to our local h(er)stories, I also see boundary crossings, as a vital feminist practice, encouraged by Mohanty in revisiting her original essay 'Under Western Eyes'.[15] In this, she calls for solidarity and sisterhood that engages with difference and yet articulates political resistance to the capitalist machinery through social movements. She cautions against easy reductive 'otherings' and is concerned about a negation of particular histories of the 'other' in an attempt to be democratic rather than colonial. As is made clear by Mohanty and Narayan, as feminists we have to strike a balance between cultural essentialism and feminist universalism. We have to be careful about not who speaks for the 'other' women, but rather how they speak about the 'other' – be the 'other' located in a different country, community, or culture. These scholars then influenced the next generation of South Asian feminist scholars, asking us to look at our own histories, in order to write it through our own lens. Yet this is not easy, or comfortable work, as even within Asia and research in our 'home' spaces, we are privileged as 'ethnographers' who come 'home' when compared to some of the women we work with in our 'fieldsites.'

As a feminist ethnographer, returning home but always negotiating between being an insider and/or outsider, I am essentially uncomfortable with what I do.[16] As I write up my first book from research with/for women in India on contraception, I often turn to Kamla Visweswran's *Fictions of Feminist Ethnography*,[17] and seminal essay 'Defining Feminist Ethnography'[18] as a space from wherein I can think about my practice and product of ethnography. In both these writings, Visweswaran, a cultural studies and women's studies scholar, asks us to remember the political potential in both fiction and ethnography, but also to remember that the romantic ideas around a perfectly egalitarian ethnography that are proposed by some feminists are fictions. It then becomes our task as contemporary feminist anthropologists, writing and working from Asia, to simultaneously lay bare the fictions of our ethnography but also write accounts full of local lives and histories.

While there is the postmodern turn in feminist ethnography,[19] there are also calls for a methodological imperative for a feminist ethnography that asks 'in whose interests an ethnographic text works?'[20] And if the answer is, in the interests of the women who give us their time, then the rephrasing from 'Can there be a feminist ethnography?' to a 'Can Asia serve as a Feminist Ethnographic Method?' allows for a particular political potency and examination of feminist ethnography with attention to h(er)stories of geography and locality – in this case Asia. Drawing on Chen's *Asia as Method* that has inspired me to think through ethnographic practice in/from/ about Asia, below I share a few moments from my feminist ethnography to hopefully suggest Asia (as one among other) as a space from where we imagine future facing feminist ethnographies.

ASIA AS (FEMINIST ETHNOGRAPHIC?) METHOD

While the debates in and about feminist ethnography are decades old, the conversation of an inter-Asian cultural studies, with implications for ethnography (alongside feminist ethnography), saw a particular resurgence in the past decade. When *Asia as Method*[21] was released in the United States under the cultural studies banner of Duke University Press in 2010, it immediately came to the attention of most students in my programme engaged with Asia. However, I was in the field and did not start hearing about the book until my return in 2011. In my programme, there were a few students from Asia (I was the only South Asian student and student studying in/about South Asia). Fan Yang was doing research in China and now has published *Faked in China*,[22] Lia Uy-Tioco was researching mobilities in Philippines and recently co-published *Mobile Media and Social Intimacies in Asia: Reconfiguring Local Ties and Enacting Global Relationships.*[23] Sangmin Kim was researching aesthetics in South Korea, Young A Jung was a Korean linguist, and Gyu Tag Lee was at the time regaling us with his research on K-pop. I was glad to be part of this community of 'Asianists', and while doing anthropological research unlike the others, I felt a certain joy when attending their seminars. Often the head nodding and the 'ah yes, it's like that in India as well' were the markers that made *Asia as Method* a call for privileging the local Asia in Fairfax, Virginia. One of the earliest conversations that remains with me from that book is the beautiful, but limited analysis on 'critical syncretism'.[24] It is a concept that I draw on here, to make sense of Asia as (feminist) ethnographic method.

In closely reading Chen, critical syncretism appears as a concept for our times as we try to create research spaces that are not beholden to colonial legacies or research that enables labelling of ourselves as 'others'. He writes:

The direction of identification put forward by a critical syncretism is outward; the intent is to become others, to actively interiorize elements of others into the subjectivity of the self so as to move beyond the boundaries and divisive positions historically constructed by colonial power relations in the form of patriarchy, capitalism, racism, chauvinism, and heterosexism, or nationalistic xenophobia.

[. . .]

Critical syncretism is a cultural strategy of identification for subaltern subject groups. Here 'others' refers not just to racial, ethnic, and national categories but also includes class, sex and gender, and geographical positions.

He is asking us to come together, separately, to create multiple points for identification across Asia, and not be constantly working within/out the colonial identification project.

For anthropologists working with communities and individuals, locating our own positionality, and being reflexive are modes of our ethnographic practice – both as a research process and product. Critical syncretism is one way which allows us to see Asia as method because it provides us tools to talk, research, and write with a particular consciousness. He writes further:

Critical syncretism takes an alternative understanding of subjectivity as its starting point. Only through multi-layered practices can one become others. The aim is not simply to rediscover the suppressed voices of the multiple subjects within social formation, but to generate a system of multiple reference points that can break away from the self-reproducing neo-colonial framework that structures the trajectories and flow of desire.[25]

It is indeed these multilayer practices that are part of any anthropologists' toolkit. However, when examined critically, these practices have continued to be located in a 'starting point' outside Asia. In the spirit of Chen's argument, I do not suggest that we ignore or write in opposition to the colonial as a starting point (which forms the basis of a lot of ethnography), but rather write and research with multiply located points within Asia. To ground our anthropological practice, in an Asian complex reality will not make research easier, but it will make it richer.

These two conversations on feminist ethnography and Asia as method (briefly outlined above) may appear as parallel conversations to some scholars; however, in my reading they are deeply entangled. In this spirit of ethnographic detail and narratives, I begin each of the following sections with stories from the field. The two areas I elaborate in this chapter are the research realities of women's mobility, and rethinking 'studying up'. These moments in the field helped me slow down and think about the ethnographic realities of fieldwork in contemporary Asia. I foreground the realities that helped me think about methodologies of feminist ethnography in Asia, outside the boundedness of my Euro-American training.

MOBILITY AND MOVEMENT: RESHAPING ETHNOGRAPHIC REALITIES

Often researchers (anthropologists in particular because of our legacies of 'arriving' on an island to study its inhabitants) think of the research partici-pants and the communities we work with as waiting for us. The romanticism of building a relationship with a village or family or community, and return-ing there year after year, is etched into the ethos of ethnographic endeavour. The community and people we work with stay, and we, the researchers, come and go - sometimes with gifts, and at other times with promises for our interlocutors to come visit us. We build relationships and look forward to going back to find our friends and our 'fieldsite families'. I want to recast that relationship to one where the mobility afforded to the researcher is also available to our interlocutors – particularly in contemporary Asia. Women's movement in Asia is something that has been examined in relation to moving out of Asia for love, labour, or the labour of love. However, internal migra-tion and movement is something that has not garnered much anthropological attention. For me, however, to see the movement of women allowed me to think about the fiction of ethnographic practice that afforded the researcher mobility, but not the researched.

In 2010, circumstances led me to do research in two cities – Delhi and Dehradun. In Delhi I had a rented apartment and in Dehradun, I lived in my parents' house. This was a new house they had constructed post-retirement in 2010, so I enjoyed seeing the place they were making a home, after the movement of my childhood: growing up in a military home and moving every two years, to moving with my family to the United States for work and educational opportunities for us (their children) and then moving within the United States for graduate school. Virginia, outside Washington, DC, where I lived when I did my PhD, was the first time I had lived in any area for longer than three years. I was there from 2005 to 2010, when I left to do fieldwork in India. Even within the five-year period, I moved three times from one rented apartment to another. As a middle-class Asian student in America, this movement (and mobility) was a reality of my economics and friendships. And yet, ethnographic texts that I was reading often told of returned journeys and thick descriptions emerging from multiple engagements with the same people and ideas. I still clearly remember creating the romantic field where I would spend time with women and build community, even as I wrote my grant application. And while I was able to build community, my expectation of my interlocutors always being there each time I returned was not the case. Maybe it was because of the demographic I was working with on my research on contraception – younger women, some of who were unmarried at the time of the research. Even as I moved between Delhi and Dehradun, there were movements – women returning to their rural villages and homes for a visit, or shifting jobs within the city. This also resulted in not being able to interact with the same level of regularity or intimacy as when I was on the floor of the NGO where we all first met.

However, this mobility and movement was brought home to me most starkly in 2017, when I returned to Dehradun after a gap of two years. The last bit of fieldwork I had done had been at the end of 2015. I Facebook messaged Meena (a pseudonym), one of the women I had known during my field research in India. I messaged to ask if she was around and keen to catch up. I explained that I had found out that the manager of the NGO we met and worked at had left Dehradun and it was being run by a new team. I assumed that the manager had moved, but some of the women in the leading roles would still be there. This is the Facebook exchange with Meena:

Me: Hi Meena . . . I am now finally back in DDun . . . and thinking of going to the office to say hi to everyone. Are you still there and who else is still working there?
Meena: Hello
    : No I left dun
    : And also preeti di
    : office also change
    : I didn't no [*sic*] what's the add
    : Arunima, deepa, Vaishali, mamata they all change jobs and married too
Me: Oh wow . . . so many changes.
    : Sorry to miss you here Meena
    : Who is running the office now
Meena: I don't know
    : It's long time not connected
Me: Oh wow . . . who was running it when you left?
Meena: I am at Udaipur raj now
    : Arunima di and deepa di
Me: And Preeti left when
Meena: Yes, she lived now in naderland [sic]

Preeti had moved to the Netherlands, and not many people I knew originally were still there. Meena and I continued to chat for a bit, but nothing substantial could be discussed further on Facebook. As I got the news, I started to revaluate my follow-up research plan. Everyone I knew in that NGO had moved. Some of the middle-class women I had interviewed in Dehradun had moved to other cities in the country for marriage or work. I was friends with some of them on Facebook, but there was no fieldsite for me to return to see how things had changed. Some of the women I had interviewed in Delhi had moved on and I can only keep in touch with a few who I have Facebook contacts with. My fieldsites were not what I imagined them to be when I started fieldwork with the idea of being able to continually follow-up and learn more. Things had changed, but not in the way I could map them in the same location with the same people.

This movement of people in and out of my fieldsite made me think seriously about the romantic expectations around fieldwork and communities to go 'back' to after a certain break. I realise this mobility is a condition of globalisation, of which I too am a product. However, within Asia there are large and subtle movements, most of them initiated after liberalisation of Asian nations, as people moved out of rural settings into urban ones for work, amenities, and pleasure. While a lot of this movement is masculine, that is, men moving and leaving families behind, there is an equal measure of movement of women as well – both for starting families through marriage in other places and for jobs to sustain families that stay in the same places. The gendered aspect of movement (beyond border crossing, which is articulated brilliantly by scholars like Dr. Malini Sur[26]) is what I think makes a feminist ethnographic reading of this mobility rife with potential as a theoretical space.

This is not extraordinary movement, but rather extremely ordinary. It is not nation border crossing, or refugee movement, or even a repeat of the horrors of partition, but rather an everyday part of women's lives in Asia. As a feminist ethnographer, it became imperative for me to train my lens to see mobility and movement as methodologically shaping. I learned to go to a city to meet up for just a few hours (easy to do, since Jaipur is a few hours from Delhi) to see if I could talk more about life with Meena, but also to understand that the thick description that I was hoping to think and write through would have to look different if the women who participated in my research are moving beyond my field. I had to redefine the field, something social media has enabled as well (as I engage with below). But in defining the field and creating multiple places from wherein my methodological training finally settled as being constantly unsettled, I felt my Asian site contributing to a conversation on Asia as feminist ethnography of/in/from the contemporary mobile world(s).

RE-THINKING STUDYING 'UP' AND
POWER IN THE FIELD: SHARING THE
RESEARCH AND SOCIAL MEDIA

It was only the second time that I was meeting Mr. Ravindra Sethia (a pseudonym); however, the level of comfort I felt in talking to him meant it did not feel like I was meeting a relative stranger but rather somebody I had known for a while. I first met him the previous month at a stem cell therapy conference where we briefly exchanged information, and then continued to stay in touch regularly over phone and email. Mr. Sethia's involvement with stem cells, the topic of my postdoctoral research, was a long-term commitment that he took on when his son was diagnosed with Duchenne Muscular Dystrophy (DMD). His experiences in dealing with stem cell therapy[27] as a patient advocate were clearly valuable. It was even more interesting to talk to and learn from him as a research participant because of the extensive breadth of his knowledge of how the stem cell regulatory framework in India was organised, and his self-taught grasp of the science that drives such therapies in India. I was in India to do fieldwork on issues around governance and ethics of stem cell research and therapies, and Mr. Sethia was a parent who navigated these issues on an everyday basis to ensure the best care for his son's diagnosis. We were likely partners in our quest to understand and navigate this biomedical terrain; however, what made this partnership unique was that it allowed me to reflexively unpack the complexities of the power dynamics between researchers and their interlocutors during fieldwork.

I saw my interactions with Mr. Sethia and his narrative as informative and offering methodological nuance for what I was out to study. Working with him allowed me to open up a point of inquiry in my research that I needed to explore as a methodologically important learning moment – the idea that when it came to stem cells I was constantly studying up even if working with patients (and not just high ranking physicians) and the implications of this for my research.

Anthropology as a field of knowledge and academic tradition has evolved to critically examine (and remedy) its own methods, biases, traditions, and writing. For anthropologists, methods are almost as important as the data collected, and most fieldwork now contains a nuanced reflexivity that gives this field of knowledge a grasp on particular topics, that might be missed by other methods. Within anthropological literature, the power dynamics and differentials between the researchers and researched often become visible and the discipline has faced some criticism on this account. As methods developed and anthropologists started analysing topics 'at home', studying the self (as in their local communities), or new technological developments (both locally and globally), as opposed to traditional research of 'other cultures' in exotic faraway places, the idea of 'studying up' became part of the anthropological vocabulary. Added to this was a batch of anthropologists, trained in US or UK academic traditions that went back 'home' to study 'their home culture'. In the going back home, beyond being able to offer some local insights or nuanced readings of a familiar culture, through the lens of an 'insider/outsider', these 'native' researchers also became aware of and pointed out the lack of reflexivity of their 'outsider' anthropological colleagues. I have previously written about my insider/outsider status as a researcher and how that affected my anthropological understanding of phenomena[28] and my interactions with Mr. Sethia were an opportunity to examine a methodologically important question of how studying up impacts my/our work as ethnographer(s). While there is ample anthropological literature on the relationship between anthropologists and their interlocutors, I have often gone back and read Sidney Mintz's accounts (and the criticisms) of his relationship with his interlocutor Taso,[29] and use that model for my analysis and writing in this piece.

My interactions with Mr. Sethia made me come to terms with the fact that, when studying biomedicine and working with its various interlocutors, I was often given established narratives and asked questions in equal proportion to the questions I wanted to ask and the narratives I wanted to develop through my data. It became evident that while I was 'studying up' in the biomedical terrain in India, I was often going to have to reconfigure my understandings of 'studying up' on a contemporary topic and ask to what extent does my anthropological work differ when I study up versus when I do not?

At a second meeting with Mr. Sethia, when we agreed to do our first official interview, I arrived with consent forms in hand and audio recording device ready. Mr. Sethia, a few minutes behind schedule, arrived with a big smile and generous demeanour to share his narrative. However, before we could record or sign forms, he said:

> Now before we start talking about stem cell, tell me a bit about yourself. Where did you grow up and where is your family from? What's your story and how is that you became so involved with stem cells? (Paraphrased from conversation, prior to audio recording)

I was quiet for a second, as I was generally used to the first question from my interlocutors to be about what a medical anthropologist does and details of my current project. However, after the initial hesitation (on my part), it was a comfortable conversation, one that I may have with a new colleague or friend. We discovered that we had similar background (military brats) and were roughly the same age. As we chatted, and I allowed myself to talk about my life experiences as honestly as I expected him to about his life and medical experiences vis-à-vis stem cells, I understood that this was a research relationship among equals. However, even as a friendship developed and I became more personally empathetic towards his son's illness, I wondered if I had to try and be the 'objective' social scientist at some point. I had to remind myself that this was an important relationship for me, since because of Mr. Sethia's extensive knowledge and experience with stem cells in India he was an 'expert lay-person' for the research. I did not want him to take me too casually, as a friend, and not share important details. But also, I did not want too formal a relationship where I was cast as a distant researcher either.

Once we started to audio-record the interview, he shared immense details with me about how he, his wife, and his extended family had been through multiple layers of knowledge gaining in order to combat their son's DMD. I saw various examples of the multiple layers of knowledge gaining, where self-taught patients and patient advocates learn about their disease, prognosis, cures, and treatments through various channels of learning. Using the Internet, news media, conversations with other patients (and caregivers) and journal publications, this process is multilayered, with the earliest stage being a superficial but thorough review of the issue. As the search continues, they spend longer scanning the news media and Internet for more details, and eventually work themselves up to the level of reading academic and scientific journals. This is particularly important to keep in mind when you consider the highly specialised and scientific knowledge that is shared in academic open access journals. These patients/patient advocates grasp (and utilise) the knowledge shared there without training in the particular specialisation. These multiple layers of knowledge gaining then leads to people I like to call 'expert-layperson'.

Mr. Sethia was a self-taught expert who now also used his knowledge to suggest stem cell therapy protocols to friends and other people within the informal network. His professional background with over twenty years of experience in financial management, where he had worked for leading multinational companies and was part of senior management, definitely allowed him to approach the data for his son's prognosis in a scientific manner. However, two years into his son's diagnosis, Mr. Sethia decided to step away from his high-profile career (which required large amounts of travelling and limited time at home for caring for his son) and devote himself to his son's care. While his wife continued to work (with a more flexible schedule), he became his son's primary caregiver. This shift corresponded with him reading extensively about stem cell therapy as a possibility for treatment of DMD. Mr. Sethia devoted himself to learning more about the potentialities and problems of stem cell therapies over a ten-year period, substantially more time than I had on this research project (one year in at that point). This made evident that hitherto established dichotomies between studying up and down based on studying physicians or patients, respectively, were perhaps no longer applicable in the biomedical terrain in India.

However, the early (and important interactions) with Mr. Sethia during my research on stem cell research and therapies made amply evident to me that I would be studying up among researchers and physicians, but also studying alongside in terms of my interactions with patients and patient advocates. The immense amount of knowledge, the ability to activate informational networks, and to leverage this knowledge and network to seek out the appropriate therapies for themselves were evidence of an emerging modality of the consumer/patient of personalised biomedicine in contemporary India. Mr. Sethia became a co-collaborator in my project by patiently helping me understand the stem cell terrain in India. Reflecting on his honest exchanges and sometimes carefully organised information sharing, has allowed me to examine my relationship to my participants and interlocutors. While I was cognisant of the fact that studying up was the only way I would be able to get access to data that I needed to understand the ethical and regulatory life of stem cell research and therapy in life, it was the ethnographic realities of working with Mr. Sethia that allowed me to realise that this process of studying up does not need to at any point be a blind friendship that derails any critical thinking, nor a vehement suspicion of the narratives that my interlocutors were interpreting for me. Instead, I realised, in order to understand the contemporary biomedical terrain in India, I was constantly studying up even if my training had prepared me to think of 'up' to exist only in certain privileged spaces and with only certain people.

When I first conceptualised this bit of writing, I emailed Mr. Sethia and asked him if he was free to get together for a cup of tea so I could discuss with him what I had written. At this point, I had stopped paying attention to whether this was our fifth or fifteenth meeting, but that it was okay for me to ask him out for a cup of tea, discuss his son's health, ask about his wife's job, and have a conversation. I read him what I had written and then emailed him the final version just in case he wanted me to re-think any part of this narrative that I have outlined here. Mr. Sethia was in no way average, and his narrative was partly self-constructed and partly pieced together by me. Like Mintz and Taso's relationship, ours too was based on some construct of a friendship. And just as Mintz struggled with his critics (and his inner self) about how to write about Taso, I too wondered if Mr. Sethia's narrative (among others) should or would overshadow my analysis or whether my construction of this narrative should be foregrounded versus his own words. This is an ongoing struggle as I write up my research; however, it is evident to me that thinking and writing about Mr. Sethia early in my research forced me to think about the impact of a particular ethnographic methodology of studying up and its impact on our work. As the boundaries of studying up or down shift, based on the topics and spaces we work within, we need to be self-reflexive about not only collecting data, but also about the nature of our anthropological inquiry itself.

The conversations in ethnography about 'studying up'[30] were initiated when Euro-American anthropologists turned away from studying others in 'exotic' lands, to studying power among themselves. While I did undertake research in this traditional idea of 'studying up' when working with neurosurgeons and other trained researchers, I was also studying with and about patients like Mr. Sethia. This was a reminder that the idea of 'studying up' looks different in contemporary (South) Asia and India specifically. Even when researchers enter the field thinking they are going to work with a community or interview an individual who does not match the academic training, and while these interlocutors are fully respected by the researchers, these are never imagined as sites of 'studying up'. The Euro-American anthropological imaginary, deeply embedded in colonial pasts, does not recognise that all ethnographic work in essence is studying up, since the community or individual sharing information is a specialist and the ethnographer not. Contemporary South Asia, and India in particular, as a site of ethnographic inquiry allows us to decentre this archaic notion of studying up being limited to studying privilege and power, by instead dispersing the power and seeing all ethnographic work as studying up. What we see as 'ethnographic refusal'[31] today is but one way communities remind us that we as ethnographers are always learning from others and so even when sitting on the floor of a one-bedroom home, we are studying up, as people in that home are the knowledge holders sharing with us what we need to learn.

Within this context, I have purposefully focused on the story of Mr. Sethia to suggest that a feminist ethnographic inquiry and critical engagement on 'studying up' can emerge from spaces which are not directly or exclusively inhabited by women (and negotiations with women on power). While most of my work is with women, I occasionally worked with men – and as in this narrative above – in talking with the men, women's lives were also made more visible to me. Mr. Sethia's wife's life (who I never interviewed – and while she told me often it was because she was busy with work and care work, I think she was hesitant to be part of the research project) was often a part of the conversations Mr. Sethia and I had on illness and its implications for 'home' life. She was ever present in our meetings and interviewers, and the easy friendship between Mr. Sethia allows me to think of this engagement as feminist ethnographic research, more than just ethnographic. Friendship, respectful collaboration, and ethnographic representation are some of the key tenants of feminist ethnography. And it is in these friendships that emerge across power hierarchies, we are given access to 'study up'. He never spoke *for* her, but rather about her. I do not write about her, or imagine her life, but rather use Mr. Sethia's life as a feminist reading of caregivers (with power).

Here it is also important for me to note that meeting Mr. Sethia was not an isolated instance of me being made aware of my privileged status, and then the tables being turned when my interlocutors wanted to take that researcher power away from me – to perhaps kindly remind me that knowledge and power resides everywhere. In each interview or meeting where that happened, I was increasingly more grateful. The more confident I became as a feminist ethnographer, the more I appreciated being asked and informed about the equal playing field we operated on. Now, I should be clear, this was not always the case. There were places where I worked with women who were loving and kind, but always treated me with a certain level of deference. However, between 2008 and 2018, my fieldwork changed thanks to the Internet and social media. In one of the meetings, I was meeting a journalist who had written an amazing story on emergency contraception in India for a popular magazine. I follow her on social media, and while she is not writing about contraception, her analysis in each of her stories is stellar and a window she kindly opens for me, a researcher and audience member, to read. She was a good ten years younger than me, but a better writer by leaps and bounds. We set up a meeting via email and we met on the campus of Jawaharlal Nehru University. When I started talking about my project and my research background, she smiled and said, ah yes, I know, I saw your university profile. Clearly, the research process, in the days of the Internet, social media, and online profiles, was making even the playing field. I may be the researcher, interviewing a junior/younger woman journalist in South Asia, but I was not studying down. I was studying up, even though in some articulations I may not be. If we are to seriously consider taking Asia as feminist and/or ethnographic method, we will first have to decentre the narrative about who is up, down, or equal. This requires acknowledging that the knowledge holders are always up in relation to the researcher even if they may not appear so in some colonial imaginary, and seeing the equaliisng role of social media and online knowledge as the dynamics of researcher–researched relationship are changing.

CONCLUSION: CHANGING RESEARCH SITES AND RESEARCH METHODS

The conversation that began (in some part) in 1988 when Judith Stacey asked 'can there be a feminist ethnography?'[32] is an ongoing one. Not because feminists ethnographers do not have an answer, but rather, as I show above using Asia as a site of #unsettling and #decentring, that feminist ethnography and its ethnographers are not keen to settle the conversation. In keeping this question open, in constantly re-visiting the space where feminist ethnographies happen as fiction[33] or in the ruins[34], we are committed to an intellectual, symbolic, and everyday non-violent radical vulnerability. Continually working through what and where feminist ethnographies happen may be the true answer to the question asked in 1988. So yes, there can be a feminist ethnography, but maybe it happens in Asia? The question then, in 2020, of Asia as feminist methods, should perhaps be a starting provocation rather than a quest for answers. It should be a site from wherein new feminist ethnographic realities are articulated with multiple reference points.

Anthropologists need to stay attuned to multiple reference points - both in the field and also in our writing. To this day, when I see scholarship where *Writing Culture is* cited without *Women Writing Culture* included in the conversation, I know the kind of attention I will *not* pay to that scholarship. While that may seem like an easy commitment to a feminist citational politics, I am extremely careful to be wary of and pay attention to whose voices are included and excluded when talking about women's lives. A 'male voice' does not automatically make the project non-feminist for me, but sometimes a woman's does, for example, when white feminists who profess to speak for non-white women as our saviours, but never really hear us. Non-feminist projects are those voices that work to drown out the voices of other women (and men) who for reasons of location of birth have been marginalised historically. My commitment to a feminist ethnography is political and suggesting that Asia serve as a method of/for feminist ethnography is not an exclusionary project to say Latin American feminists or black feminists, but rather to move beyond white feminists who always situate the feminist ethnography in relationship with coloniality. It is not a negation or denial of white feminism, but rather to take Chen seriously and create multiple reference points for wherein feminist ethnographies emerge in relationality with each other and their own histories, as opposed to always in relation (even if oppositional) to the White Euro-American feminist imaginary.

As a junior feminist scholar, I see it as fitting that it was Stacey who asked 'Can there be a feminist ethnography?' and then Abu-Lughod asked the very same question again. It is not a repetition, but rather a re-claiming that moves the feminist project to a space from where women of colour can take that question as one spoken to them about them, and the answers they give mattering. To look, study, work, and research in and about Asia then requires continually being willing to 'roll with the punches' in our rapidly evolving fieldsite, and not use the old cannons to explain the world to us or our interlocutors, but rather the other way around.

* * *

ACKNOWLEDGEMENT

This research and writing has been supported by the National Science Foundation's Doctoral Dissertation Research Improvement Grant in the Science, Technology, and Society (STS) Program (Award No. 1026682) and

George Mason University's Dean's Dissertation Completion Fellowship. I would like to thank my post-doc PI (Aditya Bharadwaj) for allocating time for me to work on this project as part of my postdoctoral fellowship on the ERC grant (ID: 313769). I would also like to thank Caroline Bennett for her helpful suggestions for restructuring this chapter and its argument, and Michael Appleton for copyediting this (and all of my work). Finally, and above all, thank you to the amazing women and men who give me their time and shared so generously of themselves. I hope I represent your everyday accurately, and in your service.

NOTES

1. Amy Pollard, "Field of Screams: Difficulty and Ethnographic Fieldwork," *Anthropology Matters* 11, no. 2 (October 6, 2009), https://www.anthropologymatters.com/index.php/anth_matters/article/view/10.

2. Nayantara Sheoran Appleton, and Lorena Gibson, "Introduction: Labours of Collaboration," *Commoning Ethnography* 2, no. 1 (December 19, 2019): 88–97, https://doi.org/10.26686/ce.v2i1.6256.

3. Nayantara Sheoran, "Reading the I-Pill Advertisement: The Pleasures and Pressures of Contemporary Contraceptive Advertising in India," in *Global Media, Culture, and Identity: Theory, Cases, and Approaches*, ed. Rohit Chopra, and Radhika Gajjala (New York: Routledge, 2011), 85–99; Nayantara Sheoran Appleton, "Get Back to Life': Contradictions in and of Emergency Contraceptive Advertisements in Contemporary India," *Economic and Political Weekly* 45, no. 4 (January 2019): 35–42; Nayantara Sheoran Appleton, and Aditya Bharadwaj, "Biocrossing Heterotopia: Revisiting Contemporary Stem Cell Research and Therapy in India," in *Global Perspectives on Stem Cell Technologies*, ed. Aditya Bharadwaj (Cham: Palgrave Macmillan, 2017), 195–214, https://doi.org/10.1007/978-3-319-6 3787-7_9; Appleton, and Bharadwaj "Biocrossing Heterotopia"; Nayantara Sheoran, "'Stratified Contraception': Emergency Contraceptive Pills and Women's Differential Experiences in Contemporary India," *Medical Anthropology* 34, no. 3 (May 1, 2015): 243–258, https://doi.org/10.1080/01459740.2014.922081.

4. Richa Nagar, and Roozbeh Shirazi, "Radical Vulnerability," in *Keywords in Radical Geography: Antipode at 50* (John Wiley & Sons, Ltd, 2019), 236–242, https://doi.org/10.1002/9781119558071.ch44.

5. Kuan-Hsing Chen, *Asia as Method: Toward Deimperialization* (Durham: Duke University Press, 2010); "Takeuchi Yoshimi's 1960 'Asia as Method' Lecture: Inter-Asia Cultural Studies: Vol 13, No 2," accessed January 24, 2020, https://www.tandfonline.com/doi/full/10.1080/14649373.2012.662937.

6. Judith Stacey, "Can There Be a Feminist Ethnography?," *Women's Studies International Forum* 11, no. 1 (January 1, 1988): 21–27, https://doi.org/10.1016/0277-5395(88)90004-0.

7. Lila Abu-Lughod, "Can There Be a Feminist Ethnography?," *Women & Performance: A Journal of Feminist Theory* 5, no. 1 (January 1, 1990): 7–27, https://doi.org/10.1080/07407709008571138.

8. Chandra Talpade Mohanty, *Feminism Without Borders: Decolonizing Theory, Practicing Solidarity* (Durham: Duke University Press, 2003).

9. Mohanty, 72.

10. Chandra Talpade Mohanty, "Under Western Eyes: Feminist Scholarship and Colonial Discourses," *Feminist Review* no. 30 (Autumn 1988): 61–88.

11. Mohanty, 81.

12. Mohanty, 79.

13. Uma Narayan, *Dislocating Cultures: Identities, Traditions, and Third-World Feminism, Thinking Gender* (New York: Routledge, 1997).

14. Uma Narayan, "Contesting Cultures: 'Westernization,' Respect for Cultures, and Third-World Feminists," in *Dislocating Cultures: Identities, Traditions, and Third-World Feminism*, ed. Uma Narayan (New York: Routledge, 1997). https://philarchive.org.

15. Chandra Talpade Mohanty, "'Under Western Eyes' Revisited: Feminist Solidarity through Anticapitalist Struggles," *Signs* 28, no. 2 (Winter 2003): 499–535.

16. Nayantara Sheoran, "Once an Insider, Always an Outsider: (Re)Negotiating Boundaries When Researchers Return 'Home' for Research," *Anthropology News* 53, no. 2 (February 2012).

17. Kamala Visweswaran, *Fictions of Feminist Ethnography* (Minneapolis: University of Minnesota Press, 1994).

18. Kamala Visweswaran, "Defining Feminist Ethnography," *Turning Points in Qualitative Research: Tying Knots in a Handkerchief*, ed. Yvonna S. Lincoln, and Norman K. Denzin (London: Altimira Press, 2003), 73–94.

19. Patti Lather, "Postbook: Working the Ruins of Feminist Ethnography," *Signs* 27, no. 1 (Autumn 2001): 199–227.

20. Richelle D. Schrock, "The Methodological Imperatives of Feminist Ethnography," *Journal of Feminist Scholarship* no. 5 (December 1, 2013): 48–60.

21. Chen, *Asia as Method*.

22. Fan Yang, *Faked in China: Nation Branding, Counterfeit Culture, and Globalization*, Global Research Studies (Bloomington, IN: Indiana University Press, 2016).

23. Jason Vincent A. Cabañes, and Cecilia S. Uy-Tioco, ed. *Mobile Media and Social Intimacies in Asia: Reconfiguring Local Ties and Enacting Global Relationships* (Netherlands: Springer, 2020). https://doi.org/10.1007/978-94-024-1790-6.

24. Chen, *Asia as Method*, 99.

25. Ibid. 101.

26. Malini Sur, "Bamboo Baskets and Barricades: Gendered Landscapes at the India-Bangladesh Border," *Transnational Flows and Permissive Polities: Ethnographies of Human Mobilities in Asia*, ed. Barak Kalir, and Malini Sur (Amsterdam: Amsterdam University Press, 2012), 127–150; Malini Sur, "Divided

Bodies: Crossing the India-Bangladesh Border," *Economic and Political Weekly* 49, no. 13 (March 2014): 31–35.

27. Stem Cell therapy means treatment protocols using stem cells for diseases and injuries.

28. Nayantara Sheoran, "Once an Insider, Always an Outsider: (Re)Negotiating Boundaries When Researchers Return 'Home' for Research," *Anthropology News* 53, no. 2 (February 2012).

29. Sidney W. Mintz, "The Sensation of Moving, While Standing Still," *American Ethnologist* 16, no. 4 (November 1, 1989): 786–796, https://doi.org/10.2307/645121.

30. Hugh Gusterson, "Studying Up Revisited," *PoLAR: Political and Legal Anthropology Review* 20, no. 1 (May 1, 1997): 114–119, https://doi.org/10.1525/pol.1997.20.1.114; Laura Nader, "Up the Anthropologist: Perspectives Gained from Studying Up," in *Reinventing Anthropology*, ed. Dell Hymes (New York: Pantheon Books, 1972), 284–311; Sherry B. Ortner, "Access: Reflections on Studying up in Hollywood," *Ethnography* 11, no. 2 (June 2010): 211–233; Esther Priyadharshini, "Coming Unstuck: Thinking Otherwise about 'Studying Up,'" *Anthropology & Education Quarterly* 34, no. 4 (January 2003): 420–437, https://doi.org/10.1525/aeq.2003.34.4.420; Gusterson, "Studying Up Revisited."

31. Sherry B. Ortner, "Resistance and the Problem of Ethnographic Refusal," *Comparative Studies in Society and History* 37, no. 1 (January 1995): 173–193; Carole McGranahan, "Theorizing Refusal: An Introduction," *Cultural Anthropology* 31, no. 3 (2016): 319–325; Audra Simpson, "On Ethnographic Refusal: Indigeneity, 'Voice' and Colonial Citizenship," *Junctures: The Journal for Thematic Dialogue* no. 9 (December 2007).

32. Judith Stacey, "Can There Be a Feminist Ethnography?," *Women's Studies International Forum* 11, no. 1 (January 1, 1988): 21–27, https://doi.org/10.1016/0277-5395(88)90004-0.

33. Kamala Visweswaran, *Fictions of Feminist Ethnography* (Minneapolis: University of Minnesota Press, 1994).

34. Patti Lather, "Postbook: Working the Ruins of Feminist Ethnography," *Signs* 27, no. 1 (2001): 199–227.

REFERENCES

Abu-Lughod, Lila. "Can There Be a Feminist Ethnography?" *Women & Performance: A Journal of Feminist Theory* 5, no. 1 (January 1, 1990): 7–27.

Appleton, Nayantara Sheoran. "Get Back to Life': Contradictions in and of Emergency Contraceptive Advertisements in Contemporary India." *Economic and Political Weekly* 45, no. 4 (January 2019): 35–42.

Appleton, Nayantara Sheoran, and Aditya Bharadwaj. "Biocrossing Heterotopia: Revisiting Contemporary Stem Cell Research and Therapy in India." In *Global*

Perspectives on Stem Cell Technologies, edited by Aditya Bharadwaj, 195–214. Cham: Palgrave Macmillan, 2017.

Appleton, Nayantara Sheoran, and Lorena Gibson. "Introduction: Labours of Collaboration." *Commoning Ethnography* 2, no. 1 (December 19, 2019): 88–97.

Cabañes, Jason Vincent A., and Cecilia S. Uy-Tioco, ed. *Mobile Media and Social Intimacies in Asia: Reconfiguring Local Ties and Enacting Global Relationships.* Netherlands: Springer, 2020.

Chen, Kuan-Hsing. *Asia as Method: Toward Deimperialization.* Durham: Duke University Press, 2010.

Gusterson, Hugh. "Studying Up Revisited." *PoLAR: Political and Legal Anthropology Review* 20, no. 1 (May 1, 1997): 114–119.

Lather, Patti. "Postbook: Working the Ruins of Feminist Ethnography." *Signs* 27, no. 1 (Autumn 2001): 199–227.

McGranahan, Carole. "Theorizing Refusal: An Introduction." *Cultural Anthropology* 31, no. 3 (2016): 319–325.

Mintz, Sidney W. "The Sensation of Moving, While Standing Still." *American Ethnologist* 16, no. 4 (November 1, 1989): 786–796.

Mohanty, Chandra Talpade. *Feminism Without Borders: Decolonizing Theory, Practicing Solidarity.* Durham: Duke University Press, 2003.

———. "Under Western Eyes: Feminist Scholarship and Colonial Discourses." *Feminist Review* no. 30 (Autumn 1988): 61–88.

———. "'Under Western Eyes' Revisited: Feminist Solidarity through Anticapitalist Struggles." *Signs* 28, no. 2 (Winter 2003): 499–535.

Nader, Laura. "Up the Anthropologist: Perspectives Gained from Studying Up." In *Reinventing Anthropology*, edited by Dell Hymes, 284–311. New York: Pantheon Books, 1972.

Nagar, Richa, and Roozbeh Shirazi. "Radical Vulnerability." In *Keywords in Radical Geography: Antipode at 50*, 236–242. John Wiley & Sons, Ltd, 2019.

Narayan, Uma. "Contesting Cultures: 'Westernization,' Respect for Cultures, and Third-World Feminists." In *Dislocating Cultures: Identities, Traditions, and Third-World Feminism*, edited by Uma Narayan. New York: Routledge 1997. https://philarchive.org.

———. *Dislocating Cultures: Identities, Traditions, and Third-World Feminism.* Thinking Gender. New York: Routledge, 1997.

Ortner, Sherry B. "Access: Reflections on Studying up in Hollywood." *Ethnography* 11, no. 2 (June 2010): 211–233.

———. "Resistance and the Problem of Ethnographic Refusal." *Comparative Studies in Society and History* 37, no. 1 (January 1995): 173–193.

Pollard, Amy. "Field of Screams: Difficulty and Ethnographic Fieldwork." *Anthropology Matters* 11, no. 2 (October 6, 2009). https://www.anthropologym atters.com/index.php/anth_matters/article/view/10.

Priyadharshini, Esther. "Coming Unstuck: Thinking Otherwise about 'Studying Up.'" *Anthropology & Education Quarterly* 34, no. 4 (January 2008): 420–437.

Rajaram, Poorva. "Sexing THE PILL." *Tehelka Magazine*, March 5, 2011. http://www.tehelka.com/story_main49.asp?filename=hub050311THEPILL.asp.

Schrock, Richelle D. "The Methodological Imperatives of Feminist Ethnography." *Journal of Feminist Scholarship* no. 5 (December 1, 2013): 48–60.

Sheoran, Nayantara. "Once an Insider, Always an Outsider: (Re)Negotiating Boundaries When Researchers Return 'Home' for Research." *Anthropology News* 53, no. 2 (February 2012).

———. "Reading the I-Pill Advertisement: The Pleasures and Pressures of Contemporary Contraceptive Advertising in India." In *Global Media, Culture, and Identity: Theory, Cases, and Approaches*, edited by Rohit Chopra, and Radhika Gajjala, 85–99. New York: Routledge, 2011.

———. "'Stratified Contraception': Emergency Contraceptive Pills and Women's Differential Experiences in Contemporary India." *Medical Anthropology* 34, no. 3 (May 1, 2015): 243–258.

Simpson, Audra. "On Ethnographic Refusal: Indigeneity, 'Voice' and Colonial Citizenship." *Junctures: The Journal for Thematic Dialogue* no. 9 (December 2007): 67 - 80.

Stacey, Judith. "Can There Be a Feminist Ethnography?" *Women's Studies International Forum* 11, no. 1 (January 1, 1988): 21–27.

Sur, Malini. "Bamboo Baskets and Barricades: Gendered Landscapes at the India-Bangladesh Border." *Transnational Flows and Permissive Polities: Ethnographies of Human Mobilities in Asia*, edited by Barak Kalir, and Malini Sur, 127–150. Amsterdam: Amsterdam University Press, 2012.

———. "Divided Bodies: Crossing the India-Bangladesh Border." *Economic and Political Weekly* 49, no. 13 (March 2014): 31–35.

"Takeuchi Yoshimi's 1960 'Asia as Method' Lecture: Inter-Asia Cultural Studies: Vol 13, No 2." n.d. https://www.tandfonline.com/doi/full/10.1080/14649373.2012.662937.

Visweswaran, Kamala. "Defining Feminist Ethnography." *Turning Points in Qualitative Research: Tying Knots in a Handkerchief*, edited by Yvonna S. Lincoln, and Norman K. Denzin, 73–94. London: AltaMira Press, 2003.

———. *Fictions of Feminist Ethnography*. Minneapolis: University of Minnesota Press, 1994.

Yang, Fan. *Faked in China: Nation Branding, Counterfeit Culture, and Globalization*. Global Research Studies. Bloomington, IN: Indiana University Press, 2016.

Chapter 10

Identity Politics, Fieldworkers, and Globalisation

A Japanese Company in Hong Kong as a Fieldsite

Yi Zhu

ABSTRACT

The major aim of the chapter is to analyse the changing dynamics of anthropological fieldwork in relation to the discourse of identity politics, business, and globalisation through a description of fieldwork in a Japanese company in Hong Kong. The chapter is primarily concerned with the process of long-term fieldwork conducted in Hong Kong by the mainland China-born researcher who was raised and educated both in mainland China and Japan. By reconstructing the process of fieldwork and presenting the ethnography of a fieldworker in the company, the chapter demonstrates how anthropological fieldwork helps us understand the inter-Asia translocality embedded in the socio-political sphere as well as the transformation of self in the process of fieldwork. The chapter examines how anti-China sentiment that arose after the handover of Hong Kong sovereignty in 1997 has influenced the emergence of local identity and how local consumption of Japanese culture has, to some extent, contributed to serve as 'external' yet 'superior' culture for reconstructing local identity. This has contributed to the construction of a translocal workplace environment in Ichi Hong Kong. The chapter then discusses how the fieldworker transformed herself based on her interpretation of the complexity of identity politics reflected in the workplace as well as her own experiences to establish ways to strategically cope with this environment. The complexity, as the chapter shows, must be understood in relation to the formation of the local Hong Kong identity vis-à-vis China and the influence of Japanese culture in Hong Kong.

Additionally, it shows that fieldworkers may need to acquire flexibility and skills to adapt to the changing dynamics of the field. In the conclusion, the author explains the relevance of anthropological fieldwork in identifying the connections between local and regional/global contexts and between fieldworker and the field.

* * *

Increasingly the flow of globalising businesses, people, and resources in the world has impacted the meanings and methods of anthropological fieldwork, as a long-term observation of one or more particular groups of people to address the system of their culture. Under these influences, the relationship between the researching subject and researched object has also been evolving, which has correspondingly altered the encounters and expectations of ethnographers: they must not only immerse themselves into a single site for a long-term period, but also flexibly cope with the changing new environment(s). A number of publications have begun addressing the psychological and subjective aspects of fieldworkers – who were traditionally expected not to disturb and change the field – illustrating how their subjective experiences, including factors such as gender, personal history, and ethnicity, can contribute to a better understanding of what is actually occurring. This chapter aims to present the inner state and struggles of a fieldworker attempting to become an *insider* in the cosmopolitan urbanity of Hong Kong.

When we discuss globalisation and its impacts, we can no longer neglect the emergence of power dynamics in Asia such as the Japanese economic miracle from the 1950s to 1980s (when Japan recorded rapid economic growth and became the second largest economy after the United States) and the economic boom in other Asian countries and regions (some of which are still experiencing rapid economic growth), including South Korea, China, and India in the 1990s. Politics in the Asian region have also been in the spotlight in terms of Asia's complex identity politics, (post)colonialism, nationalism, and imperialism. In addition, culture, and its influence in different locations (such as the consumption of Japanese popular culture across Asia), plays a significant role in (re)constructing local identity. These changes bring attention to the complex political, social, and cultural spheres within Asia, which have led to the pursuit of inter-referencing Asian cultural studies. Indeed, Asian countries have strong ties in terms of geographic closeness and historical cultural events as well as through cooperation in frequent economic activities over the years, which have created overlapping and sometimes mutually constitutive customs and ideas. However, historical development, economic activities, systems of belief, and political debates have been largely (re)configured to the countries' own systems and ideas.

To explain the relevance of anthropological fieldwork in identifying the connections between local and regional/global contexts and researcher/ researched in the Asian region, this chapter introduces fieldwork at a Japanese multinational apparel company (called Ichi in this chapter) located in Hong Kong. Through the description of fieldwork at the company, this chapter first discusses the changing picture of identity recognition of local people after the handover of Hong Kong's sovereignty to China in 1997 and how the consumption of Japanese culture has somewhat contributed to the reconstruction of local identity and complex identity politics. Second, it shows the unique relationship between researcher and the researched, by exploring the coping strategies of a fieldworker who was born in mainland China but raised and educated in mainland China and Japan. It discusses in detail how the fieldworker interpreted the identity politics on site and how she behaved in a particular way in an attempt to disguise or distort her ethnic identity as mainland Chinese to be accepted in the field. The discussion in this chapter is devoted to debating how local identity reconstruction reflects the complicated political sphere of Hong Kong and how it relates to Japanese culture. It also addresses how the relationship between the researcher and researched can be understood in the context of changing dynamics in Asia, particularly in relation to China's relations to Hong Kong, and Hong Kong's relations to Japan, by considering how I, as a person born in China, educated first in Japan and then in China, and coming to do fieldwork in Hong Kong, struggled to discover and enrich my multiple identities and strategies to cope with a changing and new environment. Finally, I discuss the importance of conducting fieldwork in businesses to identify the connections between local and regional/global contexts and between business and culture in the context of Hong Kong, China, and Japan. Although I am aware of the impact of the colonial period, this chapter focuses on the post-colonial era, particularly after the handover of Hong Kong from Britain to China in 1997.

GLOBALISATION AND CONDUCTING FIELDWORK IN BUSINESS

Numerous studies have been published on the changing nature of fieldwork practices in the context of globalisation and contemporary anthropology.[1] Globalisation has been widely debated in terms of technological advance- ment, change in space and place, and the dichotomy of global and local. Along with the increasing sophistication of technology, the ways people connect and communicate have significantly changed. Beginning with the classic work of Manuel Castells,[2] numerous publications have argued that information technology and information capitalism have resulted in the rise of the network society, which affects the choice of technological tools used in fieldwork as well as the way students are educated on how to use them.[3]

Globalisation has also changed the concept of space and place. Anthony Giddens argued that along with globalisation, time and space has been compressed because advanced technology allows people located far away from each other to obtain the latest information almost instantly.[4] The concept of the global city,[5] proposed by Saskia Sassen, is an example of the transformation and change in the space and meaning of a city.[6] This too has impacted the ways in which fieldworkers interpret the changing dynamics in the field. In terms of the dichotomy of global and local contexts, representative research includes that of Robertson,[7] who argued that along with the increasing discussion of globalisation, heated debates about what is local have increased, and Appadurai,[8] who claimed that translocality can be seen in various circumstances where the notion of locality in one nation-state can exist beyond its local context (such as in tourism). Culture that is cultivated in this process also clarifies the difference between 'territorial culture' and 'translocal culture' as Pieterse argued:[9] the former indicating a situation where culture has been essentially territorially based while the latter refers to culture acquired during a translocal learning process. In more recent publications, there has been discussion on the connection between locality and global position.[10] As for the concept of global ethnography, Burawoy and his colleagues discussed how locally situated ethnography can sharpen the abstractions of Globalisation theories into more precise and meaningful conceptual tools,[11] by illustrating the penetration of global processes and subsequent restructuring of localities organically linking local realities to global processes. Discussions of the global/local and local/global contexts have provided fieldworkers with additional frameworks to debate issues occurring locally and their global influences and impacts, and vice versa.

Along with these changes, the position of Asia has emerged as a critical aspect of the context of the global/local, related to which there has been a trend of examining Asian studies in Asia. Partially inspired by Takeuchi Yoshimi's 'Asia as Method',[12] Kuan-Hsing Chen used the history of East Asia to deimperialise the West, given the region's historical complexity. Many publications have examined various issues using this method.[13] Other studies have centred on how the daily lives of people in Asia have changed as a result of globalisation.[14] This chapter pursues this direction by discussing the daily practices of employees working in a Japanese company located in Hong Kong to reveal a situation in which translocal culture has been cultivated in a complex web of the region, mainland China, and Japan.

To engage with Stocking's argument about anthropology's fundamental 'methodological values' being taken for granted without critical analysis,[15] this section aims to explore how, under the impact of globalisation, anthropological fieldwork has evolved in terms of its meanings and methods as well as the relationship between the researcher and researched. In the early 1970s, scholars began using a deconstructive lens to critically reflect upon the time when anthropologists were expected to provide tools or guidance for the coloniser to better manage the colonised by exploring Indigenous and native cultures.[16] This lens criticises anthropology's culpability in European colonialism and specifically points out the possibility of influence by ethnographers in the findings they report.[17] This so-called reflexive turn refers to ethnographies becoming the sources of reflection because they include, almost as a requirement, meditations on the conditions of their production.[18]

With this in mind and considering the increasing compactness of the world through advanced technology, fieldwork methods have begun to change. One example is a shift from single to multi-sited fieldwork. This change, which seems to contradict the idea of classic ethnography defined by Clifford,[19] who argues that fieldworkers immersing themselves into a single field for a relatively long time, is the hallmark of the discipline. Instead, it is an argument in favour of 'cross-cut[ting] dichotomies such as the "local" and the "global," the "lifeworld" and the "system"' described.[20] This method does not shorten the fieldwork period, but rather advocates that fieldworkers should be prepared to adapt fieldwork methods and scales based on encounters with various sets of social units and social relations,[21] thus attending, and adapting to, the realities of ethnographic encounters in today's world.

As globalisation affected the way fieldwork was conducted, it also influenced the type of locales seen as appropriate for research. Along with the emergence of modern business organisations under the influence of globalisation and economic and societal development, fieldwork sites have expanded from remote places to include urban communities and organisations, including profit-oriented corporations. The use of anthropological methods in business contexts is generally considered to have initiated with experiments in the 1920s and 1930s at the Hawthorne telephone works, which aimed to explore alternative explanations for employee motivation besides 'scientific management',[22] a concept proposed by Frederic Taylor based on the assumption that people act consistent with the 'economic man'.[23] In the 'Bank Wiring Observation Room experiment', anthropologist Lloyd Warner and fellow researchers conducted fieldwork to determine whether there is any gap between what employees *say* they do and what they actually *do* on site, and examined whether payment incentives affect productivity. When it actually decreased, this experiment demonstrated that management's assumption that all employees act consistently with the 'economic man' was incorrect,

indicating that the assumptions made by groups of people do not necessarily reflect reality. Later on, various ethnographies in business organisations
showed gaps between corporate ideology/reality, global/local dichotomy, and
the crafting of identity and complexity of human relations.[24] In recent years,
along with the increasing importance on customer-centric strategy, human-
centred design, and UX research (user experience), collaboration between
industry and academia has increased, resulting in publications not only for
academia, but also business professionals.[25]

Another major change in fieldwork studies is the relationship between the
researching subject and researched object. In recent years, more publications have discussed the issue of subjectivity and changes in the emotions
of fieldworkers or their *status of being*, which is slightly different from the
'traditional empiricism' focus on not interrupting the field and being as objective as possible by creating distance with the 'researched'. In *Emotions in the
Field: The Psychology and Anthropology of Fieldwork Experience*, James
Davies and Dimitrina Spencer argued that a researcher's emotional experience can actually present opportunities for understanding an intersubjective
and experiential fieldwork.[26] Fieldwork is not simply about participant observation; fieldworkers must be critically conscious of what they are doing as
they are doing it. Crapanzano[27] argues that what John Keats calls the negative
capability of fieldworkers – that is, the ability to identify with a character
without losing the fieldworkers' identity, position, and confidence – does not
fully represent fieldworkers because fieldworkers' views can be modified by
the local context without destroying their own. Schumaker[28] also argues that
fieldworkers can become the centre of a production process that they do not
entirely control; therefore, they need to reflectively observe their responses
to a constantly changing environment, which is quite different from the
rather passive concept of fieldworkers as sensitive and intuitive observers
and participants.

Other trends in ethnography examine the transformation of self and
self-fashioning for social recognition or even personal gain. Publications
include *Crafting Selves: Power, Gender and Discourses of Identity in a
Japanese Workplace*,[29] *Ocasião: The Marquis and the Anthropologist, a
Collaboration*,[30] *Creating a Multivocal Self: Autoethnography as Method*,[31]
*Organizational Autoethnographies: Power and Identity in Our Working
Lives*,[32] and many others. As Marcus and Fischer discussed in *Anthropology as
Cultural Critique*,[33] the process of tracing and exploring personal experience
during fieldwork also contributes to the discussion of how fieldwork has
changed in relation to Globalisation and changes in our society. There have
also been discussions related to how life story narratives can provide dialogue
for the ideas of 'landscape of action' and 'landscape of consciousness' as
argued by Bruner,[34] as well as 'landscape of transformation' as claimed by

Dyson.[35] The level of action reflects what actually happened, and the level of consciousness reflects the experiences of the actors. Adding to these two ideas, Dyson examined how exploring personal transformation through self-reflection will allow us to reach the level of transformation where 'we reach a stage when we begin to see things differently to that which we first thought, or perceived'.[36]

It is clear that globalisation and changes in fieldwork have impacted anthropologists who study Asia; however, how have political issues and culture influenced the emergence of identity politics and changes in fieldwork and fieldworkers? This chapter aims to reveal the situation where translocal knowledge has been cultivated in the power dynamic in Asia through the example of identity politics in Hong Kong based on its relationship with mainland China and Japan.

IDENTITY POLITICS IN HONG KONG

Hong Kong has been associated with many concepts and meanings. On the one hand, Hong Kong is considered a place that reflects modern capitalism, cosmopolitanism, urbanity, and commercialism as well as a chaotic society full of diverse ethnic groups. As Hong Kong government's slogan 'Asia's World City' demonstrates, the region has exerted strong efforts in promoting Hong Kong as one of the most urban cities. Many people view Hong Kong as a place that combines tradition and cosmopolitanism, where Asia meets the West, and where residents can speak English and Cantonese. The government aims for Hong Kong to continue its diversity, to be open to innovation, and to grow its economy with increasing money from China through various projects including the opening of the high-speed rail link and the Hong Kong–Zhuhai–Macau Bridge in 2018. According to Hong Kong's Trade Development Council, the region is the world's freest economy in Asia as of 2018.[37] Hong Kong also topped the Euromonitor's list of the 'Top 100 City Destinations 2018',[38] and it was reported that 'Hong Kong is the most obvious beneficiary of the Chinese outbound boom'.[39] On the other hand, Chunking Mansions and its surroundings show another side of Hong Kong, that is, its 'ghetto'. This area was once surrounded by luxurious hotels and shopping malls, and was considered the most globalised spot on the planet.[40]

Identity politics refers to the tendency of groups of people with particular backgrounds, such as age, religion, and ethnicity, to form political alliances based on injustices due to not being part of majority groups. In addition to being influenced by its colonial history and sentiment, Hong Kong's local identity has a close connection with influences from mainland China, particularly after its handover in 1997, which increased the sentiment of being local and facilitated various movements in Hong Kong along with increasing political and social contact between the two places. Abbas described how, although the major ethnicity of Hong Kong people is Chinese, colonial history made Hong Kong Chinese people culturally and politically distinct from mainland Chinese.[41] A poll conducted by the University of Hong Kong in June 2019 asking participants how they self-identify for ethnicity showed the majority of people identify themselves as Hongkonger ('Hoeng gong jan' in Cantonese, meaning Hong Kong people, 52.9%) or Hongkonger in China (23.5%) rather than Chinese (10.8%) or Chinese in Hong Kong (12.3%). These results indicate that the majority of the population of Hong Kong (or at least those sampled in the poll) consider being Chinese or Hongkonger as different ethnic identities. This shows that locality is of rising importance in Hong Kong identity, particularly after the handover. A major influence in identity creation in Hong Kong today is the post-colonial period, which started after the handover of Hong Kong from the British to China in 1997. Exploring the relationship between mainland China and Hong Kong, and then considering the possible impact of the consumption of Japanese culture on Hong Kong's local identity, I lay the foundation for the fieldworker's struggles in becoming an insider and her coping strategies.

Hong Kong and Mainland China

Since Hong Kong's sovereignty was returned to China from the UK on 1 July 1997[42] with the promise of continuing 'one country, two systems' for fifty years (Hong Kong can maintain its own economic and administrative systems as a Special Administrative Region of China), the relationship between Hong Kong and mainland China has been complicated as it embeds both opportunities and threats. Opportunities include economic benefits from closer ties with mainland China, and a booming retail industry thanks to the increasing number of tourists from mainland China: 51 million of the total 65.1 million tourists recorded in 2018.[43] Since the handover, Hong Kong's economy has survived several external shocks, and meanwhile, mainland China's economy has continuously grown. In 2003, six years after the handover, a free trade agreement called the Closer Economic Partnership Arrangement was signed between mainland China and Hong Kong. This agreement includes the new Individual Visit Scheme travel policy, which resulted in loosening visa restrictions for tourists from mainland China travelling to Hong Kong. This largely contributed to a boom in Hong Kong's retail industry, and it is expected that 'Hong Kong will continue to enjoy a 10 to 15 % growth in Chinese visitor arrivals per year'.[44] To accommodate the incoming tourists, in 2012 international retailers opened more shops in Hong Kong than anywhere else in the Asia-Pacific region.[45]

It is evident that there have been significant economic benefits for Hong Kong after the handover; however, there have also been significant tensions in terms of control and sovereignty. An early example emerged two months after the handover, with the implementation of a mandatory change in the teaching language at the junior secondary level from English to Chinese, which triggered critical political debates. Although some schools applied for an exemption, news of this change shocked students and their parents.[46] English plays a significant role in Hong Kong not only in securing decent employment but also in terms of status. Due to the role language plays in structuring one's identity and society, the request from the Chinese central government was not simply a change to the medium of instruction, but rather an attempt to change local residents' identities. Chan attributed the failure of the central government to implement this policy with full support from the locals in part due to its lack of sensitivity to the nature and social functions of language.[47] Later examples relate to movements for political freedom organised in Hong Kong, such as the 2014 Hong Kong protests (i.e., the Yellow Umbrella movements), and the more recent protests against a proposed extradition law amendment in 2019. The Yellow Umbrella movements, based on the theme of Occupy Central with Love and Peace, received global media attention. During the protests, a large number of protesters sat in the streets to advocate for the resignation of then chief executive of Hong Kong, Leung Chun-ying, and protest against the new reforms to the Hong Kong electoral system. The latest conflicts, occurring under Hong Kong's management by Chief Executive Carrie Lam Cheng Yuet-ngor, began in July 2019, and a series of demonstrations have occurred in many places in Hong Kong, which have continued for several months.

Other sources of tension relate to the increasing number of people travelling from mainland China to Hong Kong, which has been linked to several issues causing social anxiety. These include a reported shortage of milk powder in 2013, threatening basic healthcare for people in Hong Kong, when a strong yuan, as well as mainland China's melamine-tainted scandal, led to some visitors making extremely large purchases of formula either as gifts, for their own use, or for resale back in China.[48] The rise of so-called birth tourism which indicates tourists from mainland China were claimed to give birth to an 'anchor baby (雙非嬰兒)' for the right of abode in Hong Kong. This would enable their children to receive better education (in particular, education in English), to cultivate international perspectives, and to have access to more secure social welfare. Related to this social anxiety, in 2013, Chief Executive Leung Chun-ying announced a policy to ban women from mainland China from having babies in Hong Kong. In 2016, around 800 cross-border babies were delivered by women from mainland China arriving at the city's emergency wards in the late stages of pregnancy. Although we cannot know for certain the reason for these births in Hong Kong, this was reported as evidence of people from mainland China deliberately breaking this law,[49] fuelling the already existing social anxiety and the divisions between the communities and countries. Related to this, a shortage of qualified hospitals for giving birth was also reported to be an issue, because it was claimed that the increasing number of people giving birth in Hong Kong had reduced the number of hospitals including public and private for giving birth, making it difficult for local women to find a suitable hospital they needed.[50]

The increasing number of such cases had seemed to alert some customs officers during my research. Arriving with my Chinese passport at the airport on two of the three trips I made from Japan to Hong Kong between 2016 and 2018, my stomach was observed, and I was asked directly if I was pregnant. An undergraduate student in her early twenties, also from China but living in Japan, told me that she was also asked the same question in late 2019. These experiences might not represent the case of all Chinese passport holders, but it made me reflect on the meaning of having a Chinese passport for women of certain ages (myself included).

Social morality is another issue that has been debated along with the increasing number of tourists from mainland China. People in Hong Kong have reported that some of the behaviours of mainland Chinese, such as spitting, littering, jaywalking, and cutting in line, were inappropriate.[51] It has been widely reported that China has expended great efforts and investment on a new moral education campaign by promoting the necessity, and ways of, behaving in 'civilized' ways;[52] however, these efforts have not yet largely changed the way Chinese were portrayed in Hong Kong.

Although Hong Kong has reaped economic benefits since the handover, many locals in Hong Kong have experienced negative political and societal impacts. These feelings have prompted locals to pursue an 'alternative culture', since the cultural logic of Hong Kong is to deny the unifying cultural foundations,[53] and the consumption of Japanese culture could be considered a way in which they do so.

Consumption of Japanese Culture

Consumption of Japanese culture in other Asian countries, including Hong Kong, has long been discussed.[54] While some scholars have pointed out the possible influence of Japan's colonial history in Hong Kong – a period of three years and eight months during World War II, from 1941 to 1945 – Chan claimed that the wartime occupation has limited influence on the current younger generations because of their lack of interest.[55] Echoing her argument, anti-Japanese sentiments were rarely discussed or even mentioned among young local employees at the company where I conducted fieldwork; instead, Japan was often associated with images of sophistication and modernity. As Iwabuchi discussed in his book

Recentering Globalization: Popular Culture and Japanese Transnationalism,[56] Japanese culture has been placed 'in but above', or 'similar but superior to', the rest of the Asian region, which also applies to how many Hong Kong people view Japan. This can be seen in Hong Kong's 'love of Japan' in terms of tourism and the popularity of Japanese products or Made-in-Japan brands in Hong Kong. In fact, Japan was the top-scoring country as a brand out of seventy-five countries, according to consulting firm Future Brand in 2015.[57]

First, Japan is a popular travel destination for the Hong Kong people, who account for one of the top groups for repeat tourists in Japan.[58] Statistics from the Japanese Tourism Agency from 2017 shows the huge popularity of Japan for Hong Kong tourists: in that year the number of visitors from Hong Kong increased 21.3% compared to the previous year. Almost one-third of all Hong Kong residents visited Japan in 2017, with more than 85% of those visiting more than twice, and 25% of the visitors visiting more than ten times. This means that visitors from Hong Kong accounted for one of the highest percentage of visitors in Japan.

During my fieldwork, I often heard local employees discuss their affection for Japan, but that they could not travel there often due to how expensive it is; instead, they mostly travelled to Taiwan where they could experience a sense of Japan on a lower budget. I also overhead many times at Ichi that long before the company entered the Hong Kong market, the reputation of the brand already existed in Hong Kong and some employees would buy the products for their friends as a nice gift. Many locals learned Japanese popular culture not only from the media, but also by visiting Japan.

Second, Hong Kong people have a strong tendency to support Japanese products or Made-in-Japan brands. According to a Japanese marketing solution company, among fourteen cities in Asia, Hong Kong residents have most trusted Japanese products and have a higher tendency to purchase Made-in-Japan branded goods, although this does not necessarily mean that the products were in fact made in Japan.[59] Zhu argued that this phenomenon, to some extent, contributes to the success of Japanese companies in Hong Kong who well utilise this as a brand strategy.[60] Hong Kong is also the largest importer of Japanese agricultural goods, which increased 15.2% in 2018 compared to the same period in 2017.[61] Japanese restaurants and retailers also significantly contribute to transforming the meaning and style of consumption in Hong Kong. Wong analysed how a Japanese retailer, Yaohan, introduced a new business model in Hong Kong to allow local residents to experience modern retail and to change the way they consider food and retail.[62] Chan described how the influence of Japanese-styled consumer culture, such as department stores (Sogo, Mitsukoshi, Seibu, etc.), formed Hong Kong's post-colonial culture.[63] Such studies have shown the strong impact of Japanese products on local consumption and how the introduction of modern commercial culture was widely welcomed by local people.

The above discussion suggests ways in which Japanese culture plays a role as an 'additional' or 'external' culture for reconstructing local identity in Hong Kong. Related to the cultural logic of denying the 'unifying cultural foundations' of China and Hong Kong,[64] people in Hong Kong asserted difference, partly through the embrace of the consumption of the Japanese brand and its goods, related to a desire for the sophistication and trustworthy image represented by the Made-in-Japan products the desire of Japanese culture does not mean that the people of Hong Kong accept it uncritically. Chan explains that along with the denial 'they want or need to embrace and ridicule at the same time'. In other words, some Hong Kong people may consider Japanese culture as sophisticated and superior to parts of their culture; however, there is no acculturation but rather a respect of diverse cultural foundations. Hong Kong has cosmopolitan values embedded in the diverse cultural foundations of local identities.

Synthesising the above discussions on the relationship between Hong Kong and mainland China, and the consumption of Japanese culture, we can conclude that there has been strong conflict between Hong Kong and mainland China due to fears of losing sovereignty and freedom after the handover, and social anxieties related to this. To reconfigure who they are, the Hong Kong people seem to have proactively incorporated various external cultures such as Japanese culture, which instilled a modern consumption culture as well as something 'similar but superior' and 'in but above' Hong Kong's own culture. However, this does not mean that Hong Kong has entirely changed its local identity, but rather it has reorganised and restructured it. Discussion of the issue of identity construction and changes in Hong Kong have contributed to understanding the difference between translocal culture and territorial culture as Pieterse described, and the process of how knowledge has been accumulated in the translocal manner.[65]

Discussions of the identity issue have also introduced the spatial atmosphere of the workplace placed upon Ichi employees as well as the fieldworker. How then are these identity politics reflected in and influenced by fieldwork? The following section discusses the daily work life in a Japanese retailer in Hong Kong to demonstrate the transformation of the fieldworker in a translocal environment and what strategies a fieldworker who is aiming to become an insider can adopt.

IDENTITY POLITICS IN A JAPANESE
APPAREL COMPANY

I was fortunate enough to be accepted by Ichi[66] as an intern for the purpose of conducting my fieldwork from August 2010 to December 2011. Ichi is a

Japanese company that began by operating fashion retail shops in Japan in the 1980s. Although it began operating in rural areas in the domestic market, the company expanded to overseas markets in the early 2000s. With a motto of selling affordable, high quality casual wear and an emphasis on customer service, Ichi now operates thousands of retail stores in more than ten overseas markets. I initially wanted to study how the company was able to globalise and how human resource management and cross-culture management had contributed to this process.

Ichi first entered Hong Kong in the early 2000s, and it was the first overseas market that earned a profit from the very beginning. With prior failures in Western and other Asian markets, Ichi's top management began to lose confidence in its overseas operations; however, high popularity and a profit from its early stages in Hong Kong prompted the company's subsequent expansion abroad. Indeed, Ichi Hong Kong has become one of Ichi's most profitable markets. Recently, Ichi began integrating all of its human resource policies, such as recruitment, evaluation, and promotion, and following the standard format created in Ichi Japan. The company also assigned several Japanese store managers to stores in Hong Kong in an attempt to disseminate Ichi corporate ideology in Hong Kong. My fieldwork was conducted during these changes, in an environment when Ichi was aiming to transform itself from a Japanese, to a global, company.

My journey at Ichi started with a one-day training at the head office in Hong Kong in 2009. Afterwards, I was assigned to one local retail shop for several months, and then worked at several other store locations for shorter periods of time. My shifts were the same as a full-time salesperson: five days a week, 8 hours a day. During my fieldwork, Ichi was well known for long working hours due to the popularity of its stores; however, I had the freedom to choose whether I wanted to work overtime, which may have influenced my analysis on some related issues.

Daily work at Ichi was slightly more difficult than I expected. For the first few months, I was busy memorising each practical task, including the required greeting words (three to four sets) in the local language (Cantonese), and various rules such as those related to customer service (prohibited phrases, external appearance, etc.), replenishment (ordering correct colours and sizes), and customer requests (for maintaining the stock, etc.). While trying to become more relaxed with my daily work routine, during lunch time, I started interviewing some of the part-time employees who dominated 70% of the labour force. At the same time, I also received access to the formal organisational structure to understand the store's structure. For the first few weeks of my interviews, employees were rather hesitant to provide direct answers to my questions, likely because I was still considered an outsider but perhaps because I spoke Mandarin instead of Cantonese, the lingua franca of Hong Kong. Even after several months, and in fact, during the entire fieldwork, I did not speak Cantonese with other employees – although I learned several words to interact with the customers – because I did not want people to label me as a 'foreigner' or 'mainland Chinese' with broken language ability.

This feeling was partly because of a fear of standing out due to my differences, but also because of my experience of living in Japan as a foreigner, where I felt inferior being '*chuugokujin*' (refers to Chinese, in Japanese). When I lived in Japan from six to twelve years old, I was the only non-Japanese student in my local primary school as well as my neighbourhood. This special identity sometimes made me the target of bullying, and I also felt frustrated whenever I had to explain my name and story to others. I became fluent in Japanese, and learned many ways to behave correctly as a Japanese person, which might be apparent from the fact I was always mistaken as Japanese in Japan. Now, I am also fluent in Mandarin thanks to the education I received in China from twelve to eighteen years old; however, when I was living in Japan for primary school, I was also hesitant to speak Chinese with my parents both in public and at home. This may not be unique in terms of childhood education and language learning for a non-native child, but the surrounding environment in Japan, particularly the increasing anti-Chinese sentiment, to some extent influenced my hesitancy.[67] It is highly possible that my strong or sometimes overt consciousness of being mainland Chinese, and my understanding of the ongoing political issues in Hong Kong, made me hesitant to present my ethnic identity at the company.

Conflicts between the ethnic majority and minorities also exist in Hong Kong but in a more complicated way. People in Hong Kong seem to have more opportunities to immerse themselves with various external cultures due to a large number of residents entering and leaving the islands. Thus, it is sometimes difficult to connect people's identity with tangible criteria such as external appearance and behaviours. Having said that, as an ethnographer, becoming an insider was a requirement, and feeling inferior as mainland Chinese prompted me to adjust in a way that locals desired or expected. In the first several weeks, I was afraid of being discriminated against due to my ethnicity, but I did not observe any discrimination lodged in my direction. However, after several months, I had more social media connections with Ichi employees, such as Facebook friends, and I noticed some of their comments about mainland China. Sometimes the comments were not racial attacks, but simply their way of expressing frustration towards the Hong Kong government. Nevertheless, I had a clearer image of what types of conversations they had online and what news they followed, of which I was unaware prior to connecting with them on social media. After that, I started to practice a conscious self-fashioning. In many contexts, people intentionally or unconsciously manipulate some aspects of themselves for social recognition or personal gain. In my case, based on how I interpreted the way in which locals viewed mainland Chinese and Japanese, I proactively adjusted some tangible aspects, including language, external appearance, manner of speech, and experience in Japan, aiming to show my immersion in the local context.

Firstly, in terms of language, I spoke Mandarin with a Southern accent to suggest to others that I was Taiwanese. Interestingly, when I was in China speaking fluent Mandarin, others believed I was 'non-Chinese' or 'overseas Chinese', but I was never confused as Taiwanese. A male salesperson in his early twenties once asked me where I was from, and after hearing my story, said, 'maybe you should tell others you are Taiwanese, instead of mainland Chinese'. His comment appeared to stem from kindness, and his advice was based on a belief shared by other employees. It seems that my 'imperfect' Mandarin, compared to 'standard' or Northern Mandarin, projected a more neutral image in Hong Kong because Northern Mandarin is associated with mainland Chinese or people from Beijing and, in turn, the central government. One of my friends from Australia told me he was not treated well in Taiwan since he spoke Northern Mandarin, while another friend from Scotland said his Southern Mandarin gave him an advantage while he was living in Taiwan. This suggests that accent plays a significant role when speaking Mandarin. Thus, I saw this as an opportunity to get *inside* and grasped it by fully embracing a Southern accent.

The second thing I did to immerse in the local context was to present an external appearance similar to Japanese or Taiwanese by wearing makeup. Applying and wearing makeup was not difficult for me because I have loved makeup since I studied as an undergraduate in Japan, where it is fairly common for women to wear makeup at that age. In many locations in China, women do not wear makeup, and thus wearing makeup is one way to distinguish oneself from mainland Chinese. Although Taiwanese are not well known for their makeup use, people in Hong Kong will often make assumptions about people's country, based on whether they are wearing makeup. I recall hearing a mainland Chinese woman and a Hong Kong woman, who both worked at a Japanese bank, discuss makeup in an elevator. The mainland Chinese woman said, 'I don't understand why people are wearing makeup. I am fine with doing nothing'. The Hong Kong woman replied, 'Well, we are working, and it is a Japanese company'. Although mainland Chinese women are spending more money on cosmetics and makeup compared to decades ago,[68] more than half of Japanese women from their twenties to sixties frequently wear makeup for all occasions.[69] Therefore, wearing makeup was one way to reflect an identity as non-mainland Chinese.

The third way I attempted to gain acceptance was to speak in an overly politely way with a 'perfect' smile. Having lived in Japan for more than a decade, I learned to speak politely in a Japanese manner. Interestingly, when I speak Mandarin, others are often reminded of Japanese because I use many polite words. Take 'Xiexie' (thank you, in Mandarin) as an example. Whenever a fellow employee helped me, I would say 'thank you' to them, even it was a small favour. Although locals often used 'Mhgoi (唔該)' or 'Dojeh (多謝)', I believe the difference in my usage was the frequency and way in which I used these terms. Therefore, whenever I thanked other employees, I also smiled to express my genuine appreciation. I knew it was not common in Chinese society to frequently use these words, but I purposely used these words quite often with other employees. The reason I became aware of this difference was that when I was studying in junior high school in China, my grandmother told me, 'You don't need to thank me. Family does not have to say, "Thank you"'. She meant that if you are close to someone, it is unnecessary to verbally thank that person. Thanking someone would categorise the person as an 'outsider'. I was shocked to learn this because in Japan, it is a common practice for children to verbally thank their parents; although both of my parents are from mainland China, I learned that this was not common in Chinese society.

I also proactively shared my life in and knowledge of Japan to remind local employees of my attachment to Japan. During my anthropological fieldwork, one of the ways I became acquainted with other employees was by sharing my experiences living in Japan and discussing the country because many of them had a strong desire to visit Japan in the near future or were repeat visitors. Some of them also came to me and shared their other work experience at Japanese companies. My understanding of Japanese culture also seemed to help me be accepted in other ways. For instance, because I had lived and been educated in Japan and understood both the language and the indirect methods of communication, local store managers sometimes asked me to translate what the Japanese expatriates were attempting to say because the store managers could not understand the full message by simply reading their emails.

The above showed how my early childhood living in a country as a non-native constructed my overt worries about being a non-native at Ichi, how I gradually realised the 'real' sentiment of locals towards mainland Chinese, and how I, considering all of these factors, concluded that self-fashioning was a better way to present myself at Ichi. In this process, I transformed myself by adopting several strategies – related to language, accent, makeup, and sharing my knowledge of Japan – in an effort to fit in. My desire to be accepted and to fit in came from not only my need to complete my fieldwork and thesis, but also my aspiration of being perceived as 'normal' to overcome my insecurities. The above discussion is an example of self-transformation in the process of building a relationship between the researcher and researched.

I felt comfortable and secure having multiple identities during fieldwork – Chinese, Japanese, and (assumed) Taiwanese. I was Chinese when I was talking to my parents. I changed identity to Japanese when I met a Japanese employee at my fieldwork site. I change again to appearing Taiwanese when interacting with local employees on site. My experience of negative attitudes towards people from mainland China led me to disguise my own ethnicity, and being Taiwanese was the most natural way for me to do this, since Taiwan has traits of traditional Chinese culture as well as elements of Japan, and also they speak Mandarin. Being comfortable with switching my assumed identity to Taiwanese to some extent indicates a type of defence mechanism; I wanted to protect myself from being labelled as either Chinese or Japanese, because of the sour experiences that I had in the past, and because of experiences of negative attitudes towards people from mainland China in Hong Kong. Being asked if I was pregnant by the customs officer simply because I had Chinese passport was not the first negative experience. During fights with my classmates while studying in a Japanese primary school, people often told me to go back to China. While at Chinese high school, some classmates accused me of being a 'Japanese devil' (*riben guizi* in Mandarin) – a derogatory term used to describe Japanese people. Although I did not feel traumatised by having negativity directed towards me in Hong Kong, I was always aware of my outsider status. Being through such experiences, sometimes I lost my sense of belongingness. Am I Chinese or what? Despite these complex feelings, the thing I struggled with the most during fieldwork was that I often had more negative opinions of mainland Chinese people than Japanese people. This again made my identity more complicated because I also had negative feelings about Chinese ethnicity, but this complexity helped me become insider, because I could sympathise with what Hong Kong people were going through.

My experience shows that the surrounding political and societal environment, as well as the researcher's background, was hugely influential in the way I conducted fieldwork and interpreted data. Thus, the following question arises: what can the Ichi case teach in terms of Asia's role in globalisation and the changing sphere of fieldwork?

Based on the discussion of identity politics in Hong Kong and self-transformation in the process of fieldwork, I hope to make contributions to the discussions of globalisation and Asian studies and the changes of self in fieldwork. First, setting the field in a Japanese company in Hong Kong provided a platform to explore the process of cultivating translocal culture in various Asian countries and regions. Hong Kong is often described as having a rich economy with complicated political and historical factors, but many have not well articulated how the latter could have influenced the former in a globalising business environment, and some simply conclude that it is where East meets West.[70] The case of Ichi has demonstrated that the structure of local identity is the mixture of passive attitudes towards an ideology about mainland China and the positive consumption of Japanese commercial culture. This does not mean that Hong Kong accepts Japanese culture as superior and definite, but that it simply considers it as an 'additional' element for composing its local identity. Ichi, as a Japanese company operating in Hong Kong, is a crossroads of such translocality and represents an interweaving of complex feelings and sentiments of the local people, including Ichi's employees.

Second, this fieldwork provides a detailed case scenario to discuss the transformation of self and prompts a debate on how a fieldworker can cope in the contemporary anthropological field where their own identity is one that receives much negative attention in their fieldsite. The case of Ichi presents one fieldworker, with her own personal history and ethnic identity, who has practiced self-fashioning by adopting various strategies, such as those related to language, external appearance, and ethnicity, in an attempt to become a native insider. This case facilitates the discussion of questions such as the following: How can a fieldworker understand the environment surrounding her/himself? How could the fieldworker at Ichi have conducted herself differently? Were there any alternative strategies? This case reconfirms that the core principles of conducting anthropological fieldwork – such as observing, listening, understanding, and analysing – remain valid even where the field is a modernised corporate empire.

Third, the skills developed by an ethnographer who aims to become a real insider to access data may be beneficial to employees in their attempts to better adjust to a changing business environment. Many management scientists have tried to discover a single solution for pursuing efficiency and reproducibility, and incorrectly focused on purported fundamental skills, while often overlooking the importance of diversity in a changing world. Being an ethnographer in a workplace is somewhat similar to the situation of an employee (including top management) being sent to an unfamiliar workplace. Although many things encountered might be new, it is important to be a *stranger* throughout the work to better understand what is really going on to understand what actually needs to be improved. Observing, listening to, understanding, and analysing situations are simple but significant processes not only for fieldworkers and business professionals, but also other people living in this world. In business contexts, these skills may benefit managers and those who are managed to increase their understanding of each other, clearly and correctly diagnose issues, and take proactive measures to pursue personal and collective gains.

CONCLUSION: GLOBALISED SHIFTING
POSITIONS IN FIELDWORK

Through its discussion of fieldwork in a Japanese company in Hong Kong, this chapter first discussed the debates in the prior literature in terms of globalisation and the rise of Asian studies and its impact on anthropological fieldwork. Specifically, it examined the context of translocality and exploration of cultural systems within organisations, including modern profit-oriented corporations, which served as the field in this chapter. It also addressed the transformation of self in the process of fieldwork and the relationship between the researching subject and the researched object from the perspective of the subjective experiences of fieldworkers and their impacts on understanding the field.

This chapter began with the examination of identity politics in Hong Kong by exploring the relationship between mainland China and Hong Kong, and the consumption of Japanese culture by local people to show how both have to some extent contributed to reconstructing local identity. Political issues after the handover to mainland China – particularly anti-China sentiments of distrust and fear – have sparked the people of Hong Kong to revisit who they truly are, and consumption of Japanese culture has become a way to pursue 'external' culture to supplement their local identity. The combination of these two factors clearly represents the picture of identity politics in Hong Kong and highlights the tension between global and local contexts. Such translocal activities in East Asia provide a platform to further explore the meaning of Asian studies. Complex feelings towards mainland China and Japan's special role have also influenced the way local employees see me, a mainland Chinese fieldworker, and how I constructed my own strategies to cope with this situation.

The fieldwork at Ichi in Hong Kong was described from the perspective of the fieldworker and focused largely on my complex life history and how I interpreted the situations of political identity in Hong Kong and behaved 'strategically' or self-fashioned in certain ways. My consciousness of being an outsider in the past years (living in Japan as Chinese, and then living in China as Chinese from Japan) had shaped my multiple identities and increased my desire to fit in. These strategies of becoming insider in the fieldwork site were not conceived at the beginning, but developed through interaction and long-term observation at the company, including communication with employees via social media. With a deeper understanding of the local employees' complicated feelings, I presented an identity more preferable for them – Japanese, Taiwanese, or non-mainland Chinese – using various strategies including using a Southern Mandarin accent, wearing makeup, and proactively sharing my ties to Japan. In other words, as a fieldworker in a translocal environment, I used identity politics as a positive strategy to conduct fieldwork rather than succumbing to feeling like a target of anti-Chinese sentiment. I was able to shift between identities largely because of my prior experiences of struggling to fit in. This implies that with the changing dynamics of the field, such as the case of Hong Kong where strong identity politics exist, it is time for fieldworkers to think ahead and develop strategies for being a proactive ethnographer with a flexible mind, which may also require self-reflection.

This chapter does not ignore the implications of evolving anthropological fieldwork in the contemporary and global/local contexts; instead, it provides practical implications for business professionals to acquire skills of ethnographers, who observe, listen to, understand, and analyse situations and people in the field. This applies to both managers and those who are managed as well as to other people who may have opportunities to encounter and interpret different mindsets and ideas. Recognising differences and understanding how to use such differences strategically are also essential skills for fieldworkers. These skills can allow fieldworkers to achieve their goals and can also be used to enrich individuals and society.

* * *

NOTES

1. See Akhil Gupta, and James Ferguson, ed., *Culture, Power, Place: Explorations in Critical Anthropology* (North Carolina: Duke University Press, 1997); George. E. Marcus, "Ethnography In/Of the World System: The Emergence of Multi-Sited Ethnography," *Annual Review of Anthropology* 24, no. 1 (1995): 95–117; Paul Rabinow, *Reflections on Fieldwork in Morocco: with a New Preface by the Author* (California: University of California Press, 2007).

2. Manuel Castells, *The Rise of the Network Society*. Vol. 1 (Oxford: Blackwell, 1996).

3. See Katharine E. Welsh, Alice L. Mauchline, Julian R. Park, W. Brian Whalley, and Derek France, "Enhancing Fieldwork Learning with Technology: Practitioner's Perspectives," *Journal of Geography in Higher Education* 37, no. 3 (2013): 399–415; Michael R. Glass, "Enhancing Field Research Methods with Mobile Survey Technology," *Journal of Geography in Higher Education* 39, no. 2 (2015): 288–298; Claire Jarvis, Nicholas Tate, Jennifer Dickie, and Gavin Brown, "Mobile Learning in a Human Geography Field Course," *Journal of Geography* 115, no. 2 (2016): 61–71.

4. Anthony Giddens, *The Consequences of Modernity* (New Jersey: John Wiley & Sons, 2013).

5. The term global city indicates cities such as New York and Tokyo which acts as a primary node in the global economic system thus having cross-border dynamics and the ability to influence other cities and form strategic transnational networks.

6. Saskia Sassen, *The Global City: New York, London, Tokyo* (New Jersey: Princeton University Press, 2013).

7. Roland Robertson, "Glocalization: Time-Space and Homogeneity-Heterogeneity," in *Global Modernities*, ed. Mike Featherstone, Scott Lash, and Roland Robertson (London: Sage Publications, 1995), 25–44.

8. Arjun Appadurai, "Disjuncture and Difference in the Global Cultural Economy," *Theory, Culture & Society* 7, no. 2–3 (1990): 295–310.

9. Jan Nederveen Pieterse, "Globalization as Hybridization," in *Global Modernities*, ed. Mike Featherstone, Scott Lash, and Roland Robertson (London: Sage Publications, 1995), 45–68.

10. See Eva-Maria Hardtmann, *The Dalit Movement in India: Local Practices, Global Connections* (Oxford: Oxford University Press, 2009); Mark Pluciennik, and Quentin Drew, "'Only Connect': Global and Local Networks, Contexts and Fieldwork," *Ecumene* 7, no. 1 (2000): 67–104; Kirsten Hastrup, "Scales of Attention in Fieldwork: Global Connections and Local Concerns in the Arctic," *Ethnography* 14, no. 2 (2013): 145–164.

11. Michael Burawoy, Joseph A. Blum, Sheba George, Zsuzsa Gille, and Millie Thayer, *Global Ethnography: Forces, Connections, and Imaginations in a Postmodern World* (California: University of California Press, 2000).

12. See Kuan-Hsing Chen, "Takeuchi Yoshimi's 1960 'Asia as Method' lecture," *Inter-Asia Cultural Studies* 13, no. 2 (2012): 317–324.

13. See Angel M. Y. Lin, "Towards Transformation of Knowledge and Subjectivity in Curriculum Inquiry: Insights from Chen Kuan-Hsing's "Asia as Method," *Curriculum Inquiry* 42, no. 1 (2012): 153–178; Warwick Anderson, "Asia as Method in Science and Technology Studies," *East Asian Science, Technology and Society: An International Journal* 6, no. 4 (2012): 445–451; Hongzhi Zhang, Philip Wing Keung Chan, and Jane Kenway, ed., *Asia as Method in Education Studies: A Defiant Research Imagination* (London and New York: Routledge, 2015).

14. See Shinji Yamashita, and Jeremy Seymour Eades, *Globalization in Southeast Asia: Local, National, and Transnational Perspectives* (New York: Berghahn Books, 2003); Marcelo M. Suárez-Orozco Desirée Qin, *Globalization: Culture and Education in the New Millennium* (California: University of California Press, 2004).

15. George W. Stocking, *The Ethnographer's Magic and Other Essays in the History of Anthropology* (Wisconsin: University of Wisconsin Press, 1992).

16. Simon Coleman, and Peter Collins, ed., *Religion, Identity and Change: Perspectives on Global Transformations* (London and New York: Routledge, 2017).

17. See Clifford, James, and George E. Marcus, ed. *Writing Culture: The Poetics and Politics of Ethnography* (California: University of California Press, 1986);

George E. Marcus, and Michael M.J. Fischer, *Anthropology as Cultural Critique: An Experimental Moment in the Human Sciences* (Chicago: University of Chicago Press, 2014).

18. James Davies, and Dimitrina Spencer, *Emotions in the Field: The Psychology and Anthropology of Fieldwork Experience* (California: Stanford University Press, 2010).

19. James Clifford, *The Predicament of Culture: Twentieth-Century Ethnography, Literature, and Art* (Boston: Harvard University Press, 1988).

20. George. E Marcus, "Ethnography In/Of the World System: The Emergence of Multi-Sited Ethnography," *Annual Review of Anthropology* 24, no. 1 (1995): 95–117.

21. Anna Tsing, "The Global Situation," *Cultural Anthropology* 15, no. 3 (2000): 327–360.

22. 'Scientific management' is a management theory, founded by Frederic Winslow Taylor, which analyses workflows in a systematic way aiming to improve economic efficiency, particularly relating to labour.

23. 'Economic man' suggests groups of people who think rationally and pursue their own gain in a narrowly self-interested way.

24. See Heung Wah Wong, *Japanese Bosses, Chinese Workers: Power and Control in a Hong Kong Megastore* (Richmond: Curzon, 1999); Mitchell Sedgwick, *Globalisation and Japanese Organisational Culture: An Ethnography of a Japanese Corporation in France* (London and New York: Routledge, 2007); Ann T. Jordan, *Business Anthropology* (Illinois: Waveland Press, 2012); Hirochika Nakamaki, Koichiro Hioki, Izumi Mitsui, and Yoshiyuki Takeuchi, ed. *Enterprise as an Instrument of Civilization* (Tokyo: Springer, 2016); Yi Zhu, "Cultural Conflicts in the Process of Embedding Mission Statements," *Transcultural Management Review* 15 (2019): 55–70.

25. See Rita M. Denny, and Patricia L. Sunderland, eds. *Handbook of Anthropology in Business* (London and New York: Routledge, 2016); Christine Miller, *Design+ Anthropology: Converging Pathways in Anthropology and Design* (London and New York: Routledge, 2017).

26. James Davies, and Dimitrina Spencer, *Emotions in the Field: The Psychology and Anthropology of Fieldwork Experience* (California: Stanford University Press, 2010).

27. Vincent Crapanzano, "At the Heart of the Discipline," in *Emotions in the Field: The Psychology and Anthropology of Fieldwork Experience*, ed. James Davies, and Dimitrina Spencer, 55–78. (California: Stanford University Press, 2010).

28. Lyn Schumaker, *Africanizing Anthropology: Fieldwork, Networks, and the Making of Cultural Knowledge in Central Africa* (Durham: Duke University Press, 2001).

29. Dorinne K Kondo, *Crafting Selves: Power, Gender and Discourses of Identity in a Japanese Workplace* (Chicago: The University of Chicago Press, 1990).

30. George. E. Marcus, and Mascarenhas, Fernando, *Ocasião: The Marquis and the Anthropologist, a Collaboration*. Vol. 4 (Maryland: Rowman & Littlefield, 2005).

31. Julie Choi, *Creating a Multivocal Self: Autoethnography as Method* (London and New York: Routledge, 2016).

32. Andrew Herrmann, *Organizational Autoethnographies: Power and Identity in Our Working Lives* (London: Taylor & Francis, 2017).

33. George E. Marcus, and Michael M. J. Fischer, *Anthropology as Cultural Critique: An Experimental Moment in the Human Sciences* (Chicago: University of Chicago Press, 2014).

34. Jerome Seymour Bruner, *Acts of Meaning* (Cambridge: Harvard University Press, 1990).

35. Michael Dyson, "My Story in a Profession of Stories: Auto Ethnography-An Empowering Methodology for Educators," *Australian Journal of Teacher Education* 32, no. 1 (2007): 3.

36. Ibid, 45.

37. "Economic and Trade Information on Hong Kong," *Hong Kong Trade Development Council*, last modified January 2, 2020. http://hong-kong-economy-research.hktdc.com/business-news/article/Market-Environment/Economic-and-Trade-Information-on-Hong-Kong/etihk/en/1/1X000000/1X09OVUL.htm.

38. Wouter Geerts, "Top 100 City Destinations 2018: The Irresistible Draw of Cities," *Euromonitor International*, last modified July 12, 2018. https://blog.euromonitor.com/top-100-city-destinations-2018-the-irresistible-draw-of-cities/.

39. Euromonitor, "Asia Leads Top City Destinations Ranking, Says Euromonitor International," *Euromonitor International*, last modified March 12, 2018. https://blog.euromonitor.com/asia-leads-top-city-destinations-ranking-says-euromonitor-international/.

40. Gordon Mathews, *Ghetto at the Center of the World: Chungking Mansions* (Hong Kong: University of Chicago Press, 2011).

41. M. Ackbar Abbas, "Cosmopolitan De-Scriptions: Shanghai and Hong Kong," *Public Culture* 12, no. 3 (Fall 2000): 769–786.

42. Hong Kong was a colony of the British Empire since 1842 until the territory was returned to China in 1997 (excepting a short period during World War II when it was occupied by Japan).

43. Xinhua, "Hong Kong's Annual Visitor Number Soars to 65 Million in 2018." *Xinhua Net*, last modified January 31, 2019. http://www.xinhuanet.com/english/2019-01/31/c_137790274.htm.

44. Jeanny Yu, "Hong Kong Still No.1 for Mainland Chinese Tourists," *South China Morning Post*, last modified November 13, 2012. http://www.scmp.com/news/hongkong/article/1081729/hk-still-no-1-mainland-tourists.

45. Paggie Leung, "More Than 50 Global Retail Brands Set Up Shop in Hong Kong in 2012," *South Morning China*, last modified May 8, 2013. http://www.scmp.com/property/hong-kong-china/article/1232393/more-50-global-retail-brands-set-shop-hong-kong-2012.

46. Angela Ng, Yi Yeung, and Gloria Lee, "Cantonese, Putonghua or English? The Language Politics of Hong Kong's School System," *Hong Kong Free Press*, last modified April 9, 2017. https://www.hongkongfp.com/2017/04/09/cantonese-putonghua-english-language-politics-hong-kongs-school-system/.

47. Annie Hau-nung Chan, "Consumption, Popular Culture, and Cultural Identity: Japan in Post-Colonial Hong Kong," *Studies in Popular Culture* 23, no. 1 (October 2000): 35–55.

48. Chris Hogg, "China Demand Means HK Parents Cannot Get Baby Milk," *BBC*, last modified February 1, 2011. https://www.bbc.com/news/world-asia-pacific-12336975. As a result, legislation was passed in 2013 banning people leaving Hong Kong with more than two tins (see Su Xinqi, "Hong Kong's Limit on Baby Milk Formula to Stay as Fears Grow Demand from Mainland China Could Cause Repeat of Shortage," *South China Morning Post*, last modified February 25, 2019. https://www.scmp.com/news/hong-kong/hong-kong-economy/article/2187581/hong-kongs-two-tin-ban-baby-milk-formula-stay-amid.

49. Emily Tsang, "Mainland Women Gatecrashing Hong Kong's Maternity Wards, 3 Years After CY Leung's 'Zero-Quota' Policy," *South China Morning Post*, last modified April 25, 2016. https://www.scmp.com/news/hong-kong/health-environment/article/1938268/mainland-women-gatecrashing-hong-kongs-maternity.

50. Ibid.

51. Sharon LaFraniere, "Mainland Chinese Flock to Hong Kong to Give Birth," *The New York Times*, last modified February 22, 2012. https://www.nytimes.com/2012/02/23/world/asia/mainland-chinese-flock-to-hong-kong-to-have-babies.html.

52. Kerry Brown, "China's New Moral Education Campaign," Last modified September 21, 2015. https://thediplomat.com/2015/09/chinas-new-moral-education-campaign/.

53. Chan, "Consumption".

54. See Koichi Iwabuchi, *Recentering Globalization: Popular Culture and Japanese Transnationalism* (Durham: Duke University Press, 2002); Peter J Katzenstein, *A World of Regions: Asia and Europe in the American Imperium* (New York: Cornell University Press, 2015); Anne Allison, *Millennial Monsters: Japanese Toys and the Global Imagination*. Vol. 13 (California: University of California Press, 2006); Daya Kishan Thussu, *International Communication: Continuity and Change* (London: Bloomsbury Publishing, 2018); Terry Flew, *Understanding Global Media* (London: Macmillan International Higher Education, 2018).

55. Chan, "Consumption," 40.

56. Koichi Iwabuchi, *Recentering Globalization: Popular Culture and Japanese Transnationalism* (Durham: Duke University Press, 2002).

57. Out of 75 countries, Future Brand considers 22 countries as 'brands' (Country Brand Index 2015).

58. "Hounichi gaikokujin ryokousha no hounichi kaisuu to shouhikoudou no kankei nituite [Relationship Between the Number of Foreign Visits and Their Consumption Patterns]," *Ministry of Land, Infrastructure, Transport and Tourism*, last modified 2017. https://www.mlit.go.jp/common/001230647.pdf

59. Hakuhodo. "Ajia 14 Toshi ni Okeru Nihon Seihin Ime-ji [Image of Japanese Products in 14 Asian Cities]," *Hakuhodo*, last modified February 10, 2012. http://www.hakuhodo.co.jp/uploads/2012/02/20120210GlobalHABIT.pdf.

60. Zhu, Yi, "Re-imagining Corporate Branding: National Culture as a Marketing Competence," *The Journal of International Public Policy* 37 (2016): 53–66.

61. "Kuni chiikibetsu no nourin suisanbutsu shokuhin no yushutu kakudai sen-ryaku [Strategy on Expanding Export of Agriculture and Food Worldwide]," *Prime Minister's Office of Japan*, last modified 2015. https://www.kantei.go.jp/jp/singi/n ousui/pdf/all_country.pdf.

62. Heung Wah Wong, "Colonization in a Japanese Company in Hong Kong: The Nature of the Managerial Control of Yaohan," *Tōyō Bunka* 89 (2009): 270–298.

63. Chan, "Consumption".

64. Ibid., 53.

65. Jan Nederveen Pieterse, "Globalization as Hybridization," in *Global Modernities*, ed. Mike Featherstone, Scott Lash, and Roland Robertson (London: Sage Publications, 1995), 45–68.

66. The name 'Ichi' and the personnel related to the company are pseudonyms.

67. Of course, many Japanese respect China's long history and culture. However, a 2019 poll showed that 85% of Japanese people reported unfavourable attitudes towards China, which is higher than reported in other Asian countries. In addition, there has been a decrease in the percentage of Japanese people reporting favourable attitudes towards China, from 55% in 2002 to 14% in 2019 (Pew Research Center 2019).

68. Ho, David, "In the Mirror: Face of China's Cosmetics Market," *China Daily*, last modified June 18, 2018. https://www.chinadaily.com.cn/a/201806/18/WS5b2740 b2a310010f8f59d69c.html.

69. VLC, "Market Research on Cosmetics in Japan," *VLC*, last modified 2008. https://www.vlcank.com/mr/report/013/.

70. Paul S. N. Lee, "The Absorption and Indigenization of Foreign Media Cultures a Study on a Cultural Meeting Point of the East and West: Hong Kong," *Asian Journal of Communication* 1, no. 2 (1991): 52–72; Donelson R. Forsyth, Ernest H. O'Boyle, and Michael A. McDaniel, "East Meets West: A Meta-Analytic Investigation of Cultural Variations in Idealism and Relativism," *Journal of Business Ethics* 83, no. 4 (February 2008): 813–833.

REFERENCES

Abbas, M. Ackbar. "Cosmopolitan De-scriptions: Shanghai and Hong Kong." *Public Culture* 12, no. 3 (Fall 2000): 769–786.

Allison, Anne. *Millennial Monsters: Japanese Toys and the Global Imagination*. Vol. 13. Berkeley: University of California Press, 2006.

Anderson, Warwick. "Asia as Method in Science and Technology Studies." *East Asian Science, Technology and Society: An International Journal* 6, no. 4 (2012): 445–451.

Appadurai, Arjun. "Disjuncture and Difference in the Global Cultural Economy." *Theory, Culture & Society* 7, no. 2–3 (1990): 295–310.

Baba, Marietta. "Anthropology and Business." In *Encyclopedia of Anthropology*, edited by H. James Birx, 83–117. Newbury Park, CA: Sage Publications, 2006.

Brown, Kerry. "China's New Moral Education Campaign." Last modified Sep 21, 2015. https://thediplomat.com/2015/09/chinas-new-moral-education-campaign/.

Bruner, Jerome Seymour. *Acts of Meaning*. Cambridge: Harvard University Press, 1990.

Burawoy, Michael, Joseph A. Blum, Sheba George, Zsuzsa Gille, and Millie Thayer. *Global Ethnography: Forces, Connections, and Imaginations in a Postmodern World*. Berkeley: University of California Press, 2000.

Castells, Manuel. *The Rise of the Network Society*. Vol. 1. Oxford: Blackwell, 1996.

Chan, Annie Hau-nung. "Consumption, Popular Culture, and Cultural Identity: Japan in Post-Colonial Hong Kong." *Studies in Popular Culture* 23, no. 1 (October 2000): 35–55.

Chen, Kuan-Hsing. "Takeuchi Yoshimi's 1960 'Asia as Method' Lecture." *Inter-Asia Cultural Studies* 13, no. 2 (2012): 317–324.

Chlopczyk, Jacques, and Christine Erlach. *Transforming Organizations*. Basel: Springer, 2019.

Choi, Julie. *Creating a Multivocal Self: Autoethnography as Method*. London and New York: Routledge, 2016.

Clifford, James. *The Predicament of Culture: Twentieth-Century Ethnography, Literature, and Art*. Boston: Harvard University Press, 1988.

Clifford, James, and George E. Marcus, ed. *Writing Culture: The Poetics and Politics of Ethnography*. Berkeley: University of California Press, 1986.

Coleman, Simon, and Peter Collins, ed. *Religion, Identity and Change: Perspectives on Global Transformations*. London and New York: Routledge, 2017.

"Country Brand Index 2014–2015." *Future Brand*, last modified 2015. https://www.futurebrand.com/uploads/CBI2014-5.pdf.

Crapanzano, Vincent. "At the Heart of the Discipline." In *Emotions in the Field: The Psychology and Anthropology of Fieldwork Experience*, edited by James Davies, and Dimitrina Spencer, 55–78. Redwood City: Stanford University Press, 2010.

Davies, James, and Dimitrina Spencer. *Emotions in the Field: The Psychology and Anthropology of Fieldwork Experience*. Redwood City: Stanford University Press, 2010.

Denny, Rita M., and Patricia L. Sunderland, ed. *Handbook of Anthropology in Business*. London and New York: Routledge, 2016.

Dyson, Michael. "My Story in a Profession of Stories: Auto Ethnography-an Empowering Methodology for Educators." *Australian Journal of Teacher Education* 32, no.1 (2007): 36–48.

Euromonitor. "Asia Leads Top City Destinations Ranking, Says Euromonitor International." *Euromonitor International*, last modified Mar 12, 2018. https://blog.euromonitor.com/asia-leads-top-city-destinations-ranking-says-euromonitor-international/.

Flew, Terry. *Understanding Global Media*. London: Macmillan International Higher Education, 2018.

Forsyth, Donelson R., Ernest H. O'Boyle, and Michael A. McDaniel. "East Meets West: A Meta-Analytic Investigation of Cultural Variations in Idealism and Relativism." *Journal of Business Ethics* 83, no. 4 (February 2008): 813–833.

Geerts, Wouter. "Top 100 City Destinations 2018: The Irresistible Draw of Cities." *Euromonitor International*, last modified Jul 12, 2018. https://blog.euromonitor. com/top-100-city-destinations-2018-the-irresistible-draw-of-cities/.

Giddens, Anthony. *The Consequences of Modernity*. New Jersey: John Wiley & Sons, 2013.

Glass, Michael R. "Enhancing Field Research Methods with Mobile Survey Technology." *Journal of Geography in Higher Education* 39, no. 2 (2015): 288–298.

Gupta, Akhil, and James Ferguson. ed. *Culture, Power, Place: Explorations in Critical Anthropology*. North Carolina: Duke University Press, 1997.

Hakuhodo. "Ajia 14 Toshi ni Okeru Nihon Seihin Ime-ji [Image of Japanese Products in 14 Asian Cities]." *Hakuhodo*, last modified Feb 10, 2012. http://www.hakuhodo. co.jp/uploads/2012/02/20120210GlobalHABIT.pdf.

Hardtmann, Eva-Maria. *The Dalit Movement in India: Local Practices, Global Connections*. Oxford: Oxford University Press, 2009.

Hastrup, Kirsten. "Scales of Attention in Fieldwork: Global Connections and Local Concerns in the Arctic." *Ethnography* 14, no. 2 (2013): 145–164.

Herrmann, Andrew. *Organizational Autoethnographies: Power and Identity in Our Working Lives*. London: Taylor & Francis, 2017.

Ho, David. 2018. "In the Mirror: Face of China's Cosmetics Market." *China Daily*, last modified Jun 18, 2018. https://www.chinadaily.com.cn/a/201806/18/WS5 b2740b2a310010f8f59d69c.html.

Hogg, Chris. "China Demand Means HK Parents Cannot Get Baby Milk." *BBC*, last modified Feb 1, 2011. https://www.bbc.com/news/world-asia-pacific-12336975.

Hong Kong Trade Development Council. "Economic and Trade Information on Hong Kong." *Hong Kong Trade Development Council*, last modified Jan 2, 2020. http: //hong-kong-economy-research.hktdc.com/business-news/article/Market-Environ ment/Economic-and-Trade-Information-on-Hong-Kong/etihk/en/1/1X000000/1 X09OVUL.htm.

"Hounichi gaikokujin ryokousha no hounichi kaisuu to shouhikoudou no kankei nituite [Relationship Between the Number of Foreign Visits and Their Consumption Patterns]." *Ministry of Land, Infrastructure, Transport and Tourism*, last modified 2017. https://www.mlit.go.jp/common/001230647.pdf.

Iwabuchi, Koichi. *Recentering Globalization: Popular Culture and Japanese Transnationalism*. Durham: Duke University Press, 2002.

Jarvis, Claire, Nicholas Tate, Jennifer Dickie, and Gavin Brown. "Mobile Learning in a Human Geography Field Course." *Journal of Geography* 115, no. 2 (2016): 61–71.

Jordan, Ann. T. *Business Anthropology*. Illinois: Waveland Press, 2012.

Katzenstein, Peter J. *A World of Regions: Asia and Europe in the American Imperium*. New York: Cornell University Press, 2015.

Kondo, Dorinne K. *Crafting Selves: Power, Gender and Discourses of Identity in a Japanese Workplace*. Chicago: University of Chicago Press, 1990.

LaFraniere, Sharon. "Mainland Chinese Flock to Hong Kong to Give Birth." *The New York Times*, last modified Feb 22, 2012. https://www.nytimes.com/2012/02/23/world/asia/mainland-chinese-flock-to-hong-kong-to-have-babies.html.

Lee, Paul S. N. "The Absorption and Indigenization of Foreign Media Cultures a Study on a Cultural Meeting Point of the East and West: Hong Kong." *Asian Journal of Communication* 1, no. 2 (1991): 52–72.

Leung, Paggie. "More than 50 Global Retail Brands Set Up Shop in Hong Kong in 2012." *South Morning China*, last modified May 8, 2013. http://www.scmp.com/property/hong-kong-china/article/1232393/more-50-global-retail-brands-set-shop-hong-kong-2012

Lin, Angel M. Y. "Towards Transformation of Knowledge and Subjectivity in Curriculum Inquiry: Insights from Chen Kuan Hsing's "Asia as Method." *Curriculum Inquiry* 42, no. 1 (2012): 153–178.

Marcus, George E. "Ethnography in/of the World System: The Emergence of Multi-Sited Ethnography." *Annual Review of Anthropology* 24, no. 1 (1995): 95–117.

Marcus, George E., and Mascarenhas, Fernando. *Ocasião: The Marquis and the Anthropologist, a Collaboration.* Vol. 4. Maryland: Rowman & Littlefield, 2005.

Marcus, George E., and Michael M. J. Fischer. *Anthropology as Cultural Critique: An Experimental Moment in the Human Sciences.* Chicago: University of Chicago Press, 2014.

Mathews, Gordon. *Ghetto at the Center of the World: Chungking Mansions, Hong Kong.* Chicago: University of Chicago Press, 2011.

Miller, Christine. *Design + Anthropology: Converging Pathways in Anthropology and Design.* London and New York: Routledge, 2017.

Nakamaki, Hirochika, Koichiro Hioki, Izumi Mitsui, and Yoshiyuki Takeuchi. ed. *Enterprise as an Instrument of Civilization.* Tokyo: Springer, 2016.

Ng, Angela, Yi Yeung, and Gloria Lee. "Cantonese, Putonghua or English? The Language Politics of Hong Kong's School System." *Hong Kong Free Press*, last modified April 9, 2017. https://www.hongkongfp.com/2017/04/09/cantonese-putonghua-english-language-politics-hong-kongs-school-system/.

Pew Research Center. "Japanese Back Global Engagement Despite Concern About Domestic Economy." *Pew Research Center*, last modified Oct 31, 2016. http://www.pewglobal.org/2016/10/31/japanese-back-global-engagement-despite-concern-about-domestic-economy/.

———. "Positive Evaluations of China on the Decline in the Asia-Pacific. Pew Research." *Pew Research Center*, last modified Sep 27, 2019. https://www.pewresearch.org/fact-tank/2019/09/30/people-around-the-globe-are-divided-in-their-opinions-of-china/ft_19-09-30_china_positive-evaluations-china-decline-asia-pacific/.

Pieterse, Jan Nederveen. "Globalisation as Hybridization." In *Global Modernities*, edited by Mike Featherstone, Scott Lash, and Roland Robertson, 45–68. London: Sage Publications, 1995.

Pluciennik, Mark, and Quentin Drew. "Only Connect': Global and Local Networks, Contexts and Fieldwork." *Ecumene* 7, no. 1 (2000): 67–104.

Qin, Marcelo M., and Suárez-Orozco Desirée. *Globalization: Culture and Education in the New Millennium.* California: University of California Press, 2004.

Rabinow, Paul. *Reflections on Fieldwork in Morocco: With a New Preface by the Author.* California: University of California Press, 2007.

Rhee, Jeong-eun. "Methodology of Leaving America for Asia: Reading South Korea's Social Studies Textbooks through ChenKuan-Hsing's Asia as Method." *Qualitative Research in Education* 2, no. 3 (2013): 328–354.

Robertson, Roland. "Glocalization: Time-Space and Homogeneity-Heterogeneity." In *Global Modernities*, edited by Featherstone, Mike, Scott Lash, and Roland Robertson, 25–44. California: Sage, 1995.

Sassen, Saskia. *The Global City: New York, London, Tokyo.* New Jersey: Princeton University Press, 2013.

Schumaker, Lyn. *Africanizing Anthropology: Fieldwork, Networks, and the Making of Cultural Knowledge in Central Africa.* Durham: Duke University Press, 2001.

Sedgwick, Mitchell. *Globalization and Japanese Organisational Culture: An Ethnography of a Japanese Corporation in France.* London and New York: Routledge, 2007.

Stocking, George W. *The Ethnographer's Magic and Other Essays in the History of Anthropology.* Wisconsin: University of Wisconsin Press, 1992.

Su Xinqi. "Hong Kong's Limit on Baby Milk Formula to Stay as Fears Grow Demand from Mainland China Could Cause Repeat of Shortage." *South China Morning Post*, last modified Feb 25, 2019. https://www.scmp.com/news/hong-kong/hong-kong-economy/article/2187581/hong-kongs-two-tin-ban-baby-milk-formula-stay-amid.

Tam, Angela Choi Fung. "Teaching Chinese in Putonghua in Post-Colonial Hong Kong: Problems and Challenges for Teachers and Administrators." *Language, Culture and Curriculum* 25, no. 2 (2012): 1–20.

Tsang, Emily. "Mainland Women Gatecrashing Hong Kong's Maternity Wards, 3 Years after CY Leung's 'Zero-Quota' Policy." *South China Morning Post*, last modified Apr 25, 2016. https://www.scmp.com/news/hong-kong/health-environment/article/1938268/mainland-women-gatecrashing-hong-kongs-maternity.

Tsing, Anna. "The Global Situation." *Cultural Anthropology* 15, no. 3 (2000): 327–360.

Thussu, Daya Kishan. *International Communication: Continuity and Change.* London: Bloomsbury Publishing, 2018.

University of Hong Kong. "People's Ethnic Identity." *Public Opinion Program at the website of the University of Hong Kong*, last modified July 2019. https://www.hku pop.hku.hk/english/popexpress/ethnic/.

VLC. "Market Research on Cosmetics in Japan." *VLC*, last modified 2008. https://www.vlcank.com/mr/report/013/.

Welsh, Katharine E., Alice L. Mauchline, Julian R. Park, W. Brian Whalley, and Derek France. "Enhancing Fieldwork Learning with Technology: Practitioner's Perspectives." *Journal of Geography in Higher Education* 37, no. 3 (2013): 399–415.

Wong, Heung Wah. *Japanese Bosses, Chinese Workers: Power and Control in a Hong Kong Megastore*. Richmond: Curzon, 1999.

————. "Colonization in a Japanese Company in Hong Kong: The Nature of the Managerial Control of Yaohan." *Tōyō Bunka* 89 (2009): 270–298.

Xinhua. "Hong Kong's Annual Visitor Number Soars to 65 Million in 2018." *Xinhua Net*, last modified Jan 31, 2019. http://www.xinhuanet.com/english/2019-01/31/c _137790274.htm.

Yamashita, Shinji, and Eades, Jeremy Seymour. *Globalization in Southeast Asia: Local, National, and Transnational Perspectives*. New York: Berghahn Books, 2003.

Yu, Jeanny. "Hong Kong Still No.1 for Mainland Chinese Tourists." *South China Morning Post*, last modified November 13, 2012. http://www.scmp.com/news/ hong-kong/article/1081729/hk-still-no-1-mainland-tourists.

Zhang, Hongzhi, Philip Wing Keung Chan, and Jane Kenway. eds. *Asia as Method in Education Studies: A Defiant Research Imagination*. London and New York: Routledge, 2015.

Zhu, Yi. "Re-imagining Corporate Branding: National Culture as a Marketing Competence." *The Journal of International Public Policy* 37 (2016): 53–66.

————. "Creation of Corporate Identity: The Role of Rites and Symbol in Management." *International Journal of Business Anthropology* 7, no. 2 (2017): 39–65.

————. "Cultural Conflicts in the Process of Embedding Mission Statements." *Transcultural Management Review* 15 (2019): 55–70.

Chapter 11

Comprador, Translator, or Cartographer?

Thoughts on Methodological Positions

Jia-shin Chen

ABSTRACT

This chapter raises two issues related to the positioning of the researcher during fieldwork and paper writing: the insider/outsider distinction and the role of a returning researcher as a comprador, translator, or cartographer. The first issue finds its significance in feminist writings about the 'outsider within' position. This position problematises the dichotomy of insiders versus outsiders and reflects the relationship between the position of the researcher and the knowledge he/she produces. The second issue echoes a long-standing discussion in Taiwan on the position of academic scholars vis-à-vis the theoretical influences of the West. Critical thoughts, including those within feminism and postcolonialism, laid the foundation for debates on intellectual positions in non-Western countries, such as Taiwan. The present chapter discusses how these issues influence the practice of a foreign-trained fieldworker, who studies phenomena in his/her home country. The analysis shows that these methodological questions are related to the identity of an ethnographic researcher. This chapter highlights three roles – comprador, translator, and cartographer – and discusses their positions in terms of knowledge production. The role of the researcher as a cartographer is particularly elaborated, because this position is believed to best illustrate the notion of 'Asia as method' raised by Kuan-Hsing Chen. Examples are given to address the ways in which research subjects become methodological inspirations and the reasons why this approach may help non-Western ethnographers re-orient themselves when doing fieldwork and writing up research findings.

* * *

In light of the multiple positions, selves, and identities at play in the research process, the subjectivity of the researcher, as much as that of the researched, became foregrounded, an indication of the blurring phenomenological and epistemological boundaries between the researcher and the researched.

– Virginia L. Olesen, 'Feminism and Qualitative Research at and into the Millennium'[1]

I conducted my first interview for my doctoral dissertation about the harm reduction policy in Taiwan in September 2007. My interviewee was a psychiatrist of a mental institution that housed a methadone clinic, the largest in the country at that time. He participated in building this clinic, and I wanted to ask his views on the policy. I was also interested in his professional experiences with the government, his colleagues, and drug users. At one point during the interview, the psychiatrist commented: 'Some users shifted from injecting to smoking [heroin]. This shift is also harm reduction'. I responded, 'We used to treat their addiction with tramadol, which is also harm reduction . . . by shifting injection to oral use'. He nodded and said, 'Tramadol . . . yes'.

When I looked back at the interview, I felt that I was transgressing but pretending to maintain an invisible line – a line that separated insiders from outsiders. The distinction could be easily perceived as being experienced (an insider) or not (an outsider). However, on a second thought, experienced in what? At the time I was taking a break from my psychiatry practice, during which I had treated people with drug addictions (particularly heroin addiction) to undertake research for a doctoral degree in sociology. Sociologists and psychiatrists typically do not mingle, and the fact that I belong to both fields is sometimes disconcerting to others in terms of defining my position. I am conscious of the line between insiders and outsiders every time I see their puzzled looks.

The interviewee was actually an acquaintance from my residency training. I was, in every sense, an insider in the field of psychiatric treatment for addiction. Speaking like a rookie when doing fieldwork was impossible for me. However, the so-called insider position depends on the context of the interview and research. When I visited the Centers for Disease Control (CDC)[2] to understand how this government agency managed the harm reduction policy to minimise the HIV/AIDS transmission caused by injection drug use, I was obviously an outsider to them because their undertakings were entirely beyond my knowledge. These tasks included preventing the spread of communicable diseases, educating the public, and administering feasible policies. I could only listen to what my CDC respondents said, uttering 'uh-huh' for most of the interview.

Afterwards, an increasing number of similar field experiences had compelled me to ask myself the following questions: Who am I? For someone who studies abroad to return and research a phenomenon 'at home', what defines the inside and the outside? What is my relationship with my research? What does my study mean to those involved and to the interviewees? How should I position myself vis-à-vis my respondents? How do I define the knowledge that I generate through my research?

These questions rendered research a soul-searching process for me, although I did not initially consider this issue a significant one. As I mentioned, I was a psychiatrist studying the harm reduction policy[3] in Taiwan for a PhD project, with a focus on science and technology studies (STS). I had previously obtained a master's degree in History of Science. During graduate school, I took courses from both departments of sociology and anthropology, and my doctoral dissertation committee consisted of two sociologists and two anthropologists. It was natural and necessary for me to accommodate different disciplinary backgrounds into my work, along with their perspectives and frameworks.

However, the creation of knowledge implies making moral choices about which knowledge is worth creating. Thus, a framework for interpreting empirical findings is one that produces *good* (well, at least *good enough*) knowledge. Researchers, as people who produce knowledge through their framework, become arbiters of the meaning of this goodness. If my mosaic training backgrounds contribute to what I define as good scholarship, what value do I advocate, and more importantly, what role do I assume? This awareness led me to wonder, 'Is a theoretical framework for research also a framework for the self-positioning of the researcher?'

Hence, I found my research connected with my identity. Qualitative researchers, particularly those who are influenced by feminist theory, have addressed the effects of researcher attributes on the research.[4] However, my concerns went deeper and were associated with post-colonial reflections on extant epistemologies. I wondered how balance could be achieved between Western and Asian perspectives. I did not want to be an academic comprador who simply 'sells' Western theories to the Taiwanese audience, but what can I re-/present?

THE INSIDER/OUTSIDER DILEMMA

[H]e confronts all of these with a distinctly 'objective' attitude, an attitude that does not signify mere detachment and nonparticipation, but is a distinct structure composed of remoteness and nearness, indifference and involvement.

– Georg Simmel, 'The Stranger'[5]

I was confronted with two dilemmas in various aspects. The first is the insider versus outsider position of a researcher, and the second is the epistemic and perspectival choice between the West and the rest. The former began to trouble me immediately after I started my fieldwork. By contrast, the latter gradually appeared over the course of my research. In the end, I found that both dilemmas were interwoven into my research and selfhood. This section will focus on the first dilemma.

The position of a researcher as an insider or outsider is determined by his/her relationship with the subject under study. However, this relationship is difficult to define because telling who is 'in the know' can be done in too many ways, including gaining familiarity with the issue or people involved, acquiring a license or certificate, or having permission from an authority, to name a few. These varying meanings boil down to a fundamental question: What does it take to be viewed as an insider or an outsider, and by whom?

The last part of the question implies that determining whether a researcher is an insider or an outsider eventually depends on subjective evaluation. For the psychiatrist mentioned in the first section, I definitely *appeared* as an insider, because, just like him, I am a board-certified psychiatrist with experience in addiction treatments. Moreover, I was still 'in the trade', which means that I was practicing psychiatry at the time of the interview. However, are these conditions sufficient to justify my position as an insider? Who is the one that decides my position? Given that my experience was based on tramadol, I clearly did not know how methadone works on heroin users, although both medications are opioid agonists, meaning they act on opioid receptors, just as heroin does. Would I be considered an insider, if the interview took place after I quit my clinical work to focus on fieldwork?

The insider/outsider dichotomy has been addressed in early sociological works, such as Georg Simmel's notion of the *Stranger* (part of which is cited above), Alfred Schulz's elaboration of this concept in social psychology,[6] Howard Becker's notion of the *Outsider*,[7] and Robert Merton's thesis in the sociology of knowledge.[8] This methodological reflection can be observed in cases where the researchers are not in the mainstream, for example, when they are female, belong to minority groups, or have conflicts of interest with the research subjects. In a classic article about the sociological significance of black feminist thought, Patricia Hill Collins addressed the 'outsider within' position of black women in academia and how their 'stranger' status (in Simmel's term) shaped and was shaped by their standpoint.[9] These scholars either noted the omission and distortion of facts and perspectives that adequately represent African American women, or they questioned statements that seem universal but are actually biased in terms of race or gender. These insights challenge the bases of existing concepts and theories, thereby making theoretical revision necessary.[10] However, this 'stranger' situation due to the 'insider *and* outsider' status is different from the traditional 'insider *or* outsider' distinction in ethnography, which usually refers to whether the researcher is native or not. However, as Kirin Narayan contends,[11] the 'native/non-native' distinction has lost ground since the targets, scopes, and practitioners of anthropology changed. It is pivotal to know that the shifting identities and relationships in fieldwork enact hybridity and make situated knowledge.

This insider/outsider distinction is certainly more than an epistemological concern as it also reflects the distinction among power operations. As Nancy Naples asserts,[12] the outsider phenomenon does not merely identify a particular identity but also refers to the 'interactions between shifting power relations' in the research context. In my experience, being a 'returning' researcher from abroad might win you a chance, but it cannot guarantee the door is always open. When I visited a certain government agency to interview the director, I was led into a conference room, where hot tea was served. However, once the interview began, courtesy turned into distance. Although the director answered every question, he disclosed nothing outside the governmental propaganda. In addition, he addressed me in a polite form (您, nin) rather than in a casual form (你, ni). The difference is similar to that of *Sie* and *du* in German. I was politely let in, but insidiously pushed out. These awkward exchanges would sometimes occur when I appeared unfamiliar with the names or terms used by my respondents. The situation would make me cautious about posing further questions and obtaining additional information. By contrast, such anxiety was reduced when I talked in an insider mode. However, being an insider will not necessarily bring forth a unified and stable set of knowledge,[13] because an insider position is a product of constant negotiation that rarely gets settled.[14] Even in a single interview, I might be regarded as an insider when the topic remains on addiction treatment in general, but I will likely be viewed as an outsider when focus shifts to the administrative details of a methadone clinic of which I have no experience at all. The distinction between insiders and outsiders (or in anthropological terms, natives and non-natives) is fluid and changeable; hence, conceptualising the distinction as a tentative state that transforms is preferable given that the researcher's relationship to multiple dimensions of the research subject varies in each interaction. That is, the distinction is not something to be endowed, but something that should be used by the researcher. It is part of the negotiation process.

The negotiation process occasionally persists through the writing phase of research and even years after the manuscript has been published. Moreover, negotiation does not only involve the identity of the researcher but also those of the research subjects. David Mosse described that he encountered fierce objections from irate colleagues and informants in the international aid organisation where he worked, which was also one of the objects of his critical ethnography.[15]

These informants believed his book would sabotage their hard-won establish-ments and claimed that it was unethical. To address the difficulties of this 'insider ethnography', Mosse situated his ethnographic work on public policy and organisations within the trend that has swept academia in the UK since the 1980s:

> As researchers, we resolved the intractable problems of access to closed organi-zational worlds through membership of the communities we ended up studying. But in doing we so [*sic*] substituted a set of boundaries that kept us *out* (the problem of access) with another set that kept us *in*. Those who made themselves professional insiders in this way faced the problem not of entering a different world so as to be able to imagine or infer the taken-for-granted (and therefore hidden) way in which 'individual action and collective illusions are interlinked' (Hastrup 2004: 469), but of exiting a known world for the same purpose.[16] (Italics in original)

Although I have not encountered oppositions or accusations regarding my published papers, hesitations between entering or exiting are undeniably present during fieldwork. My anxiety was comparatively milder when I approached government officials, because I did not consider myself one of them and I believe they did not, either. However, tension grew exponentially when I attended professional conferences, sat among other psychiatrists (some of whom were my previous colleagues), and enthusiastically wrote down field notes and critical reflections that separated me from the others. Such experience was simultaneously splitting and integrating for me, particularly when I was still practicing psychiatry. I wonder whether this anxiety was part of the reason why I ended my clinical practice to focus on fieldwork. Thus, I was able to avoid further identity confusion.

RESEARCHERS AS KNOWLEDGE PRODUCERS: COMPRADORS, TRANSLATORS, AND CARTOGRAPHERS

If sitting among previous colleagues provokes anxiety, writing research out-comes elicits ambivalence. Worries regarding the positioning of one's work have plagued some, if not all, Taiwanese intellectuals since the 1980s.[17] Such concerns were triggered partly by the critical thoughts among a number of social scientists concerning the academic position of Taiwan. These critical thoughts aimed to establish an academia that did not merely replicate what had been done and said in academically advanced countries perceived by these intellectuals, such as the United States. These efforts were not without criticism, but the trend of seeking Taiwanese subjectivity appeared in sync with the search for Taiwan's place in the international community, which became even more apparent after the abolition of Taiwan's martial law in 1987. Various political opinions and protests have flourished ever since.[18]

For a researcher like me who was born and raised during the 1970s and 1980s, the shift from an authoritarian regime to a burgeoning democracy that led to the search for Taiwanese subjectivity provoked mixed feelings about Eurocentrism. By Eurocentrism I mean the impacts of theories and perspectives originating from the West on 'the rest', as Stuart Hall argued.[19] It particularly affects the ways in which researchers in 'the rest' see themselves ('Who are we?'), frame their studies ('What is special about our research?'), and present their findings ('Who will be our audience?'). A frequent outcome of this Eurocentric ideology is that the phenomena found in 'the rest' can only be understood, legitimated, and appreciated from the perspective of the West. In this sense, refuting Eurocentrism involves listening to the voices among us without outer interference, telling stories with our own frame, and perceiving the world through our own eyes. Asian studies are not supposed to be area studies through Western lenses.

Perhaps no other discipline has fuelled the unwavering quest for self-identity than those belonging to the social sciences, which tend to raise issues regarding the questionable universality of theories. Students are likely to encounter questions such as, 'How can you be sure that the theories can be applied to the case of Taiwan if they are built from the context of the West?' or 'What makes this study unique in the sense that it is not just another example of Western theories?'

This determination to problematise a West-centred perspective or episteme may sometimes manifest itself in various terms, each of which bears a different point of emphasis. Such terms are viewed as epistemic attempts to reorganise Asian countries in a manner that is not subservient to the ideals of the West. Although this inherent dichotomised contrast still presumes the antagonism between the West and the rest, these terms challenged the ways scholars understand and examine emergent situations in Asia. For example, *East Asian Science, Technology and Society: An International Journal* is a publication sponsored by the Ministry of Science and Technology of Taiwan and published by Duke University Press. As the title indicates, East Asia is the overarching concept that distinguishes the journal from the others in the field of STS. In its first issue, Editor-in-Chief Daiwie Fu explicitly addressed this issue through the following statement: 'We wondered whether a distinctive historical experience and thus probably a shared East Asian STS theoretical perspective could serve as the basis of this journal project'.[20] This position paper provoked a series of repercussions, and I contributed a paper to the discussion.[21]

Re-examining one's position in relation to 'the West', or other dominant epistemic orientations, is not a claim peculiar to the rest. In fact, this emphasis is supported even in Western academia, particularly among those feminist and post-colonial views that problematised long-held social, political, and epistemological understandings, which are currently regarded as implicitly biased views on race and gender. Such radical thinking also unsettled the field of STS in which I specialise. For example, Sandra Harding, a renowned feminist STS scholar, argues that science frequently claims to uphold the value of neutrality. However, this claimed neutrality actually masks patriarchal and West-centred framings and assumptions that are often made invisible in scientific propositions. She contends that neutrality does not necessarily lead to objectivity. By contrast, it is only by incorporating the standpoints of oppressed or neglected minority groups, including women and people from post-colonial settings, that 'strong objectivity' can be achieved.[22]

The desire for a non-Western voice in terms of research epistemology and theory is not limited to STS and can be regarded as a pervasive phenomenon that develops in response to contemporary globalisation. This aspiration is noted for its emphasis on locality over globality, and sometimes it runs the risk of unnecessarily glorifying and essentialising local knowledge and tradition.[23] This potential risk may be the reason why some critics unveiled apprehension regarding the aforementioned notion of East Asia. For example, Fa-ti Fan suggested that the notion of East Asia be problematised by re-directing scholarly attention to the borderlands where diverse cultures and social forces encounter and collide with each other; such efforts would eventually define what East Asia should be.[24] Warwick Anderson recommended,[25] and Fan concurred,[26] that the notion of 'Asia as method' by Kuan-Hsing Chen be used as reference to build the idea of East Asia.

However, the 'Asia as method' approach, just like the earlier 'provincializing Europe' approach,[27] meant something more. This approach concerned my position, my identity, and what I do as a knowledge producer. During fieldwork, I repeatedly asked myself questions like these: Where in the world should I position myself when I study my hometown given the knowledge and perspective that I learned from the West? Am I a comprador or a translator?

I often suffered from these questions when I conducted interviews and wrote my thesis. Compradors definitely differ from translators. Compradors were people who mediated and facilitated transactions between local people and foreign businessmen during the early days of commercial dealings between China and Western countries. They were often hired by foreigners, and profited from creating business opportunities that they brokered. Therefore, they are frequently viewed as agents that represent foreign employers rather than their own countrymen. Although compradors were pivotal in achieving local prosperity,[28] the term continues to bear negative connotations. In Taiwan, no formal definition for an academic comprador is available, but this term circulates among intellectuals. Ming-Hwei Perng

(彭明輝), a mechanical engineering professor who became a social critic after his retirement, addressed higher education problems in Taiwan as follows:

> In the blind pursuit of the mass-production of publications in international journals, Taiwan has unconsciously turned into an academic colony of the Anglophone world. Scholars study American problems, but Americans just do not care. Many distinguished research award winners and chair professors become academic compradors voluntarily and seek mass production [of scholarly publications] by any means, thereby causing those scholars with integrity to withdraw themselves.[29] (Original in Chinese. My translation.)

Although Perng did not specify whom he was referring to and whether the comments he made was applicable to other areas apart from the engineering field, his depiction of an academic comprador combined two components that were repeatedly presented in the common usage of the term. The first component is the bias towards the West (or specifically, the Anglophone world, in the words of Professor Perng) in terms of research themes, methodology, and publication language selection. The second component is the pursuit of numerous publications in high-impact journals, for either fame or fortune, without attending to local needs. The commonality shared by these two positions is that they overlook the applicability of research results to local practice. Although this trend may be seen as part of the audit culture[30] that has expanded into the Taiwanese academia, Perng's remark reveals strong and persistent anxiety towards the pursuit for high impact and global exposure, which are related to the survival and sustainability of higher education worldwide. Naturally, a foreign-trained student like me studying local society will feel ambivalent towards being labelled an academic comprador.

Another frequently evoked image for researchers is that of a translator. This image comes in various guises. A translator helps other people understand something in another language by making it intelligible to them. Although translation may suggest a certain level of semantic equivalence, it often leads to an equivocation, according to anthropologist Eduardo Viveiros de Castro.[31] However, equivocation does not preclude or negate the necessity of translation, but instead prompts one to appreciate a world that is different without one's own preconceptions and worldviews. As he clarified,[32]

> An equivocation is not just a 'failure to understand' (Oxford English Dictionary, 1989), but a failure to understand that understandings are necessarily not the same, and that they are not related to imaginary ways of 'seeing the world' but to the real worlds that are being seen.

Thus, a translator may be a more modest role for me to assume even if translation is almost an impossible job. However, the whole point of translation is to stimulate and multiply dialogues instead of terminating them with some definitive closures. In other words, if my dissertation enabled my committee members and future readers to find out what was going on in Taiwan's harm reduction policy, it could work in the reverse direction. That is, I would act as a mediator who introduces to my audience in Taiwan the notion of harm reduction, which was not popular when I conducted my research, thereby clarifying its policy orientation and underlying ideology for them. Translation is not about telling one world about another, but telling both worlds about each other.[33] In this sense, a translator works both ways, which implies the likelihood of establishing balanced viewpoints and manners of communication.

For STS scholars, translation in the sense of actor-network theory is an important concept. The theory originally refers to the acts of recruiting allies, aligning interests, forming liaisons, and expanding resultant networks. Scientific truth is established through successful translation.[34] Bruno Latour demonstrated the effects of translation by recounting Louis Pasteur's attempts of persuading French farmers that the microbes in his laboratory held the key to curing anthrax that decimated their cattle.[35] In this Latourian depiction, a translator is a recruiter who intervenes by turning his/her listeners into believers.

However, research as a form of translation implies an inherent conflict.[36] How can researchers position themselves vis-à-vis the subject? Although Ian Hacking argued that representation can also be intervention,[37] the idea of translation as a form of intervention still bothers me as a researcher. How should I present my case study? To whom should I present it? Furthermore, by presenting Taiwan's harm reduction policy in English, with what assumed positions and political projects will I be aligned, both within and beyond Taiwan? What change will my study cause? Although the act of translating appears more equally grounded between the source and the result of translation, it is inevitably a product of power manoeuvring, because not everyone can be a legitimate translator and not every translation can be approved.

Unfortunately, neither the role of a comprador nor that of a translator can portray what I intend to do and where I prefer to stand. Although compradors broker Western knowledge for their own interests, translators can do the same even if their job is not to 'sell' knowledge or theories. Translation can sometimes be unfaithful,[38] but the work of translators is inevitably limited by the subject they are obliged to translate. Thus, the potential of a translator in creating a space for dialogue, dispute, and collective contemplation is constrained.

By contrast, tinkering with the troubling insider/outsider boundary can be a form of translation. When feminists address the importance of being 'outsiders within' in academia, they are attesting to the inherent function of 'outsiders within' as two-way translators of the truth about the state of inequalities against women and minorities. In this sense, translation is, à la Clausewitz (and Latour!), politics by other means.[39]

In the middle of my research, I began to yearn for some type of self-portrayal other than a comprador or a translator. I grew tired of thinking of myself as either an insider or an outsider. These descriptive terms, thought-provoking as they appear, failed to liberate me. They defined me from the outer attributes I possessed but failed to depict me from the inner drives that led me to conduct this research. I needed to find that strength from within.

Retrospectively, that was the moment when the notion of 'Asia as method' struck me. Although the 'Asia as method' claim of Kuan-Hsing Chen is epistemological and political,[40] it echoes the desire that prompted me to seek inner strength. This approach refers to the search for a means to develop Asia's own perspective through three critical endeavours: decolonization, de-Cold War, and deimperialization. Chen suggests that a locally grounded theory that can distinguish itself from its counterparts in the rest of the world is possible when scholars in Asia communicate with, and learn from, each other. Only through a critical examination of the effects of colonization, Cold War, and imperialization can a scholar appreciate Asia as a site that generates theory and not as a mere subject for which theory is applied. More importantly, this critical attitude does not aim to erase the impacts of the West totally, but 'to multiply frames of reference in our subjectivity and worldview, so that our anxiety over the West can be diluted, and productive critical work can move forward'.[41]

For me, the 'Asia as method' approach implies a novel idea that a researcher may adopt a role aside from that of an academic comprador or translator, both of which still feed on existing theories, concepts, and perspectives. Instead, 'Asia as method' shows that researchers can categorically generate innovative theoretical insights from studying local people, events, and phenomena. Researchers can draw a map of their own insights, for their use, and if situations allow, for those who are interested and willing to discuss it. They are not bound by such a map; instead, they own it; they are its cartographers.

This idea is enlightening because the image of a cartographer frees me from my anxiety of negotiating the knowledge system that I learned in graduate school and the settings that circumscribed me in the field. I drew a conceptual map of the harm reduction policy wherein people, ideas, and things move in and out to make a policy assemblage work.[42] At the same time, this map generated through my research may use one of the theories appropriated from the West, but it uses this theory with local wit (or twist?), if not wisdom. Ergo, I argue that the idea of assemblage, although borrowed from Gilles Deleuze and Félix Guattari (two figures from the West), can be applied to understand the harm reduction policy of Taiwan.[43] This application does not mean that this policy is just another example of assemblage. In my case, the heterogeneity and instability of the policy components mobilised the notion of assemblage in a dialogic sense. 'Provincializing Europe' does not have to fall prey to nationalism or regionalism; instead, it ought to transcend them. Moreover, this idea not only applies to those 'at home' studies by returning scholars, but it also applies to those scholars themselves.

Nevertheless, some issues warrant further clarification. Certainly, cartography was once an imperial tool, be it military or corporate.[44] Take the Mercator projection map for example. Widely used for navigational purposes since the days of colonisation, the map is often criticised for being biased, that is, enlarging the North and shrinking the South.[45] That being said, I have no intention of awakening the imperial past of cartography when I position myself as a cartographer. Instead, I treat it as a means of putting things in order (or out of order?). I have no qualms about making maps that are not 100% real. One thing distinguishes my use of cartography from that of imperialism, that is, in my view, a cartographer must be true to his/her map, but the map does not necessarily have to reflect reality or claim authority. Instead, it aims to stimulate readers to think what is real, especially when they cannot see what they expect on the map. To be sure, maps are forms of translating, but the thing is, translating what? The problem does not lie in the limitations of cartographic technology that claims to represent reality (such as the inevitable drawbacks of every projection method), but in the fact that too many realities exist and too many means to represent each of these realities are available. This scenario describes my case perfectly. I stay true to all my data and the derived inferences that I map out. However, I cannot guarantee that such a locally situated interpretation be applicable to all settings, even though this uncertainty does not mean that the interpretation cannot be discussed and understood by other people apart from Taiwanese, Asians, or academics. Pragmatically speaking, a map is a map mainly because it directs people to wherever they want to go, not because it claims to be correct.

Susan Leigh Star described an incident during her early fieldwork that illustrates my point. She found a paper by a neuroanatomist named David Ferrer in the historical archives of the *Royal Society*. The paper plotted human brain functions by experimenting on monkey brains. Evidently, the map outlined in the paper cannot be viewed as an exact equivalent of the human brain map. Nonetheless, the paper was a huge success. Why did a monkey brain map satisfy people when they were looking for a map for the human brain? She answered:

[T]he map did not *need* to be accurate to be useful. It could serve as the basis for conversation, for sharing data, for pointing to things – without actually demarcating any real territory. It was a good communicative device across, for example, the goal is [*sic*] worlds of clinical and of basic research. Its mediational qualities seemed to be that it 'sat in the middle' between different groups, very ill structured or sketchy in the common usage.[46]

Accordingly, researchers, as cartographers, do appropriate what they learn elsewhere and what people consider true knowledge and legitimate perspective when they draw up what they see in the field. However, they remain clear that their views, regardless of how neutral they may appear, are partial at best. The most important thing for researchers is not whether they successfully broker theories and viewpoints or if they translate precisely, correctly, and effectively. Instead, it is whether their work generates dialogues, reflections, and collaborative efforts. This objective is what I intend to achieve. Such thought has relieved my tension considerably and made me stop asking 'Who am I?' Instead, it has led me to find out 'What can I *do*?'

Unexpected as it may seem, the pragmatic attitude of my interviewees echoed the notion of 'Asia as method'. A high-rank CDC officer candidly told me, 'Although it is true that we cling to the US, but I would ask, do we have to copy them in every way? Not necessarily. Harm reduction is itself a very un-American example'. Many others shared this view, because they wanted to make 'the difference that made a difference'[47] and the United States was regarded as a bad example for its uneven and irregular implementation of harm reduction. Overall Taiwan's harm reduction policy drew more from Australia and Hong Kong. These policymakers certainly did not invent a policy all by themselves; they simply focused on available administrative resources and policy choices, tailoring them to local needs. They were smart enough to know where to seek help, what to appropriate, and when to improvise. To follow the West, or not to follow the West: that was not the question. Bearing 'what to do' in mind, they always took the side that made the policy work. It takes pragmatism and creativity to decolonise oneself from persistent and prevalent ideas/ideals for both the researcher and the researched.

In addition, some surprises during fieldwork also alerted me to the possibility of developing a local perspective without losing sight of global implications. Another CDC interviewee showed me the education sheet he designed for drug criminals about to be discharged from jail. It listed all accredited institutes that offered addiction treatments. The wording of the sheet mimicked that of a divine poem, which is common in Taiwanese temples. Excited, he read the poem to me:

The first incense comes in strong.
Accidents are so often heard.
'Cause a trip by water is risky,
Needles are not to be shared.
Taking methadone is free,
O healthy wanderers.
Use a condom when you do it,
Keeping away from disorders.
(Original in Chinese. My translation.)[48]

Jargon shared among drug users abounds in this poem. For example, 'first incense' (the first shot after a long period of non-use) and 'a trip by water' (intravenous injection). The 'incense' metaphor compares the devouring craving for heroin to the devout ceremony for gods. Some words are literal Mandarin translations of local Taiwanese, but with minor semantic changes. For example, 'wanderers' (迌人, tshit-thô-lâng) in colloquial Taiwanese refers to idlers or people who engage in gang activities, herein alluding to drug offenders. 迌 (tshit-thô) also means 'play' in Taiwanese, so this term implies the idea of 'lust/fun seekers' that are subject to HIV/AIDS infection. Furthermore, in an exegesis that he wrote, he stated:

Sweet rain comes after a long drought,
Like good medicine for an illness.
Your body has changed upon discharge,
And never use the same dose,
Or death will immediately befall.
To counteract the craving for heroin,
Take methadone instead.
Salvation lies in whatever is difficult.
(Original in Chinese. My translation.)[49]

Frankly, the wording and rhyming of this education sheet were not satisfying, but the idea that it conveyed in the form of a divine poem meant something important. Apart from creatively drawing inspiration from local religious practices in reaching out to its target population (i.e., injection drug users), most of whom were familiar with these materials, the poem showed me that these policymakers transformed themselves from researched subjects to methodological inspirations. Their innovative perspectives and deeds exemplify the notion of 'Asia as method' and make the harm reduction policy Taiwanese. Disputes may arise. On the one hand, one may treat this presentation as one of the many locally available means to communicate universal health information with potential targets, but this manner of understanding forestalls the possibility of discovering theoretical innovations from this case. Additionally, it repeats the old thinking that this case is nothing but an Asian example of health policy, the study of which has its own themes, theories, and boundaries that remain unchallenged. On the other hand, one may conceive of health education in this case as having formed an unexpected liaison with local religion; hence, this health sheet becomes a truly divine poem. This reflection brings to light the usually unquestioned boundary between divinity and health. For example, it intrigues me, following Metzl and Kirkland:[50] which is more sacred or moral now, divinity or health? Certainly, this manner of conceptualisation is not an act of straightforward translation; instead, it is a sophisticated way to mark the lines amid all likely equivocations and accordingly map the concepts therein. To me, it is great cartography, and it *draws* from Asia (pun intended).

Furthermore, Latour's research motto of 'following the scientists/actors' has a new meaning now.[51] I urge researchers to follow their subjects, who will eventually inform them both content and method. In addition, the idea of theorising from one another in the notion of 'Asia as method' implies that ethnography is a means to mediate between the subjects and the researcher's self, inspire someone else just as the researcher is inspired in the field, and assemble a world map wherein the existing order can be challenged, adjusted, or even reset.

CONCLUSION: THOUGHTS ON METHODOLOGICAL POSITIONS

Although I have articulated my reflections along my quest for self-identity and research position in this chapter, there is no means of determining if the quest is permanently over. This chapter is a manifestation of my shifting positions as my research proceeds – from data collection to paper publication. I was initially intrigued and even puzzled about my position: sometimes as an insider, sometimes as an outsider, and sometimes both. I pondered how to remain distant when everyone thought I was close and how to push myself into the game when I felt alienated. On certain occasions, I carefully chose my words and avoided direct confrontation when I heard 您 (nin) instead of 你 (ni). In other situations, I intentionally asked entry-level questions to elicit fresh responses from familiar respondents, such as 'What is harm reduction to you, anyway?'

Reactions to the insider/outsider deliberation may seem technical, as they centre on how a researcher like me speaks and behaves to maximise the empirical harvest and intellectual insight that could possibly arise from hard-won fieldwork. Although it is definitely a good thing for fieldworkers to make the most of their 'outsider within' status, this reflection should not merely stay in the terrain of epistemological politics. Instead, it should be understood as a way to explore the researcher's self-positioning as a knowledge definer, producer, and negotiator. During fieldwork, I was compelled more than once to respond to questions about my standing in terms of analytic perspective, theoretical orientation, and scholarly subjectivity. The more I immersed myself in the field, the more concerned I became about my position: Was I a comprador, a translator, or a cartographer?

The three positions discussed in this chapter indicate a shared situation for non-Western scholars who sensed and embraced the emergent needs to provincialise Europe.[52] The particular position inhabited cannot be chosen at will, and the divisions among these positions are frequently blurred and displaced. Without turning research findings into fragmentary local narratives or nationalist/regionalist propaganda, a researcher like me must eventually balance what he/she studies in the West and learns from the rest. Fortunately, if there is anything from my experience that can be shared, it is the actions of research subjects that demonstrate incredible creativity and pragmatism with theoretical ramifications and practical implications. A fieldwork aiming at Others is a fieldwork leading to our selves. Mapping the actions and positions of Others simultaneously maps our own. To really capture the ethnographic moment like this,[53] we have to be symmetrically critical and analytically reflexive at all times. Being ambitious yet humble, I therefore believe that there are numerous implications beyond my intended cartography. On the one hand, this chapter demonstrates a manner of self-searching, an endeavour on methodology, and a theoretical situation that constantly attempts a better solution. On the other hand, this chapter is open to anyone who tries to take (or tackle) their subjects as method. This chapter, along with the cartography herein, invites people to discuss, revise, and even refute its arguments. 'Salvation lies in whatever is difficult', so let there be no fear and let the conversation begin, however difficult it may be.

***

ACKNOWLEDGEMENT

The paper is partly sponsored by a research grant from Taiwan's Ministry of Science and Technology (MOST 104-2410-H-010-007-MY2). Adele Clarke carefully read through an earlier draft and provided invaluable suggestions, to which I am deeply thankful. In addition, I sincerely thank Caroline and Nayantara for their editorial advice and the anonymous reviewer for their insightful comments.

NOTES

1. Virginia L. Oleson, "Feminisms and Qualitative Research at and into the Millennium," in *Handbook of Qualitative Research*. 2nd edition, eds. Donald K. Norman, and Yvonne S. Lincoln (Thousand Oaks, CA: Sage, 2000), 227.

2. The CDC of Taiwan is an agency in the Ministry of Health and Welfare (or the Department of Health at the time of my research) that manages the threats of various communicable diseases.

3. Harm reduction policy refers to public health measures that aim to minimise the physical, social, legal, and economic harms of drug use. In the context of my research, the harm specifically meant the spread of HIV, which was the reason why the CDC initiated the policy.

4. Ruth Frankenberg, and Lata Mani, "Crosscurrents, Crosstalk: Race, 'Postcoloniality' and the Politics of Location," *Cultural Studies* 7, no. 2 (March 1993): 292–310; Oleson, "Feminisms and Qualitative Research," 215–255.

5. Georg Simmel, "The Stranger," in *Georg Simmel on Individuality and Social Forms*, ed. Donald Levine (Chicago, IL: University of Chicago Press, 1971[1908]), 145.

6. Alfred Schuetz, "The Stranger: An Essay in Social Psychology," *American Journal of Sociology* 49, no. 6 (May 1944): 499–507.

7. Howard Becker, *Outsiders: Studies in the Sociology of Deviance* (New York: The Free Press, 1973).

8. Robert K. Merton, "Insiders and Outsiders: A Chapter in the Sociology of Knowledge," *American Journal of Sociology* 78, no. 1 (July 1972): 9–47.

9. Patricia Hill Collins, "Learning from the Outsider Within: The Sociological Significance of Black Feminist Thought," *Social Problems* 33, no. 6 (December 1986): S14–S32.

10. Collins, "Learning from the Outsider Within," S14–S32.

11. Kirin Narayan, "How Native is a 'Native' Anthropologist?" *American Anthropologist* 95, no. 3 (September 1993): 671–686.

12. Nancy Naples, "A Feminist Revisiting of the Insider/Outsider Debate: The 'Outsider Phenomenon' in Rural Iowa," *Qualitative Sociology* 19, no. 1 (March 1996): 85.

13. Oleson, "Feminism and Qualitative Research," 215–255.

14. Narantaya Sheoran, "Once an Insider, Always an Outsider: (Re)Negotiating Boundaries when Researchers Return 'Home,'" *Anthropology News* 53, no. 2 (February 2012).

15. David Mosse, *Cultivating Development: An Ethnography of Aid Policy and Practice* (London: Pluto Press, 2005); David Mosse, "Anti-social Anthropology? Objectivity, Objection, and the Ethnography of Public Policy and Professional Communities," *Journal of the Royal Anthropological Institute* 12, no. 4 (December 2006): 935–956.

16. Mosse, "Anti-social Anthropology," 936.

17. Chyuan-Jenq Shiau, "The Indigenization of Social Sciences in Taiwan," *Taiwanese Journal of Political Science* 13 (2000): 1–26 (in Chinese).

18. Denny Roy, *Taiwan: A Political History* (Cornell: Cornell University Press, 2003); Murray A. Rubinstein, *Taiwan: A New History* (New York: Routledge, 2007).

19. Stuart Hall, "The West and the Rest," in *Modernity: An Introduction to Modern Societies*, eds. Stuart Hall, David Held, Don Hubert, and Kenneth Thompson (Malden, MA: Blackwell, 1996), 184–201.

20. Daiwie Fu, "How Far Can East Asian STS Go?" *East Asian Science, Technology and Society: An International Journal* 1, no. 1 (March 2007): 4.

21. Jia-shin Chen, "Rethinking the East Asian Distinction: An Example of Taiwan's Harm Reduction Policy," *East Asian Science, Technology, and Society: An International Journal* 6, no. 4 (December 2012): 453–464.

22. Sandra Harding, "'Strong Objectivity': A Response to the New Objectivity Question," *Synthese* 104, no. 3 (September 1995): 331–349; Sandra Harding, *Sciences from Below: Feminisms, Postcolonialities, and Modernities* (Durham, NC: Duke University Press, 2008).

23. Warwick Anderson, "From Subjugated Knowledge to Subjugated Subjects: Science and Globalization, or Postcolonial Studies of Science?," *Postcolonial Studies* 12, no. 4 (December 2009): 389–400.

24. Fa-Ti Fan, "East Asian STS: Fox or Hedgehog?," *East Asian Science, Technology and Society: An International Journal* 1, no. 2 (June 2007): 243–247.

25. Warwick Anderson, "Asia as Method in Science and Technology Studies," *East Asian Science, Technology and Society* 6, no. 4 (December 2012): 445–451.

26. Fa-ti Fan, "Modernity, Region, and Technoscience: One Small Cheer for Asia as Method," *Cultural Sociology* 10, no. 3 (April 2016): 352–368.

27. Dipesh Chakrabarty, *Provincializing Europe: Postcolonial Thought and Historical Difference* (Princeton: Princeton University Press, 2000).

28. Marie-Claire Bergere, *The Golden Age of the Chinese Bourgeoisie, 1911–1937* (Cambridge: Cambridge University Press, 1989).

29. Ming-Hwei Perng, *The Dangers and Challenges of Taiwan in 2020* [2020 台灣的危機與轉機] (Taipei: Linking Publishing, 2012), 193.

30. Marilyn Starthern, ed., *Audit Culture* (New York: Routledge, 2000).

31. Eduardo Viveiros de Castro, "Perspectival Anthropology and the Method of Controlled Equivocation," *Tipiti: Journal of the Society for the Anthropology of Lowland South America* 2, no. 1 (January 2004): 3–22.

32. Viveiros de Castro, "Perspectival Anthropology," 11.

33. Renato Rosaldo, "Lessons from the Space Between Languages: Notes on Poetry and Ethnography," in *Theorizing Fieldwork in the Humanities: Methods, Reflections, and Approaches to the Global South*, eds. Shalini Puri, and Debra A. Catillo (New York: Palgrave Macmillan, 2016), 183–189.

34. Bruno Latour, *Science in Action: How to Follow Scientists and Engineers Through Society* (Cambridge, MA: Harvard University Press, 1987).

35. Bruno Latour, *The Pasteurization of France*, trans. Alan Sheridan, and John Law (Cambridge, MA and London: Harvard University Press, 1988).

36. Marisol De la Cadena, Marianne E. Lien, Caspaer Bruun Jensen, Tess Lea, Atsuro Morita, Heather Swanson, Gro B. Ween, Pisge West, and Margaret Winer, "Anthropology and STS: Generative Interfaces, Multiple Locations," *HAU: Journal of Ethnographic Theory* 5, no. 1 (March 2015): 437–475.

37. Ian Hacking, *Representing and Intervening: Introductory Topics in the Philosophy of Natural Science* (Cambridge: Cambridge University Press, 1983).

38. John Law, "Traduction/Trahison: Notes on ANT," Lancaster University, 2003, https://www.lancaster.ac.uk/fass/resources/sociology-online-papers/papers/law -traduction-trahison.pdf.

39. Latour, *The Pasteurization of France.*

40. Kuan-Hsing Chen, *Asia as Method: Toward Deimperialization* (Durham, NC: Duke University Press, 2010).

41. Chen, *Asia as Method*, 223.

42. Jia-shin Chen, "Assembling Harm Reduction Policy in Taiwan" (PhD diss., University of California, San Francisco, 2009).

43. Gilles Deleuze, and Félix Guattari, *A Thousand Plateaus* (Minneapolis, MN: University of Minnesota Press, 1987); Chen, "Rethinking," 453–464.

44. Steven J. Harris, "Long-Distance Corporations, Bid Sciences, and the Geography of Knowledge," in *Postcolonial Science and Technology Studies Reader*, ed. Sandra Harding (Durham, NC: Duke University Press, 2011), 61–83.

45. John M. Hobson, "Discovering the Oriental West," in *Postcolonial Science and Technology Studies Reader*, ed. Sandra Harding (Durham, NC: Duke University Press, 2011), 39–60.

46. Susan Leigh Star, "This Is Not a Boundary Object: Reflections on the Origin of a Concept," *Science, Technology and Human Values* 35, no. 5 (September 2010): 608.

47. Aihwa Ong, *Fungible Life: Experiment in the Asian City of Life* (Durham, NC: Duke University Press, 2016), xvii.

48. The Chinese version is as follows: 頭香力道強，意外時有聞。水路風險高，針具不共用。暢飲美沙冬，健康𨑨迌人，辦事有一套，保險不染病。

49. The Chinese version is as follows: 久旱逢雨，病逢妙藥，出監體質變，忌如前量施打，恐登時斃命，抵癮海洛因，改服美沙冬，凡事難中有救。

50. Jonathan M Metzl, and Anna Kirkland, *Against Health: How Health Became the New Morality* (New York: NYU Press, 2010).

51. Latour, *Science in Action.*

52. Charkrabarty, *Provincializing Europe.*

53. Strathern, Marilyn, *Property, Substance and Effect: Anthropological Essays on Persons and Things* (London: Athlone Press, 1999), 6.

REFERENCES

Anderson, Warwick. "From Subjugated Knowledge to Subjugated Subjects: Science and Globalization, or Postcolonial Studies of Science?" *Postcolonial Studies* 12, no. 4 (December 2009): 389–400.

———. "Asia as Method in Science and Technology Studies." *East Asian Science, Technology and Society* 6, no. 4 (December 2012): 445–451.

Becker, Howard. *Outsiders: Studies in the Sociology of Deviance.* New York: The Free Press, 1973.

Bergere, Marie-Claire. *The Golden Age of the Chinese Bourgeoisie, 1911–1937.* Cambridge: Cambridge University Press, 1989.

Chakrabarty, Dipesh. *Provincializing Europe: Postcolonial Thought and Historical Difference.* Princeton: Princeton University Press, 2000.

Chen, Jia-shin. "Assembling Harm Reduction Policy in Taiwan." PhD diss., University of California, San Francisco, 2009.

———. "Rethinking the East Asian Distinction: An Example of Taiwan's Harm Reduction Policy." *East Asian Science, Technology, and Society: An International Journal* 6, no. 4 (December 2012): 453–464.

Chen, Kuan-Hsing. *Asia as Method: Toward Deimperialization.* Durham, NC: Duke University Press, 2010.

Collins, Patricia Hill. "Learning from the Outsider Within: The Sociological Significance of Black Feminist Thought." *Social Problems* 33, no. 6 (December 1986): S14–S32.

De la Cadena, Marisol, Marianne E. Lien, Caspaer Bruun Jensen, Tess Lea, Atsuro Morita, Heather Swanson, Gro B. Ween, Pisge West, and Margaret Winer. "Anthropology and STS: Generative Interfaces, Multiple Locations." *HAU: Journal of Ethnographic Theory* 5, no. 1 (March 2015): 437–475.

Deleuze, Gilles, and Felix Guattari. *A Thousand Plateaus.* Minneapolis, MN: University of Minnesota Press, 1987.

Fan, Fa-Ti. "East Asian STS: Fox or Hedgehog?" *East Asian Science, Technology and Society: An International Journal* 1, no. 2 (June 2007): 243–247.

———. "Modernity, Region, and Technoscience: One Small Cheer for Asia as Method." *Cultural Sociology* 10, no. 3 (April 2016): 352–368.

Frankenberg, Ruth, and Lata Mani. "Crosscurrents, Crosstalk: Race, 'Postcoloniality' and the Politics of Location." *Cultural Studies* 7, no. 2 (March 1993): 292–310.

Fu, Daiwie. "How Far Can East Asian STS Go?" *East Asian Science, Technology and Society: An International Journal* 1, no. 1 (March 2007): 1–14.

Hacking, Ian. *Representing and Intervening: Introductory Topics in the Philosophy of Natural Science.* Cambridge: Cambridge University Press, 1983.

Hall, Stuart. "The West and the Rest." In *Modernity: An Introduction to Modern Societies,* edited by Stuart Hall, David Held, Don Hubert, and Kenneth Thompson, 184–201. Malden, MA: Blackwell, 1996.

Harding, Sandra. "'Strong Objectivity': A Response to the New Objectivity Question." *Synthese* 104, no. 3 (September 1995): 331–349.

———. *Sciences from Below: Feminisms, Postcolonialities, and Modernities.* Durham, NC: Duke University Press, 2008.

Harris, Steven J. "Long-Distance Corporations, Bid Sciences, and the Geography of Knowledge." In *Postcolonial Science and Technology Studies Reader,* edited by Sandra Harding, 61–83. Durham, NC: Duke University Press, 2011.

Hastrup, Kirsten. "Getting It Right: Knowledge and Evidence in Anthropology." *Anthropological Theory* 4, no. 4 (December 2004): 455–472.

Hobson, John M. "Discovering the Oriental West." In *Postcolonial Science and Technology Studies Reader,* edited by Sandra Harding, 39–60. Durham, NC: Duke University Press, 2011.

Latour, Bruno. *Science in Action: How to Follow Scientists and Engineers Through Society.* Cambridge, MA: Harvard University Press, 1987.

———. *The Pasteurization of France.* Translated by Alan Sheridan and John Law. Cambridge, MA and London: Harvard University Press, 1988.

Law, John. "Traduction/Trahison: Notes on ANT." Lancaster University, accessed 12 June, 2019. https://www.lancaster.ac.uk/fass/resources/sociology-online-paper s/papers/law-traduction-trahison.pdf.

Merton, Robert K. "Insiders and Outsiders: A Chapter in the Sociology of Knowledge." *American Journal of Sociology* 78, no. 1 (July 1972): 9–47.

Metzl, Jonathan M., and Anna Kirkland. *Against Health: How Health Became the New Morality.* New York: NYU Press, 2010.

Mosse, David. *Cultivating Development: An Ethnography of Aid Policy and Practice.* London: Pluto Press, 2005.

———. "Anti-Social Anthropology? Objectivity, Objection, and the Ethnography of Public Policy and Professional Communities." *Journal of the Royal Anthropological Institute* 12, no. 4 (December 2006): 935–956.

Naples, Nancy. "A Feminist Revisiting of the Insider/Outsider Debate: The 'Outsider Phenomenon' in Rural Iowa." *Qualitative Sociology* 19, no. 1 (March 1996): 83–106.

Narayan, Kirin. "How Native is a 'Native' Anthropologist?" *American Anthropologist* 95, no. 3 (September 1993): 671–686.

Oleson, Virginia L. "Feminisms and Qualitative Research at and into the Millennium." In *Handbook of Qualitative Research.* 2nd edition, edited by Donald K. Norman and Yvonne S. Lincoln, 215–255. Thousand Oaks, CA: Sage, 2000.

Ong, Aihwa. *Fungible Life: Experiment in the Asian City of Life.* Durham, NC: Duke University Press, 2016.

Perng, Ming-Hwei. *The Dangers and Challenges of Taiwan in 2020.* [2020 台灣的危機與轉機]. Taipei: Linking Publishing, 2012 (in Chinese).

Rosaldo, Renato. "Lessons from the Space Between Languages: Notes on Poetry and Ethnography." In *Theorizing Fieldwork in the Humanities: Methods, Reflections, and Approaches to the Global South,* edited by Shalini Puri and Debra A. Catillo, 183–189. New York: Palgrave Macmillan, 2016.

Roy, Denny. *Taiwan: A Political History.* Cornell: Cornell University Press, 2003.

Rubinstein, Murray A. *Taiwan: A New History.* New York: Routledge, 2007.

Schuetz, Alfred. "The Stranger: An Essay in Social Psychology." *American Journal of Sociology* 49, no. 6 (May 1944): 499–507.

Sheoran, Narantaya. "Once an Insider, Always an Outsider: (Re)Negotiating Boundaries when Researchers Return 'Home.'" *Anthropology News* 53, no. 2 (February 2012).

Shiau, Chyuan-Jenq "The Indigenization of Social Sciences in Taiwan." *Taiwanese Journal of Political Science* 13 (2000): 1–26. (in Chinese)

Simmel, Georg. "The Stranger." In *Georg Simmel on Individuality and Social Forms,* edited by Donald Levine, 143–149. Chicago, IL: University of Chicago Press, 1971[1908].

Star, Susan Leigh. "This is Not a Boundary Object: Reflections on the Origin of a Concept." *Science, Technology and Human Values* 35, no. 5 (September 2010): 601–617.

Strathern, Marilyn. *Property, Substance and Effect: Anthropological Essays on Persons and Things*. London: Athlone Press, 1999.

———. ed. *Audit Culture*. New York: Routledge, 2000.

Viveiros de Castro, Eduardo. "Perspectival Anthropology and the Method of Controlled Equivocation." *Tipiti: Journal of the Society for the Anthropology of Lowland South America* 2, no. 1 (January 2004): 3–22.

Index

www.ingramcontent.com/pod-product-compliance
Lightning Source LLC
Chambersburg PA
CBHW060147280326
41932CB00012B/1671